New Developments of the Exchange Rate Regimes in Developing Countries

New Developments of the Exchange Rate Regimes in Developing Countries

Edited by

Hisayuki Mitsuo

IDE-JETRO

First published 2007 by
PALGRAVE MACMILLAN
Houndmills, Basingstoke, Hampshire RG21 6XS and
175 Fifth Avenue, New York, N.Y. 10010
Companies and representatives throughout the world

PALGRAVE MACMILLAN is the global academic imprint of the
Palgrave Macmillan division of St. Martin's Press, LLC and of
Palgrave Macmillan Ltd. Macmillan® is a registered trademark in
the United States, United Kingdom and other countries. Palgrave is a
registered trademark in the European Union and other countries.

ISBN-13: 978-0-230-00473-3   hardback
ISBN-10: 0-230-00473-3   hardback

This book is printed on paper suitable for recycling and made from fully managed
and sustained forest sources.

A catalogue record for this book is available from the British Library.

Library of Congress Cataloging-in-Publication Data

New developments of the exchange rate regimes in developing
    countries/edited by Hisayuki Mitsuo.
        p. cm.
    Includes bibliographical references and index.
    ISBN 0-230-00473-3 (cloth)
    1. Foreign exchange–Developing countries. I. Mitsuo, Hisayuki, 1967–

HG3877.N47 2007
332.4′56091724–dc22

                                                            2006049465

10   9   8   7   6   5   4   3   2   1
16   15   14   13   12   11   10   09   08   07

Printed and bound in Great Britain by
Antony Rowe Ltd, Chippenham and Eastbourne

Contents

v

List of Figures

List of Tables

Preface

This book is a product of a research project on exchange rate regimes in developing countries conducted at the Institute of Developing Economies (IDE), Japan External Trade Organization (JETRO), from April 2003 to March 2005.

Exchange rate regimes can be represented on a spectrum that constitutes hard pegs (currency union, dollarization, currency board), conventional fixed pegs, intermediate regimes (band, basket peg, and crawling peg), managed floating, and independent floating according to the degree of fixity of exchange rates.

Some developing countries have experienced major changes in their exchange rate regimes since the 1990s. Argentina adopted a currency board (1991–2002). Some Baltic and Eastern European countries also adopted currency boards in the 1990s. East Asian and Latin American countries experienced currency crises and after the crises moved to floating exchange regimes. Ecuador dollarized in 2000. On the other hand, based on a rapid integration in trade and finance, a concern for monetary integration in East Asia is rising. We term changes of exchange rate regimes in developing countries as represented above as new developments.

Our objective in this book is to present theoretical and empirical analyses of the new developments since the 1990s. Because this book addresses a variety of exchange rate regimes from hard peg to floating, and various regions of East Asia, Latin America, and Eastern Europe, we can observe diverse cases of how various exchange rate regimes relate to the national economy in developing countries.

We would like to thank all copyright holders for granting us permission. We have made every effort to trace all copyright holders. But if any have been unintentionally overlooked, the publisher will be pleased to make the necessary arrangements at the first opportunity.

We would like to express our sincere thanks to all those who helped our project, especially to the anonymous referees who provided us with helpful comments.

Hisayuki Mitsuo

Notes on the Contributors

Taro Esaka is an Associate Professor at Kobe City University of Foreign Studies. He holds a PhD from Osaka University. His main research interests are the behavior of exchange rates, central bank intervention, exchange rate policies in emerging market economies, international capital flows, and the international monetary system. His recent publications include "The Louvre Accord and Central Bank Intervention: Was There a Target Zone?" *Japan and the World Economy*, 12, May: 107–126 (2000) and "Was It Really a Dollar Peg?: the Exchange Rate Policies of East Asian Countries, 1980–97", *Journal of Asian Economics* 13, January: 787–809 (2003).

Kaku Furuya is an Associate Professor of Economics at Daito Bunka University, where he has taught since 2001. He has also been a research associate for various research projects at IDE-JETRO. From 1996 to 2001, he was an Assistant Professor of Economics at U.C. Irvine. He received his BA and MA in international relations from University of Tokyo and received his PhD in economics from U.C. Berkeley. His areas of research include macroeconomics, international economics, and labor economics.

Masanaga Kumakura is an Associate Professor of International Economics at Osaka City University. Professor Kumakura holds a PhD in economics from the University of Cambridge, UK, and works extensively on issues related to trade and exchange rates. His recent publications include "Exchange Rate Regimes in Asia: Dispelling the Myth of Soft Dollar Pegs," *Journal of the Asia Pacific Economy*, 10 (1): 69–95 (2005) and "Is the Yen/Dollar Exchange Rate Really Responsible for East Asia's Export and Business Cycles? A Commentary on McKinnon and Schnabl (2003)," *The World Economy*, 28 (1): 1509–37 (2005).

Hisayuki Mitsuo is a researcher at IDE-JETRO. He studies monetary and exchange rate policy in developing countries, from the perspective of monetary policy regimes: frameworks of monetary policy that comprise domestic monetary policy typically represented as control of the monetary base and exchange rate arrangements. He edited *Monetary Policy Regimes and Currency Crises: Experiences and Challenges in Developing Countries*, IDE-JETRO, 2003 (in Japanese).

Shoji Nishijima is Director and Vice President of Kobe University in Japan and a Professor at the Research Institute for Economics and Business Administration. He is a former President of the Japan Society of Social Science on Latin America. He received a PhD in Economics from Kobe University. His recent books are *East Asia and Latin America: the Unlikely Alliance,* coedited, Rowman & Littlefield, 2003, *Policy Reforms in Latin America,* coedited, Kobe University, 2003 (in Japanese), and *Brazilian Macro Economy in the 1990s,* Kobe University, 2002 (in Japanese).

Kiyotaka Sato is Associate Professor of Economics, Yokohama National University, Japan. He holds a PhD in economics from the University of Tokyo. His main research interest is the issue of regional monetary integration in East Asia, exchange rate pass-through and currency invoicing of Japanese and East Asian exporters, and exchange rate policies in East Asian economies. He has published articles in journals such as *The World Economy, Applied Economics,* and *Asian Economic Journal.*

Introduction: New Developments of the Exchange Rate Regimes in Developing Countries

Hisayuki Mitsuo

1. Objective and analytical foundation

Exchange rate regimes can be represented on a spectrum that constitutes hard pegs (currency union, dollarization, currency board), conventional fixed peg, intermediate regimes (band, basket peg, and crawling peg), managed floating, and independent floating according to the degree of fixity of exchange rates.

Some developing countries have experienced major changes in their exchange rate regimes since the 1990s. Argentina adopted a currency board (1991–2002). Some Baltic and Eastern European countries also adopted currency boards in the 1990s. East Asian and Latin American countries experienced currency crises after which they moved to floating exchange rate regimes. Ecuador dollarized in 2000. On the other hand, based on rapid integration in trade and finance, a concern for monetary integration in East Asia is rising. We term changes of exchange rate regimes in developing countries as represented above as new developments. Our objective in this book is to present theoretical and empirical analyses of the new developments since the 1990s. Because this book addresses a variety of exchange rate regimes from hard peg to floating, and various regions of East Asia, Latin America, and Eastern Europe, we can observe diverse cases of how various exchange rate regimes relate to the national economy in developing countries.

In analyzing diverse experiences under a variety of exchange rate regimes in developing countries, we base our arguments on the following analytical framework. In an environment under which finance and trade are fully integrated, an economy which adopts a fixed exchange rate regime must have monetary policy autonomy largely restricted. This economy must bear the cost of restricted monetary policy autonomy, and must lose the means of correcting current account imbalance by exchange rate changes. On the other hand, an economy with a flexible exchange rate regime would have monetary policy autonomy and have the means to correct current account imbalance. Thus, the effect of a choice of exchange rate regimes on a national economy crucially depends upon how important money affects real production,[1] and how important exchange rate flexibility is in the adjustment of current account balance. These two criteria on the effect of a choice of exchange rate regime on a national economy can be applied to the discussion of an optimum currency area, a domain under which a common monetary policy bears few costs.

The relationship between an exchange rate regime and a national economy is multifaceted; the exchange rate regime relates to a national economy through the structural characteristics of an economy, namely monetary and fiscal policies, external trade, the degree of foreign currency denomination of external debts, foreign indebtedness, nominal wage rigidity, productivities and the structures of industries, etc. Moreover, a national economy is subject to real or nominal shocks, originating both inside and outside of its national borders.

These structural characteristics and shocks affect a national economy through the exchange rate regime. The causality does not run in one direction; the structural characteristics and shocks, in turn, affect the choice of exchange rate regimes in developing countries.

Thus, in our studies of exchange rate regimes, we focused on structural characteristics and the nature and the degree of shocks in developing countries; how they affect a national economy through the exchange rate regimes and how they affect choices of the regimes. In what follows, based on the analytical foundation explained above, we show in each chapter the relationship of structural characteristics and/or shocks to the choice of exchange rate regimes in developing countries.

One structural characteristic of developing countries is the difficulty in borrowing in terms of their own currencies, which was pointed out by Eichengreen and Hausmann (1999). As a result, currency mismatches on the balance sheet, where liabilities denominated in foreign currencies outweigh assets denominated in domestic currencies on balance sheets, occur. In order to avoid the large amplitude of business cycles caused by net worth changes due to exchange rate fluctuations, exchange rate fluctuations in emerging market countries are kept smaller than expected under the flexible exchange rate regimes. This phenomenon was called "fear of floating" by Calvo and Reinhart (2002). *Chapter 1* presents econometric evidence of this argument.

East Asian exchange rate regimes before the currency crisis are often characterized as a dollar peg. Under this assumption, McKinnon and Schnabl (2003) argue that a nominal shock of yen/dollar fluctuations has been a major determinant for East Asian business cycles. Instead, *Chapter 4* argues that the real shock of global demand cycles for electronic goods has been more important than the nominal shock of yen/dollar fluctuations for East Asian business cycles. Furthermore, most East Asian countries' exchange rate regimes were not a simple dollar peg. Rather, East Asian exchange rate policies were more pragmatic than commonly thought; they may have monitored the effective value of their currencies.

Many developing countries adopted an inflation targeting regime after moving to a flexible exchange rate regime. Inflation targeting is a monetary policy regime under which the Central Bank tries to attain preannounced inflation rates by changing short-term interest rates. Inflation targeting accompanies a flexible exchange rate regime so that the Central Bank can manage short-term interest rates. However, developing countries have a structural characteristic that might make inflation targeting less effective. If a large amount of government debt is held by foreign investors and if debt default is a concern, deterioration in the government's ability to service the debt causes capital outflow. Capital outflows translate into exchange rate depreciation and a rise in inflation.

Brazil is an example. Brazil moved to a flexible exchange rate regime in 1999. Lacking an exchange rate anchor for inflation, Brazil adopted an inflation targeting regime in the same year. Brazil has a structural characteristic of relatively large government debt held by foreigners. In 2002, the exchange rate depreciated as government debts increased. This depreciation raised the inflation rate. The Central Bank of Brazil quickly raised interest rates in order to stop depreciation and acceleration of inflation. However, raising interest rates may increase the debt burden and accelerate capital outflows and exchange rate depreciation. The Central Bank of Brazil quickly lowered interest rates after inflation expectations were lowered. *Chapter 3* presents econometric evidence that the Central Bank controlled short-term interest rates with a consideration of country risk and government debt. It should be noted that the high interest rate under inflation targeting lowered production; the GDP growth rate, which registered 1.9 percent in 2002, fell to 0.5 percent in 2003.

Argentina had a similar structural characteristic; a large amount of government debt is held by foreign investors. From 1991 Argentina adopted a currency board, which forms in principle a monetary base to move proportionately with foreign exchange reserves. An external shock caused by Brazil's currency crisis in 1999 reduced external demand for Argentina due to a real exchange rate appreciation. As recession started, government finances deteriorated and net capital inflow declined. This caused the growth of the monetary base to stagnate. If an increase in money supply can raise output, the currency board worsened recession. *Chapter 2* reports protracted recession since 1999 and the eventual collapse of the currency board in 2002.

Price regulation in the nontradable sector is another structural characteristic in developing countries. A model under which exchange rate revaluation causes real exchange rate *depreciation* is developed in *Chapter 7*. In the model, exchange rate revaluation will cause a decline in tradable prices and a rise in the relative price of nontradable goods. Because of the price constraint in the nontradables, firms faced with a rise in their own relative price will increase quality. This will lower the consumer price index and cause real exchange rate depreciation.

Price regulation in the nontradable sector still remains in China. The model will have an implication on the effect of a possible exchange rate revaluation in China.

Due to rapid economic integration in trade and finance in East Asian countries, a concern over the possibility of monetary integration in East Asia has been growing recently. Which country grouping is appropriate for monetary integration, under which a country pegs her exchange rate or adopts a common currency? In order to answer this question, we have to look at the theory of an optimum currency area. According to the theory, if economies are subject to common shocks, there will be less need to conduct independent monetary policy. *Chapter 5* investigates the correlation of supply shocks among East Asian countries, and finds that a grouping of four countries/regions (Taiwan, Hong Kong, Singapore, and Malaysia) had similar supply shocks.

Chapter 6 investigates the trade structure in East Asia based upon the new indices of trade competition, reflecting intra-industry trade between domestic and a foreign country and competition in third countries' markets. They show increasing export rivalry in East Asia and East Asian countries' declining rivalry against the United States. They provide a basis in considering exchange rate regimes of a common basket peg or monetary integration in East Asia.

Although Ecuador attained monetary integration with the United States, *Chapter 2* documents that Ecuador's economic performance is largely dependent on oil prices. The effect of changes in oil prices would be asymmetric between Ecuador and the United States, which implies that Ecuador may not be suited to make monetary integration with the United States, and future sustainability of the dollarization regime is questionable.

2. Structure and contents

Chapter 1 investigates de facto exchange rate regimes of developed, emerging markets, and developing countries, all of which are IMF member countries. This chapter investigates the evolution of exchange rate regimes during 1990–2001, based on surveys of recent literature on classification of exchange rate regimes. First, it investigates whether an exchange rate regime exhibited a significant change into either hard pegs (dollarization, currency boards, or currency union) or independent floating. In emerging markets as a whole, this trend is not clear. Second, discrepancies between *de jure* (the IMF's official classification) and de facto exchange rate regimes were examined. Among the discrepancies, *fear of floating* was observed more often in emerging markets and developing countries than in developed ones. Furthermore, this chapter provides an econometric analysis of the determinants of fear of floating, a situation in which a country that says it is making its exchange rate float, in fact does not do so. During 1990–98, for 32 emerging market countries and developing countries and 11 developed countries that exhibited fear of floating, it was found that currency mismatches in the balance sheet and the inability to borrow internationally in domestic currencies were the main determinants of fear of floating.

Chapter 2 investigates the macroeconomic structure and performance of developing and transition countries that have adopted hard peg exchange rate regimes since the 1990s. These countries are Argentina, Estonia, and Bulgaria which adopted currency boards and Ecuador which adopted a dollarization regime. First, it was found that hard peg exchange rate regimes were introduced as stabilization devices for high inflation. Hard pegs are shown to be effective in containing inflation. Second, adoption of hard pegs is associated with smaller budget deficits for Estonia, Bulgaria, Ecuador and for Argentina at least before the start of recession in 1999.

A similarity of the functions and roles of currency boards in Argentina, Estonia, and Bulgaria was found. They have all retained some monetary policy discretion, which a "pure" currency board does not have. Under the stabilized environment, these countries received capital inflows. In Estonia and Bulgaria, coupled with governments' efforts to reduce budget deficits that the adoption of a currency necessitates, foreign direct investments promoted economic transition to a market economy.

The collapse of the currency board in Argentina has shown that under the currency board, capital outflow or declining capital inflow may induce recession through a declining monetary base. If future economic prospects are dim, expectations may be realized though net capital outflow under the currency board. This shows that keeping the budget in balance may not be a sufficient condition for sustainability of the currency board.

Ecuador decided to dollarize in 2000 under the banking, currency, and external debt crisis. Since Ecuador's economic performance depends largely on oil prices, not only keeping the budget balanced but also the productivity enhancement of oil and other export industries are necessary in order to sustain a dollarization regime.

Chapter 3 analyzes Brazilian monetary and exchange rate policy after the currency crisis in 1999. After that crisis, Brazil's exchange rate regime changed to a floating regime from the previous regime under which the exchange rate was used to anchor inflation. To compensate for this loss of an anchor for inflation, an inflation targeting policy was adopted. Due to the rise in the country risk index which reflects the level of government debt and concern about the outcome of the presidential election, the exchange rate depreciated significantly in 2002. As a result of the depreciation, the target rate of inflation was breached. The Central Bank of Brazil raised short-term interest rates to combat inflation, and as inflation subsided, interest rates were lowered after a year.

Based on a theoretical model of the inflation targeting policy with government debt and an exchange rate risk premium, an interest rate response function was estimated. The result shows that interest rates are associated with deviation of the expected inflation and the target rate (positively), country risk (positively) and government debt (negatively). They suggest that the Central Bank of Brazil managed interest rates in consideration of not only deviation of the expected inflation and the target rate but also country risk and government debts.

Chapter 4 discusses East Asian exchange rate regimes before and after the 1997 Asian crisis. The author criticizes the argument that (1) yen/dollar fluctuations have dominantly created synchronized business cycles in East Asia, and (2) most East Asian countries pegged to the US dollar before the currency crisis and even after the currency crisis still peg to the US dollar. As for the first argument, the author presents econometric evidence that global IT cycles have been more important than yen/dollar fluctuations for East Asian business cycles. In addition, the author shows that electronics goods (including IT goods and components) have been an important factor in explaining the exports of East Asian countries. As to the second argument, the author admits the result of the Frankel–Wei regression using high frequency data as evidence that most East Asian countries do smooth exchange rate fluctuations against the US dollar in the short run. However, the author refutes the result as evidence of an exchange rate regime of East Asian countries over the intermediate term. Instead, using semiannual data, he shows the simulated paths of exchange rates if East Asian countries had targeted nominal effective exchange rates or if they had adopted a common basket peg policy. These paths provide evidence that East Asian countries' exchange rate policies have been pragmatic rather than the often claimed "dollar peg."

Chapter 5 investigates a possible grouping of an optimum currency area in East Asia. The author asserts that one criterion of an optimum currency area is the similarity of supply shocks. Stochastic disturbance terms that have a permanent effect on income (supply shocks) among East Asian countries are estimated. It is found that the correlations of supply shocks in Taiwan, Hong Kong, Singapore, and Malaysia are positively significant, and the author contends that these four countries/regions are candidates for forming an optimum currency area.

Chapter 6 develops indices that measure the degree of trade rivalry, reflecting that the traditional indices, such as share of bilateral trade out of total trade of home and foreign country, or correlation of export value between home and foreign country, do not always represent the degree of trade rivalry appropriately. The indices developed show bilateral rivalry using modified intra-industry trade between home and a foreign country. They also show overall rivalry not only directly bilaterally but also taking intro account rivalry in third market countries. They were calculated for nine countries in East Asia. They show that Asian countries' rivalry in trade with the United States is becoming increasingly less. On the other hand, many Asian countries have increased rivalries with neighboring Asian countries. These observations provide us with a basis for regional exchange rate regimes including the idea of a common currency in Asia. Finally, based on the index, real effective exchange rates for Asian countries were calculated.

Chapter 7 presents a theoretical model of exchange rate revaluation under a price ceiling. In the model, contrary to what is usually considered, revaluation causes real depreciation if the real exchange rate is measured using a quality adjusted consumer price index, and if revaluation induces quality improvement in the nontradable sector. Before revaluation, the nontradable sector's quality level was suboptimal due to the price ceiling. Exchange rate revaluation will relieve the constraint on the relative price, and enables firms in the nontradable sector to upgrade their quality. Quality upgrading translates to a decline in the CPI index and real depreciation results. Under the model, the effect on the current account from revaluation is then shown to be positive under certain conditions. An application of the model to a revaluation of the Chinese renminbi is discussed.

Note

1   If money is neutral, the problem of a regime choice of an exchange rate, the external value of money, will ultimately become irrelevant.

References

Calvo, G. and C. M. Reinhart, 2002, "Fear of Floating," *Quarterly Journal of Economics* 117(2), May: 379–408.
Eichengreen, B. and R. Hausmann, 1999, "Exchange Rates and Financial Fragility," NBER Working Paper No. 7418, November.
McKinnon, R. and G. Schnabl, 2003. "Synchronized Business Cycles in East Asia and Fluctuations in the Yen/Dollar Exchange Rate," *The World Economy*, 26(8): 1067–88.

1
De Facto Exchange Rate Regimes in Emerging Market Countries, 1990–2001: Some Empirical Evidence

Taro Esaka

1.1 Introduction

The choice of exchange rate regime is one of the most important topics in international economics that have been studied and debated over recent decades. This topic has gained momentum following the major currency crises seen in the 1990s (e.g. the European Monetary System (EMS) crisis in 1992–93, the Mexican crisis in 1994–95, and the Asian crisis in 1997–98). In a world with increasingly integrated capital markets, we are led to pose the question "what sort of exchange rate regime is sustainable?" Recently, some researchers have suggested that, in a world of increasing international capital mobility, only the two extreme exchange rate regimes (either hard pegs such as dollarization, currency boards or monetary unions, or a freely floating regime) are likely to be sustainable (Eichengreen 1994, Obstfeld and Rogoff 1995, Summers 2000, Fischer 2001). Conversely, intermediate exchange rate regimes (such as adjustable pegs, basket pegs, crawling pegs, or bands)[1] are likely to be unsustainable and will disappear. This view has come to be known as the "bipolar view" or the "hollowing-out" hypothesis.

Fischer (2001) has examined the transition of exchange rate regimes in IMF member countries by comparing the distribution of exchange rate regimes in 1991 with that in 1999, on the basis of the data of the IMF official classification. His study has shown that, of 159 countries in 1991 and 185 countries in 1999 in the sample, the proportion of hard pegs increased from 16 percent in 1991 to 24 percent in 1999, that of intermediate regimes decreased from 62 percent in 1991 to 34 percent in 1999, and that of floating regimes increased from 23 percent in 1991 to 42 percent in 1999 (Figure 1.1).[2,3] This evidence shows that, in the last decade, intermediate regimes have hollowed out and hard pegs and floating regimes have increased, indicating that the bipolar view holds.

Before 1998, the IMF official classification system classified IMF member countries on the basis of their own official statements about the degree of

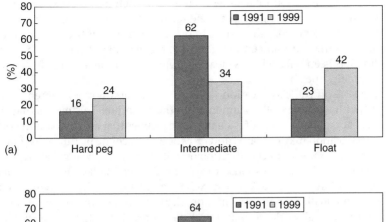

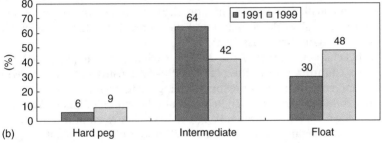

Figure 1.1   The transition of exchange rate regimes, 1991 and 1999, according to Fischer (2001): (a) all countries; (b) emerging market countries
Note: Fischer (2001) defines economies with no separate currency or those with currency boards as "hard pegs," economies with conventional fixed pegs, crawling pegs, horizontal bands, and crawling bands as "intermediate regimes," and economies with a managed float with no specified central rate or those with independent floating as "floating regimes."
Source: (a) Fischer (2001: Figure 1); (b) author's own, based on Table 2 of Fischer (2001).

exchange rate flexibility. Many empirical studies of exchange rate regimes (e.g. the relationship between exchange rate regime and macroeconomic perform-ance (such as inflation rate, interest rate, and output growth) and the deter-minants of the choice of exchange rate regime) relied on the IMF classification of exchange rate regimes, because the classification system provides classifi-cation data of many countries over a long time span.[4]

However, it is well known that several countries' actual (de facto) exchange rate regimes are inconsistent with their official (*de jure*) exchange rate regimes. For example, according to the IMF classification, Thailand had a basket peg, Korea, Indonesia, Malaysia, and Singapore had a managed float, and the Philippines even had an independent float before the Asian currency crisis of 1997. However, it is said that their currencies were effectively pegged to the US dollar.[5] Calvo and Reinhart (2002) suggest that, in reality, many countries that claim to have floating regimes do not allow their nominal exchange rate to float freely. This finding has been referred to as "fear of floating." Levy-Yeyati and Sturzenegger (2002) show that, in practice, many countries adopt a fixed regime, but they announce a more flexible regime (do not claim to fix). This finding has been referred to as "fear of pegging" (or more accurately "fear of announcing a peg").[6]

Thus, the official classification suffers from important measurement problems that have been well documented in the literature. This means that the results of empirical studies of exchange rate regimes that are based on the official classification may be biased and provide an inaccurate picture of exchange rate regimes. A means of classification describing actual exchange rate regimes has been called for. In response to this need, over the last few years some researchers have begun to classify exchange rate regimes by applying quantitative and qualitative analyses in order to arrive at a description more appropriate to the real world situation and have provided databases of de facto regimes based on these classifications.[7]

In this chapter, we survey the de facto exchange rate regimes of the IMF member countries during the period 1990–2001 using databases provided by recent empirical literature on exchange rate regime classification by Bubula and Ötker-Robe (2002), Reinhart and Rogoff (2002), Levy-Yeyati and Sturzenegger (2002), and Shambaugh (2003).[8] Many empirical analyses of exchange rate regimes will use these classifications of exchange rate regimes,[9] both because they make such de facto classification data public and because they cover a large number of countries over a long time period. Thus, it is useful to review methodologies for classifying exchange rate regimes and investigate the structure of the data so provided.

Accordingly, Section 1.2 will present a brief survey of the methodologies for classifying exchange rate regimes under the IMF classification system (Bubula and Ötker-Robe 2002, Reinhart and Rogoff 2002, Levy-Yeyati and Sturzenegger 2002, Shambaugh 2003). Section 1.3 will present the evolution of exchange rate regimes over the period 1990–2001 in order to examine whether the bipolar view holds in the sense that the proportions of hard pegs and freely floating regimes considerably increased and that of intermediate regimes considerably decreased throughout the sample period, by examining the de facto classification data.

By comparing de facto classifications with the *de jure* classification provided by the IMF, Section 1.4 will investigate the degree of deviation of actual regimes from official regimes and examine the exchange rate policies labeled "fear of floating" and "fear of announcing a peg." Furthermore, Section 1.5 will statistically identify the determinants of fear of floating by using logit models. Section 1.6 will present a summary and concluding remarks. Finally, the list of countries and the sources and nature of the data are presented in the Appendix.

1.2 The methodology of classifying exchange rate regimes

In this chapter, we examine the de facto exchange rate regimes of the IMF
member countries during 1990–2001 on the basis of exchange rate regime
classification data. Before we show the de facto exchange rate regimes, let us
first present a brief survey of the methodologies used for classifying exchange
rate regimes under the IMF classification system (Bubula and Ötker-Robe 2002,
Reinhart and Rogoff 2002, Levy-Yeyati and Sturzenegger 2002, Shambaugh
2003). The methodologies of classifying exchange rate regimes are summarized
in Table 1.1.

1.2.1 The IMF classification

Before 1998, the (old) IMF official classification system classified members'
exchange rate regimes on the basis of their own official statements. Regimes
were mainly classified into three categories: (1) peg (a peg to a single currency or
a composite of currencies), (2) limited flexibility, and (3) more flexible (managed
floating and independently floating). Many empirical studies of exchange rate
regimes relied on the IMF classification data, because this classification system
had long provided quarterly and annual classification data for many countries.

However, it is well known that several countries' actual exchange rate regimes
were inconsistent with the official exchange rate regimes recorded under the
IMF classification. For example, according to the IMF classification, Thailand
had a basket peg, Korea, Indonesia, Malaysia, and Singapore had a managed
float, and the Philippines even had an independent float before the Asian
currency crisis of 1997. However, it is widely recognized that their currencies
were effectively pegged to the US dollar. Thus, this suggests significant draw-
backs in this classification system.

To correct this shortcoming, the IMF has adopted a new classification system
based on the IMF members' de facto regimes since January 1999. According
to Bubula and Ötker-Robe (2002), the new classification system classifies the
IMF members' regimes on the basis of the degree of flexibility of the arrangement or a formal or informal commitment to a given exchange rate path. It
is also based on the information obtained by provision of technical assistance
to member countries and regular contact with IMF country economists. These
views are supported by analyses of observed exchange rate and reserves
behavior.

The new IMF system classifies member countries into eight categories: (1)
exchange arrangements with no separate legal tender, including formal dollarization and currency unions, (2) currency boards, (3) other conventional
fixed pegs, (4) pegged exchange rates within horizontal bands, (5) crawling peg,
(6) exchange rates within crawling bands, (7) managed floating with no predetermined path for the exchange rate, and (8) independently floating. The
old and new IMF classifications are given in the IMF's *Annual Report on Exchange*

Table 1.1 Summary of the methodologies of classifying exchange rate regimes

Classification	Sample, frequency, and country coverage	Method or criterion	Data of classification	Categories of classification
The old IMF classification system	IMF members before 1998	This classification system is based on members' official statements about the degree of exchange rate flexibility	Quarterly and annual classifications	Three categories: (1) peg (a peg to single currency and a composite of currencies), (2) limited flexibility, and (3) more flexible (managed floating and independently floating)
The new IMF classification system	IMF members since 1999	This classification system classifies exchange rate regimes on the basis of the degree of flexibility of the arrangement or a formal or informal commitment to a given exchange rate path. This classification system is also based on information obtained by provision of technical assistance to member countries and regular contacts with IMF country economists. These views are supported by an analysis of observed exchange rate and reserves behavior (Bubula and Ötker-Robe 2002)	Quarterly and annual classifications	Eight categories: (1) exchange arrangements with no separate legal tender, including formal dollarization and currency unions, (2) currency boards, (3) other conventional fixed pegs, (4) pegged exchange rates within horizontal bands, (5) crawling peg, (6) exchange rates within crawling bands, (7) managed floating with no predetermined path for the exchange rate, and (8) independently floating
Bubula and Ötker-Robe (2002)	IMF members from 1990 to 2001	Following the new IMF classification system, they construct a historical database on de facto regimes. That is to say, this classification system is based on the information obtained by provision of technical assistance to member countries and regular contacts with the IMF country economists. These views are supported by an analysis of observed exchange rate and reserves behavior	Monthly and annual classifications	Thirteen categories: (1) formal dollarization, (2) currency union, (3) currency board, (4) conventional fixed peg to single currency, (5) conventional fixed peg to basket, (6) pegged within a horizontal band, (7) forward-looking crawling peg, (8) forward-looking crawling band, (9) backward-looking crawling peg, (10) backward-looking crawling band, (11) tightly managed floating, (12) other managed float with no predetermined exchange rate path, and (13) independently floating

Classification	1	2	3	4	Categories of classification
Reinhart and Rogoff (2002)	Monthly data of official and market-determined (dual and parallel) exchange rates and inflation data for 153 countries from 1946 to 2001	Several measures of exchange rate variability. Twelve-month rate of inflation	They classify exchange rate regimes by using detailed country chronologies and a broad variety of descriptive statistics	Monthly and annual classifications	Fourteen categories: (1) no separate legal tender, (2) preannounced peg or currency board arrangement, (3) preannounced horizontal band that is narrower than or equal to +/−2%, (4) de facto peg, (5) preannounced crawling peg, (6) preannounced crawling band that is narrower than or equal to +/−2%, (7) de facto crawling peg, (8) preannounced crawling band that is wider than or equal to +/−2%, (9) de facto crawling band that is narrower than or equal to +/−2%, (10) de facto crawling band that is narrower than or equal to +/−5%, (11) moving band that is narrower than or equal to +/−2%, (12) managed floating, (13) freely floating, and (14) freely falling. They create a new separate category for a country whose 12-month rate of inflation is above 40%. This country is classified as freely falling
Levy-Yeyati and Sturzenegger (2002)	Monthly data of exchange rates, international reserves and monetary bases for 183 countries from 1974 to 2000	Three classification variables: (1) exchange rate volatility, (2) the volatility of exchange rate changes and (3) the volatility of reserves	Cluster analysis. For the criteria, see Table 1.2	Annual classification	Four categories: (1) fix, (2) crawling peg, (3) dirty float, and (4) flexible, plus an "inconclusive" category
Shambaugh (2003)	Monthly data of exchange rates for 155 countries from 1973 to 2000	The level of the exchange rate	Simple statistical analysis	Annual classification	Five categories: (1) 0% change in the exchange rate, (2) stays within 1% bands, (3) stays within 2% bands, (4) realignment, but zero change in 11 of 12 months, and (5) no peg. He determines if the exchange rate stayed within +/−1% (+/−2%) bands against the base currency

1 Sample, frequency and country coverage; 2 Classification variables; 3 Method or criterion; 4 Data of classification.

Arrangements and Exchange Restrictions (*AREAER*) and *International Financial Statistics* (*IFS*).

1.2.2   The Bubula and Ötker-Robe (2002) classification

Many researchers find the lack of historical data available under the new IMF classification a serious impediment to study. Following the new IMF classification system, Bubula and Ötker-Robe (2002) accordingly constructed historical (monthly and annual) data on de facto regimes for all the IMF member countries for the period from 1990 to 2001. As in the new IMF classification, they classify the members' regimes on the basis of the degree of flexibility of the arrangement or a formal or informal commitment to a given exchange rate path. This classification is also based on information obtained through provision of technical assistance to member countries and regular contact with IMF country economists. These views are supplemented with other sources of information, including press reports, news articles, and other relevant papers, and are also supported by analyses of observed exchange rate and reserves behavior.

Bubula and Ötker-Robe (2002) classify the IMF member countries into 13 categories: (1) formal dollarization, (2) currency union, (3) currency board, (4) conventional fixed peg to a single currency, (5) conventional fixed peg to basket, (6) pegged within a horizontal band, (7) forward-looking crawling peg, (8) backward-looking crawling peg, (9) forward-looking crawling band, (10) backward -looking crawling band, (11) tightly managed floating, (12) other managed float with no predetermined exchange rate path, and (13) independently floating. The data of the Bubula and Ötker-Robe (2002) classification can be obtained from Table 7 in their paper.

1.2.3   The Reinhart and Rogoff (2002) classification

Reinhart and Rogoff (2002) constructed a historical (monthly and annual) database on de facto exchange rate regimes for 153 countries over the period 1946–2001. They classify exchange rate regimes by applying detailed country chronologies and a broad variety of descriptive statistics of official and market-determined (dual and parallel) exchange rates.

The basic procedure of their classification is as follows. First, they verify whether there existed a unified rate or dual or multiple rates, or parallel markets, by using detailed country chronologies. Second, if there is no dual or parallel market, they check if there is an official announcement for the exchange rate. If there is, they confirm whether the announced exchange rate passes a statistical verification test. If the regime is verified, it is classified as a peg, band, and so on. If the announcement fails verification, they statistically classify the regime by using their de facto statistical sort. Third, if there is no announcement for the exchange rate, or the announced regime fails to conform to the data, they statistically classify the regime by using a broad variety of descriptive statistics of market-determined exchange rates. Fourth, a characteristic difference from all other classifications is that they create a new separate category for a country whose 12-month rate of inflation is above 40 percent. This country is classified as "freely falling."

Following the procedure, Reinhart and Rogoff (2002) classify countries into 14 categories: (1) no separate legal tender, (2) preannounced peg or currency board arrangement, (3) preannounced horizontal band that is narrower than or equal to +/−2 percent, (4) de facto peg, (5) preannounced crawling peg, (6) preannounced crawling band that is narrower than or equal to +/−2 percent, (7) de facto crawling peg, (8) preannounced crawling band that is wider than or equal to +/−2 percent, (9) de facto crawling band that is narrower than or equal to +/−2 percent, (10) de facto crawling band that is narrower than or equal to +/−5 percent, (11) moving band that is narrower than or equal to +/−2 percent, (12) managed floating, (13) freely floating, and (14) freely falling. The data of the Reinhart and Rogoff (2002) classification can be obtained from http://www.puaf.umd.edu/faculty/papers/reinhart/papers.htm.

1.2.4   The Levy-Yeyati and Sturzenegger (2002) classification

Levy-Yeyati and Sturzenegger (2002) constructed an annual database of de facto exchange rate regimes for 183 countries from 1974 to 2000. This classification is based on the following three variables related to exchange rate behavior: (1) exchange rate volatility, (2) the volatility of exchange rate changes, and (3) the volatility of reserves. Exchange rate volatility is computed as the average of the absolute monthly percentage changes in the nominal exchange rate during a calendar year, the volatility of exchange rate changes is computed as the standard deviation of the monthly percentage changes in the exchange rate, and the volatility of reserves is the average of the absolute monthly change in net dollar international reserves relative to the monetary base in the previous month.

The criterion of their classification is represented in Table 1.2. According to Table 1.2, for example, flexible exchange rate regimes are characterized by little intervention in the foreign exchange market (i.e. low volatility of reserves) with high exchange rate volatility. By contrast, fixed exchange rate regimes are characterized by heavy intervention (i.e. high volatility of reserves) with low exchange rate volatility. Furthermore, crawling peg regimes are characterized by high volatility of reserves with low exchange rate change volatility and high exchange rate volatility, because a country that adopts a crawling peg actively intervenes in the exchange market and the exchange rate depreciates at a uniform pace.

Levy-Yeyati and Sturzenegger (2002) classify 183 countries into four exchange rate regimes: (1) fix, (2) crawling peg, (3) dirty float, and (4) flexible, plus an "inconclusive" category, by applying a K-means cluster analysis to exchange rate volatility, the volatility of exchange rate changes, and the volatility of reserves. The data of the Levy-Yeyati and Sturzenegger (2002) classification can be obtained from http://www.utdt.edu/~ely/.

Table 1.2　The criterion of the Levy-Yeyati and Sturzenegger (2002) classification

	Exchange rate volatility (σ_e)	Volatility of exchange rate changes ($\sigma_{\Delta e}$)	Volatility of reserves (σ_r)
Inconclusive	Low	Low	Low
Flexible	High	High	Low
Dirty float	High	High	High
Crawling peg	High	Low	High
Fixed	Low	Low	High

Note: Exchange rate volatility (σ_e) is computed as the average of the absolute monthly percentage changes in the nominal exchange rate during a calendar year. The volatility of exchange rate changes ($\sigma_{\Delta e}$) is computed as the standard deviation of the monthly percentage changes in the exchange rate. The volatility of reserves (σ_r) is the average of the absolute monthly change in net dollar international reserves relative to the monetary base in the previous month (also in dollars).
Source: Levy-Yeyati and Sturzenegger (2002: Table 1).

In the case where a country stabilizes the exchange rate without any direct purchase or sale of foreign exchange in the market, this classification would be inappropriate, because the country would be classified as "inconclusive" when the volatilities of exchange rate and reserves are low (Table 1.2).[10] In developing countries with small and shallow foreign exchange markets, the authorities actually limit exchange rate volatility through administrative foreign exchange controls and regulations or moral suasion (Bubula and Ötker-Robe 2002).

1.2.5　The Shambaugh (2003) classification

To examine how a degree of fixed exchange rate regime affects monetary autonomy, Shambaugh (2003) mainly classifies countries as pegged or nonpegged exchange rate regimes. His classification covers 155 countries over the period 1973–2000. The criterion of classifying exchange rate regimes is to verify whether the exchange rate stayed within +/–1 percent (+/–2 percent) bands against the base currency.

Following the criterion, he classifies countries into five groups: (1) zero percent change in the exchange rate, (2) stays within 1 percent bands, (3) stays within 2 percent bands, (4) realignment, but zero change in 11 of 12 months, and (5) no peg. His category (4) can generally be considered as fixed regimes. The data of the Shambaugh (2003) classification can be obtained from http://www.dartmouth.edu/~economic/faculty/Shambaugh/index.htm.

As presented above, while Shambaugh (2003) classifies countries into pegged and nonpegged regimes, he does not definitely distinguish hard pegs or intermediate regimes from pegged regimes. For this reason, we cannot examine whether the bipolar view holds, by using this data classification.

1.3   The evolution of exchange rate regimes, 1990–2001: does the bipolar view hold?

As shown above, the bipolar view of exchange rate regimes suggests that, in a world of increasing international capital mobility, only the two extreme exchange rate regimes (either hard pegs such as dollarization, currency boards, or monetary unions, or a freely floating regime) are likely to be sustainable, and then intermediate regimes (such as adjustable pegs, basket pegs, crawling pegs, or bands) are likely to be unsustainable and will disappear. In this section, by using the databases of the de facto classifications, we present the evolution of exchange rate regimes of the IMF member countries over the period 1990–2001 in order to examine whether the bipolar view holds in the sense that the proportions of hard pegs and freely floating regimes considerably increased, while that of intermediate regimes considerably decreased, with the result that the share of intermediate regimes has fallen below that of hard pegs or freely floating regimes during the sample period.

For this purpose, we first group exchange rate regimes into three categories: (1) "hard pegs," (2) "intermediate regimes" (soft pegs), and (3) "independently floating regimes" (freely floating regimes), in each of the de facto classifications. Then, we observe the transition of exchange rate regimes in the IMF member countries during 1990–2001 on the basis of the data of the de facto classifications. If hard pegs and freely floating regimes significantly increased and intermediate regimes significantly declined over the sample period, it can be considered as evidence that the bipolar view holds.

From the standpoint of the bipolar view, it may be surmised that developed countries and emerging market economies are apt to have hard pegs or freely floating regimes, because they can be considered as more integrated or integrating into international capital markets than developing countries. Following Fischer (2001) and Bubula and Ötker-Robe (2002),[11] we thus classify all the IMF members into three groups: developed countries, emerging market countries or regions, and developing countries or regions (see Appendix 1A).

1.3.1   The Bubula and Ötker-Robe (2002) classification

Tables 1.3 and 1.4 and Figure 1.2 show the evolution of exchange rate regimes over the period 1990–2001, on the basis of the database of the Bubula and Ötker-Robe (2002) classification.[12] Here, we define their categories (1)–(3) as "hard pegs," (4)–(12) as "intermediate regimes," and (13) as "independently floating regimes" to examine the bipolar view. From these tables and figure, we first observe that, for all countries, while the proportion of hard pegs and independently floating regimes increased over the sample period, the proportion of intermediate regimes decreased over the sample period.

Second, for developed countries, the proportion of hard pegs markedly increased from 0 percent in 1990 to 52.2 percent in 2001 and that of independently floating regimes increased from 21.7 percent in 1990 to 39.1 percent

Table 1.3 The evolution of exchange rate regimes, 1990–2001, according to Bubula and Ötker-Robe (2002) (%)

Categories	1990	1991	1992	1993	1994	1995	1996	1997	1998	1999	2000	2001
1	1.899	1.875	6.145	2.762	2.717	2.717	2.717	3.243	3.243	3.243	3.784	4.324
2	12.03	11.88	10.61	10.5	10.33	10.33	10.33	10.81	10.81	16.76	16.76	17.3
3	1.899	2.5	2.793	2.762	3.261	3.261	3.261	4.324	4.324	4.324	4.324	4.324
4	24.05	21.25	18.44	19.34	20.11	21.2	19.57	20	18.92	18.38	17.84	16.22
5	19.62	17.5	15.08	13.81	10.33	8.696	7.609	7.027	5.946	5.405	5.405	5.405
6	8.861	8.125	6.145	7.182	8.152	7.065	9.783	8.649	8.649	2.703	3.243	2.703
7	1.899	1.875	1.117	2.21	2.717	2.717	2.717	2.703	1.622	2.162	3.243	1.622
8	0.633	2.5	2.235	2.21	2.174	3.261	4.348	4.324	4.865	3.243	2.703	3.243
9	7.595	7.5	6.145	6.63	3.804	3.804	3.804	4.324	4.324	2.703	0.541	0.541
10	1.266	1.25	0.559	1.105	1.087	2.174	2.174	1.081	0.541	0.541	0.541	0
11	5.063	6.25	6.145	6.077	8.696	9.783	8.152	4.865	3.243	5.405	7.568	8.649
12	9.494	10	11.73	11.6	13.59	10.87	13.04	14.05	16.22	16.76	14.59	15.14
13	5.696	7.5	12.85	13.81	13.04	14.13	12.5	14.59	17.3	18.38	19.46	20.54
Total	100	100	100	100	100	100	100	100	100	100	100	100

Note: Thirteen categories: (1) formal dollarization, (2) currency union, (3) currency board, (4) conventional fixed peg to single currency, (5) conventional fixed peg to basket, (6) pegged within a horizontal band, (7) forward-looking crawling peg, (8) backward-looking crawling peg, (9) forward-looking crawling band, (10) backward-looking crawling band, (11) tightly managed floating, (12) other managed float with no predetermined exchange rate path, and (13) independently floating.

Source: The database of the Bubula and Ötker-Robe (2002) classification.

Table 1.4 Test of the bipolar view by using the data of Bubula and Ötker-Robe (2002) (%)

	1990	1991	1992	1993	1994	1995	1996	1997	1998	1999	2000	2001
All												
Hard pegs	15.8	16.3	19.6	16	16.3	16.3	16.3	18.4	18.4	24.3	24.9	25.9
Intermediate regimes	78.5	76.3	67.6	70.2	70.7	69.6	71.2	67	64.3	57.3	55.7	53.5
Independently floating	5.7	7.5	12.8	13.8	13	14.1	12.5	14.6	17.3	18.4	19.5	20.5
Total	100	100	100	100	100	100	100	100	100	100	100	100
Developed												
Hard pegs	0	0	0	0	0	0	0	0	0	47.8	47.8	52.2
Intermediate regimes	78.3	78.3	56.5	60.9	60.9	60.9	69.6	69.6	65.2	17.4	17.4	8.7
Independently floating	21.7	21.7	43.5	39.1	39.1	39.1	30.4	30.4	34.8	34.8	34.8	39.1
Total	100	100	100	100	100	100	100	100	100	100	100	100
Emerging												
Hard pegs	6.45	9.68	9.38	9.09	9.09	9.09	9.09	12.1	12.1	12.1	15.2	15.2
Intermediate regimes	87.1	83.9	87.5	90.9	87.9	87.9	84.8	75.8	72.7	60.6	54.5	54.5
Independently floating	6.45	6.45	3.13	0	3.03	3.03	6.06	12.1	15.2	27.3	30.3	30.3
Total	100	100	100	100	100	100	100	100	100	100	100	100
Developing												
Hard pegs	22.1	21.7	25.8	20.8	21.1	21.1	21.1	23.3	23.3	23.3	23.3	24
Intermediate regimes	76	73.6	64.5	66.4	68	66.4	68	64.3	62	63.6	62.8	61.2
Independently floating	1.92	4.72	9.68	12.8	10.9	12.5	10.9	12.4	14.7	13.2	14	14.7
Total	100	100	100	100	100	100	100	100	100	100	100	100

Note: In order to examine the bipolar view, we define their categories (1)–(3) as "hard pegs," (4)–(12) as "intermediate regimes," and (13) as "independently floating regimes."

Source: Author's estimates based on the data of Bubula and Ötker-Robe (2002).

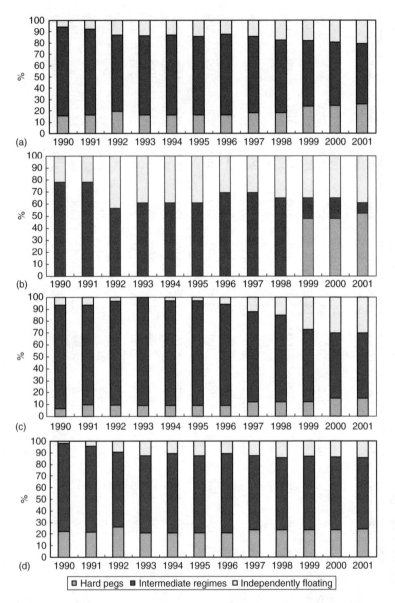

Figure 1.2 The evolution of exchange rate regimes, 1990–2001, according to Bubula and Ötker-Robe (2002): (a) all countries; (b) developed countries; (c) emerging market economies; (d) developing countries
Note: In order to examine the bipolar view, we define their categories (1)–(3) as "hard pegs," (4)–(12) as "intermediate regimes," and (13) as "independently floating regimes."
Source: As for Table 1.4.

in 2001. On the other hand, the proportion of intermediate regimes dramatically decreased from 78.3 percent in 1990 to 8.7 percent in 2001. Naturally, the fact that 12 European countries entered into Economic and Monetary Union (EMU) from 1999 to 2001 underlies this result. At the end of 2001, in practice, there were two countries (Denmark and Norway) with intermediate regimes (see Table 1.5). Hence, we can be reasonably sure that the bipolar view strongly holds for developed countries.

Third, for emerging market economies, the share of hard pegs increased from 6.45 percent in 1990 to 15.2 percent in 2001 and that of independently floating regimes increased sharply from 6.45 percent in 1990 to 30.3 percent in 2001. On the other hand, the share of intermediate regimes decreased from 87.1 percent in 1990 to 54.5 percent in 2001. In particular, from 1997 to 2001, intermediate regimes substantially decreased and independently floating regimes significantly increased. This result is partly supported by the fact that currency crises (e.g. the Asian crisis in 1997–98) caused emerging market economies to move away from soft pegs toward freely floating regimes. We observe from Table 1.5 that, while most emerging economies adopted intermediate regimes in 2001, many countries moved toward the two edges (i.e. conventional fixed peg and other managed float) although still remaining as intermediate regimes.

However, the proportion of intermediate regimes was more than 50 percent in 2001 and was significantly higher than those of hard pegs (15.2 percent) and freely floating regimes (30.3 percent) in 2001. From this result, we cannot conclude that the bipolar view strictly holds for emerging market economies, even though hard pegs and freely floating regimes increased and intermediate regimes decreased over the sample period, on the basis of the database of the Bubula and Ötker-Robe (2002) classification.[13]

1.3.2   The Reinhart and Rogoff (2002) classification

Tables 1.6 and 1.7 and Figure 1.3 show the evolution of exchange rate regimes over the period 1990–2001, on the basis of the database of the Reinhart and Rogoff (2002) classification.[14] Here, we define their categories (1)–(2) as "hard pegs," (3)–(12) as "intermediate regimes," and (13)–(14) as "independently floating regimes" to examine the bipolar view. From these tables and figure, we first observe that, for all countries, while the proportion of hard pegs increased over the sample period, those of intermediate regimes and freely floating regimes showed little change.

Second, for developed countries, the proportion of hard pegs dramatically increased from 0 percent in 1990 to 52.1 percent in 2001 and that of freely floating regimes slightly decreased from 17.4 percent in 1990 to 13.0 percent in 2001. On the other hand, the proportion of intermediate regimes registered a marked decrease from 82.6 percent in 1990 to 34.8 percent in 2001. While there were eight countries with intermediate regimes, five countries (Iceland, New Zealand, Norway, Sweden, and the United Kingdom) had a managed floating regime in 2001 (see Table 1.8).

Table 1.5 Exchange rate arrangements, 1990 and 2001: developed countries and emerging market economies, according to Bubula and Ötker-Robe (2002)

Exchange rate regimes		1990	2001
Developed countries			
Hard pegs	(1)		
	(2)		Austria, Belgium, Finland, France, Germany, Greece, Ireland, Italy, Luxembourg, Netherlands, Portugal, Spain
	(3)		
Intermediate regimes	(4)	Austria, Luxembourg, Netherlands	
	(5)		
	(6)	Belgium, Denmark, Finland, France, Germany, Iceland, Ireland, Italy, Norway, Spain, Sweden, United Kingdom	Denmark
	(7)	Greece	
	(8)	Portugal	
	(9)		
	(10)		
	(11)		
	(12)	Canada	Norway
Independently floating	(13)	Australia, Japan, New Zealand, Switzerland, United States	Australia, Canada, Iceland, Japan, New Zealand, Sweden, Switzerland, United Kingdom, United States
Emerging market economies			
Hard pegs	(1)	Panama	Ecuador, Panama
	(2)		
	(3)	Hong Kong	Argentina, Bulgaria, Hong Kong
Intermediate regimes	(4)	China, Egypt, Philippines, Poland, Qatar	China, Jordan, Malaysia, Qatar
	(5)	Bulgaria, Hungary, Jordan, Malaysia, Morocco, Thailand	Morocco
	(6)	India, Israel	Egypt, Hungary
	(7)	Ecuador, Mexico	
	(8)		Israel, Venezuela
	(9)	Colombia, Indonesia, Sri Lanka, Turkey	
	(10)	Chile	
	(11)	Korea, Nigeria, Pakistan, Singapore	India, Nigeria, Singapore
	(12)	Brazil, South Africa, Venezuela	Czech Republic, Indonesia, Pakistan, Russia, Sri Lanka, Thailand
Independently floating	(13)	Argentina, Peru	Brazil, Chile, Colombia, Korea, Mexico, Peru, Philippines, Poland, South Africa, Turkey

Note: Thirteen categories: (1) formal dollarization, (2) currency union, (3) currency board, (4) conventional fixed peg to single currency, (5) conventional fixed peg to basket, (6) pegged within a horizontal band, (7) forward-looking crawling peg, (8) backward-looking crawling peg, (9) forward-looking crawling band, (10) backward-looking crawling band, (11) tightly managed floating, (12) other managed float with no predetermined exchange rate path, and (13) independently floating.
Source: The database of the Bubula and Ötker-Robe (2002) classification.

Table 1.6 The evolution of exchange rate regimes, 1990–2001, according to Reinhart and Rogoff (2002) (%)

Categories	1990	1991	1992	1993	1994	1995	1996	1997	1998	1999	2000	2001
1	4.065	3.788	3.731	3.65	3.623	3.521	3.521	3.571	3.597	12.23	13.04	13.14
2	19.51	16.67	16.42	16.79	18.12	19.01	19.01	20.71	21.58	21.58	21.74	21.9
3	0	0.758	0.746	0	0	0	0	0	0	0	0	0
4	8.13	7.576	10.45	10.95	12.32	11.97	13.38	14.29	12.95	6.475	7.971	7.299
5	1.626	1.515	0.746	0.73	0	0	0	0	0	0	0	0
6	0.813	1.515	0.746	0.73	0.725	1.408	1.408	2.143	2.158	1.439	0.725	0.73
7	5.691	7.576	7.463	9.489	9.42	10.56	11.27	11.43	10.07	9.353	7.971	8.029
8	0.813	0.758	0	0	0.725	0	0	0	0	1.439	0.725	0.73
9	15.45	15.15	14.18	15.33	15.22	16.9	17.61	16.43	15.11	13.67	15.94	16.06
10	8.943	9.091	9.701	8.029	8.696	9.155	9.155	7.857	8.633	7.194	5.797	5.839
11	1.626	2.273	2.239	0.73	0.725	0.704	0.704	0.714	0.719	0.719	0.725	0.73
12	10.57	7.576	6.716	6.569	4.348	4.93	7.042	8.571	9.353	10.79	14.49	16.06
13	5.691	5.303	4.478	3.65	3.623	4.93	5.634	5	6.475	6.475	6.522	6.569
14	17.07	20.45	22.39	24.09	22.46	16.9	11.27	9.286	9.353	8.633	4.348	2.92
Total	100	100	100	100	100	100	100	100	100	100	100	100

Note: Fourteen categories: (1) no separate legal tender, (2) preannounced peg or currency board arrangement, (3) preannounced horizontal band that is narrower than or equal to +/−2%, (4) de facto peg, (5) preannounced crawling peg, (6) preannounced crawling band that is narrower than or equal to +/−2%, (7) de facto crawling peg, (8) preannounced crawling band that is wider than or equal to +/−2%, (9) de facto crawling band that is narrower than or equal to +/−2%, (10) de facto crawling band that is narrower than or equal to +/−5%, (11) moving band that is narrower than or equal to +/−2%, (12) managed floating, (13) freely floating, and (14) freely falling.

Source: The database of the Reinhart and Rogoff (2002) classification.

Table 1.7 Test of the bipolar view by using the data of Reinhart and Rogoff (2002) (%)

	1990	1991	1992	1993	1994	1995	1996	1997	1998	1999	2000	2001
All												
Hard pegs	23.58	20.45	20.15	20.44	21.74	22.54	22.54	24.29	25.18	33.81	34.78	35.04
Intermediate regimes	53.66	53.79	52.99	51.82	52.17	55.63	60.56	61.43	58.99	51.08	54.35	55.47
Freely floating	5.691	5.303	4.478	3.65	3.623	4.93	5.634	5	6.475	6.475	6.522	6.569
Freely falling	17.07	20.45	22.39	24.09	22.46	16.9	11.27	9.286	9.353	8.633	4.348	2.92
Total	100	100	100	100	100	100	100	100	100	100	100	100
Developed												
Hard pegs	0	0	0	0	0	0	0	0	0	52.17	52.17	52.17
Intermediate regimes	82.61	82.61	82.61	82.61	82.61	82.61	82.61	82.61	82.61	34.78	34.78	34.78
Freely floating	17.39	17.39	17.39	17.39	17.39	17.39	17.39	17.39	17.39	13.04	13.04	13.04
Freely falling	0	0	0	0	0	0	0	0	0	0	0	0
Total	100	100	100	100	100	100	100	100	100	100	100	100
Emerging												
Hard pegs	13.33	10	9.677	10	10	9.375	9.375	12.9	12.9	15.63	18.75	18.75
Intermediate regimes	66.67	66.67	64.52	63.33	70	68.75	75	77.42	70.97	65.63	71.88	68.75
Freely floating	0	0	0	0	0	3.125	3.125	3.226	6.452	9.375	9.375	9.375
Freely falling	20	23.33	25.81	26.67	20	18.75	12.5	6.452	9.677	9.375	0	3.125
Total	100	100	100	100	100	100	100	100	100	100	100	100
Developing												
Hard pegs	36.23	30.77	30.38	30.12	32.14	33.72	33.72	35.29	36.9	36.14	36.59	37.04
Intermediate regimes	39.13	39.74	39.24	38.55	36.9	43.02	48.84	49.41	47.62	49.4	52.44	55.56
Freely floating	4.348	3.846	2.532	1.205	1.19	2.326	3.488	2.353	3.571	3.614	3.659	3.704
Freely falling	20.29	25.64	27.85	30.12	29.76	20.93	13.95	12.94	11.9	10.84	7.317	3.704
Total	100	100	100	100	100	100	100	100	100	100	100	100

Note: In order to examine the bipolar view, we define their categories (1)–(2) as "hard pegs," (3)–(12) as "intermediate regimes," and categories (13) (freely floating) and (14) (freely falling) as "independently floating regimes."
Source: Author's estimates based on the data of Reinhart and Rogoff (2002).

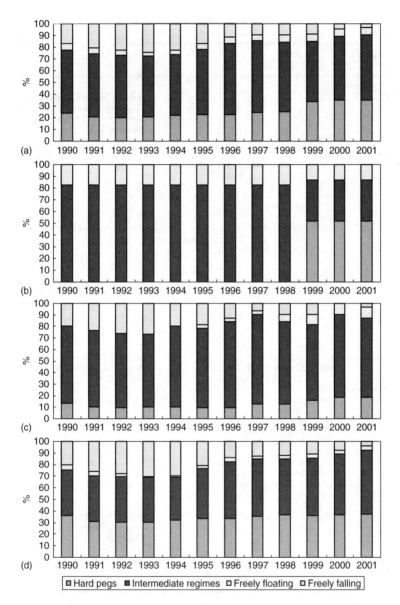

Figure 1.3 The evolution of exchange rate regimes, 1990–2001, according to Reinhart and Rogoff (2002): (a) all countries; (b) developed countries; (c) emerging market economies; (d) developing countries

Note: In order to examine the bipolar view, we define their categories (1)–(2) as "hard pegs," (3)–(12) as "intermediate regimes," and categories (13)–(14) as "independently floating regimes."

Source: As for Table 1.7.

Table 1.8 Exchange rate arrangements, 1990 and 2001: developed countries and emerging market economies, according to Reinhart and Rogoff (2002)

Exchange rate regimes		1990	2001
Developed countries			
Hard pegs	(1)		Austria, Belgium, Finland, France, Germany, Greece, Ireland, Italy, Luxembourg, Netherlands, Portugal, Spain
	(2)		
Intermediate regimes	(3)		
	(4)	Austria, Belgium, France, Greece, Luxembourg, Netherlands	Denmark
	(5)		
	(6)		
	(7)	Denmark	
	(8)		
	(9)	Canada, Finland, Iceland, Ireland, Italy, Portugal, Spain, Sweden, Switzerland	Canada, Switzerland
	(10)		
	(11)	Norway	
	(12)	New Zealand, United Kingdom	Iceland, New Zealand, Norway, Sweden, United Kingdom
Independently floating	(13)	Australia, Germany, Japan, United States	Australia, Japan, United States
	(14)		
Emerging market economies			
Hard pegs	(1)	Panama	Ecuador, Panama
	(2)	Hong Kong, Poland, Sri Lanka	Argentina, Bulgaria, Hong Kong, Malaysia
Intermediate regimes	(3)		
	(4)	Thailand	China, Egypt, Jordan, Peru
	(5)	Mexico	
	(6)	Korea	Venezuela
	(7)	India, Indonesia, Pakistan, Philippines	India
	(8)	Chile	Hungary
	(9)	Czech Republic, Israel, Malaysia, Morocco, Singapore	Morocco, Pakistan, Russia
	(10)	Colombia, Egypt, Hungary, Jordan	Israel, Sri Lanka
	(11)		
	(12)	China, Nigeria, Venezuela	Brazil, Chile, Colombia, Czech Republic, Mexico, Nigeria, Philippines, Poland, Singapore, Thailand
Independently floating	(13)		Indonesia, Korea, South Africa
	(14)	Argentina, Brazil, Bulgaria, Ecuador, Peru, Turkey	Turkey

Note: Fourteen categories: (1) no separate legal tender, (2) preannounced per or currency board arrangement, (3) preannounced horizontal band that is narrower than or equal to +/−2%, (4) de facto peg, (5) preannounced crawling peg, (6) preannounced crawling band that is narrower than or equal to +/−2%, (7) de facto crawling peg, (8) preannounced crawling band that is wider than or equal to +/−2%, (9) de facto crawling band that is narrower than or equal to +/−2%, (10) de facto crawling band that is narrower than or equal to +/−5%, (11) moving band that is narrower than or equal to +/−2%, (12) managed floating, (13) freely floating, and (14) freely falling.
Source: The database of the Reinhart and Rogoff (2002) classification.

Third, for emerging market economies, the share of hard pegs increased from 13.3 percent in 1990 to 18.8 percent in 2001, that of freely floating regimes increased from 0 percent in 1990 to 9.37 percent in 2001, and that of freely falling regimes decreased considerably from 20 percent in 1990 to 3.1 percent in 2001[15] (i.e. the share of independently floating regimes decreased from 20 percent in 1990 to 12.5 percent in 2001). On the other hand, the share of intermediate regimes showed virtually no change (66.7 percent in 1990 and 68.7 percent in 2001). We observe from Table 1.8 that 22 emerging market economies adopted intermediate regimes in 2001 and 10 countries had a managed floating regime in 2001.

From these results, we can reasonably conclude that the bipolar view holds for developed countries, in the sense that the proportion of hard pegs significantly increased and that of intermediate regimes significantly decreased over the sample period. On the other hand, the bipolar view for emerging market economies cannot be supported by the Reinhart and Rogoff (2002) classification data, because the proportion of intermediate regimes did not change to any great extent between 1990 and 2001 and remained at a significantly high level (68.7 percent in 2001).[16]

1.3.3 The Levy-Yeyati and Sturzenegger (2002) classification

Table 1.9 and Figure 1.4 show the evolution of exchange rate regimes over the period 1990–2000, on the basis of the database of the Levy-Yeyati and Sturzenegger (2002) classification. From this table and figure, we first see that, for all countries, the proportion of the floating regimes increased and that of intermediate regimes[17] decreased over the sample period, while that of the pegs was stable at 57.9 percent. The proportion of intermediate regimes (16.4 percent) was considerably lower than that of the peg (57.9 percent) or the floating regime (25.7 percent) in 2000.

Second, for developed countries, the proportion of the pegs markedly increased from 33.3 percent in 1990 to 68.2 percent in 2000 and that of floating regimes decreased from 50 percent in 1990 to 27.3 percent in 2001. On the other hand, the proportion of intermediate regimes decreased from 16.7 percent in 1990 to 4.5 percent in 2000. Third, for emerging market economies, the proportion of the pegs increased from 26.9 percent in 1990 to 34.5 percent in 2000 and that of floating regimes increased considerably from 30.8 percent in 1990 to 48.3 percent in 2000. On the other hand, the proportion of intermediate regimes decreased considerably from 42.3 percent in 1990 to 17.2 percent in 2000.

To test for the bipolar view, we define their category (1) fixed regimes as "hard pegs," (2) crawling pegs and (3) a dirty float as "intermediate regimes," and (4) float as "freely floating regimes," while Levy-Yeyati and Sturzenegger (2002) did not distinguish clearly between hard pegs (such as dollarization, currency boards, and monetary unions) and conventional fixed regimes. These results

Table 1.9 The evolution of exchange rate regimes, 1990–2000, according to Levy-Yeyati and Sturzenegger (2002) (%)

	1990	1991	1992	1993	1994	1995	1996	1997	1998	1999	2000
All											
Fix	57.98	56.67	59.17	59.38	49.24	52.7	55.78	51.97	56.58	58.28	57.89
Dirty/crawling peg	9.244	17.5	11.67	10.16	11.36	10.14	15.65	13.82	10.53	11.26	11.18
Dirty float	14.29	9.167	7.5	4.688	21.97	12.16	6.122	7.237	6.579	6.623	5.263
Float	18.49	16.67	21.67	25.78	17.42	25	22.45	26.97	26.32	23.84	25.66
Total	100	100	100	100	100	100	100	100	100	100	100
Developed											
Fix	33.33	36.84	54.55	54.55	61.9	42.86	57.14	50	63.16	68.18	68.18
Dirty/crawling peg	5.556	15.79	0	0	4.762	0	4.762	0	0	4.545	0
Dirty float	11.11	15.79	9.091	4.545	0	14.29	4.762	16.67	5.263	0	4.545
Float	50	31.58	36.36	40.91	33.33	42.86	33.33	33.33	31.58	27.27	27.27
Total	100	100	100	100	100	100	100	100	100	100	100
Emerging											
Fix	26.92	26.92	25	36	34.78	21.43	29.63	24.14	40	33.33	34.48
Dirty/crawling peg	11.54	34.62	33.33	20	26.09	17.86	25.93	24.14	10	11.11	13.79
Dirty float	30.77	11.54	16.67	8	17.39	17.86	7.407	6.897	6.667	11.11	3.448
Float	30.77	26.92	25	36	21.74	42.86	37.04	44.83	43.33	44.44	48.28
Total	100	100	100	100	100	100	100	100	100	100	100
Developing											
Fix	74.67	72	71.62	67.9	50	63.64	62.63	60	60.19	62.75	62.38
Dirty/crawling peg	9.333	12	8.108	9.877	9.091	10.1	15.15	13.33	12.62	12.75	12.87
Dirty float	9.333	6.667	4.054	3.704	28.41	10.1	6.061	5.714	6.796	6.863	5.941
Float	6.667	9.333	16.22	18.52	12.5	16.16	16.16	20.95	20.39	17.65	18.81
Total	100	100	100	100	100	100	100	100	100	100	100

Note: Four categories: (1) peg, (2) dirty/crawling peg, (3) dirty float, and (4) float.
Source: The database of the Levy-Yeyati and Sturzenegger (2002) classification.

29

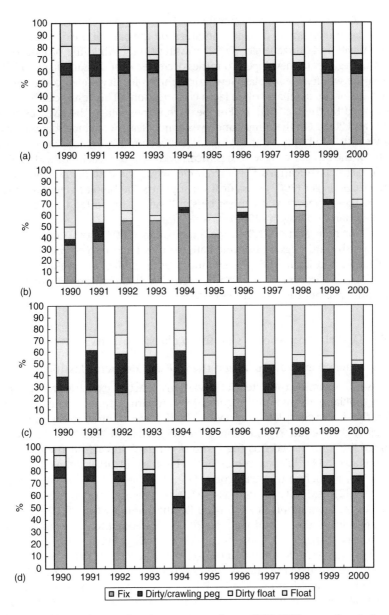

Figure 1.4 The evolution of exchange rate regimes, 1990–2000, according to Levy-Yeyati and Sturzenegger (2002): (a) all countries; (b) developed countries; (c) emerging market economies; (d) developing countries
Source: As for Table 1.9.

from Table 1.9 and Figure 1.4 indicate that the bipolar view holds for developed countries and emerging market economies, on the basis of the database of the Levy-Yeyati and Sturzenegger (2002) classification,[18] while the proportion of floating regimes for developed countries decreased over the sample period.[19]

On the whole, the bipolar view strictly holds for developed countries, on the basis of the databases of de facto classifications. This result can be partly explained by the fact that 12 European countries joined the EMU between 1999 and 2001. On the other hand, we cannot clearly conclude that the bipolar view strictly holds for emerging market economies, because the results of tests for the bipolar view were significantly different in each of the databases of de facto classifications.[20] For example, while the data of the Levy-Yeyati and Sturzenegger (2002) classification supports the bipolar view for emerging market economies, it cannot be significantly supported by the data of the Reinhart and Rogoff (2002) classification.

As shown in Section 1.2, since Shambaugh (2003) does not definitely distinguish hard pegs or intermediate regimes from pegged regimes, from Table 1.10 and Figure 1.5 (the evolution of exchange rate regimes, on the basis of the database of the Shambaugh (2003) classification), we cannot examine whether the bipolar view holds.

1.4 IMF classification vs de facto classifications

1.4.1 The mismatches between the IMF and de facto classifications

Let us now examine the extent of deviations of actual exchange rate regimes from official exchange rate regimes by comparing de facto classifications with the *de jure* classification provided by the IMF. In order to do so, we first group exchange rate regimes into four categories: (1) "peg," (2) "flexibility limited," (3) "managed floating," and (4) "float," in each of the classifications (Table 1.11).[21] For example, for the Bubula and Ötker-Robe (2002) classification, we define their categories (1)–(5) as category (1) peg; (6)–(10) as category (2) flexibility limited; (11)–(12) as category (3) managed floating; and (13) as category (4) float. For the Reinhart and Rogoff (2002) classification, following Alesina and Wagner (2003), we define their categories (1)–(4) as category (1) peg; (5)–(9) as category (2) flexibility limited; (10)–(12) as category (3) managed floating; and (13)–(14) as category (4) float.[22]

Then, we estimate the rates of the mismatches (matches) between the IMF and de facto classifications. Tables 1.12–1.14 compare the IMF and de facto classifications.[23] The rows show the exchange rate regimes of the IMF classification. The exchange rate regimes of the de facto classification are shown in columns. Hence, the diagonal of these tables shows the coincidence between both classifications and both sides of the diagonal show deviations of actual regimes from official regimes. Moreover, the elements below the diagonal indicate that, in practice, some countries have a peg more than they announce

Table 1.10 The evolution of exchange rate regimes, 1990–2000, according to Shambaugh (2003) (%)

	1990	1991	1992	1993	1994	1995	1996	1997	1998	1999	2000
All											
Categories (1) and (4)	23.23	20.65	21.29	20.65	19.35	20	21.29	21.29	23.38	20.13	22.58
Category (2)	16.13	14.84	16.77	14.19	20	18.71	19.35	21.29	20.13	23.38	19.35
Category (3)	6.452	7.097	5.806	7.742	6.452	8.387	7.742	4.516	1.948	3.247	3.226
Category (5)	54.19	57.42	56.13	57.42	54.19	52.9	51.61	52.9	54.55	53.25	54.84
Total	100	100	100	100	100	100	100	100	100	100	100
Developed											
Categories (1) and (4)	4.348	4.348	4.348	4.348	4.348	4.348	4.348	0	4.348	4.348	4.348
Category (2)	26.09	17.39	26.09	8.696	26.09	13.04	17.39	34.78	43.48	43.48	43.48
Category (3)	17.39	26.09	0	4.348	0	8.696	13.04	8.696	0	4.348	4.348
Category (5)	52.17	52.17	69.57	82.61	69.57	73.91	65.22	56.52	52.17	47.83	47.83
Total	100	100	100	100	100	100	100	100	100	100	100
Emerging											
Categories (1) and (4)	10	6.667	6.667	6.667	6.667	6.667	10	13.33	20	16.67	16.67
Category (2)	6.667	3.333	10	16.67	13.33	16.67	20	13.33	6.667	10	6.667
Category (3)	6.667	13.33	16.67	10	10	13.33	6.667	3.333	3.333	6.667	6.667
Category (5)	76.67	76.67	66.67	66.67	70	63.33	63.33	70	70	66.67	70
Total	100	100	100	100	100	100	100	100	100	100	100
Developing											
Categories (1) and (4)	31.37	28.43	29.41	28.43	26.47	27.45	28.43	28.43	28.71	24.75	28.43
Category (2)	16.67	17.65	16.67	14.71	20.59	20.59	19.61	20.59	18.81	22.77	17.65
Category (3)	3.922	0.98	3.922	7.843	6.863	6.863	6.863	3.922	1.98	1.98	1.961
Category (5)	48.04	52.94	50	49.02	46.08	45.1	45.1	47.06	50.5	50.5	51.96
Total	100	100	100	100	100	100	100	100	100	100	100

Note: Five categories: (1) zero percent change in the exchange rate, (2) stays within 1% bands, (3) stays within 2% bands, (4) realignment, but zero change in 11 of 12 months, and (5) no peg.

Source: The database of the Shambaugh (2003) classification.

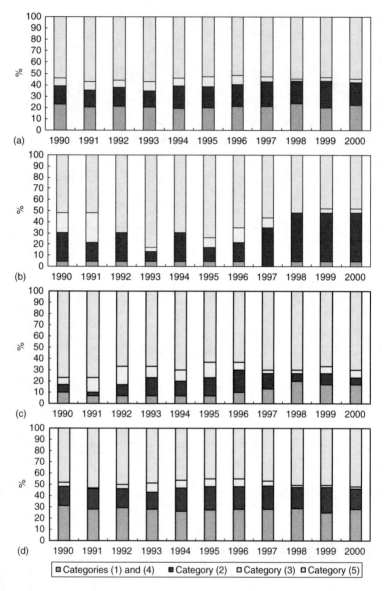

Figure 1.5 The evolution of exchange rate regimes, 1990–2000, according to Shambaugh (2003): (a) all countries; (b) developed countries; (c) emerging market economies; (d) developing countries

Note: Shambaugh (2003) classifies exchange rate regimes into five categories: (1) zero percent change in the exchange rate, (2) stays within 1% bands, (3) stays within 2% bands, (4) realignment, but zero change in 11 of 12 months, and (5) no peg.

Source: As for Table 1.10.

Table 1.11 Classification of the four classifications of exchange rate regimes

	IMF	Bubula and Ötker-Robe (2002)	Reinhart and Rogoff (2002)	Levy-Yeyati and Sturzenegger (2002)
1 Peg	Pegged to single currency or composite of currencies	(1) Formal dollarization up to (5) Conventional fixed peg to basket	(1) No separate legal tender up to (4) De facto peg	(1) Fix
2 Limited	Flexibility limited	(6) Pegged within a horizontal band up to (10) Backward-looking crawling band	(5) Preannounced crawling peg up to (9) De facto crawling band that is narrower than or equal to +/−2%	(2) Dirty/crawling peg
3 Managed	Managed floating	(11) Tightly managed floating or (12) Other managed float with no predetermined exchange rate path	(10) De facto crawling band that is narrower than or equal to +/−5% up to (12) Managed floating	(3) Dirty float
4 Float	Independently floating	(13) Independently floating	(13) Freely floating or (14) Freely falling	(4) Float

Note: Following the basis of Alesina and Wagner (2003), we classify exchange rate regimes into four categories: (1) "peg," (2) "flexibility limited," (3) "managed floating," and (4) "float," in order to compare the classifications.

Table 1.12 IMF classification vs Bubula and Ötker-Robe (2002) classification, 1990–98

IMF classification	De facto classification				Total numbers	Mismatch
	1 Peg	2 Limited	3 Managed	4 Float		
All countries						
1 Peg	627	40	22	0	689	62
	(91.0)	(5.8)	(3.2)	(0)		(9.0)
2 Limited	60	94	0	1	155	61
	(38.7)	(60.6)	(0)	(0.7)		(39.4)
3 Managed	62	155	111	4	332	221
	(18.7)	(46.7)	(33.4)	(1.20)		(66.6)
4 Float	33	27	166	194	420	226
	(7.9)	(6.4)	(39.5)	(46.2)		(53.8)
Total numbers	782	316	299	199	1596	570 (35.7)
Developed countries						
1 Peg	4	14	0	0	18	14
	(22.2)	(77.8)	(0)	(0)		(77.8)
2 Limited	23	75	0	0	98	23
	(23.5)	(76.5)	(0)	(0)		(23.5)
3 Managed	0	8	4	0	12	8
	(0)	(66.7)	(33.3)	(0)		(66.7)
4 Float	0	0	10	69	79	10
	(0)	(0)	(12.7)	(87.3)		(12.7)
Total numbers	27	97	14	69	207	55 (26.6)
Emerging market economies						
1 Peg	60	3	4	0	67	7
	(89.6)	(4.4)	(6.0)	(0)		(10.4)
2 Limited	9	9	0	0	18	9
	(50)	(50)	(0)	(0)		(50)
3 Managed	17	84	38	0	139	101
	(12.2)	(60.4)	(27.3)	(0)		(72.7)
4 Float	9	5	36	18	68	50
	(13.2)	(7.4)	(52.9)	(26.5)		(73.5)
Total numbers	95	101	78	18	292	167 (57.2)
Developing countries						
1 Peg	563	23	18	0	604	41
	(93.2)	(3.8)	(3.0)	(0)		(6.8)
2 Limited	28	10	0	1	39	29
	(71.8)	(25.6)	(0)	(2.6)		(74.4)
3 Managed	45	63	69	4	181	112
	(24.9)	(34.8)	(38.1)	(2.2)		(61.9)
4 Float	24	22	120	107	273	166
	(8.8)	(8.1)	(43.9)	(39.2)		(60.8)
Total numbers	660	118	207	112	1097	348 (31.7)

Note: The figures in parentheses indicate the percentage of the number of countries in the given row category.

Source: Author's estimates based on the data of Bubula and Ötker-Robe (2002) and AREAER.

Table 1.13   IMF classification vs Reinhart and Rogoff (2002) classification, 1990–2001

IMF classification	De facto classification				Total numbers	Mismatch
	1 *Peg*	*2* *Limited*	*3* *Managed*	*4* *Float*		
All countries						
1 Peg	422	84	88	39	633	211
	(66.7)	(13.3)	(13.9)	(6.1)		(33.3)
2 Limited	81	61	16	12	170	109
	(47.6)	(35.9)	(9.4)	(7.1)		(64.1)
3 Managed	40	163	86	69	358	272
	(11.2)	(45.5)	(24.0)	(19.3)		(76.0)
4 Float	29	127	107	186	449	263
	(6.5)	(28.3)	(23.8)	(41.4)		(58.6)
Total numbers	572	435	297	306	1610	855 (53.1)
Developed countries						
1 Peg	38	12	2	0	52	14
	(73.1)	(23.1)	(3.8)	(0)		(26.9)
2 Limited	66	29	1	9	105	76
	(62.9)	(27.6)	(0.9)	(8.6)		(72.4)
3 Managed	7	1	7	0	15	8
	(46.7)	(6.6)	(46.7)	(0)		(53.3)
4 Float	2	32	34	36	104	68
	(1.9)	(30.8)	(32.7)	(34.6)		(65.4)
Total numbers	113	74	44	45	276	166 (60.1)
Emerging market economies						
1 Peg	57	24	10	5	96	39
	(59.4)	(25)	(10.4)	(5.2)		(40.6)
2 Limited	1	10	12	1	24	14
	(4.2)	(41.7)	(50)	(4.1)		(58.3)
3 Managed	23	66	45	20	154	109
	(14.9)	(42.9)	(29.2)	(13.0)		(70.8)
4 Float	7	18	30	42	97	55
	(7.2)	(18.6)	(30.9)	(43.3)		(56.7)
Total numbers	88	118	97	68	371	217 (58.4)
Developing countries						
1 Peg	315	60	78	36	489	174
	(64.4)	(12.3)	(15.9)	(7.4)		(35.6)
2 Limited	14	22	3	2	41	19
	(34.1)	(53.7)	(7.3)	(4.9)		(46.3)
3 Managed	10	96	38	49	193	155
	(5.2)	(49.7)	(19.7)	(25.4)		(80.3)
4 Float	20	77	44	111	252	141
	(7.9)	(30.6)	(17.5)	(44.0)		(56.0)
Total numbers	359	255	163	198	975	489 (50.2)

Note: The figures in parentheses indicate the percentage of the number of countries in the given row category.
Source: Author's estimates based on the data of Reinhart and Rogoff (2002) and AREAER.

36

Table 1.14 IMF classification vs Levy-Yeyati and Sturzenegger (2002) classification, 1990–2000

IMF classification	De facto classification				Total numbers	Mismatch
	1 Peg	2 Limited	3 Managed	4 Float		
All countries						
1 Peg	565	27	24	17	633	68
	(89.3)	(4.2)	(3.8)	(2.7)		(10.7)
2 Limited	108	19	7	32	166	147
	(65.1)	(11.4)	(4.2)	(19.3)		(88.6)
3 Managed	59	66	46	121	292	246
	(20.2)	(22.6)	(15.8)	(41.4)		(84.2)
4 Float	110	71	61	180	422	242
	(26.1)	(16.8)	(14.4)	(42.7)		(57.3)
Total numbers	842	183	138	350	1513	703 (46.5)
Developed countries						
1 Peg	27	0	1	0	28	1
	(96.4)	(0)	(3.6)	(0)		(3.6)
2 Limited	65	4	3	16	88	84
	(73.9)	(4.5)	(3.4)	(18.2)		(95.5)
3 Managed	10	0	4	0	14	10
	(71.4)	(0)	(28.6)	(0)		(71.4)
4 Float	20	3	9	63	95	32
	(21.0)	(3.2)	(9.5)	(66.3)		(33.7)
Total numbers	122	7	17	79	225	127 (56.4)
Emerging market economies						
1 Peg	41	16	4	3	64	23
	(64.1)	(25)	(6.2)	(4.7)		(35.9)
2 Limited	12	1	2	11	26	25
	(46.2)	(3.8)	(7.7)	(42.3)		(96.2)
3 Managed	24	25	18	55	122	104
	(19.7)	(20.5)	(14.8)	(45.0)		(85.2)
4 Float	12	18	12	40	82	42
	(14.6)	(22.0)	(14.6)	(48.8)		(51.2)
Total numbers	89	60	36	109	294	194 (66.0)
Developing countries						
1 Peg	497	11	19	14	541	44
	(91.9)	(2.0)	(3.5)	(2.6)		(8.1)
2 Limited	31	14	2	5	52	38
	(59.6)	(26.9)	(3.8)	(9.6)		(73.1)
3 Managed	25	41	24	66	156	132
	(16.0)	(26.3)	(15.4)	(42.3)		(84.6)
4 Float	78	50	40	77	245	168
	(31.8)	(20.4)	(16.3)	(31.4)		(68.6)
Total numbers	631	116	85	162	994	372 (37.4)

Note: The figures in parentheses indicate the percentage of the number of countries in the given row category.
Source: Author's estimates based on the data of Levy-Yeyati and Sturzenegger (2002) and AREAER.

Table 1.15 The comparison between de facto classification data

	De facto classification				Total numbers
	1 *Peg*	*2* *Limited*	*3* *Managed*	*4* *Float*	
All countries					
Bubula and Ötker-Robe (2002)	1048 (48.7)	371 (17.3)	424 (19.7)	307 (14.3)	2150
Reinhart and Rogoff (2002)	572 (35.5)	435 (27.0)	297 (18.4)	306 (19.0)	1610
Levy-Yeyati and Sturzenegger (2002)	842 (55.7)	183 (12.1)	138 (9.1)	350 (23.1)	1513
Developed countries					
Bubula and Ötker-Robe (2002)	61 (22.1)	104 (37.7)	17 (6.2)	94 (34.0)	276
Reinhart and Rogoff (2002)	113 (40.9)	74 (26.8)	44 (15.9)	45 (16.3)	276
Levy-Yeyati and Sturzenegger (2002)	122 (54.2)	7 (3.1)	17 (7.5)	79 (35.1)	225
Emerging market economies					
Bubula and Ötker-Robe (2002)	125 (32.0)	116 (29.7)	103 (26.3)	47 (12.0)	391
Reinhart and Rogoff (2002)	88 (23.7)	118 (31.8)	97 (26.1)	68 (18.3)	371
Levy-Yeyati and Sturzenegger (2002)	89 (30.3)	60 (20.4)	36 (12.2)	109 (37.1)	294
Developing countries					
Bubula and Ötker-Robe (2002)	862 (58.1)	151 (10.2)	304 (20.5)	166 (11.2)	1483
Reinhart and Rogoff (2002)	359 (36.8)	255 (26.2)	163 (16.7)	198 (20.3)	975
Levy-Yeyati and Sturzenegger (2002)	631 (63.5)	116 (11.7)	85 (8.5)	162 (16.3)	994

Note: The sample of the data of Bubula and Ötker-Robe (2002) and Reinhart and Rogoff (2002) is from 1990 to 2001 and the sample of the data of Levy-Yeyati and Sturzenegger (2002) is from 1990 to 2000 in this table. The figures in parentheses indicate the percentage of the number of countries in the given classification.

and the elements above the diagonal indicate that some countries actually permit floating to a greater degree than they announce.

Table 1.12 shows the comparison between the IMF classification and the Bubula and Ötker-Robe (2002) classification over the period 1990–98.[24] From this table, we can see that the rate of mismatch was 35.7 percent for all countries, 26.6 percent for developed countries, 57.2 percent for emerging market economies, and 31.7 percent for developing countries, respectively. For the comparison between the IMF classification and the Reinhart and Rogoff (2002) classification during 1990–2001, we can observe from Table 1.13 that the rate of mismatch was 53.1 percent for all countries, 60.1 percent for developed countries, 58.4 percent for emerging market economies, and 50.2 percent for developing countries, respectively.

Table 1.14 shows the comparison between the IMF classification and the Levy-Yeyati and Sturzenegger (2002) classification over the period 1990–2000. From this table, we can see that the rate of mismatch was 46.5 percent for all countries, 56.4 percent for developed countries, 66.0 percent for emerging market economies, and 37.4 percent for developing countries, respectively.

Overall, Tables 1.12–1.14 yield several interesting observations. First, the rates of mismatches between the IMF and de facto classifications were significantly large, ranging between 36 and 53 percent for all countries. This indicates that, in practice, some countries had a more fixed regime than announced or others actually allowed their currencies to float to a greater degree than announced. Second, in particular, many countries had a peg more than they announced. Third, the rates of mismatches for emerging market economies were larger (ranging between 57 and 66 percent) than those for developed and developing countries. Fourth, by contrast, the degree to which fixed regimes' IMF and de facto classifications matched was very high. This suggests that, in practice, many countries that claimed to have fixed regimes did indeed adopt fixed regimes in order to raise the credibility of their monetary and exchange rate policies.

1.4.2 Fear of floating and fear of announcing a peg

Next, we investigate the following phenomena of exchange rate policies: fear of floating and fear of announcing a peg, by comparing de facto classification data and the IMF classification data. "Fear of floating" can be defined as a behavior (policy) that, in fact, a country that claims to have a floating regime does not allow its nominal exchange rate to float to any great degree (Calvo and Reinhart 2002). "Fear of announcing a peg" can be defined as a behavior (policy) that a country that in practice adopts a fixed regime announces more flexible regimes (Levy-Yeyati and Sturzenegger 2002). Following Alesina and Wagner (2003), the notions of fear of floating and fear of announcing a peg can be represented in Figure 1.6.

Table 1.16 reports the rates of fear of floating and fear of announcing a peg. Here, the rates of fear of floating 1 and 2 and the rate of fear of announcing a peg are defined as

$$
\begin{bmatrix} \text{Rate of fear} \\ \text{of floating 1} \end{bmatrix} = \frac{\begin{bmatrix} \text{the number of } \textit{de jure} \text{ freely floats} \\ \text{which are not de facto freely floats} \end{bmatrix}}{[\text{the number of } \textit{de jure} \text{ freely floats}]}
$$

$$
\begin{bmatrix} \text{Rate of fear} \\ \text{of floating 2} \end{bmatrix} = \frac{\begin{bmatrix} \text{the number of } \textit{de jure} \text{ freely and managed floats} \\ \text{which adopt de facto more fixed than announced} \end{bmatrix}}{\begin{bmatrix} \text{the number of } \textit{de jure} \text{ freely and} \\ \text{managed floats} \end{bmatrix}}
$$

$$
\begin{bmatrix} \text{Rate of fear of} \\ \text{announcing a peg} \end{bmatrix} = \frac{\begin{bmatrix} \text{the number of de facto pegs} \\ \text{which are not } \textit{de jure} \text{ pegs} \end{bmatrix}}{[\text{the number of de facto pegs}]}
$$

First, we can see from Table 1.16 that, for the data of Bubula and Ötker-Robe (2002), the rates of fear of floating 2 for emerging economies (72.9 percent) and developing countries (60.4 percent) were markedly higher than that for developed countries (19.8 percent). On the other hand, the rates of fear of announcing a peg for developed countries (85.2 percent) and emerging market economies (36.8 percent) were considerably higher than that for developing countries (14.7 percent).

Second, we can also observe from Table 1.16 that, for the data of Reinhart and Rogoff (2002), the rates of fear of floating 2 for developed countries (63.9 percent), emerging market economies (57.4 percent), and developing countries (55.5 percent) were significantly high. On the other hand, the rates of fear of announcing a peg for developed countries (66.4 percent) and emerging market economies (35.2 percent) were considerably higher than that for developing countries (12.2 percent).

Third, for the data of Levy-Yeyati and Sturzenegger (2002), the rates of fear of floating 2 for emerging economies (44.6 percent) and developing countries (58.4 percent) were considerably higher than that for developed countries (38.5 percent). On the other hand, the rates of fear of announcing a peg for developed countries (77.9 percent) and emerging market economies (53.9 percent) were markedly higher than that for developing countries (21.2 percent).[25]

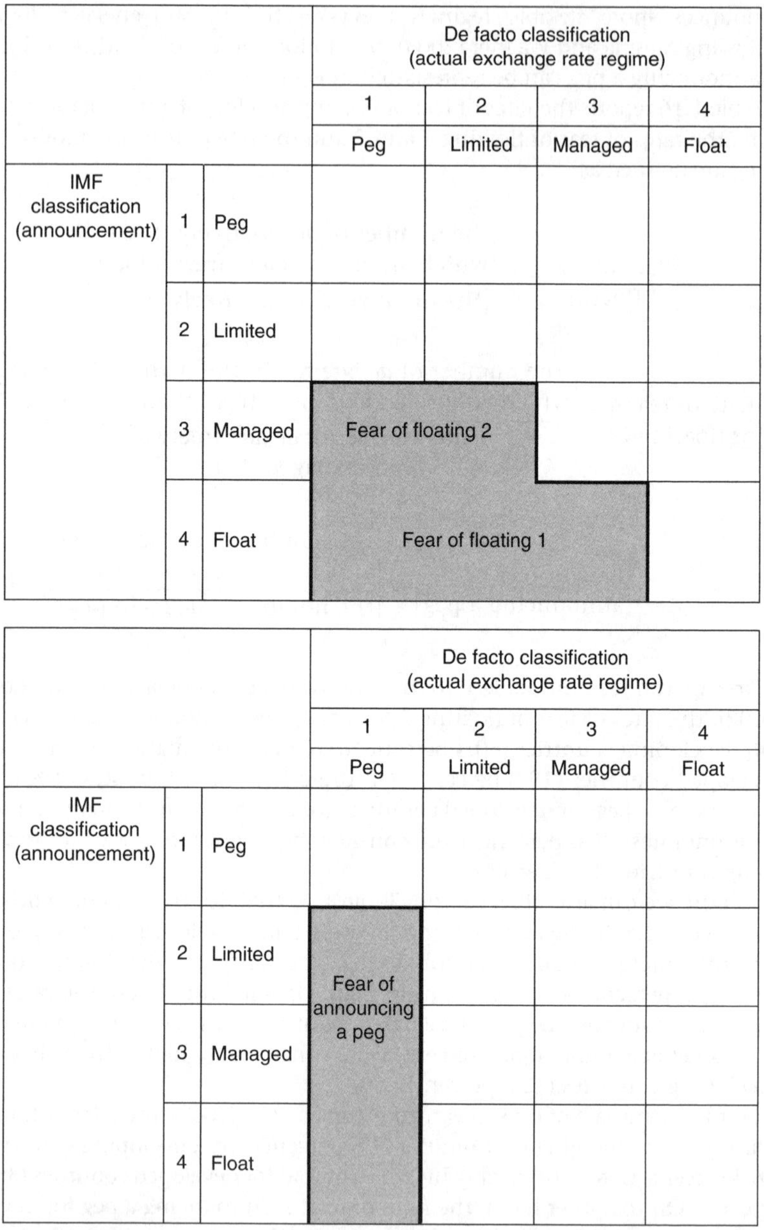

		De facto classification (actual exchange rate regime)			
		1	2	3	4
		Peg	Limited	Managed	Float
IMF classification (announcement)	1 Peg				
	2 Limited				
	3 Managed	Fear of floating 2			
	4 Float	Fear of floating 1			

		De facto classification (actual exchange rate regime)			
		1	2	3	4
		Peg	Limited	Managed	Float
IMF classification (announcement)	1 Peg				
	2 Limited	Fear of announcing a peg			
	3 Managed				
	4 Float				

Figure 1.6 The notions of fear of floating and fear of announcing a peg
Note: Following Calvo and Reinhart (2002), Levy-Yeyati and Sturzenegger (2002), and Alesina and Wagner (2003), we define the policies of "fear of floating" and "fear of announcing a peg".
Source: Modified from Figure 1 of Alesina and Wagner (2003).

Table 1.16   Rates of fear of floating and fear of announcing a peg (%)

Classification data		Fear of floating		Fear of announcing a peg
		Fear of floating 1	Fear of floating 2	
Bubula and	All	53.8	58.9	19.8
Ötker-Robe (2002)	Developed	12.7	19.8	85.2
	Emerging	73.5	72.9	36.8
	Developing	60.8	60.4	14.7
Reinhart and	All	58.6	57.7	26.2
Rogoff (2002)	Developed	65.4	63.9	66.4
	Emerging	56.7	57.4	35.2
	Developing	56	55.5	12.2
Levy-Yeyati and	All	57.3	51.4	32.9
Sturzenegger (2002)	Developed	33.7	38.5	77.9
	Emerging	51.2	44.6	53.9
	Developing	68.6	58.4	21.2

On the whole, these results from the rates of fear of floating 1 and 2 suggest that emerging market economies and developing countries exhibited a greater fear of floating behavior than developed countries, because the rates of fear of floating for emerging market economies and developing countries were a lot higher (about 50 percent) than those for developed countries. Moreover, these results from the rate of fear of announcing a peg indicate that developed countries and emerging market economies exhibited a greater fear of announcing a peg behavior than developing countries, because the rates of fear of announcing a peg for developed countries and emerging market economies were considerably higher than those for developing countries.

Calvo and Reinhart (2002) and Hausmann et al. (2001) theoretically suggest that the phenomenon of fear of floating may arise from a lack of ability of a country to borrow abroad in its own currency and a high pass-through from exchange rates to prices.[26] In the case where a country (domestic economy) cannot borrow internationally in its own currency,[27] there are large currency mismatches in the balance sheets of firms, banks, households, or the government. In this situation, as depreciation can damage those exposed to foreign currency liabilities, the authorities limit exchange rate volatility even if they claim to have floating regimes. Similarly, in the case of a high level of pass-through from exchange rates to prices, as depreciation can substantially raise domestic prices, the authorities limit exchange rate movements through heavy intervention even if they claim to have floating regimes.

Generally speaking, the currency mismatches in the balance sheets in emerging market economies and developing countries may be considerably larger than those in developed countries, because of the lack of ability to borrow abroad in the domestic currency.[28] Moreover, it may be thought that the levels of the pass-through in emerging market economies and developing countries are higher than those in developed countries. Hence, the results for the rates of fear of floating may be related to the cause of the behavior of fear of floating suggested by Calvo and Reinhart (2002) and Hausmann et al. (2001).

Levy-Yeyati and Sturzenegger (2002) suggest that the phenomenon of fear of announcing a peg may arise from an attempt to reduce the exposure to speculative attacks associated with explicit commitments to maintain a predetermined fixed rate. It is likely that, in a world of increasing international capital mobility, such countries do in fact adopt a fixed regime, but announce a more flexible regime (without assuming an explicit commitment with a predetermined parity), because official pegs may become targets of speculative attacks.

It can generally be considered that developed countries and emerging market economies are more integrated, or in the process of integrating, into international capital markets than developing countries. Hence, the results for the rates of fear of announcing a peg may be related to the cause of the behavior of fear of announcing a peg suggested by Levy-Yeyati and Sturzenegger (2002).

1.5 Determinants of fear of floating: an empirical analysis

Why do countries adopt a fear of floating policy? In order to answer the question, we make use of a logit model to identify the determinants of fear of floating by using the IMF and de facto classifications data in this section.

1.5.1 Measuring fear of floating

Hausmann et al. (2001), Levy-Yeyati et al. (2003), and Alesina and Wagner (2003) empirically examine the determinants of fear of floating.[29] However, the measures of fear of floating (dependent variables of regressions of fear of floating) are different in each of their studies. For example, Levy-Yeyati et al. (2003) restrict their data to countries that claim to have freely floated (*de jure* free floaters) and apply the fear of floating dummy that takes a value of one if the country that claims to have freely floated actually adopts a more fixed regime.[30] Alesina and Wagner (2003) apply the fear of floating dummy that takes a value of one if the country actually has a more fixed regime than announced, whatever *de jure* regimes are adopted.[31] Therefore, our first task is to measure fear of floating in order to statistically examine the determinants of fear of floating.

First, we restrict our data to countries that claim to adopt a free float or managed float (i.e. *de jure* free or managed floaters). Thus, we use annual data for 43 countries (11 developed countries and 32 emerging and developing countries) over the period 1990–98 (see Appendix 1B).[32] All sample countries are classified as managed floating or independently floating by the IMF classification.

Then, we construct the fear of floating dummy variable (dependent variable of the logit model) by comparing de facto classifications with the *de jure* classification provided by the IMF. Following Calvo and Reinhart (2002), we assume that the fear of floating dummy (FFD) variable takes a value of one if the country that claims to have a free float or managed float actually adopts a more fixed regime than announced and zero otherwise. Hence, the fear of floating dummy variable is a discrete qualitative variable. This definition corresponds to the notion of fear of floating 2 in Figure 1.6.

1.5.2   The data of balance sheet, currency mismatch, and original sin

As noted above, recent theoretical contributions suggest that the phenomenon of fear of floating may arise from large currency mismatches in the balance sheets (the balance sheet effects) due to the lack of ability to borrow abroad in the domestic currency and a high pass-through from exchange rates to prices (Calvo and Reinhart 2002, Hausmann et al. 2001). In order to test this hypothesis, we thus need to have a measure of the balance sheet effects and obtain the pass-through coefficients.

To measure the balance sheet effects, we use the lagged ratio of foreign liabilities to money stocks (FLM1), which we take as a proxy for currency mismatches in the balance sheets, as in Levy-Yeyati et al. (2003) and Alesina and Wagner (2003). To mitigate potential endogenous problems stemming from the reverse causality from the fear of floating policy to currency mismatches in the balance sheets, we use the lagged variable of currency mismatches. According to this hypothesis, we expect that a larger FLM1 is positively associated with the probability of choosing the fear of floating policy.

It is important to measure the ability of a country to borrow abroad in its own currency, because large currency mismatches in the balance sheets may result from the inability of the country to borrow abroad in its own currency. Thus, we also apply the two indicators of the ability to borrow abroad in the domestic currency, developed (provided) by Eichengreen et al. (2003).[33]

They give the following indicators of original sin (a situation where a country cannot borrow internationally in its own currency):

$$\text{OSIN1}_i = 1 - \frac{\text{Securities issued by country } i \text{ in currency } i}{\text{Securities issued by country } i}$$

$$\text{OSIN3}_i = \max\left(1 - \frac{\text{Securities in currency } i}{\text{Securities issued by country } i}, 0\right)$$

The indicator of OSIN1 is defined as one minus the ratio of the stock of international securities issued by a country in its own currency to the total stock of international securities issued by the country. If the country issues all its securities in own currency, OSIN1 takes a value of zero. On the other hand, if the country issues all of them in foreign currency, OSIN1 takes a value of one. Hence, the higher the value, the greater the original sin.

The indicator of OSIN3 is constructed in consideration of an opportunity for countries to hedge currency exposures via the swap market. If the ratio of the stock of international securities issued by the country and the other countries in currency i to the total stock of international securities issued by the country i is large, OSIN3 is close to zero. Hence, the higher the value, the greater the original sin.[34] According to the hypothesis of fear of floating, we expect that higher OSIN1 and OSIN3 are positively associated with the probability of choosing the fear of floating policy.[35]

Next, we need to obtain the coefficients of pass-through from exchange rates to prices. However, it is difficult to obtain accurate and stable coefficients of pass-through, because the estimated coefficients are significantly different, depending on the specifications, methods, and samples (Calvo and Reinhart 2000, Hausmann et al. 2001). Since the results of empirical studies that used inaccurate coefficients of pass-through may be biased, we exclude the coefficients of pass-through from the explanatory variables in the analysis.

1.5.3   Control variables

As control variables, we use the following: trade openness, financial openness, economic size, economic development, as well as a dummy variable for emerging and developing countries, emphasized in the literature on the determinants of the choice of exchange rate regime. We measure trade openness by using the lagged ratio of (export + import)/2 over GDP (TOPEN1). For de facto financial openness, we calculate the indices of financial openness by using the lagged ratio of total actual foreign assets and liabilities to GDP (FOPEN1).[36] The data of actual foreign assets and liabilities is obtained from Lane and Milesi-Ferretti (2001).

We also include variables for economic size and economic development. Economic size is measured as the country's GDP in dollars relative to US GDP

(SIZE) and economic development is measured as a logarithm of GDP per capita (ED). Moreover, we use a dummy variable (EMDD) for emerging or developing countries (EMDD takes a value of one if the country is an emerging or developing country) to verify whether emerging market economies and developing countries exhibit a greater fear of floating behavior than developed countries, as shown in Section 1.4.[37]

1.5.4   Empirical results

In order to empirically examine why countries adopt the fear of floating policy, we estimate a variety of logit models of the determinants of fear of floating during the period 1990–98, using the maximum likelihood (ML) method.[38] Here, the dependent variable is the fear of floating dummy (FFD) that captures whether the country in question, in a certain year, adopts a fear of floating policy or not. The explanatory variables include potential variables (FLM1, OSIN1, or OSIN3) for determinants of adopting fear of floating and control variables (TOPEN1, FOPEN1, SIZE, ED, and EMDD).[39] In the logit model, a positive coefficient suggests that the explanatory variable increases the likelihood of adopting the fear of floating policy. According to Calvo and Reinhart (2002), we expect that larger FLM1, OSIN1, and OSIN3 are shown to increase the probability of the choice of the fear of floating policy.

To check whether the results of the logit model for the determinants of choosing fear of floating depend on the classifications data of exchange rate regimes, we apply some data of comparing de facto classifications (Bubula and Ötker-Robe (2002), Reinhart and Rogoff (2002), and Levy-Yeyati and Sturzenegger (2002) classifications) with the *de jure* IMF classification. If the estimated results by some classifications are the same, we can obtain robust results for the determinants of adopting the fear of floating policy.

Table 1.17 shows the results of estimating the logit models of the determinants of fear of floating by using the IMF and the Bubula and Ötker-Robe (2002) classifications data. From this table, we note that the coefficients of FLM1 are significantly positive for all models (1)–(4), indicating that the probability of the choice of fear of floating is likely to increase with larger currency mismatches in the balance sheets. The coefficients of OSIN1 and OSIN3 are significantly positive, except for model (8), indicating that the probability of the choice of fear of floating is likely to increase with the lack of ability to borrow abroad in its own currency. It is statistically confirmed that fear of floating arose from large currency mismatches in the balance sheets that resulted from the lack of ability to borrow abroad in the domestic currency (the situation of original sin).

For control variables, the coefficients of TOPEN1 are statistically significant and negative, indicating that higher trade openness tends to decrease the likelihood of adopting the fear of floating policy.[40] The coefficients of SIZE and ED are significantly negative, indicating that smaller economic size and lower level of economic development tend to increase the probability of

Table 1.17 Determinants of fear of floating: the Bubula and Ötker-Robe (2002) classification

	(1)	(2)	(3)	(4)	(5)	(6)	(7)	(8)	(9)
FLM1	3.239*** (0.664)	1.768*** (0.575)	1.539*** (0.556)	1.261** (0.550)					
OSIN1					11.496*** (2.720)	5.963** (2.483)			
OSIN3							3.889*** (0.745)	1.686 (1.100)	2.707*** (0.872)
TOPEN1			-3.838*** (1.209)	-2.035** (1.004)		-3.895*** (1.286)		-5.236*** (1.471)	-4.167*** (1.325)
FOPEN1			-2.717*** (0.793)	-1.177 (0.806)		-0.662 (0.920)		-2.452*** (0.945)	-0.804 (0.946)
SIZE			-16.433*** (5.154)					-20.384*** (7.800)	
ED				-0.812*** (0.152)		-0.657*** (0.178)			-0.610*** (0.180)
EMDD		2.656*** (0.416)							
Constant	-0.111 (0.145)	-2.024*** (0.377)	2.540*** (0.461)	7.845*** (1.350)	-10.829*** (2.674)	1.461 (3.187)	-3.169*** (0.703)	1.645 (1.210)	4.542** (1.868)
Observations	318	313	318	318	230	230	230	230	230
Fraction of correct predictions	0.711	0.770	0.818	0.827	0.704	0.804	0.696	0.800	0.787
Scaled R-squared	0.140	0.311	0.399	0.362	0.208	0.405	0.212	0.412	0.414

Note: The logit models are estimated by the maximum likelihood method. The numbers in parentheses are robust standard errors.
* Significant at the 10% level.
** Significant at the 5% level.
*** Significant at the 1% level.

choosing a fear of floating policy. In the case of EMDD, the coefficient is significantly positive, indicating that emerging market economies and developing countries have been more inclined to adopt a fear of floating policy than developed countries.

Table 1.18 shows the results of estimating the logit models for the determinants of fear of floating by using the IMF and the Reinhart and Rogoff (2002) classifications data. We can see from this table that the coefficients of FLM1 are all significantly positive, indicating that larger currency mismatches in the balance sheets are likely to increase the probability of adopting the fear of floating policy. The coefficients of OSIN1 and OSIN3 are significantly positive, except for models (9) and (10), indicating that lower ability to borrow abroad in the domestic currency tends to increase the probability of the choice of the fear of floating policy. We statistically confirmed that countries that had some problems with large currency mismatches in the balance sheets significantly adopted the fear of floating policy.

While the coefficients of TOPEN1 are significantly negative for the Bubula and Ötker-Robe (2002) classification data, they are significantly positive for the Reinhart and Rogoff (2002) classification data. Moreover, the coefficients of FOPEN1 are significantly positive for the Reinhart and Rogoff (2002) classification data. This result suggests that higher trade and financial openness tend to increase the likelihood of choosing the fear of floating policy. The coefficients of SIZE and ED are significantly negative, indicating that smaller economic size and lower level of economic development tend to increase the probability of the choice of the fear of floating policy.[41]

Table 1.19 presents the results of the logit models for the IMF and the Levy-Yeyati and Sturzenegger (2002) classifications data. From this table, we note that the coefficients of FLM1, OSIN1, and OSIN3 are always significantly positive, indicating that larger currency mismatches in the balance sheets due to inability to borrow internationally in its own currency tend to increase the probability of having the fear of floating policy. Moreover, the coefficients of SIZE are negative, although it is not statistically significant in model (6), indicating that smaller economies adopted the fear of floating policy.[42]

In Table 1.20, we present the combined results for the determinants of fear of floating to find robust results in some classifications of exchange rate regimes. For the balance sheet effects, the coefficients of FLM1 are always significantly positive. For the ability to borrow abroad in the domestic currency, the coefficients of OSIN1 and OSIN3 are significantly positive, except for OSIN3 of the Reinhart and Rogoff (2002) classification. Robust results suggest that countries with large currency mismatches in the balance sheets due to inability to borrow internationally in the domestic currencies did adopt the fear of floating policy. That is, they actually adopted more fixed regimes than announced freely floating or managed float. Hence, these results are consistent with the predicted theoretical effect of currency mismatches in the balance sheets on the choice of exchange rate regimes.

Table 1.18 Determinants of fear of floating: the Reinhart and Rogoff (2002) classification

	(1)	(2)	(3)	(4)	(5)	(6)	(7)	(8)	(9)	(10)
FLM1	1.418*** (0.503)	1.117** (0.503)	1.178** (0.519)	0.959* (0.515)						
OSIN1					4.650*** (1.067)	5.307* (3.208)	3.394* (2.101)			
OSIN3								1.765*** (0.446)		
TOPEN1			5.140*** (1.548)	5.984*** (1.556)		3.400** (1.741)	4.392** (1.992)		3.674** (1.727)	5.730*** (2.076)
FOPEN1			0.614 (0.662)	1.819** (0.844)		1.871* (1.140)	3.676*** (1.078)		0.823 (0.828)	3.039*** (0.972)
SIZE			−3.493*** (1.340)			−1.037 (2.626)			−3.608* (2.075)	
ED				−0.7E-04*** (0.2E-04)			−0.846*** (0.189)			−0.939*** (0.195)
EMDD		0.576* (0.310)								
Constant	0.754*** (0.152)	0.377 (0.249)	−0.487 (0.442)	−0.575 (0.439)	−3.084*** (0.994)	−5.132 (3.321)	2.986 (2.771)	−0.216 (0.380)	−0.350 (1.061)	6.595*** (1.911)
Observations	313	313	313	313	228	228	228	228	228	228
Fraction of correct predictions	0.738	0.738	0.760	0.767	0.794	0.820	0.807	0.781	0.811	0.785
Scaled R-squared	0.036	0.047	0.218	0.224	0.099	0.191	0.285	0.068	0.180	0.271

Note: The logit models are estimated by the maximum likelihood method. The numbers in parentheses are robust standard errors.
* Significant at the 10% level.
** Significant at the 5% level.
*** Significant at the 1% level.

Table 1.19   Determinants of fear of floating: the Levy-Yeyati and Sturzenegger (2002) classification

	(1)	(2)	(3)	(4)	(5)	(6)	(7)	(8)
FLM1	1.701*** (0.386)	1.385*** (0.387)	1.208*** (0.376)	1.308*** (0.390)				
OSIN1					6.824*** (1.819)	9.368*** (3.233)		
OSIN3							1.196*** (0.456)	1.523** (0.650)
TOPEN1			0.081 (0.605)	0.615 (0.569)		−1.291* (0.742)		−0.135 (0.708)
FOPEN1			−0.818 (0.608)	−0.746 (0.683)		1.455** (0.697)		0.033 (0.640)
SIZE			−6.119** (2.780)			−1.558 (4.345)		
ED				−0.203* (0.125)				0.107 (0.149)
EMDD		0.797** (0.325)						
Constant	−0.533*** (0.143)	−1.099*** (0.281)	0.001 (0.241)	1.205 (1.011)	−6.567*** (1.774)	−8.987*** (3.242)	−1.067*** (0.413)	−2.198 (1.508)
Observations	306	306	306	306	223	223	223	223
Fraction of correct predictions	0.624	0.624	0.592	0.618	0.570	0.574	0.570	0.556
Scaled R-squared	0.085	0.105	0.157	0.113	0.118	0.142	0.034	0.036

Note: The logit models are estimated by the maximum likelihood method. The numbers in parentheses are robust standard errors.
* Significant at the 10% level.
** Significant at the 5% level.
*** Significant at the 1% level.

Table 1.20   Combined results of determinants of fear of floating

Classification	Fear of floating dummy		
	Bubula and Ötker-Robe (2002)	*Reinhart and Rogoff (2002)*	*Levy-Yeyati and Sturzenegger (2002)*
FLM1	+ (significance)	+ (significance)	+ (significance)
OSIN1	+ (significance)	+ (significance)	+ (significance)
OSIN3	+ (significance)	+	+ (significance)
TOPEN1	− (significance)	+ (significance)	+/−
FOPEN1	−	+ (significance)	+/−
SIZE	− (significance)	− (significance)	− (significance)
ED	− (significance)	− (significance)	+/−
EMDD	+ (significance)	+ (significance)	+ (significance)

Note: + (−) indicates that the coefficient of the explanatory variable is positive (negative), +/− indicates that the coefficient is either positive or negative depending on the specifications, and "significance" indicates that the coefficient is statistically significant in most cases.

In the cases of trade and financial openness, we cannot obtain robust results, because the coefficients are either positive or negative and significant or insignificant, depending on the classifications of exchange rate regimes. On the other hand, for economic size and the level of economic development, we can obtain robust results, because the coefficients are significantly negative, except for ED of the Levy-Yeyati and Sturzenegger (2002) classification data. This result suggests that small economies and countries with a low level of economic development actually adopted the fear of floating policy.

1.6   Summary and concluding remarks

In this chapter, we have surveyed the de facto exchange rate regimes of the IMF member countries over the period 1990–2001 on the basis of the data of classifying exchange rate regimes. First, we have presented the evolution of exchange rate regimes over the period 1990–2001 in order to examine whether the "bipolar view" holds, by using the data of de facto classifications of exchange rate regimes. It was shown that the bipolar view strictly holds for developed countries. This result can be partly explained by the fact that 12 European countries joined the EMU between 1999 and 2001.

On the other hand, we cannot clearly conclude that the bipolar view strictly holds for emerging market economies, because the results of tests for the bipolar view were significantly different in each of the databases of the de facto classifications. For example, while the data of the Levy-Yeyati and Sturzenegger (2002) classification supports the bipolar view for emerging market economies, it cannot be significantly supported by the data of the Reinhart and Rogoff (2002) classification.

Second, we have compared de facto classifications with the *de jure* classification provided by the IMF. By doing so, we have ascertained the extent of deviations of actual regimes from official regimes. It was found that the rates of mismatches between the IMF and de facto classifications were significantly large, ranging between 36 and 56 percent for all countries. This result indicates that, in practice, some countries had adopted a peg to a greater degree than announced, while others actually allowed their currencies to float to a greater degree than announced. In particular, the rates of mismatches for emerging market economies were larger than those for developed and developing countries, and many emerging market economies actually pegged their currencies to a greater degree than announced.

Third, we have investigated the exchange rate policies of "fear of floating" and "fear of announcing a peg," by estimating the rates of fear of floating and fear of announcing a peg. It is true that emerging market economies and developing countries exhibited a greater fear of floating behavior than developed countries. This result clearly confirms the stylized finding of Calvo and Reinhart (2002). It was also found that emerging market economies and developed countries exhibited a greater fear of announcing a peg behavior than developing countries. As Levy-Yeyati and Sturzenegger (2002) suggested, this result may arise from an attempt to reduce the exposure to speculative attacks associated with explicit commitments to maintain a predetermined fixed rate in a world of increasing international capital mobility.

Finally, we have statistically examined the determinants of fear of floating during the period 1990–98, by using the data of some classifications of exchange rate regimes. It was shown that countries with large currency mismatches in their balance sheets due to inability to borrow internationally in the domestic currency did adopt a fear of floating policy. Hence, this result is consistent with the fear of floating theory presented by Calvo and Reinhart (2002) and Hausmann et al. (2001).

Appendix 1A   List of countries in Sections 1.3 and 1.4

In Sections 1.3 and 1.4, following Fischer (2001) and Bubula and Ötker-Robe (2002), we classified all the IMF members into three groups: developed countries, emerging market countries or regions, and developing countries or regions.

Developed countries (23)

Australia, Austria, Belgium, Canada, Denmark, Finland, France, Germany, Greece, Iceland, Ireland, Italy, Japan, Luxembourg, Netherlands, New Zealand, Norway, Portugal, Spain, Sweden, Switzerland, United Kingdom, United States.

Emerging market countries or regions (33)

Argentina, Brazil, Bulgaria, Chile, China, Colombia, the Czech Republic, Ecuador, Egypt, Hong Kong SAR, Hungary, India, Indonesia, Israel, Jordan,

Korea, Malaysia, Mexico, Morocco, Nigeria, Pakistan, Panama, Peru, the Philippines, Poland, Qatar, Russia, Singapore, South Africa, Sri Lanka, Thailand, Turkey, Venezuela.

Developing countries or regions (131)

Afghanistan, Albania, Algeria, Angola, Antigua and Barbuda, Armenia, Aruba, Azerbaijan, the Bahamas, Bahrain, Bangladesh, Barbados, Belarus, Belize, Benin, Bhutan, Bolivia, Bosnia and Herzegovina, Botswana, Brunei Darussalam, Burkina Faso, Burundi, Cambodia, Cameroon, Cape Verde, Central African Republic, Chad, Comoros, Democratic Republic of the Congo, Republic of Congo, Costa Rica, Cote d'Ivoire, Croatia, Cyprus, Czech Republic, Djibouti, Dominica, Dominican Republic, El Salvador, Equatorial Guinea, Eritrea, Estonia, Ethiopia, Fiji, Gabon, the Gambia, Georgia, Ghana, Grenada, Guatemala, Guinea, Guinea-Bissau, Guyana, Haiti, Honduras, India, Iran, Iraq, Jamaica, Kazakhstan, Kenya, Kiribati, Kuwait, Kyrgyzstan, Laos, Latvia, Lebanon, Lesotho, Liberia, Libya, Lithuania, Macedonia, Madagascar, Malawi, Maldives, Mali, Malta, Marshall Islands, Mauritania, Mauritius, Micronesia, Moldova, Mongolia, Mozambique, Myanmar, Namibia, Nepal, Netherlands Antilles, Nicaragua, Niger, Oman, Palau, Papua New Guinea, Paraguay, Romania, Rwanda, Samoa, San Marino, São Tomé and Principe, Saudi Arabia, Senegal, Seychelles, Sierra Leone, Slovak Republic, Slovenia, Solomon Islands, Somalia, St Kitts and Nevis, St Lucia, St Vincent and Grenadines, Sudan, Suriname, Swaziland, Syrian Arab Republic, Tajikistan, Tanzania, Togo, Tonga, Trinidad and Tobago, Tunisia, Turkmenistan, Uganda, Ukraine, United Arab Emirates, Uruguay, Uzbekistan, Vanuatu, Viet Nam, Yemen Arab Republic, Yugoslavia, Zambia, Zimbabwe.

Appendix 1B   List of countries in Section 1.5

In Section 1.5, we used annual data for 43 countries (11 developed countries and 32 emerging and developing countries) over the period 1990–98. The sample countries were as follows: Algeria (the period of *de jure* free or managed floats, 1992–98), Australia (1990–98), Bolivia (1990–97), Brazil (1990–98), Canada (1990–98), Chile (1990–97), Colombia (1990–97), Costa Rica (1990–97), Dominican Republic (1991–98), Ecuador (1990–97), Egypt (1990–97), El Salvador (1990–97), Finland (1992–95), Guatemala (1990–98), India (1990–98), Indonesia (1990–98), Israel (1991–97), Italy (1992–95), Jamaica (1990–98), Japan (1990–98), Korea (1990–98), Malaysia (1992–97), Mauritius (1994–98), Mexico (1990–98), New Zealand (1990–98), Norway (1992–98), Pakistan (1990–98), Paraguay (1990–98), Peru (1990–98), Philippines (1990–98), Singapore (1990–98), South Africa (1990–98), Sri Lanka (1990–97), Sweden (1992–98), Switzerland (1990–98), Thailand (1997–98), Tunisia (1990–97), Turkey (1990–97), United Kingdom (1992–98), United States (1990–98), Uruguay (1990–97), Venezuela (1990–93 and 1996–97), and Zimbabwe (1994–98).

Appendix 1C   List of variables, definitions, and data sources in Section 1.5

Dependent variables

- Fear of floating dummy (FFD): 1 if the country that claims to have a free float or managed float actually adopts more fixed regimes than announced, 0 otherwise.

Explanatory variables

The data of balance sheet, currency mismatch, and original sin:

- FLM1: lagged ratio of foreign liabilities to money. Source: IFS.
- OSIN1: $OSIN1_i = 1 - \dfrac{\text{Securities issued by country } i \text{ in currency } i}{\text{Securities issued by country } i}$.
- OSIN3: $OSIN3_i = \max\left[1 - \dfrac{\text{Securities in currency } i}{\text{Securities issued by country } i}, 0\right]$.

Source: Eichengreen et al. (2003).

Control variables

- TOPEN1: trade openness. Lagged ratio of (export + import)/2 to GDP. Source: IFS.
- FOPEN1: financial openness. Lagged ratio of gross actual foreign assets and liabilities to GDP. Source: Lane and Milesi-Ferretti (2001).
- SIZE: economic size. GDP in dollars over USA GDP. Source: World Bank, *World Development Indicators* (WDI).
- ED: economic development. Logarithm of GDP per capita. Source: WDI.
- EMDD: dummy variable for emerging and developing countries.

Acknowledgments

The author would like to thank Andrea Bubula, Philip Lane, Eduardo Levy-Yeyati, İnci Ötker-Robe, Carmen Reinhart, and Jay Shambaugh for making their data available. However, the author alone is responsible for any remaining errors.

Notes

1   Intermediate exchange rate regimes are referred to as "soft pegs."
2   Fischer (2001) defined economies with no separate currency or those with currency boards as "hard pegs," economies with conventional fixed pegs, crawling pegs, horizontal bands, and crawling bands as "intermediate regimes," and economies

with a managed float with no specified central rate or those with independent floating as "floating regimes." From the standpoint of the bipolar view, however, his classification would be inappropriate, because the managed float was not defined as an "intermediate regime."

3   According to Fischer (2001), of the 33 emerging market countries over the 1990s, the share of hard pegs increased from 6 percent in 1991 to 9 percent in 1999, that of intermediate regimes decreased from 64 percent in 1991 to 42 percent in 1999, and that of floating regimes increased from 30 percent in 1991 to 48 percent in 1999 (Figure 1.1).

4   As notable empirical studies, Ghosh et al. (2002) examined the relationship between exchange rate regimes and macroeconomic performance using the data of *de jure* and de facto classifications. Juhn and Mauro (2002) reviewed the empirical studies of the determinants of choosing exchange rate regimes.

5   For the exchange rate policies of East Asian countries before the Asian currency crisis of 1997, see, for example, Ito et al. (1998) and Esaka (2003).

6   While Levy-Yeyati and Sturzenegger (2002) call this behavior "fear of pegging," Alesina and Wagner (2003) call it "fear of announcing a peg." In this chapter, following Alesina and Wagner (2003), we mainly call it "fear of announcing a peg."

7   As shown in Section 1.2, the IMF has adopted a new classification system based on members' de facto regimes, which has become the official arrangement since January 1999.

8   Some of these articles will be published in the top economic journals.

9   For empirical analyses of exchange rate regimes by using de facto classifications, see, for example, Levy-Yeyati and Sturzenegger (2001, 2003), Alesina and Wagner (2003), and Rogoff et al. (2004). Levy-Yeyati and Sturzenegger (2001) examined the effects of different exchange rate regimes on macroeconomic performance by using the de facto classification data of Levy-Yeyati and Sturzenegger (2002). Alesina and Wagner (2003) examined the determinants of the choice of exchange rate regimes by using the de facto classification data of Reinhart and Rogoff (2002).

10   In addition, there were many countries (cases) that could not be classified by the Levy-Yeyati and Sturzenegger (2002) classification, because of the lack of reserve data in IMF member countries.

11   On the basis of the IFS, Emerging Markets Bond Index Plus (EMBI+), and Morgan Stanley Capital International (MSCI) index, Fischer (2001) and Bubula and Ötker-Robe (2002) classified the IMF members into three groups: developed countries, emerging market countries or regions, and all other countries (developing countries).

12   Bubula and Ötker-Robe (2002) examined the bipolar view by using their classification data. From the standpoint of the bipolar view, however, their definition would be inappropriate, because the managed floating regime was not coded as "intermediate regimes."

13   For developing countries, the share of hard pegs slightly increased from 22.1 percent in 1990 to 24 percent in 2001 and that of freely floating regimes considerably increased from 1.9 percent in 1990 to 14.7 percent in 2001. On the other hand, the share of intermediate regimes decreased from 76 percent in 1990 to 61.2 percent in 2001 (Table 1.4).

14   Rogoff et al. (2004) empirically examined the evolution and performance of exchange rate regimes by using the Reinhart and Rogoff (2002) classification data. They suggested that the bipolar view of exchange rate regimes does not hold for emerging market economies and developing countries.

15 The marked decline in freely falling regimes suggests that prices have become stable throughout the period 1990–2001.

16 For developing countries, the proportion of hard pegs virtually did not change (36.2 percent in 1990 and 37.0 percent in 2001). On the other hand, the proportion of independently floating regimes decreased from 24.6 percent in 1990 to 7.4 percent in 2001, and that of intermediate regimes increased considerably from 39.1 percent in 1990 to 55.6 percent in 2001 (Table 1.7).

17 We defined their categories of crawling pegs and the dirty float as "intermediate regimes."

18 For developing countries, the proportion of pegs decreased from 74.7 percent in 1990 to 62.4 percent in 2000 and that of floating regimes increased from 6.7 percent in 1990 to 18.8 percent in 2001. On the other hand, the proportion of intermediate regimes virtually did not change (Table 1.9).

19 For developed countries, the proportion of intermediate regimes (4.5 percent) was remarkably lower than that of the pegs (68.2 percent) or the floating regimes (27.3 percent) in 2000 (Table 1.9).

20 It is shown that the bipolar view for developing countries cannot be significantly supported by the data of some de facto classifications.

21 For the new IMF classification, we define categories (1)–(3) as category (1) peg; (4)–(6) as category (2) flexibility limited; (7) as category (3) managed floating; and (8) as category (4) float.

22 In the case of the Levy-Yeyati and Sturzenegger (2002) classification, following Alesina and Wagner (2003), we define their category (1) as category (1) peg; (2) as category (2) flexibility limited; (3) as category (3) managed floating; and (4) as category (4) float.

23 Table 1.15 shows the comparison between de facto classification data. From this table, we find that there were significant differences between de facto classification data. First, for the Bubula and Ötker-Robe (2002) and the Levy-Yeyati and Sturzenegger (2002) classifications, 50 percent of observations were classified as peg. Second, in the case of the Reinhart and Rogoff (2002) classification, 45 percent of observations were grouped as flexibility limited or managed floating.

24 Following the new IMF classification system, Bubula and Ötker-Robe (2002) constructed a historical database on de facto exchange rate regimes during 1990–2001. Accordingly, we compared their classification data with the IMF classification data during 1990–98.

25 As compared with the rates of fear of floating 2, the results of the rates of fear of floating 1 were substantially the same.

26 Calvo and Reinhart (2002) also suggested that the phenomenon of fear of floating may arise from lack of credibility and execution of inflation targets.

27 This situation has been referred to as "original sin" (Eichengreen and Hausmann 1999).

28 As noted in note 38, there is significant positive correlation between emerging and developing countries dummy variables and the variable of original sin. It can be surmised that emerging and developing countries cannot borrow abroad in the domestic currency.

29 For example, Levy-Yeyati et al. (2003) used the Levy-Yeyati and Sturzenegger (2002) classification data and Alesina and Wagner (2003) mainly used the Reinhart and Rogoff (2002) classification data.

30 Their definition corresponds to the notion of fear of floating 1 in Figure 1.6.

31 That is, Alesina and Wagner (2003) did not restrict their data to *de jure* floaters.

32 We excluded the following from the sample countries: some small countries, the Middle Eastern countries, transition economies, and other countries with incomplete data.

33 Eichengreen et al. (2003) constructed the indicators of original sin by using the data of the Bank for International Settlements (BIS) and empirically examined the effects of original sin on the stability of output, exchange rate volatility, and the level of country credit ratings by using some indicators of original sin.

34 The indices of OSIN1 and OSIN3 range from 0 (lower original sin) to 1 (higher original sin).

35 Eichengreen et al. (2003) also constructed OSIN2 as a proxy for the situation of original sin. Accordingly, we estimated the logit models by using OSIN2. The results of OSIN2 were substantially the same as OSIN3.

36 We used the lagged variables of trade and financial openness to mitigate potential simultaneity problems.

37 For the list of variables and the definitions and the sources of the data, see Appendix 1C.

38 Before proceeding to apply the logit regressions, we estimated the pairwise correlations between the explanatory variables. OSIN1 and OSIN3 were both significantly and negatively correlated with SIZE and ED, and there was significant positive correlation between SIZE and ED. In addition, OSIN1 and OSIN3 were both significantly and positively correlated with EMDD. This result suggested some potential problems of multicollinearity. Thus, we selected the combination of the explanatory variables and estimated some logit models to cope with multicollinearity.

39 Since Calvo and Reinhart (2002) also suggested that fear of floating may arise from execution of inflation targets, we also included the dummy variable of inflation targets in the logit model. However, the coefficient was not statistically significant.

40 The optimum currency area theory suggests that high trade openness is likely to be associated with fixed regimes. According to Juhn and Mauro (2002), however, previous empirical studies have not found much support for this hypothesis.

41 For the Reinhart and Rogoff (2002) classification, the coefficient of EMDD is also significantly positive, indicating that emerging market economies and developing countries exhibited a greater fear of floating behavior than developed countries.

42 In the case of the Levy-Yeyati and Sturzenegger (2002) classification, the coefficient of EMDD is also significantly positive, indicating that emerging market economies and developing countries exhibited a greater fear of floating behavior than developed countries.

References

Alesina, Alberto and Alexander Wagner, 2003, "Choosing (and Reneging on) Exchange Rate Regimes," NBER Working Paper No. 9809, June.

Bubula, Andrea and İnci Ötker-Robe, 2002, "The Evolution of Exchange Rate Regimes since 1990: Evidence from De Facto Policies," IMF Working Paper No. 02/155, September.

Calvo, Guillermo and Carmen M. Reinhart, 2000, "Fixing for Your Life," NBER Working Paper No. 8006, November 2000.

Calvo, Guillermo and Carmen M. Reinhart, 2002, "Fear of Floating," *Quarterly Journal of Economics* 117(2), May: 379–408.

Eichengreen, Barry, 1994, *International Monetary Arrangements for the 21st Century*, Washington: Brookings Institution.

Eichengreen, Barry and Ricardo Hausmann, 1999, "Exchange Rates and Financial Fragility," NBER Working Paper No. 7418, November.

Eichengreen, Barry, Ricardo Hausmann and Ugo Panizza, 2003, "The Pain of Original Sin," August. Available at http://emlab.berkeley.edu/users/eichengr/research/ospainaug21-03.pdf

Esaka, Taro, 2003, "Was It Really a Dollar Peg?: the Exchange Rate Policies of East Asian Countries, 1980–97," *Journal of Asian Economics* 13(6), January: 787–809.

Esaka, Taro, 2004, "*De Facto* Exchange Rate Regimes: Evidence from Some Classifications of Exchange Rate Regimes," in Hisayuki Mitsuo (ed.), *Exchange Rate Regimes in Developing Countries*, Institute of Developing Economies, JETRO, March, pp. 1–54.

Fischer, Stanley, 2001, "Exchange Rate Regimes: Is the Bipolar View Correct?," *Journal of Economic Perspectives* 15(2), Spring: 3–24.

Ghosh, Atish, Anne-Marie Gulde and Holger Wolf, 2002, *Exchange Rate Regimes: Choices and Consequences*, Cambridge, Mass.: MIT Press.

Hausmann, Ricardo, Ugo Panizza and Ernesto Stein, 2001, "Why Do Countries Float the Way They Float?," *Journal of Development Economics* 66(2), December: 387–414.

Ito, Takatoshi, Eiji Ogawa and Yuri Nagataki Sasaki, 1998, "How did the Dollar Peg Fall in Asia?," *Journal of the Japanese and International Economies* 12(4), December: 256–304.

International Monetary Fund, *Annual Report on Exchange Arrangements and Exchange Restrictions*, various issues, Washington: International Monetary Fund.

International Monetary Fund, *International Financial Statistics*, various issues, Washington: International Monetary Fund.

Juhn, Grace and Paolo Mauro, 2002, "Long-run Determinants of Exchange Rate Regimes: a Simple Sensitivity Analysis," IMF Working Papers 02/104, June.

Lane, Philip R. and Gian Maria Milesi-Ferretti, 2001, "The External Wealth of Nations: Measures of Foreign Assets and Liabilities for Industrial and Developing Countries," *Journal of International Economics* 55(2), December: 263–94.

Levy-Yeyati, Eduardo and Federico Sturzenegger, 2001, "Exchange Rate Regimes and Economic Performance," *International Monetary Fund Staff Papers* 47, Special Issue, 62–98.

Levy-Yeyati, Eduardo and Federico Sturzenegger, 2002, "Classifying Exchange Rate Regimes: Deeds vs. Words," Universidad Torcuato Di Tella. Available at http://www.utdt.edu/~ely/. Now available as 2005, *European Economic Review* 49(6), August: 1603–35.

Levy-Yeyati, Eduardo and Federico Sturzenegger, 2003, "To Float or to Fix: Evidence on the Impact of Exchange Rate Regimes on Growth," *American Economic Review* 93(4), September: 1173–93.

Levy-Yeyati, Eduardo, Federico Sturzenegger and Iliana Reggio, 2003, "On the Endogeneity of Exchange Rate Regimes," Universidad Torcuato Di Tella. Available at http://www.utdt.edu/~ely/

Obstfeld, Maurice and Kenneth Rogoff, 1995, "The Mirage of Fixed Exchange Rates," *Journal of Economic Perspectives* 9(4), Fall: 73–96.

Reinhart Carmen M. and Kenneth S. Rogoff, 2002, "The Modern History of Exchange Rate Arrangements: a Reinterpretation," NBER Working Paper No. 8963, May. Forthcoming in *Quarterly Journal of Economics*.

Rogoff, Kenneth S, Aasim M. Husain, Ashoka Mody, Robin Brooks and Nienke Oomes, 2004, "Evolution and Performance of Exchange Rate Regimes," International Monetary Fund Occasional Paper No. 229, May.

Shambaugh, Jay C., 2003, "The Effects of Fixed Exchange Rates on Monetary Policy," Dartmouth College. Available at http: // www. dartmouth. Edu /~economic /faculty/ Shambaugh /index.htm. Now available as 2004, *Quarterly Journal of Economics* 119(1), February: 301–52.

Summers, Lawrence H., 2000, "International Financial Crises: Causes, Prevention, and Cures," *American Economic Reviews, Papers and Proceedings* 90(2), May: 1–16.

2

Roles of Hard Pegs in Developing and Transition Countries: Cases of Argentina, Estonia, Bulgaria, and Ecuador

Hisayuki Mitsuo

2.1 Introduction

Since the 1990s, some developing and transition countries have adopted hard peg exchange rate regimes. Hard peg exchange rate regimes consist of dollarization, currency boards, and currency unions. A currency board is an exchange rate regime under which the exchange rate is fixed and the monetary base is fully backed by foreign exchange reserves. Dollarization is an exchange rate regime under which a country unilaterally lets another country's currency circulate in place of a national currency. Under both regimes, monetary policy autonomy is largely restricted.

The collapse of the Argentine currency board in 2002 shows that even a hard peg exchange rate regime may not be sustainable. This event has a particular significance in that the Argentine economy, whose monetary policy autonomy was restricted under the currency board, experienced prolonged recession prior to the currency crisis, and the cumulative loss of output together with that caused by the currency crisis was enormous. Reflecting the severity of the Argentine crisis, examination of the roles of hard peg exchange rate regimes in other developing countries as well as in Argentina will be needed. For that purpose, we have chosen three countries that adopted currency boards: Argentina (1991–2002), Estonia (1992–), Bulgaria (1997–) and one country that adopted dollarization Ecuador (2000–) as a representative sample of developing and transition countries that adopted hard peg exchange rate regimes after the 1990s.

The purpose of this chapter is to clarify the roles of hard pegs in Argentina, Estonia, Bulgaria, and Ecuador. Because the relationship between hard peg exchange rate regimes and a national economy is multifaceted, we need to clarify the roles of hard peg exchange rate regimes among various economic sectors that constitute a whole economic system. In the next section, we lay a foundation on which we analyze four cases of hard pegs. Sections 2.2–2.6 present four countries' macroeconomic performance under hard pegs. In the final section, we compare four countries' experiences under hard pegs in order to understand the roles of hard pegs in developing and transition countries since the 1990s.

2.2   Roles of a currency board and dollarization: analytical foundation

A currency board is a form of a pegged exchange rate regime. Under the currency board, the monetary base (cash and banks' reserves held at the Central Bank) is fully backed by foreign exchange reserves. Also, maintenance of a fixed exchange rate is guaranteed by law. Under the currency board, discretionary changes in monetary base are, in principle, not possible. Accordingly, the lender of last resort function that is normally expected of a Central Bank is not possible under the currency board. Two characteristics that distinguish a currency board from a conventional fixed peg are the backing rule and that the maintenance of the rate is guaranteed by law. Dollarization, by contrast, is an exchange rate regime under which a country unilaterally lets another country's currency circulate in place of the national currency. In what follows, we examine the relationships between a currency board and various economic variables and sectors, followed by an examination of dollarization.

2.2.1   Inflation

The inflation rate in the current period is determined by the difference between demand and supply in the current period. A currency board affects the current period's demand and supply directly in that the monetary base is strictly constrained by the level of foreign exchange reserves. This makes monetary authorities almost unable to issue the monetary base in a discretionary manner. A currency board also affects the current period's demand and supply by expected inflation that the public holds. The adoption of a currency board affects expected inflation in that it shows the public monetary authorities' determination both to maintain a fixed exchange rate and conduct tough monetary policy.

2.2.2   Trade and capital flow

The role of a currency board in trade and capital flows is similar to that of a conventional fixed peg, albeit the preservation of parity is more credible than in the conventional fixed peg. The increased credibility on exchange rate certainty under the currency board facilitates trade and capital flow. The benefits from exchange rate certainty are higher to the national economy with higher trade openness.

2.2.3   Interest rates

Under the currency board, without restrictions of capital movements, due to the elimination of exchange rate risks that originate from a fixed rate and higher credibility to maintain the parity, it becomes easier for capital to flow into a country. As more capital flows are provided, the interest rate tends to fall to a level similar to that of the host country. Another effect of a currency board on interest rates is that due to its effect on the expected level of inflation, nominal interest rates will be changed. Introduction of a currency board in a high inflation economy will contribute to lower expected inflation and nominal interest rates.

2.2.4 Fiscal sector

Firstly, under a currency board, the government budget is expected to balance because a monetization of the budget deficit is, in principle, not possible and because the government will try to manage its debt at a level consistent with a low fear of insolvency. Secondly, the government budget should be sound enough to be able to conduct a countercyclical policy because under the currency board monetary policy autonomy is restricted.

2.2.5 External debt

Even though monetization of government budget deficits is institutionally not possible under a currency board, governments can still finance their deficits externally. In an environment where international transactions of financial assets are made instantaneously, solvency concerns may precipitate a currency crisis. Because of the impossibility of exchange rate changes without an amendment of the law under the currency board, a quick response by monetary authorities to change exchange rates in the face of prolonged recession or a sudden outflow of capital is not possible under a currency board.

2.2.6 Real effective exchange rate

Under a currency board where the exchange rate is pegged, if domestic prices rise faster than trading partners' prices, the real exchange rates appreciate. This lowers export competitiveness. Without a compensating increase in productivity, real exchange rate appreciation cannot be corrected. If a country adopts a currency board in order to stop high inflation, real exchange rate appreciation tends to be created due to inflation inertia. The degree of appreciation under the currency board also depends upon the degree to which the initial exchange rate is undervalued; under an undervalued exchange rate, higher external demand leads to higher inflation.

2.2.7 Roles of dollarization

In the case of dollarization, the national currency is abolished and a major international currency unilaterally circulates in the national economy. Due to the loss of autonomy of monetary policy, money supply is constrained by the current account or capital inflows. The effects on inflation, interest rates, fiscal sector, external debt, and real effective exchange rates are similar to those of the currency board. Trade and capital flow will be facilitated due to the absence of transactions costs in foreign exchange markets.

2.3　Currency board in Argentina

The currency board was established in April 1991 under the Convertibility Law. Under the currency board arrangement, the peso was pegged to the US dollar at the rate of 1 US dollar = 1 peso. Devaluation required new legislation by Congress. In 1990, Argentina suffered a hyperinflation whose rate was 2315 percent annually. This hyperinflation was created by rapid money growth. The currency board was adopted primarily in order to stop excessive money growth. The currency board in Argentina was not a pure currency board in the sense that the monetary base was not entirely covered by foreign exchange reserves; up to one-third of the backing of the monetary base could be foreign currency-denominated government bonds. Figure 2.1 shows a scatter diagram of foreign exchange reserves versus monetary base during the period from April 1991 to January 2002. We can find that the monetary base and foreign exchange reserves do not exhibit a linear relationship.

2.3.1　Inflation

The inflation rate, which had been 171.7 percent in the year of the introduction of the currency board, declined to 24.9 percent in the course of the first year and to 10.6 percent after two years. Inflation was contained throughout the period under the currency board (Table 2.1). This disinflation was realized

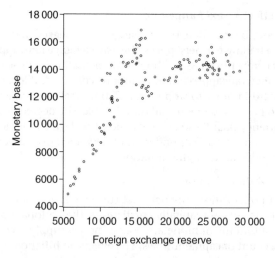

Figure 2.1　Foreign exchange reserve vs monetary base (Argentina) (millions of pesos: April 1991–January 2002)
Source: International Financial Statistics December 2004, IMF

Table 2.1 Economic indicators concerning the currency board in Argentina

	1991	1992	1993	1994	1995	1996	1997	1998	1999	2000	2001
Inflation rate (consumption price index)	171.7	24.9	10.6	4.2	3.4	0.1	0.5	0.9	−1.2	−0.9	−1.1
Exports of goods and services (% change)	−2.8	6.9	6.2	18.6	28.9	13.6	9.1	0.7	−10.5	11.5	−0.5
Imports of goods and services (% change)	68.9	67.2	13.9	23.9	−4.6	15.8	24.4	3.4	−15.2	0.5	−16.6
Money market rate	71.3	15.1	6.3	7.7	9.5	6.2	6.6	6.8	7.0	8.2	24.9
Federal funds rate (United States)	5.7	3.5	3.0	4.2	5.8	5.3	5.5	5.4	5.0	6.2	3.9
Government budget balance/GDP(%)*	n.a.	n.a.	1.2	0.0	−0.5	−2.0	−1.5	−1.4	−1.7	−2.4	−3.2
External debts†											
Total debt/gross national income (%)	35.6	30.4	27.7	29.6	39.0	41.8	44.8	48.6	52.6	52.7	52.5
Debt service/exports of goods and services (%)	33.6	27.5	30.9	25.2	30.2	39.4	50.0	57.6	75.6	70.9	66.1
Currency composition of long-term debt, US dollars (%)	54.3	55.9	68.7	64.9	59.3	57.5	61.7	63.8	64.5	62.8	60.7
Debt outstanding, total long-term (US$ billion)	49.4	49.9	52.5	63.8	71.3	81.6	90.6	105.2	111.4	112.5	102.8
Public sector, long-term (US$ billion)	45.5	45.6	46.2	50.6	55.2	62.5	67.1	77.2	84.0	86.5	71.1
Private sector, long-term (US$ billion)	3.9	4.3	6.4	13.1	16.1	19.1	23.5	27.9	27.4	26.0	31.7
Total debt stocks (US$ billion)	65.4	68.3	64.7	75.1	98.8	111.4	128.4	141.6	145.3	145.9	136.7
Real effective exchange rate‡											
Annual change (%)	−19.0	1.8	0.6	−7.4	2.9	3.3	5.1	−1.7	5.2	2.5	1.7
Rate of change from the value in 1991 (%)	0.0	1.8	2.4	−5.1	−2.4	0.9	6.0	4.2	9.7	12.4	14.3

Source: International Financial Statistics February 2004. International Monetary Fund.
* Secretariat of the Treasury. Ministry of Economy (downloaded from the Ministry of Economy and Production website).
† Global Development Finance 2004. The World Bank.
‡ JP Morgan, © Datastream.

Table 2.2 Main trading partners (% share)

	1998	1999	2000	2001	2002
Export					
Brazil	30.1	24.4	26.5	23.3	18.8
US	8.4	11.4	12.0	10.9	11.5
Chile	7.0	8.0	10.2	10.7	11.5
Import					
Brazil	22.5	21.9	25.5	25.7	28.0
US	19.8	19.6	19.1	18.6	20.1
Chile	2.3	2.5	2.4	2.5	2.0

Source: INDEC.

by a steady increase in the monetary base backed by the foreign exchange reserves. Expected inflation is supposed to decline due to the credibility of the currency board arrangement.

2.3.2 Trade and capital flow

Under the currency board exports and imports grew rapidly until 1997, helped by the reduction in exchange rate uncertainty. About a quarter of exports go to Brazil. By contrast, the country with which Argentina maintained a peg, the United States, has about a 10 percent share. The main origin of imports is Brazil and the US, whose shares are around 25 and 20 percent (Table 2.2). Export stagnation in 1999 (real exports declined by 1.3 percent) was partly brought about by Brazilian devaluation and a decline in competitiveness.

The current account deficit relative to GDP continued to widen from −0.3 percent (1991) to −4.3 percent (1994). After a short decline, it reached −4.9 percent in 1998. These relatively large deficits were financed by surges in investment. Net portfolio investment inflow reached as much as 14.3 percent of GDP in 1993. From 1999, reflecting worsening economic conditions, the net portfolio investment turned negative. The financial account started to decline in 1999, and reached −5.6 and −23.4 percent of GDP in 2001 and 2002, respectively (Table 2.3).

2.3.3 Interest rates

When expected inflation fell, and capital flowed in, money market rates declined as shown in Table 2.1. As capital inflows stared to decline in 1999, foreign exchange reserves stopped growing and the monetary base started to decline. In 2001 as capital flowed out of the country, the money market rate was raised in order to attract capital. This triggered a banking crisis in December 2001, following which the government introduced a partial deposit freeze.

Table 2.3 Current and financial accounts and net portfolio investment

	1991	1992	1993	1994	1995	1996	1997	1998	1999	2000	2001	2002
Current account/ GDP (%)	-0.3	-2.5	-3.5	-4.3	-2.0	-2.5	-4.2	-4.9	-4.2	-3.2	-1.4	8.9
Financial account/ GDP (%)	0.1	3.3	8.6	4.4	1.9	4.3	5.7	6.3	5.1	2.8	-5.6	-23.4
Net portfolio investment/ GDP (%)	0.0	2.1	14.3	3.2	0.7	3.6	3.4	2.9	-2.4	-0.9	-3.5	-6.3

Source: International Financial Statistics February 2004. International Monetary Fund.

Table 2.4 Public finance – nonfinancial public sector

	1993	1994	1995	1996	1997	1998	1999	2000	2001	2002
Unit billion peso										
Total income	45.4	48.3	49.3	46.5	54.6	56.5	57.4	55.6	50.5	55.1
Total expenses	42.7	48.3	50.6	52.0	58.9	60.6	62.2	62.4	59.2	59.6
Surplus/deficit	2.7	-0.1	-1.4	-5.5	-4.3	-4.1	-4.8	-6.8	-8.7	-4.5
Interest payments on debts	2.9	3.2	4.1	4.6	5.8	6.7	8.2	9.7	10.2	6.8
Relative to GDP (%)										
Total income	19.2	18.7	19.1	17.1	18.6	18.9	20.3	19.6	18.8	17.6
Total expenses	18.1	18.8	19.6	19.1	20.1	20.3	21.9	22.0	22.0	19.1
Surplus/deficit	1.2	0.0	-0.5	-2.0	-1.5	-1.4	-1.7	-2.4	-3.2	-1.5
Interest payments on debts	1.2	1.2	1.6	1.7	2.0	2.2	2.9	3.4	3.8	2.2

Source: Secretariat of the Treasury. Ministry of Economy (downloaded from the Ministry of Economy and Production website).

Table 2.5   Public expenditure by provincial and Buenos Aires city governments (relative to GDP (%))

1993	1994	1995	1996	1997	1998	1999	2000	2001	2002
12.5	12.4	12.7	11.9	11.8	12.4	13.7	13.5	14.5	11.7

Note: Data for 1997–2000 is preliminary. Data for 2001–2 estimated.
Source: Bureau of Consolidated Social Expenditure. Secretariat of Economic Policy (downloaded from the Ministry of Economy and Production website).

2.3.4   Fiscal sector

The government's budget balance deteriorated in the latter half of the 1990s. The nonfinancial public sectors' budget balance relative to GDP, which stood at −1.4 percent in 1998, rose to −3.2 percent in 2001. Behind this deterioration lay interest payments and recession. Interest payments relative to GDP rose from 1.7 percent in 1996 to 3.8 percent in 2001 (Table 2.4). Provincial governments' expenditure grew more rapidly than economic growth rates during the recession. Provincial governments' expenditure share against GDP which was 12.4 percent in 1998 rose to 14.5 percent in 2001 (Table 2.5).

2.3.5   External debt

Total external debt which amounted to 65.4 billion US dollars when the currency board was introduced rose to 145.9 billion US dollars in 2000. Total debt relative to gross national income changed from 35.6 percent in 1991 to 52.7 percent in 2000. The debt service ratio rose rapidly from 25.2 percent in 1994 to 75.6 percent in 1999 (Table 2.1). A partial default on external debt was announced in December 2001.

2.3.6   The real effective exchange rate

The real effective exchange rate rose by 14.3 percent from 1991 to 2001 (Table 2.1). This eroded export competitiveness. In 1999, reflecting a currency crisis in Brazil, the real effective exchange rate rose by 5.2 percent from the previous year. This lowered export growth; in real terms exports declined by −1.3 percent in 1999.

2.3.7   Currency crisis

Argentina's GDP growth stagnated from 1999; GDP growth rates were −3.4, −0.8, and −4.4 percent during this period. Argentina exited from the currency board in January 2002 and experienced a severe recession during the year; the growth rate declined to −10.9 percent (Table 2.6). From our observations on the relationships between the currency board and economic sectors, we must understand the collapse of the currency board in Argentina as a complex phenomenon. No one single factor including government debt, declining capital inflows, and real exchange rate appreciation, can be said to be the dominant factor in the collapse of the currency board.

Table 2.6   Real gross domestic product by expenditure (% growth)

	1994	1995	1996	1997	1998	1999	2000	2001	2002
Household consumption including VAT	6.1	−4.4	5.5	9.0	3.5	−2.0	−0.7	−5.7	−14.4
Public consumption	0.4	0.8	2.2	3.2	3.4	2.6	0.6	−2.1	−5.1
Gross domestic fixed investment	13.7	−13.1	8.9	17.7	6.5	−12.6	−6.8	−15.7	−36.4
Exports of real goods and services	15.3	22.5	7.6	12.2	10.6	−1.3	2.7	2.7	3.1
Imports of real goods and services	21.1	−9.8	17.5	26.9	8.4	−11.3	−0.2	−13.9	−50.1
GDP	5.8	−2.8	5.5	8.1	3.9	−3.4	−0.8	−4.4	−10.9

Source: National Bureau of National Accounts (downloaded from the Ministry of Economy and Production website).
Note: Data for 2000–2 is preliminary.

Table 2.7   Growth rates of money supply

	1994	1995	1996	1997	1998	1999	2000	2001
Monetary base	8.5	−15.4	2.1	13.6	2.6	0.8	−8.8	17.9
M1	8.2	1.6	14.6	12.8	0.0	1.6	−9.1	−20.1
M2	17.6	−2.8	18.8	25.5	10.5	4.1	1.5	−19.4

Source: International Financial Statistics February 2004. International Monetary Fund.

Partly as a result of declining capital inflows that started in 1999 and the net capital outflow that started in 2001, growth rates of the monetary base or money supply decelerated under the currency board from 1999 (Table 2.7). If a decline in money supply lowers output, one reason for the recession since 1999 may well have been the deceleration or contraction of the money supply. Lacking exchange rate flexibility under the currency board, Argentina lost price competitiveness against Brazil when that country was hit by a currency crisis in 1999. As a result, exports stagnated and GDP fell by 3.4 percent in 1999. This, together with increasing interest payments, induced the budget balance to deteriorate. A partial default on external debt was announced in December 2001, and the currency board subsequently collapsed in January 2002.

2.4   Currency board in Estonia

A currency board was established in June 1992, together with a national currency the kroon. Under the currency board arrangement, the kroon was pegged to the German mark at the rate of 1 mark = 8 EEK. From January 1999, the kroon has been fixed against the euro at the rate of 1 euro = 15.6466 EEK. In

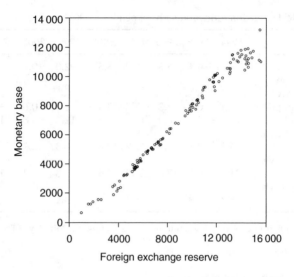

Figure 2.2   Foreign exchange reserve vs monetary base (Estonia) (millions of kroon: June 1992–December 2002)
Source: International Financial Statistics December 2004, IMF

1991, the economy contracted severely and the inflation rate soared. Shortages of goods underpinned inflation. These shortages reflected the collapse of transportation and distribution systems of the Soviet era. Against inflation, some people rushed to procure and stockpile goods (Zirnask 2002). Such anticipation of future inflation would have accelerated inflation. A currency board was introduced in order to achieve macroeconomic stability.

2.4.1   Inflation

Inflation subsided quickly after the introduction of the currency board; the inflation rate which registered 89.8 percent in 1993 decreased to 10.6 percent in 1997. This marked decline can be attributed to a decline in expected inflation and stable growth of the monetary base that is reflected in the steady accumulation of foreign exchange reserves. Figure 2.2 is a scatter diagram between foreign exchange reserves versus monetary base during the period from June 1992 to December 2002. This figure shows the close correspondence between them.

2.4.2   Trade and capital flow

Under the currency board exports and imports grew rapidly by 1998 (Table 2.8). This confirms the effect of reduced exchange rate uncertainty under a currency board. The largest trading partner is the European Union (Table 2.9). In 2002, the share of exports to the European Union and CIS were 81.7 and 5.4

Table 2.8 Economic indicators concerning the currency board in Estonia

	1993	1994	1995	1996	1997	1998	1999	2000	2001	2002
Inflation rate (consumption price index)	89.8	47.7	28.8	23.1	10.6	8.2	3.3	4.0	5.7	3.6
Exports of goods and services (% change)	22.3	50.9	38.5	6.8	26.4	17.5	-8.8	35.0	1.5	5.1
Imports of goods and services (% change)	34.5	65.3	49.4	19.8	20.6	11.5	-12.5	22.5	1.7	11.4
Current account/GDP (%)	1.2	-6.9	-4.2	-8.6	-11.4	-8.6	-5.3	-5.4	-5.7	-10.2
Government budget balance/GDP (%)	-2.0	1.3	-0.5	-0.8	2.4	-0.1	-0.1	0.1	2.4	n.a.
Money market rate	n.a.	5.7	4.9	3.5	6.5	11.7	5.4	5.7	5.3	3.9
Call money rate (Germany) or euro area interbank rate (overnight) (from 1999)	7.5	5.4	4.5	3.3	3.2	3.4	2.7	4.1	4.4	3.3
External debt*										
Total debt/gross national income (%)	3.9	4.7	5.9	35.2	50.7	50.2	48.9	52.0	53.6	76.7
Debt service/exports of goods and services (%)	1.6	1.5	0.8	3.2	4.9	7.6	12.9	8.7	7.4	13.7
Currency composition of long-term debt, US dollars (%)	42.4	32.7	27.3	21.2	18.9	16.1	17.7	16.8	19.2	3.3
Debt outstanding, total long-term (US$ billion)	0.10	0.12	0.16	0.34	1.24	1.59	1.61	1.61	1.81	3.15
Public sector, long-term (US$ billion)	0.08	0.11	0.16	0.22	0.20	0.23	0.21	0.17	0.16	0.46
Private sector, long-term (US$ billion)	0.01	0.01	0.01	0.12	1.04	1.35	1.41	1.43	1.65	2.69
Total debt stocks (US$ billion)	0.2	0.2	0.3	1.5	2.3	2.6	2.5	2.6	2.9	4.7
Real effective exchange rate†										
Annual change (%)	n.a.	10.9	18	9.7	3.3	10.4	7.3	-3.8	2	1.9
Rate of change from the value in 1993 (%)	0	10.9	30.9	43.6	48.3	63.7	75.7	69.0	72.4	75.6

Source: International Financial Statistics February 2004. International Monetary Fund.
Global Development Finance 2004. The WorldBank.
Central Bank of Estonia. (downloaded from the Central Bank of Estonia website).

Table 2.9   Main trading partners (% share)

	1999	2000	2001	2002
Export				
EU	85.6	88.1	81.3	81.7
CIS	5.9	4.0	5.1	5.4
Import				
EU	84.7	83.3	81.7	79.7
CIS	9.7	9.8	10.0	9.5

Source: Statistical Office of Estonia (downloaded from the Statistical Office of Estonia website).
Note: EU includes 25 countries since May 2004.

percent, while their shares of imports were 79.7 and 9.5 percent, respectively. The large share of the EU confirms the choice of currency peg made by Estonia, initially the German mark and subsequently the euro. Current account deficits widened during 1996–98. The size of the current account deficits relative to GDP amounted to -8.6, -11.4, and -8.6 percent during the period.

Under the currency board, capital flowed in vigorously. Most capital inflow took the form of foreign direct investment (FDI). According to Ehrlich et al. (2002), Sweden and Finland were important providers of foreign direct investment, and these countries made intensive investments in the fields of finance, transport, storage, communication, manufacturing, and wholesale and retail trade. This FDI promoted transition from a planned to a market economy through the importation of technology and business practices.

2.4.3   Interest rates

In August 1994, full current account convertibility was established. Where capital movement is free, interest rates tend to become equalized with those of the main source of capital through capital movements under the fixed exchange rate of the currency board. The money market rate was comparable to those of Germany or the euro area (Table 2.8).

However, in 1998, interest rates rose to 11.7 percent due to the Russian currency crisis. This affected real economic growth; the gross fixed capital formation and GDP declined by 15.6 and 0.1 percent respectively, in 1999 (Table 2.10).

Partly affected by the Russian crisis, in October 1998 the Bank of Estonia supplemented the loss-making Forekspank's share capital (Zirnask 2002). Under the currency board in Estonia, the lender of last resort facility, which a "pure" currency board does not have, is preserved. Lepik and Tors (2002) explain that the extent of the lender of last resort function is limited to the excess foreign reserves: the amount of foreign exchange reserve in excess of the monetary base.

Table 2.10   Real gross domestic product by expenditure (% growth)

	1994	1995	1996	1997	1998	1999	2000	2001	2002
Private consumption	0.6	5	10.1	10.5	5.2	−2.5	8.6	6.2	10.3
Government consumption	4	13.5	−3.1	−1.3	1.7	2.9	1.1	1.8	5.9
Gross fixed capital formation	9.2	5.6	9.6	19.9	14	−15.6	14.3	13	17.2
Exports	3.5	5.3	2.8	28.9	12	0.7	28.3	−0.2	0.9
Imports	11.1	6.4	7.5	29.3	12.3	−5.2	28.3	2.1	3.7
GDP	−1.6	4.5	4.5	10.5	5.2	−0.1	7.8	6.4	7.2

Source: Statistical Office of Estonia (downloaded from the Central Bank of Estonia website).

2.4.4   Fiscal sector

Estonia recorded relatively large current account deficits; from 1996 to 1998, current account deficits relative to nominal GDP were −8.6, −11.4, and −8.6 percent, respectively. The fiscal surplus widened in 1997 against these large deficits. Because widening current account deficits raise doubts about the sustainability of the currency board, fiscal tightening, by acting to reduce the current account deficit, helps maintain the currency board. From 1997 the government budget balance has been maintained in surplus, which helps with the sustainability of the currency board system.

2.4.5   External debt

The private sector share of total long-term debt exceeded the public sector share in 1997. In 2002, the private sector share of total long-term debt was 85.4 percent. External debt relative to gross national debt increased from 48.9 percent in 1999 to 76.7 percent in 2002. The debt service ratio under the currency board system was maintained at 13.7 percent in 2002.

2.4.6   Real effective exchange rate

The speed of appreciation was rapid during 1994–99, which was mainly caused by the high inflation rate. From 1993 to 1999, the rate rose by 75.7 percent. This appreciation contributed to wide current account deficits. Subsequently, the rate remained relatively stable during 2000–2.

2.5   Currency board in Bulgaria

In July 1997, Bulgaria introduced a currency board during a period of economic crisis. The monetary base increased by 826.8 percent in 1997 (Table 2.11). Behind this problem lay a financial markets problem. The government encouraged state-owned banks to lend to loss-making state-owned enterprises,[1] which worsened the banks' balance sheets. High interest payments on the

Table 2.11 Economic indicators concerning the currency board in Bulgaria

	1992	1993	1994	1995	1996	1997	1998	1999	2000	2001	2002
Inflation rate (consumption price index)	89.3	71.7	96.7	62.0	121.7	1058.2	18.7	2.6	10.3	7.4	5.8
Exports of goods and services (% change)	21.5	−2.6	6.0	30.5	−7.7	0.3	−4.7	−3.1	20.8	3.4	11.3
Imports of goods and services (% change)	25.4	9.5	−11.0	25.1	−8.5	−3.7	4.5	9.6	16.9	9.7	9.0
Government budget balance/GDP (%)	−4.9	−12.1	−4.7	−5.2	−18.9	2.0	2.7	1.5	0.6	1.9	0.0
Monetary base (% change)	50.7	22.0	55.9	52.0	91.5	826.8	10.2	17.6	11.1	30.4	8.0
Interbank rate	52.4	48.1	66.4	53.1	119.9	66.4	2.5	2.9	3.0	3.7	2.5
Call money rate (Germany) or euro area interbank rate (overnight) (from 1999)	9.4	7.5	5.4	4.5	3.3	3.2	3.4	2.7	4.1	4.4	3.3
External debts*											
Total debt/gross national income (%)	116.0	114.4	102.6	81.9	106.2	98.3	80.7	79.0	82.9	72.5	68.6
Debt service/exports of goods and services (%)	8.8	6.6	13.0	16.5	19.7	15.1	20.8	19.3	17.1	16.9	15.9
Currency composition of long-term debt, US dollars (%)	45.5	45.5	71.3	66.1	69.1	74.3	79.9	79.9	81.6	80.6	66.0
Debt outstanding, total long-term (US$ billion)	9.7	9.7	8.5	9.1	8.6	8.2	8.5	8.5	8.4	8.2	8.6
Total debt stocks (US$ billion)	11.8	12.2	9.8	10.4	10.1	9.9	10.0	10.1	10.2	9.6	10.5
Real effective exchange rate											
Annual change (%)		52.0	−9.7	14.9	−13.9	20.1	14.2	3.7	2.0	4.8	4.5
Rate of change from the value in 1997 (%)	−38.7	−6.8	−15.8	−3.3	−16.7		14.2	18.5	20.8	26.7	32.3

Source: International Financial Statistics December 2004. International Monetary Fund.
* Global Development Finance 2004. The World Bank.

government internal debts contributed to a widening in government budget deficits. As a result of growing budget deficits, the government asked for long-term direct credit from the Bulgarian National Bank, the Central Bank of Bulgaria (Mihov 2002). The exchange rate which was US$1 = 0.12 lev in May 1996 depreciated to 2.39 lev in February 1997. The rapid increase of the monetary base and exchange rate depreciation affected inflation; the inflation rate (measured by the consumer price index) rose from 62.0 percent in 1996 to 1058.2 percent in 1997.

2.5.1   Inflation

The exchange rate was set at 1000 Bulgarian lev = 1 German mark in July 1997. In January 1999, the euro replaced German mark at the rate of 1955.83 lev = 1 euro. In July 1999, the exchange rate was changed to 1.95583 lev = 1 euro with denomination of the lev. The Bulgarian currency board is composed of an issue department and a banking department. Liabilities of the issue department include banking department deposit and government deposit. Banking department deposit makes it possible for the Central Bank to perform a lender of last resort function.

Under the currency board, inflation declined rapidly; the inflation rate of 1058.2 percent in 1997 declined to 18.7 percent in 1998. Under the currency board rapid expansion of monetary base was stopped (Table 2.11). The introduction of the currency board seems to have lowered expected inflation. These two effects combined contributed to the rapid decline in inflation. Relatively

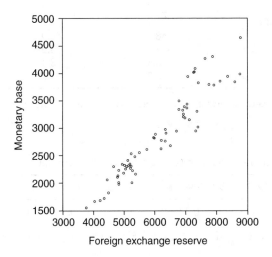

Figure 2.3   Foreign exchange reserve vs monetary base (Bulgaria) (millions of lev: July 1997–December 2002)
Source: International Financial Statistics December 2004, IMF

low inflation rates have been maintained under the currency board (Table 2.11). Figure 2.3 shows a scatter diagram of foreign exchange reserve versus monetary base during the period from July 1997 to December 2002.

2.5.2   Trade and capital flow

After the introduction of the currency board, trade started to expand. The role of the EU in trade is high; in 2001, shares of exports and imports were 54.7 and 49.3 percent, respectively (Table 2.12). From 1999, current account deficits widened to over 5 percent relative to GDP. Foreign direct investment grew rapidly. The economy attained stable growth[2] led by foreign direct investments (Tables 2.13 and 2.14).

Table 2.12   Main trading partners (% share)

	1999	2000	2001
Export			
CIS	8.5	5.7	5.5
Russian Federation	4.7	2.5	2.3
EU	52.1	51.3	54.7
Germany	9.9	9.1	9.5
Italy	13.9	14.3	15.0
Greece	8.6	7.8	8.8
Import			
CIS	23.4	27.7	23.8
Russian Federation	20.1	24.3	20.0
EU	48.4	44.0	49.3
Germany	14.9	13.9	15.3
Italy	8.4	8.4	9.6
Greece	5.7	4.9	5.7

Source: National Statistical Institute (downloaded from the National Statistical Institute website).

Table 2.13   Current account and foreign direct investment flow (% against GDP)

	1992	1993	1994	1995	1996	1997	1998	1999	2000	2001	2002
Current account	−3.6	−11.0	−0.3	−0.2	0.2	4.1	−0.5	−5.0	−5.6	−7.2	−5.3
Direct investment (inflow)	0.4	0.4	1.0	0.7	1.1	4.9	4.2	6.3	7.9	6.0	5.8

Source: International Financial Statistics December 2004. International Monetary Fund.

Table 2.14 Real gross domestic product by expenditure (% growth)

	1992	1993	1994	1995	1996	1997	1998	1999	2000	2001	2002
Individual consumption	−2.4	−2.9	−4.4	−1.9	−5.7	−10.0	2.6	9.3	4.9	4.6	3.4
Collective consumption	−9.3	−9.3	−5.6	−2.1	−33.2	−3.9	23.4	4.1	13.3	2.9	6.0
Gross fixed capital formation	−7.3	−17.5	1.1	16.1	−21.2	−20.9	35.2	20.8	15.4	23.3	8.5
Exports of goods and services	n.a.	n.a.	n.a.	n.a.	n.a.	12.8	−4.7	−5.0	16.6	10.0	7.0
Imports of goods and services	n.a.	n.a.	n.a.	n.a.	n.a.	10.9	12.1	9.3	18.6	14.8	4.9
GDP	−7.3	−1.5	1.8	2.9	−9.4	−5.6	4	2.3	5.4	4.1	4.9

Source: National Statistical Institute.

2.5.3 Interest rates

The interbank interest rate rose during the economic crisis in 1996–97. However, the rate which had been 119.9 percent in 1996 declined to 2.5 percent in 1998. The currency board was effective in bringing down expected inflation and interest rates. Under the currency board, the interbank interest rate became comparable to short-term interest rates in Germany or, after the introduction of the euro, in the euro area. In September 1998 current account convertibility was established.

2.5.4 Fiscal sector

Since the currency board was introduced, budget deficits have not been recorded (Table 2.11). This shows that the budgetary discipline necessitated by the currency board has been realized. Fiscal prudence helps to correct the "soft budget constraint" and promotes economic transition to a market economy.

2.5.5 External debt

The gross external debt relative to gross national income diminished after introduction of the currency board from 80.7 percent in 1998 to 68.6 percent in 2002. The debt service ratio continued to decline from 20.8 percent in 1998 to 15.9 percent in 2002 (Table 2.11).

2.5.6 Real effective exchange rate

The real effective exchange rate appreciated rapidly in 1998. Mainly due to higher inflation rates than trading partners, the rate rose by 32.3 percent in 2002 compared to that in 1997 (Table 2.11).

2.6   Dollarization in Ecuador

In March 2000, the Ecuador economy started to circulate the US dollar, abolishing the sucre as a national currency (dollarization). This was a significant exchange regime change from a crawling band regime. This section tries to analyze the background to dollarization and reports on economic performance and potential risks under the dollarization regime in Ecuador. The background to dollarization was the economic crisis in 1999, composed of fiscal, external debt, banking, and currency crises. A common initial shock lay behind these crises: a decline in oil prices. The economic crisis of 1999 originated from the fundamental economic structure of Ecuador: a high dependency on oil exports, high external debt burden, high share of interest payments in government expenditure, and high oil revenue share in government revenue. After the dollarization in 2000, the inflation rate fell and growth resumed. However, output growth was helped by high oil prices. The long-term sustainability of the dollarization regime ultimately hinges on productivity enhancements in the oil and other export industries.

2.6.1   Economic performance and structure of the Ecuador economy before dollarization

Table 2.15 shows real economic growth rates of GDP and demand components of GDP during the period 1994–2001. GDP fell by 7.3 percent in 1999. This severe economic decline was a precondition to the decision to dollarize in 2000. It is to be noted that real exports fell by 3.2 percent in 1998 at the onset of the economic crisis in 1999. Table 2.15 also shows the percentage share of demand components and sectors in GDP during 1994–2001. In 2001, export and import shares were 35.2 and 23.1 percent of GDP. The characteristics of the Ecuador economy are the high share of the agricultural and oil industries. Their shares were 16.8 and 14.6 percent in 2001, respectively.

Ecuador is a primary commodity exporting country. Table 2.16 shows the percentage share of main export items in 1992–2001. In 2001, the shares of crude oil, banana, shrimp, natural flowers, and cacao were 37.1, 17.8, 6.0, 4.9, and 1.2 percent, respectively. The primary products total was 73.2 percent. Table 2.17 shows the share of exports and imports by main destinations. In 2001, 38.3 percent of exports went to the United States, with 24.7 percent of imports originating from the United States. In sum, the Ecuador economy is dependent on commodity exports, mainly crude oil, and the main destination of exports and origin of imports is the United States.

2.6.2   Fiscal, monetary, and exchange rate policies, and external debt up to dollarization

Table 2.18 shows the nonfinancial public sector's expenditure and revenue during 1996–2001. The first characteristic of the fiscal sector in Ecuador is

...annual percentage of sectors (percentage growth and percentage share)

	1994	1995	1996	1997	1998	1999	2000	2001
Real gross domestic product by expenditure (% growth)								
Household consumption	2.9	2.2	1.9	2.4	2.0	-9.7	2.2	4.1
Government consumption	0.0	1.9	-1.0	-0.3	0.2	-15.5	-1.3	0.0
Gross fixed investment	4.5	5.3	1.8	4.0	6.3	-35.5	10.5	40.4
Exports of goods and services	8.7	5.0	3.6	4.3	-3.2	-0.4	-0.2	5.0
Imports of goods and services	6.0	9.8	-5.9	8.8	5.5	-39.0	18.7	33.7
GDP	4.3	2.3	2.0	3.4	0.4	-7.3	2.3	5.6
Gross domestic product by expenditure (% share)								
Household consumption	64.3	64.2	64.2	63.6	64.6	62.9	62.8	61.9
Government consumption	9.5	9.5	9.2	8.9	8.9	8.1	7.8	7.4
Gross fixed investment	14.3	14.7	14.7	14.8	15.6	10.9	11.7	15.6
Exports of goods and services	33.4	34.2	34.8	35.1	33.8	36.3	35.4	35.2
Imports of goods and services	21.8	23.4	21.6	22.8	23.9	15.7	18.3	23.1
Real gross domestic product by sectors (% growth)								
Agriculture	3.9	3.2	3.5	4.1	-1.4	-1.3	-5.3	4.5
Oil and mining	10.6	3.8	-1.9	3.5	-3.3	0.3	4.8	3.0
Manufacturing	4.4	2.2	3.3	3.5	0.4	-7.2	5.2	5.0
Electricity, gas, and water	3.1	-3.7	2.8	2.4	2.1	4.7	5.1	0.5
Construction	5.3	-1.4	2.5	2.8	6.0	-8.0	3.7	14.7
Commerce	3.6	2.2	4.4	3.3	0.9	-12.1	4.7	10.5
Transport and communications	4.2	3.0	3.1	3.9	1.6	-8.8	4.4	4.0
GDP	4.3	2.3	2.0	3.4	0.4	-7.3	2.3	5.6
Gross domestic product by sector (% share)								
Agriculture	17.1	17.2	17.5	17.6	17.3	18.4	17.0	16.8
Oil and mining	14.4	14.6	14.0	14.0	13.5	14.6	15.0	14.6
Manufacturing	15.3	15.2	15.4	15.5	15.5	15.5	15.9	15.8
Electricity, gas, and water	1.5	1.4	1.4	1.4	1.4	1.6	1.6	1.5
Construction	2.5	2.4	2.4	2.4	2.6	2.5	2.6	2.8
Commerce	14.8	14.7	15.1	15.1	15.1	14.4	14.7	15.4
Transport and communications	8.9	9.0	9.1	9.1	9.2	9.1	9.3	9.1

Source: Central Bank of Ecuador.

Table 2.16   Main export items (1992–2001) (% share)

	1992	1993	1994	1995	1996	1997	1998	1999	2000	2001
Primary products	87.9	82.2	82.2	81.2	78.2	80.8	76.1	76.1	75.1	73.2
Crude oil	40.6	37.6	30.8	31.9	31.2	26.8	18.8	29.5	43.5	37.1
Banana	22.0	18.5	18.4	19.5	19.8	24.9	25.2	21.2	16.4	17.8
Shrimp	17.5	15.4	14.3	15.4	13.0	16.8	20.8	13.6	5.8	6.0
Natural flowers	1.0	1.3	1.5	1.9	2.2	2.5	3.9	4.1	4.0	4.9
Cacao	1.1	1.6	1.7	1.9	1.9	1.1	0.5	1.4	0.8	1.2

Source: Central Bank of Ecuador.

Table 2.17   Main trading partners (% share)

	1992	1993	1994	1995	1996	1997	1998	1999	2000	2001
Exports										
USA	42.8	42.6	41.5	40.2	38.2	38.6	39.0	38.4	38.1	38.3
Colombia	2.4	4.8	5.9	5.8	6.2	6.8	6.7	5.1	5.4	7.0
Korea	10.9	9.2	6.8	6.6	6.5	3.3	2.3	4.8	6.4	5.1
Italy	3.0	4.0	4.0	4.0	4.0	5.2	6.1	4.7	3.3	4.3
Imports										
USA	33.8	33.7	26.6	31.3	31.1	30.6	30.1	30.4	25.0	24.7
Colombia	4.1	3.8	8.1	9.5	10.6	10.3	10.6	12.0	13.4	14.4
Venezuela	1.7	1.9	4.5	6.5	4.8	6.8	4.8	6.4	7.1	5.5
Brazil	4.8	3.7	6.2	4.5	4.0	2.9	3.5	3.2	3.7	3.6

Source: Central Bank of Ecuador.

Table 2.18   Public finance – nonfinancial public sector (US$ million)

	1996	1997	1998	1999	2000	2001
Petroleum revenue	1575	1270	913	1049	1460	1347
Petroleum revenue/GDP (%)	8.3	6.4	4.6	7.6	10.7	7.5
Total revenue	4656	4714	4027	3515	4126	4923
Interest payments	831	995	987	1183	1052	985
Interest payments/GDP (%)	4.4	5.0	5.0	8.6	7.7	5.5
Total expenditure	5221	5220	5145	4165	3889	4932
Budget balance	−565	−507	−1118	−650	237	−9
Budget balance/GDP (%)	−3.0	−2.6	−5.7	−4.7	1.7	−0.1

Source: Central Bank of Ecuador.

Table 2.19 External debt

	1994	1995	1996	1997	1998	1999	2000	2001	2002
Debt outstanding, total long-term (US$ billion)	10.8	12.5	12.8	13.2	13.3	15.1	12.8	12.9	13.8
Public sector, long-term (US$ billion)	10.5	12.1	12.4	12.9	13.1	13.6	11.3	11.3	11.2
Private sector, long-term (US$ billion)	0.2	0.4	0.3	0.3	0.2	1.6	1.4	1.7	2.6
Currency composition of long-term debt, US$ (%)	53.6	70.5	73.9	77.9	83.5	84.0	83.2	84.9	85.0
Short-term debt outstanding (US$ billion)	4.1	1.3	1.6	2.1	2.3	1.1	0.8	1.4	2.3
Total debt stocks (US$ billion)	15.1	14.0	14.5	15.4	15.6	16.3	13.7	14.5	16.5
Total debt/gross national income (%)	85.4	72.6	71.6	68.2	70.8	105.7	94.4	73.3	72.5
Debt service/exports of goods and services (%)	20.2	24.9	21.4	27.7	29.8	34.7	25.7	28.4	28.7
Workers' remittances and compensation of employees, received (US$ billion)	0.3	0.4	0.5	0.6	0.8	1.1	1.3	1.4	1.4
Workers' remittances and compensation of employees (share of gross national income (%))	1.6	2.0	2.4	2.9	3.6	7.1	9.1	7.2	6.3

Source: Global Development Finance 2004. The World Bank.

the high share of interest payments in GDP. This share was 4.4 percent in 1996, but it rose to 8.6 percent in 1999. Underlying the interest rate payments is the external debt. The second characteristic of the fiscal sector in Ecuador is the high level of petroleum revenue. This was 8.3 percent of GDP in 1996. Due to the decline in oil prices, petroleum revenue declined from US$1575 million in 1996 to US$913 million in 1998. Due to the increase in interest payments and decline in oil revenues, the budget deficit increased to US$1.1 billion (−5.7 percent of GDP) in 1998.

In 1997, Ecuador's total debt amounted to US$15.4 billion and the debt income ratio was 68.2 percent. However, the debt income ratio rose rapidly to 105.7 percent in 1999, when Ecuador's government debt defaulted. From 1996 to 1999, the debt service ratio increased rapidly from 21.4 to 34.7 percent (Table 2.19).

Due to capital inflows, foreign assets of the monetary authorities increased in 1994. Money supply (M_1) and quasi-money increased rapidly. The 1994 Law of the Financial System Institutions promoted interest rate liberalization. Due to the financial liberalization policy, quasi-money continued to grow rapidly. This significant expansion of quasi-money can be termed a "credit boom."

The credit boom was accompanied by deposit dollarization. In 1994, 15.6 percent of commercial banks' overall deposits were in US dollars. This ratio rose to 53.7 percent in 1999. In 1994, 15.7 percent of quasi-money was in US dollars. This ratio rose to 47.4 percent in 1999 (Table 2.20). Caused by an oil price decline that started in 1996, real exports declined by 3.2 percent in 1998. In addition, natural disasters caused by the El Niño phenomenon lowered

Table 2.20   Dollarization indicators

Year	Year-end percentage in US dollars of	
	Quasi-money	Deposits
1989	9.7	14.7
1990	7.4	13.3
1991	7.5	14.5
1992	10.8	20.0
1993	12.6	16.9
1994	15.7	15.6
1995	24.3	19.2
1996	28.0	22.3
1997	36.9	23.6
1998	43.9	36.9
1999	47.4	53.7

Source: Modified from Table 2.2. Ecuador. Dollarization indicators in Beckerman (2001).

agricultural production by 1.4 percent in 1998 (Table 2.15). These real exogenous shocks and resulting overall output decline affected the banking sector.

Banking crises began with the closure of a small bank (Solbanco) in April 1998. Runs on deposits then spread to other banks. The government declared a bank holiday in March 1999. Then the government imposed a deposit freeze. However, runs on deposits continued (Jácome 2004). The monetary base grew rapidly, and inflation accelerated, and the exchange rate continued to depreciate.

Ecuador's de facto exchange rate regime until February 1999 was basically a crawling band around the US dollar (Reinhart and Rogoff 2004). The band width of +/−5 percent was widened to +/−10 percent in March and +/−15 percent in September 1998. As the sucre started to depreciate, confidence in the sucre fell and a shift from sucre deposits to dollar deposits increased under the financial system that accompanies deposit dollarization. Currency depreciation also increased the debt burden; currency composition of long-term debt in US dollars had increased 54 percent in 1994 to 84 percent in 1998 (Table 2.19).

2.6.3 Economic performance and potential risk under dollarization

During the economic turmoil, Ecuador declared dollarization in January 2000 at the rate of 25 000 sucre to one US dollar. Although Ecuador has lost monetary policy autonomy, the Central Bank of Ecuador was preserved. Coins with a face value under one dollar are issued by the Central Bank under the name of centavos, while the US coins whose unit is cents also circulate.

Due to monetary growth stability and diminished inflation expectation, the inflation rate which was 96.1 percent in 2000 fell to 37.7 percent in 2001. Adopting the US dollar brought Ecuador benefits in reducing exchange rate uncertainties in international trade and payments, in particular with the United States. Helped by high oil prices and by the remittances of Ecuadorian workers overseas, the economy grew briskly after dollarization. The government budget deficit was reduced after dollarization. However, the sustainability of the dollarization regime in the medium term is questionable. Money supply under this regime is determined by capital inflow and ultimately by the trade balance, in particular exports. As we saw in Section 2.1, the main export item is crude oil. Since Ecuador can no longer depreciate exchange rates to cope with external shocks like a sudden decline in crude oil prices, improving productivity in the oil industry as well as other export industries will be crucial to avoid a situation in which money is insufficient for Ecuador's growth potential.

2.7 Summary and conclusion

In this section, we compare four cases of hard peg exchange rate regimes, summarize our findings, and draw policy implications.

Firstly, hard peg exchange rate regimes were introduced as stabilization devices for high inflation. Hard pegs were shown to be effective in containing inflation. These effects are attributable to the function of a currency board and dollarization; under the currency board the monetary base is basically provided proportionate with foreign exchange reserves. Under dollarization the monetary base is determined by external trade and capital inflows, which prohibits discretionary supply of the monetary base by the Central Bank. Because under both regimes, changing parity or moving to other exchange rate regimes is difficult, monetary policy achieves a higher credibility which helps to lower expected inflation.

Secondly, we found a similarity of the functions and roles of currency boards in Argentina, Estonia, and Bulgaria. They all retained limited discretion in monetary policy, which a "pure" currency board is not supposed to have.

Thirdly, adoption of hard pegs is associated with smaller budget deficits. This is because adoption of a hard peg tends to impose discipline on government budgets and because monetization of government budget deficits is not possible. However, even though Argentina's budget deficits had been kept relatively small after the introduction of the currency board, the budget deficits created by central government and growing expenditure by the provincial governments in the late 1990s induced a decline in net capital inflows. A high proportion of government debt was external and this prepared the preconditions for a currency crisis. Coupled with reduced capital flows, a reduced monetary base lowered real output. This channel is inherent in the mechanism of the currency board. In Estonia, the government budget turned into a surplus against widening current account deficits in 1997. This fiscal policy was conducive for sustaining a currency board in Estonia. In Estonia and Bulgaria, the fiscal discipline under the currency board helps to contain the "soft budget constraint" that characterized socialist economic systems and promoted economic transition to a market economy.

Fourthly, four countries' trade openness (period average) under the hard peg regime was 20.1 percent in Argentina, 156.6 percent in Estonia, 107.8 percent in Bulgaria, and 73.6 percent in Ecuador.[3] Estonia and Bulgaria's relatively high trade openness would have given those countries relatively larger gains from reduced exchange rate uncertainty under the currency board.

Notes

1 This can be interpreted as a "soft budget constraint" that characterized the socialist economic system.
2 Ialnazov (2003) evaluates a currency board affirmatively as an "external anchor," which would make Bulgaria escape from the economic turmoil of transition through a rule-based monetary policy.
3 Periods are Argentina (1991–2001), Estonia (1993–2002), Bulgaria (1997–2002), and Ecuador (2000–1).

References

Beckerman, P., 2001, "Longer-term Origins of Ecuador's 'Predollarization' Crisis," in P. Beckerman and A. Solimano (eds), *Ecuador: Crisis and Dollarization*, Washington, DC: World Bank.

Ehrlich, L., Ü. Kaasik, and A. Randveer, 2002, "The Impact of Scandinavian Economies on Estonia via Foreign Trade and Direct Investments," Working Papers of Eesti Pank, No. 4.

Ialnazov, D. S., 2003, "Can a Country Extricate Itself from its Post-Socialist Trajectory? The Role of External Anchors in Bulgaria," *Hikaku Keizai Taisei Kenkyu*, Vol. 10: 85–103.

Jácome, L. I. H., 2004, "The Late 1990s Financial Crisis in Ecuador: Institutional Weaknesses, Fiscal Rigidities, and Financial Dollarization at Work," International Monetary Fund Working Paper.

Lepik, I. and J. Tors, 2002, "Structure and Performance of Estonia's Financial Sector," in C. Thimann (ed.), *Financial Sectors in EU Accession Countries*, European Central Bank.

Mihov, I., 2002, "The Economic Transition in Bulgaria 1989–1999," in M. I. Blejer and M. Skreb (eds), *Transition: the First Decade*, MIT Press.

Reinhart, C.M. and K. Rogoff, 2004, "The Modern History of Exchange Rate Arrangements: a Reinterpretation," *Quarterly Journal of Economics* 119(1), February: 1–48.

Zirnask, V., 2002, *15 Years of New Estonian Banking – Achievements and Lessons of the Reconstruction Period*, Tallinn: Estfond.

3
Monetary Policy in Brazil under a Flexible Exchange Rate

Shoji Nishijima

3.1 Introduction

Although the Brazilian economy experienced hyperinflation from the middle of the 1980s until the beginning of the 1990s, the *Real Plan* stabilization policy implemented in July 1994 successfully eliminated high rates of inflation by adopting an exchange rate anchor system. It is very evident that the policy reforms introduced during the 1990s helped this disinflation process by liberalizing trade and capital markets, which significantly increased market competition and capital inflows. On the other hand, a stabilization policy based on a dollar peg inevitably led to overvaluations of real exchange rates, which in turn led to external imbalances and higher dependence on foreign capital.

As is well known from open macroeconomics, a country cannot simultaneously adopt fixed exchange rates, free capital movement and an independent monetary policy without experiencing involuntary adjustments like a currency crisis. In this respect, Brazil has been no exception. Faced with the currency crises prevailing in the second half of the 1990s, Brazil was eventually forced to abandon the fixed exchange rate system in January 1999 in the face of large capital outflows and speculative attacks. Under the new exchange rate regime – a flexible exchange rate system – the Brazilian government has adopted inflation targeting as the new anchor for inflation.

Between 1999 and 2000, inflation rates were contained within the target range, which created much kudos for Brazilian monetary policy. However, actual inflation rates exceeded the target range in the period from 2001 through 2003. In particular, the inflation rate reached 12.53 percent in 2002 – much higher than the upper limit of 6 percent – due to sudden shifts perceived in country risk and exchange rates that were provoked by market expectations about the presidential election. This event conforms to the accepted truth that a country in "fiscal dominance"[1] is likely to face to difficulties in managing an inflation targeting policy.

The purpose of this chapter is to discuss the main problems of the current monetary policy in Brazil under a flexible exchange rate system. Section 3.1

briefly examines some characteristics of the inflation targeting policy implemented in July 1999. Section 3.2 summarizes the institutional aspects of the policy and macroeconomic performance under this regime. Section 3.3 presents a theoretical model for inflation targeting that takes public debt and exchange rate risk premium into consideration. These two factors are very important for managing inflation targeting policy, particularly in the context of emerging markets, which suffer from the fiscal dominance problem. In Section 3.4, Brazilian inflation targeting policy is examined by estimating response functions regarding interest rates. The estimation verifies that the Central Bank determines interest rates, taking into account the changes in risk premium and public debt.

3.2 Some problems of inflation targeting under a flexible exchange rate system

Research regarding the theory and the experience of inflation targeting are found, among others, in Blejer et al. (2000), Bernanke et al. (1999), Taylor (1999), and Svensson (1999). The methodology of setting an inflation target means that the monetary authority conducts stabilization policies using traditional instruments of monetary policy – basically short-term interest rates – to realize the target rate set in advance. According to Haldane (2000), Bernanke et al. (1999), and Svensson (1997), the main advantages of inflation targeting are: (1) the monetary authority can set an inflation target as a nominal anchor for monetary policy or as a reference index for inflationary expectation, (2) it can increase not only the transparency of monetary policy but also the capacity for evaluation of monetary policy and its performance, (3) it can demonstrate to the public that monetary policy has a long-run effect on stabilization.

However, inflation targeting policy in an open economy is likely to experience problems in Latin America. Under a flexible exchange rate system, inflation targeting policy faces difficulties due to large and volatile changes in exchange rates. Changes in exchange rates affect price levels directly through import prices and indirectly through aggregate demand and supply. In turn, exchange rates are affected by external shocks and expectations. Historically in Latin American countries exchange rate changes have been quickly passed through to price levels (Mishkin and Savastano 2001).

Particularly when a country is in fiscal dominance with unsustainable public debt and budget deficits, it is inevitable that the credibility of the public debt decreases and default risk becomes serious, which immediately leads to a deterioration in the risk premium and a large depreciation. According to Blanchard (2004), while a standard argument predicts that an increase in interest rates will lead to an exchange rate appreciation by attracting foreign capital, fiscal dominance makes an inflation targeting policy difficult due to higher default risk and depreciation caused by the increase in interest rates.

In reality an inflation targeting policy does not assure fiscal discipline. The public debt of Brazil has increased significantly even following the introduction of the inflation targeting policy. Whereas the ratio of public debt to GDP in July 1999 was 46 percent, it reached a peak of 60 percent in September 2002. Moreover, about 80 percent of Brazilian debt is either denominated in dollars or indexed to exchange rates or interest rates. This means that a large depreciation increases debt payments in local currency terms, which reduces the credibility of government bonds. This, in turn, aggravates default risk and increases the risk premium, and once again leads to a vicious circle of depreciation.

Several months ahead of the presidential election of October 2002, along with expectations that the candidate Lula would win, the Brazilian EMBI + spread suddenly spiked upwards from 732 basis points in March 2002 to 2001 basis points in August. Based on his career and political attitude, the market expected that Lula would not embrace rigorous policies to reduce budget deficits and would be hostile to international financial markets. The exchange rate depreciated drastically from 2.4 real per US dollar in January 2002 to 3.9 real in August, while the inflation rate (IPCA) increased from 7.6 percent in January 2002 to 16.8 percent in April 2003. Blanchard (2004), using empirical evidence in Brazil, found a link between expected debt and the probability of default, which in turn influences the exchange rate. Favero and Giavazzi (2004) discussed the possibility of the default risk in this period reinforcing the vicious circle that made the fiscal constraint on monetary policy more stringent.

Here we discuss the effects of exchange rates on interest rates using an inflation targeting model, in which the exchange rate is incorporated into an aggregate demand and supply function (Mishkin and Savastano 2001). The aggregate supply function is given by

$$\pi_t = \pi_{t-1} + \alpha_1 y_{t-1} + \alpha_2 e_{t-1} + \varepsilon_t$$

and the aggregate demand function is given by

$$y_t = \beta_1 y_{t-1} - \beta_2 (i_{t-1} - \pi_{t-1}) + \beta_3 (e_{t-1} - e_{t-2}) + \eta_t$$

where π_t is the inflation rate, y_t is the output gap (the log of the actual to potential output), i_t is the nominal interest rate, e_t is the log of the real exchange rate (a deviation from a normal level), ε_t and η_t represent aggregate supply and demand shocks, respectively. The exchange rate is determined by

$$e_t = \varphi i_t + u_t$$

where u_t are the external shocks and φ captures the impacts of interest rates on the exchange rate. The monetary authority determines the optimal interest rate by minimizing the following intertemporal loss function:

$$E_t \sum_{\tau=1}^{\infty} \delta^{\tau-1} \{(\pi_\tau - \pi^*)^2/2 + \lambda y_\tau^2/2\}$$

where E is the operator to express expectation, δ is the government discount rate and π^* is the target inflation level. The optimal interest rate is expressed by a modified Taylor rule:

$$i_t = \pi_t + b_1(\pi_t - \pi^*) + b_2 y_t + b_3 e_t$$

The assumption concerning Latin America under flexible exchange rate regimes that changes in exchange rate significantly affect interest rates due to a relatively large pass-through is expressed by a large b_3. Moreover, considering that φ captures the extent of the effects on the exchange rate (caused, for instance, by capital inflows that are induced by interest rate differentials between home and abroad) and u_t captures the extent of such an external shock as country risk, the large magnitude of these factors indicates that the interest rate has to change to a greater degree in the inflation targeting regime.

Under such a circumstance, if a country is in fiscal dominance, an increase in interest rates will aggravate the debt payment burden. Therefore an automatic increase in interest rates due to the inflation targeting policy will have a further negative impact on the default risk of the country. This means that, even when a country is experiencing a sudden jump in default risk for some reason, it will nonetheless still face difficulty in increasing interest rates. The experience of Brazil in 2002 is a typical case in which a country in fiscal dominance was confronted with such a situation. How did the Brazilian government determine interest rates during that period? We will make an empirical investigation by estimating the response function of the Brazilian Central Bank to discuss this question in Section 3.5.

3.3   Inflation targeting policy in Brazil

3.3.1   Institutional aspects

In Brazil the inflation targeting policy was legally institutionalized by presidential decree No. 3088 from July 1, 1999 with the objective of substituting the exchange rate anchor with an inflation target as the nominal anchor. From July 1994 (when the Real Plan was implemented) to January 1999 (when the currency crisis happened), the Brazilian government maintained monetary stability through a crawling peg and high level of international reserves. When currency crises happened in Mexico, Asia, and Russia in the second half of the 1990s, Brazil could defend its exchange rate system by adopting high interest rates and intervention in exchange markets. However, in addition to the delay of fiscal reforms for the tax and pension systems, the high interest rate policies brought about huge increases in debt payments and gradually weakened the market's credibility in the Brazilian government.

Since the flexible exchange rate system was introduced on January 15, 1999, the real depreciated noticeably from R\$1.21 per US dollar in the beginning of January to R\$2.06 at the end of February. In March, the Central Bank increased interest rates and announced an alteration to procedures for their determination; the president of the Central Bank was authorized to set the interest rate without notifying the Monetary Policy Committee (Copom) in advance. Until then interest rates were determined exclusively by Copom. At the same time, the Bank announced the introduction of a new base interest rate called SELIC and the abolition of the interest rate band system (TBC/TBAN).

The main characteristics of the Brazilian inflation targeting system are as follows:

1. The target rate and tolerance range are set by the National Monetary Council (Conselho Monetário Nacional) based on proposals from the Ministry of Finance.
2. The Central Bank is mandated to implement monetary policies needed to attain the inflation target.
3. In case the target is not met, the president of the Bank has a responsibility to issue an open letter to the Minister of Finance explaining the reasons for the deviation, measures to eliminate it, and the time necessary to return the inflation rate to an acceptable level within the tolerance. However the president of the Bank is not subject to any penalty.
4. The broad-based price index (IPCA: Índice de Preços ao Consumidor Amplo) is adopted as the inflation targeting reference index. The IPCA is calculated by the Brazilian Institute for Geography and Statistics based on a price survey of consumption of families with monthly incomes ranging from 1 to 40 times the minimum wage in 11 large cities.
5. The Bank has a responsibility to issue the *Inflation Report* every quarter, in which the consequences of the monetary policy and inflation forecasts are reported.
6. The Bank makes public the basic economic concept and theory behind its inflation targeting policy, while the actual econometric model determining interest rates is not open to the public.
7. The target rate should be announced by June 30 of the year two years in advance.
8. The target rates for 1999, 2000, and 2001 were set at 8, 6, and 4 percent respectively with a 2 percent tolerance interval (upward and downward).

Because of the long history of high inflation and the low credibility of the monetary authority, the Brazilian government requires the Central Bank to follow rigorous rules in conducting inflation targeting policy, particularly by not allowing escape clauses and by adopting an inflation index that covers every item without exception. Some countries such as the UK, Canada, Australia, and New Zealand that have previously implemented inflation targeting policies commonly exclude certain specific components from the inflation indices. The reason why Brazil preferred not to create an index with exclusions to measure its inflation rates is to prevent the improper use of exclusion – an event that has frequently happened in the past – and to avoid its negative influence on the credibility of the new monetary regime. For the same reason, a new index (IPCA) was created and substituted for the old IPC index that had been widely used for a long time. The IPCA is allowed to have a 2 percent tolerance range because it is expected to show more unstable movements than that of the core inflation index.

Notwithstanding the fact that the new monetary regime was based on multiple factors and considerations, the monetary authority failed to generate adequate credibility for political reasons. For instance, although the president of the Central Bank is required to undertake certain obligatory procedures in the case of not achieving the target, he was not subject to severe punishment such as dismissal. In addition, special legislation that prohibits political intervention in Copom was not prepared. Because of this, the President of the Republic is able to restructure Copom by altering its membership and changing the interest rate setting formula.

3.3.2 Macroeconomic performance in Brazil under inflation targeting policy

Figures 3.1–3.6 indicate the monthly movements of six variables from June 1999 to September 2004; IPCA (Broad Consumer Price Index), SP (EMBI+), B (percent of public debts to GDP), R (basic interest rate SELIC), R$RATE (exchange rate), Y (capacity utilization ratio of manufacturing sectors).

One of the most salient features of this period is seen in the following fact. Along with a gradual increase in the level of public debt from 2000, Brazilian country risk and the exchange rate suddenly jumped from April 2002 due to

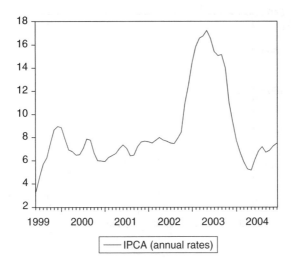

Figure 3.1   Inflation rate (broad CPI index)

concerns about the upcoming presidential election in October. At the same time, inflation rates also started to rise with a time lag of a few months. Faced with these events, the Brazilian government raised the SELIC rate to 26.5 percent in October. However, after a couple of months, due to significant changes to market perceptions about Lula, the Brazilian EMBI+ started to fall. Exchange and inflation rates also showed a sudden decrease.

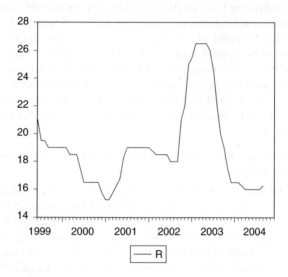

Figure 3.2   Basic interest rate (SELIC rate)

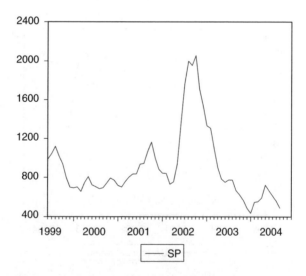

Figure 3.3   Emerging Markets Bond Index Plus (EMBI+)

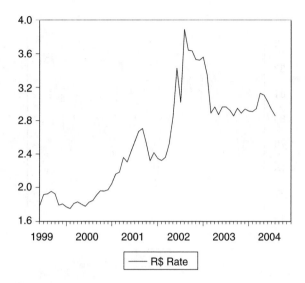

Figure 3.4 Exchange rates against US dollar

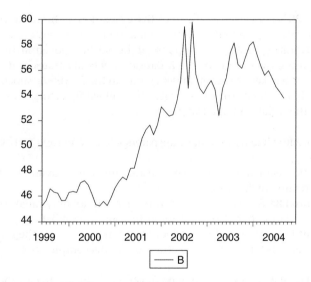

Figure 3.5 Percentage of public debts to GDP

While inflation rates were within the upper limit in 1999 and 2000, the government was unsuccessful in maintaining inflation within the limit from 2001 in the face of such preelection turbulence. It reached 7.67 percent in 2001 and 12.53 percent in 2002. Since 2003, however, inflation rates have been on a downward trend.

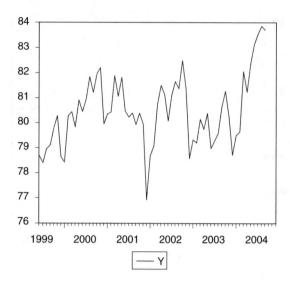

Figure 3.6   Capacity utilization rate

Mishkin (2004) has given a rather positive evaluation of this macroeconomic performance during this period. While inflation rates were greater than the targets in 2001 through 2003, "the response of the Brazilian government and central bank to the overshoots of the inflation targets illustrates that inflation targeting can help keep inflation under control in the face of big shocks like the real depreciation 2002" (p. 19). He listed the following factors to explain the success of the inflation targeting policy:

1. The procedure had tremendous transparency in determining and explaining the policy;
2. The Central Bank recognized that adjusting the target was absolutely necessary to retain credibility;
3. The Central Bank was able to demonstrate that it not only cared about controlling inflation but also cared about the output fluctuation;
4. President Lula successfully introduced legislation to reform the public pension system and fiscal policy to attain the budget surplus goal.

We need to pay some attention to point (2) above. In fact, to date the Central Bank has issued six resolutions regarding the inflation target. But, in the resolution of June 27, 2002, the Bank altered the target for 2003 to 4 percent from the level of 3.25 percent that was set on June 28, 2001. The tolerance interval was also changed from 2 to 2.5 percent. Moreover, in the resolution of June 25, 2003, the target for 2003 was increased to 5.5 percent from the level of 3.75 percent that was set in June 2002 and the tolerance interval was reduced again to

2 percent. Generally changes in the target are likely to foster market perceptions that the policy is discretionary and therefore lead to a deterioration in market credibility. In this sense, although the interpretation by Mishkin differs from the common understanding, it seems worthwhile making a further investigation.

At any rate, Brazil was confronted with a default risk triggered by political considerations. In such a circumstance, the Brazilian government was forced to respond immediately by increasing interest rates. But the increase in interest rates would eventually accelerate the default risk by raising the debt payment burden. How did the Brazilian government manage such a dilemma and retain credibility under the inflation targeting system?

3.4   A theoretical model

In this section, we introduce a model based on the works of BCB (2000), Ball (1999), and Svensson (1997) to include fiscal variables. The model particularly focuses on the effects of the risk premium and government debt on optimal monetary policy. The model was initially developed by Nishijima and Tonooka (2000).

$$y_t = \alpha_y y_{t-1} - \alpha_r r_{t-1} - \alpha_e e_{t-1} + v_{1t} \qquad 0 < \alpha_y < 1, \qquad \alpha_r, \alpha_e > 0 \qquad (3.1)$$

$$\pi_t = \pi_{t-1} + \beta_y y_{t-1} - \beta_e(e_{t-1} - e_{t-2}) + v_{2t} \qquad \beta_y, \beta_e > 0 \qquad (3.2)$$

$$e_t = \gamma_r r_t - \gamma_X X_t + v_{3t} \qquad \gamma_r, \gamma_X > 0 \qquad (3.3)$$

$$X_t = X_{t-1} + \delta_d d_t + v_{4t} \qquad \delta_d > 0 \qquad (3.4)$$

$$d_t = \varepsilon_r r_t + \varepsilon_D D_{t-1} - \varepsilon_y y_t + v_{5t} \qquad \varepsilon_r, \varepsilon_D, \varepsilon_y > 0 \qquad (3.5)$$

where y_t is the log of the output gap, π_t is the log of the inflation rate, r_t is the log of the real interest rate, e_t is the log of the real exchange rate (increase means appreciation), X_t is the log of the risk premium, d_t is the log of the budget deficit per GDP, D_t is the log of the government debt per GDP (where $D_t = D_{t-1} + d_t$), and v_i are the stochastic shocks.

Equation (3.1) measures aggregate demand, which is negatively dependent on real interest rates and real exchange rates. There is a one-period time lag to effect on real output. v_{1t} stands for demand-side stochastic shocks.

Equation (3.2) is the aggregate supply curve (Phillips curve) according to Ball (1999). The inflation rate is dependent on real output with a one-period lag and on real exchange rates through changes in import prices. The exchange rate has two-period lags because of a slow response in price setting (by a hypothesis of Ball). Inflation inertia is expressed by a one-period lag in the endogenous variable. v_{2t} represents supply shocks.

Equation (3.3) provides a relation between exchange rates and interest rates. An increase in domestic interest rates attracts foreign capital inflows, which leads to exchange rate appreciation. Increase in risk premium leads to exchange rate devaluation. v_{3t} stands for such shocks as foreign interest rate fluctuations, foreign capital market instability and other external shocks. Here we assume for simplicity that the exchange risk premium is the same as the country risk.

Equation (3.4) captures the effects of fiscal variables on risk premiums that are considered important in the context of Brazilian experience; in fact, when the currency crisis happened in 1999 and when the presidential election caused market turbulence in 2002, the Brazilian risk premium (country risk) suddenly increased. v_{4t} denotes shocks that affect the risk premium such as changes in international reserves and political instability, etc.

Equation (3.5) determines budget deficits, which depend on two components; the debt payments dependent on both interest rate and amount of the debts, and the government current balance dependent on real output. v_{5t} represents shocks regarding budget deficits.

The objective of the monetary authority is to determine the present and future optimal interest rates that minimize the expected deviations between the target rate and the future inflation rate. The objective function is expressed as

$$\min E_t 0.5 \sum_{i=0}^{\infty} \theta^i (\pi_{t+i} - \pi^*)^2 \tag{3.6}$$

where E_t is the conditional expectation based on the available information at time t, θ $(0 < \theta < 1)$ is the discount rate, and π^* is the target rate.

Using Equations (3.3), (3.4), and (3.5), we obtain Equation (3.7):

$$e_t = (\gamma_r - \gamma_X \delta_d \varepsilon_r) r_t - \gamma_X X_{t-1} - \gamma_X \delta_d \varepsilon_D D_{t-1} + \gamma_X \delta_d \varepsilon_y y_t - v_{7t}. \tag{3.7}$$

By substituting Equation (3.7) into Equations (3.1) and (3.2), and expressing π at one period ahead, we obtain

$$y_t = (\alpha_y - \alpha_e \gamma_X \delta_d \varepsilon_y) y_{t-1} - [\alpha_r + \alpha_e (\gamma_r - \gamma_X \delta_d \varepsilon_r)] r_{t-1} + \alpha_e \gamma_X X_{t-2}$$
$$+ \alpha_e \gamma_X \delta_d \varepsilon_D D_{t-2} + v_{1t} + \alpha_e v_{7t-1} \tag{3.8}$$

$$\pi_{t+1} = \pi_t + (\beta_y - \beta_e \gamma_X \delta_d \varepsilon_y) y_t + \beta_e \gamma_X \delta_d \varepsilon_y y_{t-1} - \beta_e (\gamma_r - \gamma_X \delta_d \varepsilon_r) r_t$$
$$+ \beta_e (\gamma_r - \gamma_X \delta_d \varepsilon_r) r_{t-1} + \beta_e \gamma_X X_{t-1} - \beta_e \gamma_X X_{t-2} + \beta_e \gamma_X \delta_d \varepsilon_D D_{t-1}$$
$$- \beta_e \gamma_X \delta_d \varepsilon_D D_{t-2} + v_{2t+1} + \beta_e v_{7t} - \beta_e v_{7t-1} \tag{3.9}$$

Equation (3.9) is rewritten using Equation (3.8) to obtain Equation (3.10):

$$\pi_{t+1} = \pi_t + [(\beta_y - \beta_e \gamma_X \delta_d \varepsilon_y)(\alpha_y - \alpha_e \gamma_X \delta_d \varepsilon_y) + \beta_e \gamma_X \delta_d \varepsilon_y] y_{t-1}$$
$$- \beta_e (\gamma_r - \gamma_X \delta_d \varepsilon_r) r_t - \{(\beta_y - \beta_e \gamma_X \delta_d \varepsilon_y)[\alpha_r + \alpha_e (\gamma_r - \gamma_X \delta_d \varepsilon_r)]$$
$$- \beta_e (\gamma_r - \gamma_X \delta_d \varepsilon_r)\} r_{t-1} + \beta_e \gamma_X (X_{t-1} - X_{t-2})$$
$$+ (\beta_y - \beta_e \gamma_X \delta_d \varepsilon_y) \alpha_e \gamma_X X_{t-2} + \beta_e \gamma_X \delta_d \varepsilon_D (D_{t-1} - D_{t-2})$$
$$+ (\beta_y - \beta_e \gamma_X \delta_d \varepsilon_y) \alpha_e \gamma_X \delta_d \varepsilon_D D_{t-2} + v_{2t+1} + (\beta_y - \beta_e \gamma_X \delta_d \varepsilon_y) v_{1t}$$
$$+ [(\beta_y - \beta_e \gamma_X \delta_d \varepsilon_y) \alpha_e - \beta_e] v_{7t-1} \tag{3.10}$$

Since the interest rate at time t affects the inflation rate at time $t + 1$, and the interest rate at time $t + 1$ affects the inflation rate at time $t + 2,...,$ we can find the intertemporal minimization problem for the monetary authority as the solution to the simple period-by-period minimization problem (Svensson 1997: 1139–40). The period-by-period loss function is expressed as

$$\min E_t 0.5\theta(\pi_{t+1} - \pi^*)^2 \tag{3.11}$$

Using Equation (3.10), we get the first-order condition with respect to r_t:

$$\partial E_t[0.5\theta(\pi_{t+1} - \pi^*)^2]/\partial r_t = E_t[\theta(\pi_{t+1} - \pi^*)\partial \pi_{t+1}/\partial r_t]$$
$$= -\theta\beta_e(\gamma_r - \gamma_X\delta_d\varepsilon_r)E_t(\pi_{t+1} - \pi^*) = 0$$

Therefore, under the optimal setting of the interest rate, it follows that

$$E_t\pi_{t+1} = \pi^*$$

In other words, the optimal interest rate is determined by setting the expected rate of inflation conditional upon information available at time t equal to the target rate. By obtaining the expected rate of inflation from Equation (3.10) and using the relation $E_t\pi_{t+1} = \pi^*$, we get the response function of the Central Bank:

$$
\begin{aligned}
r_t = 1/\beta_e(\gamma_r - \gamma_X\delta_d\varepsilon_r)\{(\pi_t - \pi^*) + [(\beta_y - \beta_e\gamma_X\delta_d\varepsilon_y)(\alpha_y - \alpha_e\gamma_X\delta_d\varepsilon_y) \\
+ \beta_e\gamma_X\delta_d\varepsilon_y]y_{t-1} - \{(\beta_y - \beta_e\gamma_X\delta_d\varepsilon_y)[\alpha_r + \alpha_e(\gamma_r - \gamma_X\delta_d\varepsilon_r)] \\
- \beta_e(\gamma_r - \gamma_X\delta_d\varepsilon_r)\}r_{t-1} + \beta_e\gamma_X(X_{t-1} - X_{t-2}) \\
+ (\beta_y - \beta_e\gamma_X\delta_d\varepsilon_y)\alpha_e\gamma_X X_{t-2} + \beta_e\gamma_X\delta_d\varepsilon_D(D_{t-1} - D_{t-2}) \\
+ (\beta_y - \beta_e\gamma_X\delta_d\varepsilon_y)\alpha_e\gamma_X\delta_d\varepsilon_D D_{t-2}\}
\end{aligned}
\tag{3.12}
$$

This reaction function is of the same modified form as the Taylor rule. The interest rate is positively dependent on the excess of inflation at time t over the target and on the real output with a one-period lag (here we assume the coefficients are positive). As Svensson (1997: 1119) argues, however, the interest rate depends on current inflation, not because current inflation is targeted but because current inflation together with output affect the inflation expectation in the future (current inflation is predetermined).

Equation (3.12) shows in an explicit way the effects of risk premium and government debts on the optimal instrument, which are not analyzed in Svensson (1997) and Ball (1999). Both risk premium and debts affect the optimal interest rate in the form of the rate of change ($X_{t-1} - X_{t-2}$, $D_{t-1} - D_{t-2}$) and the level (X_{t-2}, D_{t-2}). This implies that the inflation targeting policy should be conducted carefully by taking account of the technical difficulties that are caused by risk premium and government debts. At the same time, it implies that rigorous fiscal reform as a precondition is required to make the targeting policy successful.

In the next section we estimate the response function of the monetary authority with respect to interest rates based on the model in this section.

However, in the real world, it is very probable that actual policy implementation diverges from theory and is affected by various incidents. Thus, it would be necessary to modify the estimation equation taking account of the following realities:

1. According to the econometric researches of the Banco Central do Brasil (Minella et al. 2002, 2003), their results demonstrate that an interest rate is determined by referring to the expected deviation of 12 months ahead between the inflation forecast and the target, not to the deviation at time *t* as mentioned in the model.
2. In the model discussed above, an increase in government debt would lead to a deterioration in the risk premium through an increase in the budget deficit, and then lead to a depreciation in the exchange rate. This in turn brings about an increase in interest rates eventually via an increase in real output and actual inflation. However, there is a vicious circle in which an increase in the interest rate would raise the level of debt payment and the budget deficit, and thereby raise the default risk. In such a circumstance, it would be proper to think that the monetary authority would be reluctant or careful to increase interest rates taking this vicious circle into account. Therefore, we cannot deny the possibility that the sign of changes in government debt is negative.
3. On the other hand, should investor confidence in government debt collapse and a sudden outflow of foreign capital cause an overshoot in default risk, the government will be forced to increase interest rates in order to escape default.

   In the following section, we estimate the response function of the Brazilian Central Bank with respect to interest rates, taking these points into consideration.

3.5   Estimation of response function of the SELIC rate

3.5.1   Prior research

Two working papers of the Brazilian Central Bank (Minella et al. 2002, 2003) estimated the interest rate function under the inflation targeting regime.[2] In Minella et al. (2003) the basic formula for the SELIC target function is specified as

$$i_t = \alpha_1 i_{t-1} + (1 - \alpha_1)(\alpha_0 + \alpha_2(E_t \pi_{t+j} - \pi^*_{t+j}) + \alpha_3 y_{t-1} + \alpha_4 \Delta e_{t-1})$$

where i_t is the SELIC rate decided by Copom, $E_t \pi_{t+j}$ is inflation expectation at time j, π^*_{t+j} is the inflation target at time j, y_{t-1} is the output gap, and Δe_{t-1} is the nominal exchange rate variation (12-month change).

The estimation used two types of expected inflation to measure the deviations from the target rate. The first is the inflation forecast by the Bank presented in the *Inflation Report* and the other is the inflation forecast (called the market forecast) based on a daily survey conducted by the Bank. As the main results of the estimation, they found that, for both variants of the inflation forecasts, the deviations of the expected inflation from the target[3] are statistically significant in various model specifications. Therefore they concluded that the Bank has been reacting strongly to expected inflation on a forward-looking basis. In addition, they found that the output gap has the wrong sign but is nevertheless statistically significant in one of the specifications, while the exchange rate is not significant in the case of the market forecast. However, it must be noted here that the paper did not show the results of unit root tests of the data used in the estimations.

3.5.2 Confirmation of the Central Bank formula estimated in a different period

Here we estimate the same response function discussed above using a different period from January 2001 to December 2003 when the targeting policy did not contain inflation within the target range.[4] (See Table 3.1.) We specify two models using the deviations of expected inflation from the target and the deviations of actual inflation from the target:

$$i_t = \alpha_0 + \alpha_1 i_{t-1} + \alpha_2 (E_t \pi_{t+j} - \pi_{t+j}^*) + \alpha_3 y_{t-1} + \alpha_4 ex_{t-1} + u_t$$

$$i_t = \alpha_0 + \alpha_1 i_{t-1} + \alpha_2 (\pi_t - \pi_t^*) + \alpha_3 y_{t-1} + \alpha_4 ex_{t-1} + u_t$$

where i_t is the SELIC rate, $E_t \pi_{t+j}$ is the expected rate of inflation either 6 or 12 months ahead, π_{t+j}^* is the target rate either 6 or 12 months ahead, $\pi_t - \pi^*$ is a deviation of the inflation rate from the target at time t, y_t is output gap at t, and ex_{t-1} is the rate of changes of nominal exchange rate.[5] Unit root test of the variables used here is reported in note 5.[6]

Table 3.1 Actual and target inflation rates

	IPCA	Target	Lower limit	Upper limit	
1999	8.94	8	6	10	
2000	5.97	6	2	6	
2001	7.67	4	2	6	*
2002	12.53	3.5	1.0	6	*
2003	9.30	4	1.5	6.5	*
2004	6.68	5.5	3.5	7.5	

*Means the years in which the inflation rate surpassed the target.
Source: Central Bank of Brazil.

Table 3.2 reports the results of estimation. In the case that the equations specified above are estimated with respect to the period from January 2001 to December 2003 when the inflation targets were not attained, the coefficients of deviations of the inflation expectation from the target have a correct sign and are statistically significant in both $E\pi_{12} - \pi^*_{12}$ and $E\pi_6 - \pi^*_6$ cases. Moreover, the deviation at time t between the actual inflation and the target inflation is significant as well. On the other hand, output gap and exchange rate change are not statistically significant. Therefore, basically we can confirm the results of Minella et al. (2003), but it must be emphasized that both the deviations of inflation expectations 12 and 6 months ahead are statistically significant, and rate of change in nominal exchange rates is not statistically significant in determining the interest rate.

3.5.3   Estimation of response function considering risk premium and government debt

In the theoretical model the interest rate is taken to be the real interest rate. But, because unit root tests show the real interest rate to be nonstationary, we use the nominal interest rate as the dependent variable to estimate the response function of the Central Bank. The results are reported in Table 3.3.

While the model for the estimation is specified taking account of the theoretical model, we use the deviation of the expected rate of inflation from the target rate. At the same time, we use the deviation of the actual inflation rate from the target rate.

$$i_t = \alpha_0 + \alpha_1 i_{t-1} + \alpha_2(E\pi_{t+j} - \pi^*_{t+j}) + \alpha_3 y_{t-1} + \alpha_4 sptr_{t-2}$$
$$+ \alpha_5 gsp_{t-1} + \alpha_6 btr_{t-2} + \alpha_7 gb_{t-1} + u_t$$

$$i_t = \alpha_0 + \alpha_1 i_{t-1} + \alpha_2(\pi_t - \pi^*_t) + \alpha_3 y_{t-1} + \alpha_4 sptr_{t-2}$$
$$+ \alpha_5 gsp_{t-1} + \alpha_6 btr_{t-2} + \alpha_7 gb_{t-1} + u_t$$

where $sptr$ is the deviation of country risk (EMBI+) from its trend, gsp is the rate of change of country risk, btr is the deviation of government debt from its trend, and gb is the rate of change of government debt. The $sptr$ and gsp are derived as the residuals of the regressions of country risk and government debt respectively using the ARCH method applied to a cubic function.

As an alternative estimation instead of using the real interest rate, we estimate the equation by adding actual inflation rates as an explanatory variable. The results are shown in Table 3.4.[7]

$$i_t = \alpha_0 + \alpha_1 \pi + \alpha_2 i_{t-1} + \alpha_3(E\pi_{t+j} - \pi^*_{t+j}) + \alpha_4 y_{t-1}$$
$$+ \alpha_5 sptr_{t-2} + \alpha_6 gsp_{t-1} + \alpha_7 btr_{t-2} + \alpha_8 gb_{t-1} + u_t$$

Tables 3.3 and 3.4 report the results using OLS estimation. Table 3.5 shows the results obtained using the instrumental variable method to confirm the

Table 3.2 Estimation of basic formula by the Brazilian Central Bank

Dependent variable: i(SELIC)
Method: Least squares
Sample: 2001M01 2003M12

Included observations: 36
White heteroskedasticity-consistent standard errors and covariance

	(1) Coefficient t-value	(2) Coefficient t-value	(3) Coefficient t-value
c	−4.774	−6.893	2.178
	−0.487	−0.770	0.208
$i(-1)$	0.891	0.697	1.133
	25.835***	15.500***	14.799***
$i(-3)$			−0.561
			−6.730***
$E\pi_{12} - \pi_{12}^*$	0.583		
	6.979***		
$E\pi_6 - \pi_6^*$		0.346	
		7.920***	
$E\pi - \pi^*$			0.291
			2.968***
$y(-1)$	0.081	0.145	0.057
	0.682	1.367	0.499
$ex(-1)$	0.016	0.019	0.028
	0.809	1.028	1.036
R^2	0.976	0.978	0.976
Ad.R^2	0.972	0.976	0.972
LM test	Probability	Probability	Probability
lag1	0.416	0.443	0.703
lag2	0.628	0.748	0.899
lag3	0.289	0.395	0.418
lag4	0.450	0.555	0.476

Notes: Breusch-Godfrey Serial Correlation LM test. The lower berth is t-value. *** means significance at 1%.

robustness of the estimation. In addition, Table 3.3 reports the results using a different combination of explanatory variables to confirm the stability of the estimation.

The coefficients of $E\pi_{12} - \pi_{12}^*$ and $E\pi_6 - \pi_6^*$ have the correct sign and the statistical significance at 1 percent level, but that of $\pi - \pi^*$ is not statistically significant. Therefore we can confirm the results of Minella et al. (2003) that the Central Bank has been determining the interest rate taking account of the

Table 3.3   Estimation of response function of the Brazilian Central Bank

Dependent variable: i (SELIC)
Sample: 2001M01 2003M12
Included observations: 36

Method: Least squares
White heteroskedasticity-consistent standard errors and covariance

(1)

	(a) Coefficient / t-value	(b) Coefficient / t-value
c	-9.142 / -1.050	-10.661 / -1.274
$i(-1)$	0.859 / 21.166***	0.856 / 24.166***
$E\pi_{12} - \pi_{12}^*$	0.355 / 3.267***	0.398 / 3.793***
$y(-1)$	0.142 / 1.345	0.161 / 1.597
$gsp(-1)$	0.007 / 1.149	
$sptr(-2)$	0.002 / 3.261***	0.002 / 2.910***
$gb(-1)$	-0.021 / -0.609	-0.021
$btr(-2)$	-0.281 / -3.603***	-0.251 / -3.723***
R^2	0.983	0.983
Adj. R^2	0.979	0.980

LM test	(a) Probability	(b) Probability
lag1	0.211	0.204
lag2	0.464	0.453
lag3	0.306	0.552
lag4	0.241	0.617

(2)

	(c) Coefficient / t-value	(d) Coefficient / t-value
c	-8.554 / -1.144	-10.670 / -1.491
$i(-1)$	0.748 / 16.203***	0.735 / 17.433***
$E\pi_6 - \pi_6^*$	0.206 / 5.365***	0.217 / 5.464***
$y(-1)$	0.155 / 1.726*	0.185 / 2.177**
$gsp(-1)$	0.010 / 1.802*	
$sptr(-2)$	0.002 / 4.734***	0.002 / 4.328***
$gb(-1)$	-0.015 / -0.427	
$btr(-2)$	-0.240 / -3.029***	-0.226 / -3.651***
R^2	0.9859	
Adj. R^2	0.9836	

LM test	(c) Probability	(d) Probability
lag1	0.522	0.548
lag2	0.816	0.837
lag3	0.746	0.948
lag4	0.697	0.962

(3)

	(e) Coefficient / t-value	(f) Coefficient / t-value
c	-5.942 / -0.558	-10.320 / -1.044
$i(-1)$	1.073 / 8.530***	1.128 / 9.804***
$i(-2)$	-0.299 / -1.618	-0.324 / -1.947*
$E\pi - \pi^*$	0.090 / 1.080	0.061 / 0.777
$y(-1)$	0.117 / 0.983	0.167 / 1.512
$gsp(-1)$	0.012 / 1.733*	
$sptr(-2)$	0.003 / 5.934***	0.003 / 6.243***
$gb(-1)$	-0.021 / -0.540	
$btr(-2)$	-0.332 / -3.473***	-0.308 / -4.072***
R^2	0.981	0.980
Adj. R^2	0.976	0.976

LM test	(e) Probability	(f) Probability
lag1	0.778	0.885
lag2	0.625	0.500
lag3	0.539	0.709
lag4	0.215	0.708

Notes: *** means significant at 1% level, ** at 5% and * 10% level.

Table 3.4   Estimation added π as an explanatory variable

Dependent variable: i(SELIC) Method: Least squares
Sample: 2001M01 2003M12 White heteroskedasticity-consistent standard
Included observations: 36 errors and covariance

	(1) Coefficient t-value		*(2)* Coefficient t-value		*(3)* Coefficient t-value
c	−10.5404 −1.1003	c	−8.4203 −1.0385	c	−6.1671 −0.5671
π	−0.0237 −0.4105	π	0.0022 0.0455	π	−0.3430 −1.1886
$i(-1)$	0.8835 12.7572***	$i(-1)$	0.7458 11.5698***	$i(-1)$	1.0526 8.6184***
				$i(-2)$	−0.2953 −1.6189
$E\pi_{12} - \pi^*_{12}$	0.3519 3.2082***	$E\pi_6 - \pi^*_6$	0.2066 5.4648***	$E\pi - \pi^*$	0.3954 1.3633
$y(-1)$	0.1559 1.3684	$y(-1)$	0.1540 1.5998	$y(-1)$	0.1446 1.1478
$gsp(-1)$	0.0055 0.8012	$gsp(-1)$	0.0098 1.6120	$gsp(-1)$	0.0071 0.7929
$sptr(-2)$	0.0020 2.9366***	$sptr(-2)$	0.0022 4.4554***	$sptr(-2)$	0.0032 6.2359***
$gb(-1)$	−0.0210 −0.5847	$gb(-1)$	−0.0146 −0.4203	$gb(-1)$	−0.0405 −1.0040
$btr(-2)$	−0.2816 −3.3284***	$btr(-2)$	−0.2394 −2.9832***	$btr(-2)$	−0.4236 −3.5955***
R^2	0.9832	R^2	0.9869	R^2	0.982357
Adj.R^2	0.9783	Adj.R^2	0.9830	Adj.R^2	0.97625
LM test	Probability		Probability		Probability
lag1	0.2090		0.4291		0.9119
lag2	0.4398		0.7240		0.9348
lag3	0.3565		0.7245		0.6646
lag4	0.2788		0.7107		0.2958

future expected rate of inflation, not the current rate of inflation. However, $E\pi_{12} - \pi^*_{12}$ and $E\pi_6 - \pi^*_6$ have no essential statistical differences in determining the interest rate.

The output gap measured by capacity utilization is expected to have a negative sign, but the coefficient actually has the wrong sign albeit statistically insignificant. The real output was probably affected by a series of external shocks or needed more time to have an effect on interest rates. Overall, it is difficult to judge whether or not the monetary authority has disregarded the output gap in setting the interest rate.

Regarding country risk, its growth rate (*gsp*) is statistically significant at the 10 percent level in two of the three cases with a correct sign. Moreover its deviation from the trend (*sptr*) is strongly significant at the 1 percent level in three cases. These results imply that the Central Bank has decisively increased interest rates in order to avoid a default crisis when the EMBI+ overshot in 2002 in particular. When we consider the results in Table 3.2 that the exchange rate has no significant effect on interest rates, it would be safe to say that the monetary authority tried to apply its policy instrument (SELIC) directly to the country risk overshoot, not merely reacting to exchange rate changes that the theoretical model mentions.

The growth rate of government debt (*gb*) is not statistically significant and with a negative sign. Its deviation from the trend (*btr*), however, is strongly significant at the 1 percent level with a negative sign in either case. This means that the Central Bank has reduced interest rates when the debt deviated from its trend, fearing a default crisis due to the increase in government debt. At least, a decrease in interest rates is likely to lessen the debt payment burden of the government bonds that are indexed to interest rates.

Although both country risk and government debt directly affect interest rates, there is a large difference regarding the size of the coefficients; those of *btr* (negative sign) are greater than *sptr* (positive sign). This difference might be one of the reasons for having inflation rates greater than the target rates during 2001–3. In other words, the effect of *btr* to reduce the interest rate is larger than that of *sptr* to increase it, which might be one of the causes underlying inflation rates exceeding target rates. On the other hand, the result that *gb* is not significant may imply that the monetary authority was more sensitive to the deviation of debt from its trend than to its absolute growth rate, because the latter tends to fluctuate frequently and unstably due to, for instance, short-term market operations.

Table 3.4 reports the results of the estimation in which the actual inflation rate π is included as an independent variable, instead of estimating the real interest rate directly as a dependent variable. We found that there is no significant difference compared with the estimation using nominal interest rates. But, since the actual inflation rate is not statistically significant, it is not possible to judge whether the Central Bank referred to the real interest rate in setting the monetary instrument as the model indicates.

Table 3.5 shows the results of the instrumental variable method to confirm the robustness. Here the instrumental variables are defined by adding more one and two backward time lags to the explanatory variables. Compared with the results from the OLS method, there is no meaningful difference with respect to sign and significance.

Table 3.5 Estimation by instrumental variable method.

Dependent variable: i(SELIC)
Sample: 2001M01 2003M12

White heteroskedasticity-consistent standard errors and covariance
Method: Two-stage least squares

(b')
Instrumental variables:
i(−2), i(−3), Dπ12(−1), Dπ12(−2), y(−2), y(−3), sptr(−3), sptr(−4), btr(−3), btr(−4)

	Coefficient	t-Statistic	Probability
c	1.812	0.166	0.869
i(−1)	0.827	17.073	0.000***
$E\pi_{12} - \pi_{12}^{*}$	0.288	1.711	0.097*
y(−1)	0.012	0.095	0.925
sptr(−2)	0.003	2.847	0.008***
btr(−2)	−0.304	−2.246	0.032**
R^2	0.980		
Adj.R^2	0.976		

(d')
Instrumental variables:
i(−2), i(−3), Dπ6(−1), Dπ6(−2), y(−2), y(−3), sptr(−3), sptr(−4), btr(−3), btr(−4)

	Coefficient	t-Statistic	Probability
c	−2.460	−0.231	0.819
i(−1)	0.722	15.497	0.000***
$E\pi_6 - \pi_6^{*}$	0.190	3.939	0.001***
y(−1)	0.086	0.666	0.510
sptr(−2)	0.003	5.795	0.000***
btr(−2)	−0.297	−3.139	0.004***
R^2	0.984		
Adj.R^2	0.981		

(f')
Instrumental variables:
i(−2), i(−3), Dπ(−1), Dπ(−2), y(−2), y(−3), sptr(−3), sptr(−4), btr(−3), btr(−4)

	Coefficient	t-Statistic	Probability
c	−33.678	−1.395	0.173
i(−1)	1.033	6.063	0.000***
$E\pi - \pi^{*}$	−0.109	−0.971	0.340
y(−1)	0.412	1.510	0.142
sptr(−2)	0.004	7.208	0.000***
btr(−2)	−0.293	−1.778	0.086*
R^2	0.973		
Adj.R^2	0.968		

Note: Here we estimate Equation (b), (d), (f) in Table 3.2 in order to confirm the robustness. The instrumental variables are defined by adding more 1 and 2 backward time lags to the explanatory variables. Comparing with the results by the OLS method, there is no considerable difference with respect to signs and significance. Therefore we judge that the estimation in Table 3.2 has no serious correlation between independent variables and the residuals.

3.6   Conclusion

The objective of this chapter is to understand Brazilian inflation targeting policy under the flexible exchange rate system. Brazil was in a situation of so-called "fiscal dominance" in which government debt rose to critical levels and country risk became very sensitive to market expectations. For instance, the Brazilian country risk (EMBI+) suddenly jumped due to market perceptions about the presidential election, which led to large capital outflows and exchange rate depreciation in 2002. In such a situation, it is very likely that an inflation targeting policy will face serious difficulties in setting an appropriate interest rate.

We presented a theoretical model for inflation targeting in which country risk and government debt are taken into account. Based on this model, we estimated the response function of the Brazilian Central Bank with respect to interest rate setting. We selected the sample period from 2001 to 2003, during which time actual inflation rates exceeded the range of inflation targeting. The basic findings are as follows: (1) The Bank sets the interest rate referring to the deviation of the expected inflation and the target rate. (2) The exchange rate (its rate of change) is not statistically significant in determining interest rates. (3) Not only through the channel of the exchange rate, the Bank set the interest rate directly responding to the increase in country risk and government debts. When the country risk worsens, the interest rate tends to be increased; on the other hand, when government debt increases, it tends to be reduced. Therefore, it would be appropriate to think, at least in the face of serious default risk and unsustainable government debts particularly in 2001–3, that the Brazilian Central Bank flexibly set the interest rates at levels that deviated to some extent from those arising under the basic formula dictated by inflation targeting. Of course such an interpretation may be too simple to understand the actual and complicated interest rate setting process. Further investigations concerning the causal relationships between these factors and interest rates are necessary.

Notes

1   The term "fiscal dominance" was used in Sargent and Wallace (1985).
2   Garcia and Didier (2003) analyzed the relations between interest rate, exchange risk, and country risk in Brazil for the 1990s, but not in the context of inflation targeting policy.
3   Minella et al. (2003) constructed a series of data regarding the deviation of inflation from the target using a weighted average of current year and following year deviations expected.
4   All the data we use in the paper, except EMBI+, is available from the web pages of the Central Bank of Brazil (http://www.bcb.gov.br/?INDICATORS) and Instituto de Pesquisa Econômica Aplicada (http://www.ipeadata.gov.br/).
5   We adopt here a simple measure of deviation of inflation expectation from the target, that is, just a difference between $E_t \pi_{t+j}$ and π^*_{t+j}, not the measure used in Minella et al. (2003) in which current and future inflation rates are weighted. Moreover, we use the rate of changes of the nominal exchange rate instead of using the nominal

exchange rate variation (12-month change) used in Minella et al. (2003), because the data of 12-month change that we made is not stationary according to the unit root test.

6 Stationarity of the variable is examined by the Augmented Dickey-Fuller (ADF) test with a constant term during the period from September 1999 to September 2004.

		t-Statistic	Probability	
Interest rate (SELIC rate)	i	−3.199	0.025	
Nominal exchange rate change (12 months change)	Δex	−2.252	0.190	#
Rate of change in exchange rates	ex	−4.258	0.001	
Inflation rate (IPCA)	π	−4.027	0.002	
Target inflation rate	π^*	−3.518	0.011	
Expected rate of inflation 12 months ahead	$E\pi_{12}$	−3.653	0.007	
Expected rate of inflation 6 months ahead	$E\pi_6$	−3.751	0.006	
Expected deviation of $E\pi_{12}$ from the π^*	$E\pi_{12} - \pi_{12}^*$	−3.969	0.003	
Expected deviation of $E\pi_6$ from the π^*	$E\pi_6 - \pi_6^*$	−3.473	0.012	
Deviation of actual inflation rate from the target	$E\pi - \pi^*$	−2.897	0.052	
Capacity utilization ratio	y	−2.923	0.048	
Deviation of EMBI from trend	$sptr$	−3.481	0.012	
Deviation of government debt/GDP from trend	btr	−3.324	0.018	
Rate of change of EMBI	gsp	−4.405	0.001	
Rate of change of government debt/GDP	gb	−7.835	0.000	
Real interest rate	ri	−1.792	0.381	#

Note: # denotes the cases that the hypothesis (the data has unit root) is not rejected.

According to the ADF test, except for nominal exchange rate change (12-month change) and the real interest rate, all other variables are judged as stationary.

7 We did not find any essential differences in the estimation that uses the real interest rate.

References

Ball, Laurence, 1999, "Policy Rules for Open Economies," in John Taylor (ed.), *Monetary Policy Rules*, Cambridge: NBER.

BCB (Banco Central do Brasil) 2000, "Issues in the Adoption of an Inflation Targeting Framework in Brazil," in Mario Blejer et al. (eds), *Inflation Targeting in Practice: Strategic and Operational Issues and Application to Emerging Market Economies*, Washington: IMF.

Bernanke, Ben et al., 1999, *Inflation Targeting: Lessons from the International Experience*, Princeton: Princeton UP.

Blanchard, Oliver, 2004, "Fiscal Dominance and Inflation Targeting: Lesson from Brazil," NBER Working Papers No. 10389, March.

Blejer, Mario I., Alain Ize, Alfredo M. Leone and Sergio Werleng, 2000, *Inflation Targeting in Practice: Strategic and Operational Issues and Application to Emerging Market Economies*, Washington, IMF.

Favero, Carlos and Francesco Giavazzi, 2004, "Inflation Targeting and Debt: Lessons from Brazil," NBER Working Papers No. 10390, March.

Garcia, Márcio and Tatiana Didier, 2003, "Taxa de juros, risco cambial e risco Brasil," *Pesquisa e Planejamento Econômico*, 33 (2).

Haldane, Andrew, 2000, "Targeting Inflation: the UK in Retrospect," in Mario Blejer et al. (eds), *Inflation Targeting in Practice: Strategic and Operational Issues and Application to Emerging Market Economies*, Washington: IMF.

Minella, André, Paulo Singer de Freitas, Ilan Goldfajin and Marcelo Kfoury Munihos, 2002, "Inflation Targeting in Brazil: Lessons and Challenges," Banco Central do Brasil Working Paper Series 53, November.

Minella, André, Paulo Singer de Freitas, Ilan Goldfajin and Marcelo Kfoury Munihos, 2003, "Inflation Targeting in Brazil: Construction Credibility under Exchange Rate Volatility," Banco Central do Brasil Working Paper Series 77, July.

Mishkin, Frederic, 2004, "Can Inflation Targeting Work in Emerging Market Countries?" NBER Working Paper No. 10646, July.

Mishkin, Frederic and Miguel Savastano, 2001, "Monetary Policy Strategy for Latin America," *Journal of Development Economics*, 66.

Nishijima, Shoji and Eduardo Tonooka, 2000, "Inflation Targeting Policy in Brazil," *Kokumin Keizai Zasshi*, 182 (6) (in Japanese).

Sargent, Thomas-J. and Neil Wallace, 1985, "Some Unpleasant Monetarist Arithmetic," *Federal Reserve Bank of Minneapolis Quarterly Review*, 9 (1) Winter.

Svensson, Lars, 1997, "Inflation Forecast Targeting: Implementing and Monitoring Inflation Targets," *European Economic Review*, 41.

Svensson, Lars, 1999, "Inflation Targeting as a Monetary Policy Rule," *Journal of Monetary Economics*, 43.

Taylor, John (ed.), 1999, *Monetary Policy Rules*, Cambridge: NBER.

4
Fluctuations in the Yen/Dollar Exchange Rate, Business Cycles of East Asian Countries, and the Asian Financial Crisis[1]

Masanaga Kumakura

4.1   Introduction

In recent years, there has been growing interest in regional exchange rate management in East Asia. Whereas a full monetary union is generally regarded as impractical, numerous economists and policy-makers are now calling for an arrangement in which some or all East Asian countries explicitly coordinate their exchange rate policies. In some respects, this growing clamor for currency policy coordination is motivated by similar considerations to those that led European policy-makers to introduce the Exchange Rate Mechanism (ERM) in the late 1970s and ultimately to form the European Monetary Union (EMU) in 1999. These include concerns about potentially destructive competitive devaluations and disruptions of trade and investment flows due to excessive exchange rate instability.

In East Asia, however, a collective exchange rate arrangement is also called for to address a problem specific to this region: large and recurrent swings in the yen/dollar exchange rate. According to some observers, as most East Asian currencies are pegged to the dollar either officially or unofficially, fluctuations in the yen/dollar rate alter the relative export competitiveness between Japan and other East Asian countries, and generate boom-and-bust cycles in the latter's economies (Kwan 2001; McKinnon and Schnabl 2003). Some authors also blame the yen/dollar exchange rate for the 1997–98 Asian financial crisis, noting the fact that the yen fell sharply against the dollar, and many East Asian countries sank into a major export slump during the preceding years (Ito et al. 1998; Doraisami 2004). This view manifests itself in a number of proposals for regional exchange rate targeting currently under discussion.

For example, Williamson (2000) and Kawai and Takagi (2000) propose a common basket peg regime, whereby most or all East Asian countries other than Japan peg their currencies to a weighted basket of the dollar, the yen and the euro. This proposal is predicated on the view that the relatively large and closed economy of Japan is unsuited to a fixed exchange rate regime and that the other East Asian countries must accept yen/dollar fluctuations as given. However, Williamson and others argue that, by jointly pegging their currencies to the same basket of the dollar, the yen and the euro, the East Asian countries can at least alleviate the destabilizing impact of yen/dollar fluctuations on their economies while keeping the stability of the relative value of their own currencies.

Ito et al. (1998) and Kwan (2001) propose a variant of the common basket arrangement in which the yen is granted a substantially larger weight than is warranted by the East Asian countries' trade structure. Underlying this proposal is the perception that, as Japan is particularly important for other East Asian countries as an export competitor and a source of inward investment, these countries should pay special attention to the yen value of their currencies. This policy would give rise to a quasi-yen bloc in East Asia, which some authors consider to be a useful intermediate step toward an eventual regional monetary union (Ogawa 2002).

McKinnon and Schnabl (2003), however, contend that the basket arrangement makes little sense for East Asia. In their view, most East Asian countries still constitute a virtual dollar zone, in the sense that most of their international transactions are priced in dollars and their monetary authorities are keen to stabilize the dollar values of their currencies. McKinnon and Schnabl argue that a more natural arrangement is for *all* East Asian countries, including Japan, to peg their currencies formally to the dollar; with appropriate assistance from the US monetary authorities, they argue, this arrangement will be more effective in containing the destabilizing impact of yen/dollar fluctuations and promoting the region's economic integration.

This chapter challenges the view that fluctuations in the yen/dollar exchange rate constitute the primary threat to East Asia's macroeconomic stability. First, although this view rests on the assumption that most East Asian currencies are pegged to the dollar sufficiently tightly that fluctuations in the yen/dollar rate are translated directly into the relative cost competitiveness of Japan and the other Asian countries, this assumption is by no means incontrovertible. Second, while the foregoing view presumes that exchange rate-induced competitiveness shocks are the main driver of East Asia's export and output fluctuations, this is not the case in reality. As we will see, much of what is widely considered as the effect of yen/dollar fluctuations reflects export demand shocks arising from the global electronics cycle. Many of the existing proposals for regional exchange rate targeting are therefore founded on mistaken premises.

This chapter is organized as follows. In the next section, we first look at broad evidence on the East Asian countries' business cycles and show that cyclical fluctuations in the world electronics market exert a decisive impact on their economies. Section 4.3 examines the relative impact of yen/dollar fluctuations and the global electronics cycle on the export performance of the East Asian countries. As we will see, in most countries the effect of yen/dollar fluctuations has been modest, including the critical period leading to the Asian financial crisis. In Section 4.4, we look at the pre- and post-crisis behavior of the East Asian currencies. While there is substantial variation across the currencies, evidence suggests that many Asian currencies have not been pegged to the dollar as rigidly as widely presumed. Section 4.5 summarizes the findings of this chapter and their implications for the region's exchange rate arrangement in the future. In the Appendix, we provide an additional analysis of the business cycles of East Asian countries by focusing on more recent evidence.

4.2   Yen/dollar exchange rate and East Asia's business cycle

McKinnon and Schnabl (2003) note that the business cycles of eight East Asian countries (Hong Kong, Indonesia, Korea, Malaysia, the Philippines, Singapore, Taiwan, and Thailand) have been highly correlated during the past two decades, and argue that recurrent swings in the yen/dollar exchange rate were responsible for their synchronized business cycles. Table 4.1 shows the empirical correlations of the real GDP growth rates of the eight East Asian countries and other major countries. (In what follows, we refer to these eight countries as either "EA" or "EA economies" to save space; note that this group does not include the two largest regional economies, Japan and China.) The business cycles of most EA economies have indeed been highly correlated with those of the others. In contrast, the correlation of the EA business cycles with those of China, the United States and the EU is generally tenuous, although their correlation with Japan's business cycle is somewhat stronger.

To "prove" that the yen/dollar exchange rate is responsible for EA's business cycle, Kwan (2001) and McKinnon and Schnabl (2003) have estimated the following single-equation model:

$$\Delta y_{EA}(t) = \alpha_1 + \alpha_2 \Delta x(t) + \alpha_3 \Delta e_{Y/\$}(t) + \alpha_4 \Delta e_{Y/\$}(t-1) + u(t) \qquad (4.1)$$

where $\Delta y_{EA}(t)$ denotes the weighted average of the growth rate of the eight EA countries' real GDP in year t, where the weights are computed by the relative size of the eight economies' nominal US dollar GDP in year $t-1$; $\Delta x(t)$ is the rate of change in the external demand for EA's exports, proxied by the growth rate of the United States; $\Delta e_{Y/\$}(t)$ is the rate of change in the nominal yen/dollar exchange rate, defined as the price of one dollar in yen; and $u(t)$ is the disturbance term. The maintained hypothesis of Kwan (2001) and McKinnon and Schnabl (2003) is that the value of α_3 and/or α_4 are negative since a yen depreciation is expected to undermine EA's export competitiveness vis-à-vis Japan and dampen its output. Kwan (2001) estimated Equation (4.1) using annual data for 1982–97, while McKinnon and Schnabl (2003) used data for 1980–2001.

Before assessing what Kwan (2001) and McKinnon and Schnabl (2003) claim on the basis of this empirical exercise, we first reestimate Equation (4.1) using

Table 4.1 Business cycle correlation among the East Asian and other countries, 1980–2004

	EA	China	Japan	USA	EU
Hong Kong	0.684 (0.503)	0.221 (0.187)	0.353 (0.194)	0.133 (0.241)	−0.053 (0.003)
Indonesia	0.724 (0.306)	0.076 (−0.059)	0.457 (0.289)	−0.138 (−0.055)	−0.131 (−0.083)
Korea	0.602 (0.224)	0.171 (0.123)	0.373 (0.171)	0.137 (0.312)	0.216 (0.398)
Malaysia	0.793 (0.573)	0.082 (0.001)	0.347 (0.135)	−0.042 (0.062)	−0.093 (−0.031)
Philippines	0.241 (0.146)	−0.482 (−0.518)	0.052 (−0.023)	−0.236 (−0.218)	−0.032 (−0.013)
Singapore	0.699 (0.692)	0.055 (0.010)	0.328 (0.213)	0.083 (0.145)	−0.104 (−0.070)
Thailand	0.803 (0.547)	0.093 (0.007)	0.589 (0.501)	−0.092 (0.004)	0.062 (0.208)
Taiwan	0.464 (0.621)	0.325 (0.313)	0.387 (0.361)	0.394 (0.421)	0.091 (0.109)
China	0.125 (0.052)		−0.097 (−0.154)	0.367 (0.388)	−0.196 (−0.186)
Japan	0.503 (0.363)			0.009 (0.042)	0.387 (0.461)
USA	0.057 (0.249)				0.155 (0.144)
EU	0.063 (0.229)				

Notes: Coefficient of correlation between the annual real GDP growth rates of the row and column countries. Values in parentheses were computed by excluding 1998. EU growth rate is the weighted average for 13 EU member countries. The correlation coefficient for each EA country and EA is computed as correlation between the growth rate of the former and the weighted average for the other seven countries. Values larger than 0.5 are highlighted.
Sources: Author's calculation based on data from IMF IFS and CEIC database.

updated data for 1980–2004 with only minimum modification. First, although both Kwan (2001) and McKinnon and Schnabl (2003) proxy $\Delta x(t)$ by the growth rate of the United States, we also consider using a weighted average of the annual growth rates of the United States, Japan, 15 EU countries and China, recognizing the fact that these countries also constitute EA's important trade partners.[2] Second, we note that the growth rates of the EA economies during our sample period have been very high in general, with 1998 being the *only* year in which their average growth rate fell into negative territory. As the region's output collapse in 1998 was an unusual event in a number of senses, we add a year dummy for 1998 to Equation (4.1).[3]

Table 4.2 reports our estimation result. In all equations, the terms representing the export demand are not statistically significant, with the coefficients of their lagged value having the wrong sign. In contrast, most exchange rate variables are statistically significant and of the expected sign. Our estimation suggests that a 10 percent yen depreciation dampens EA's growth rate by some 1–2 percent, which seems large if one recalls, for example, the fact that the yen fell vis-à-vis the dollar by nearly 60 percent over three years between 1995 and 1998. Based on this result, Kwan claims that "fluctuations in the yen/dollar rate have replaced the US economic growth rate as the major factor determining short-term macroeconomic performance in Asian countries" (Kwan 2001: 39), while McKinnon and Schnabl conclude that "for the past two decades, fluctuations in the yen/dollar rate have generated synchronized business cycles in the smaller East Asian countries" (McKinnon and Schnabl 2003: 1068).

The preceding regression cannot be taken at face value, however, since it does not control for other factors that are potentially important for EA's macroeconomic performance. McKinnon and Schnabl (2003) argue that the business cycle synchronization of the EA economies cannot be explained by industry-specific shocks since the product mixes of these economies vary substantially. In their view, EA-wide output correlations arise from macroeconomic shocks that affect all countries across the board, such as fluctuations in the yen/dollar exchange rate. However, if what links yen/dollar fluctuations and the EA business cycle is the relative export competitiveness between Japan and EA, it should primarily be countries whose industrial structure is relatively mature and resembles that of Japan that are first affected by changes in the yen/dollar rate. For this to cause *EA-wide* output comovement, there must be a channel through which this effect is transmitted to other countries, such as trade between these countries. If this second effect is important, however, the argument that industry shocks cannot generate a region-wide output cycle does not hold.[4]

As is widely documented, the EA countries' production and export structures have changed dramatically during the past quarter of a century. Starting in the early 1980s, the newly industrializing economies of Hong Kong, Korea, Singapore, and Taiwan have emerged as the world's leading assemblers and

Table 4.2 Kwan/McKinnon/Schnabl regression, 1980–2004

Constant	Δx	$\Delta x(-1)$	$\Delta e_{Y/S}$	$\Delta e_{Y/S}(-1)$	$\Delta e_{Y/S}(-2)$	$D\,(1998)$	$R^2\,(adj.)$	D.W.
Δx = (real GDP growth rate of USA)								
0.055***	0.244					−0.117***	0.595	1.431
(0.007)	(0.202)					(0.019)		
0.059***	0.273	−0.166				−0.114***	0.585	1.325
(0.009)	(0.228)	(0.217)				(0.020)		
0.057***	0.113		−0.084**			−0.106***	0.666	1.349
(0.006)	(0.192)		(0.035)			(0.018)		
0.056***	0.096		−0.073**	−0.062*		−0.098***	0.699	1.466
(0.007)	(0.198)		(0.035)	(0.034)		(0.018)		
0.054***	0.111		−0.081**	−0.057	−0.038	−0.091***	0.702	1.706
(0.007)	(0.201)		(0.036)	(0.036)	(0.037)	(0.019)		
Δx = (average growth rate of USA, Japan, EU and China)								
0.047***	0.394					−0.114***	0.594	1.517
(0.013)	(0.332)					(0.019)		
0.054***	0.550	−0.348				−0.111***	0.587	1.317
(0.017)	(0.414)	(0.399)				(0.020)		
0.053***	0.192		−0.084**			−0.105***	0.667	1.376
(0.012)	(0.312)		(0.035)			(0.018)		
0.057***	0.037		−0.076**	−0.062*		−0.097***	0.695	1.528
(0.013)	(0.340)		(0.034)	(0.035)		(0.018)		
0.055***	0.070		−0.084**	−0.056	−0.037	−0.090***	0.697	1.749
(0.015)	(0.368)		(0.037)	(0.037)	(0.037)	(0.019)		

Notes: Standard errors in parentheses. *, ** and *** denote statistical significance at 10, 5, and 1% confidence levels.
Source: See Table 4.1.

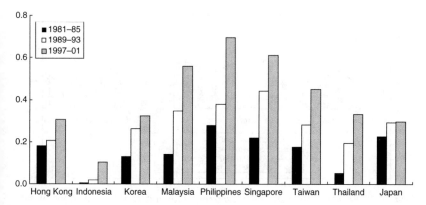

Figure 4.1 Share of electronic goods in merchandise exports
Notes: Electronics exports are computed as the sum of SITC 75, 76 and 77. The data for the Philippines is adjusted for exports of goods produced on a consignment basis and categorized in SITC 9310 (special transactions and commodities not classified elsewhere).
Source: Author's computation based on data from Statistics Canada World Trade Database and Trade Statistics of the Philippines.

exporters of electronics goods, and a few other countries (e.g. Malaysia) soon followed suit. More recently, several EA countries have sharply increased their production and exports of information and technology (IT) goods and their components, whose market is notoriously prone to cyclical boom-and-bust cycles. When the global electronics market encounters a major setback, it is likely that at least some EA economies are affected, which may conceivably be transmitted to some other countries in the region. As Figure 4.1 shows, the share of electronic goods in total exports is extremely high and still rising in most EA countries. In Figure 4.2, we find that EA's real GDP comoves closely with its exports, suggesting that the latter is a crucial determinant of the former. Figure 4.2 also indicates that the year-on-year growth rate of EA's export earnings is tightly correlated with the growth rate of world semiconductor shipments, a widely used indicator of the cyclical condition of the world electronics market (Ping et al. 2004). More interestingly, we observe that this indicator is in fact also fairly strongly correlated with the yen/dollar exchange rate.[5]

We also note that the Kwan/McKinnon/Schnabl hypothesis rests on the assumption that EA's currencies are pegged to the dollar sufficiently tightly that changes in the nominal yen/dollar exchange rate are translated immediately to those of the price competitiveness of Japanese and EA exporters. Given the widely held view that most EA currencies have been routinely pegged to the dollar, this view may not sound particularly contentious. As we will discuss in Section 4.4 however, not all EA currencies have been pegged to the dollar sufficiently closely as to make the yen/dollar exchange rate in Equation (4.1)

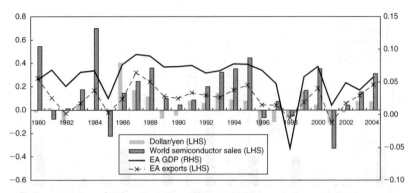

Figure 4.2   EA real GDP, yen/dollar exchange rate and world semiconductor sales (year-on-year rate of change)
Note: World semiconductor sales are valued in US dollars and exclude those shipped in/to Japan.
Source: IMF IFS, CEIC database, US Semiconductor Industry Association.

a good proxy for Japan–EA export competitiveness. Moreover, what matters for a country's external competitiveness is not the nominal but the real exchange rate of its currency. Unless EA's productivity-adjusted inflation rate remains close to that of Japan, there is a possibility that their relative export competitiveness departs from the nominal yen/dollar exchange rate, even if all EA currencies were fixed permanently to the dollar.

We next demonstrate the empirical importance of these two issues by estimating modified versions of the Kwan/McKinnon/Schnabl model. First, we replace the yen/dollar variables in Equation (4.1) with a proxy variable for the global electronics cycle and examine how doing so affects the model's explanatory power. Although the growth rate of world semiconductor sales is perhaps the most widely used indicator of the cyclical condition of the world electronics market, we need to be careful when using this value as a regressor in Equation (4.1), not least because the original sales values are denominated in dollars. To the extent that Japanese firms are major producers of semiconductor devices and related products, and that some of the products sold by Japanese producers are priced in yen, the dollar value of global semiconductor shipments may receive pure valuation effects from nominal yen/dollar fluctuations. To minimize this effect, we exclude all sales recorded in the Japanese market when computing the world aggregate, and let $\Delta elc(t)$ denote the growth rate of this value.[6] As this variable is more volatile than $\Delta e_{Y/\$}(t)$, we also consider specifications that include the square of its value to allow for a nonlinear relationship between $\Delta elc(t)$ and $\Delta y_{EA}(t)$.

The result of our estimation is shown in Table 4.3. As one can see, this modified model substantially outperforms the original Kwan/McKinnon/Schnabl

Table 4.3   Reformulated Kwan/McKinnon/Schnabl regression, 1980–2004

Constant	Δx	$\Delta x(-1)$	Δelc	$[\Delta elc]^2$	$\Delta elc\,(-1)$	$[\Delta elc\,(-1)]^2$	D (1998)	R^2 (adj.)	D.W.
$\Delta x =$ (real GDP growth rate of USA)									
0.053***	0.080		0.041**				−0.105***	0.681	1.286
(0.006)	(0.190)		(0.016)				(0.018)		
0.054***	0.118		0.080***	−0.112***			−0.106***	0.765	1.346
(0.005)	(0.163)		(0.019)	(0.038)			(0.015)		
0.054***	−0.078		0.103***	−0.129***	0.026		−0.099***	0.790	1.413
(0.006)	(0.204)		(0.025)	(0.043)	(0.019)		(0.016)		
0.060***	−0.085	−0.132	0.056***			−0.001	−0.099***	0.715	1.030
(0.008)	(0.220)	(0.180)	(0.018)			(0.046)	(0.017)		
0.056***	0.000	0.005	0.084***	−0.098**	0.026		−0.103***	0.764	1.181
(0.007)	(0.204)	(0.175)	(0.020)	(0.044)	(0.020)		(0.016)		
0.055***	−0.077	−0.041	0.102***	−0.126**		0.001	−0.098***	0.778	1.342
(0.007)	(0.210)	(0.174)	(0.026)	(0.046)		(0.048)	(0.017)		
$\Delta x =$ (average growth rate of USA, Japan, EU and China)									
0.050***	0.138		0.041**				−0.104***	0.681	1.336
(0.012)	(0.310)		(0.016)				(0.017)		
0.050***	0.202		0.080***	−0.112***			−0.105***	0.766	1.379
(0.010)	(0.266)		(0.019)	(0.038)			(0.015)		
0.059***	−0.206		0.105***	−0.129***	0.028		−0.099***	0.793	1.412
(0.011)	(0.340)		(0.025)	(0.043)	(0.019)		(0.015)		
0.061***	−0.227	0.042	0.058***			−0.001	−0.102***	0.708	1.251
(0.014)	(0.432)	(0.359)	(0.019)			(0.045)	(0.017)		
0.055***	−0.052	0.086	0.086***	−0.099**	0.028		−0.104***	0.765	1.253
(0.013)	(0.395)	(0.323)	(0.021)	(0.042)	(0.020)		(0.015)		
0.058***	−0.233	0.046	0.106***	−0.129***		−0.002	−0.099***	0.780	1.456
(0.013)	(0.398)	(0.314)	(0.026)	(0.044)		(0.046)	(0.016)		

Notes and Sources: See Tables 4.1 and 4.2.

model, with most electronics terms being highly significant and of the expected sign. The table also indicates that the electronics cycle has its effect felt on the EA economies very quickly, as none of the lagged electronics variables are significant. The quadratic term is also significant, suggesting that nonlinearity is indeed important. With the mean and the standard deviation of $\Delta elc(t)$ being 0.164 and 0.233 in our sample, a reduction in this variable by one standard deviation from its mean implies a contemporaneous fall in the EA's growth rate of around 1.2–1.5 percent.

As the electronics cycle is correlated with the yen/dollar exchange rate, however, the preceding result does not by itself invalidate the Kwan/McKinnon/Schnabl hypothesis. We thus next consider specifications that include both the yen/dollar and electronics cycle variables. As the general export demand $\Delta x(t)$ was not significant in any of the preceding regressions, we now drop this term from the set of regressors to save degrees of freedom. Although the empirical correlation between $\Delta e_{Y/\$}(t)$ and $\Delta elc(t)$ suggests that including both terms causes multicollinearity, the result still turns out to be informative. As shown in Table 4.4 (upper table), the electronics variables still remain highly significant, with the estimates of their coefficients largely invariant to the inclusion of the yen/dollar variables. Meanwhile, the latter are now either insignificant or only marginally so, and the estimated values of their coefficients are substantially lower than what we found in Table 4.1. This observation suggests that the original Kwan/McKinnon/Schnabl regression is, to a large degree, spurious.

As we noted previously, there is little a priori reason to believe that the nominal yen/dollar exchange rate provides a good proxy for the relative price competitiveness of Japanese and EA exporters. To test the validity of this assumption, we next create an index of the real effective exchange rate between the yen and the eight EA currencies and replace the yen/dollar terms in Equation (4.1) with this variable. This real exchange rate index is defined as follows:

$$\Delta s_{Y/EA}(t) \equiv \sum_{i=1}^{8} \phi_i(t)[\Delta e_{Y/i}(t) + \Delta p_i(t) - \Delta p_{JP}(t)] \qquad (4.2)$$

where $e_{Y/i}$ is the nominal exchange rate between the yen and country i's currency (price of one unit of currency i in yen), $p_i(t)$ is country i's price level, and $\phi_i(t)$ is the weight assigned to currency i in our effective exchange rate index. For p_i, we use the producer price index (PPI) for the manufacturing industry, assuming that PPI-based real exchange rates provide a better indicator of export competitiveness than those based on CPI.[7] Although the currency weight $\phi_i(t)$ is typically decided by the share of each foreign country in the home country's trade, the size of bilateral trade volume does not necessarily reflect the strength of export competition in third countries.[8] As

Table 4.4 Reformulated Kwan/McKinnon/Schnabl regression, 1980–2004

Constant	Δelc	$[\Delta elc]^2$	$\Delta elc\,(-1)$	$\Delta e_{Y/S}$	$\Delta e_{Y/S}(-1)$	$\Delta e_{Y/S}(-2)$	$D\,(1998)$	$R^2\,(adj.)$	$D.W.$
0.057***	0.071***	−0.094**		−0.032			−0.102***	0.770	1.379
(0.004)	(0.022)	(0.041)		(0.033)			(0.015)		
0.057***	0.073***	−0.101**		−0.016	−0.056*		−0.096***	0.811	1.344
(0.003)	(0.021)	(0.039)		(0.032)	(0.028)		(0.014)		
0.053***	0.084***	−0.101***		−0.017	−0.047*	−0.048*	−0.085***	0.856	1.384
(0.003)	(0.019)	(0.035)		(0.029)	(0.026)	(0.026)	(0.013)		
0.053***	0.042**		0.008	−0.051			−0.099***	0.734	1.162
(0.005)	(0.017)		(0.014)	(0.036)			(0.016)		
0.055***	0.035*		−0.002	−0.044	−0.047		−0.096***	0.741	1.237
(0.005)	(0.018)		(0.016)	(0.036)	(0.038)		(0.016)		
0.054***	0.043**		−0.020	−0.037	−0.058	−0.062	−0.082***	0.799	1.452
(0.005)	(0.016)		(0.017)	(0.033)	(0.036)	(0.031)	(0.016)		

Constant	Δelc	$[\Delta elc]^2$	$\Delta elc\,(-1)$	$\Delta S_{Y/EA}$	$\Delta S_{Y/EA}(-1)$	$\Delta S_{Y/EA}(-2)$	$D\,(1998)$	$R^2\,(adj.)$	$D.W.$
0.057***	0.081***	−0.106**		−0.011			−0.107***	0.761	1.437
(0.004)	(0.020)	(0.040)		(0.032)			(0.018)		
0.057***	0.081***	−0.104**		0.003	−0.029		−0.103***	0.777	1.254
(0.004)	(0.020)	(0.040)		(0.033)	(0.029)		(0.018)		
0.054***	0.085***	−0.105**		−0.001	−0.030	−0.031	−0.096***	0.806	1.168
(0.004)	(0.019)	(0.038)		(0.031)	(0.028)	(0.027)	(0.018)		
0.053***	0.051***		0.007	−0.022			−0.109***	0.710	1.189
(0.005)	(0.016)		(0.015)	(0.038)			(0.020)		
0.054***	0.048**		0.006	−0.020	−0.015		−0.109***	0.697	1.214
(0.005)	(0.018)		(0.016)	(0.039)	(0.034)		(0.021)		
0.053***	0.049***		−0.009	−0.013	−0.021	−0.039	−0.099***	0.719	1.092
(0.005)	(0.017)		(0.018)	(0.039)	(0.034)	(0.035)	(0.022)		

Notes and Sources: See Tables 4.1 and 4.2.

Equation (4.1) effectively regards the eight EA countries as a single economic area, here we compute $\phi_i(t)$ as follows:

$$\phi_i(t) \equiv \sum_{i=1}^{8} \frac{Y_i(t-1)}{\sum_{j=1}^{8} Y_i(t-1)}$$

where $Y_i(t-1)$ is country i's nominal US dollar GDP in $t-1$.[9] In practice, however, the way in which the currency weights are computed matters little for what we will see below.[10]

As it turns out, although our proxy for the electronics cycle is highly correlated with the nominal yen/dollar rate, the former is practically uncorrelated with our real exchange rate index.[11] Thus using the latter should allow us to better isolate the effect of exchange rate-induced competitiveness shocks from that of the electronics cycle. The result of our estimation is shown in Table 4.4 (lower table). As one can see, *none* of the exchange rate variables is statistically significant, and their estimated coefficients are numerically negligible. Thus we conclude that the bulk of what Kwan (2001) and McKinnon and Schnabl (2003) consider to be the effect of yen/dollar fluctuations is in fact that of cyclical fluctuations in the world market for electronic goods.

What we have seen in this section does not necessarily mean that the yen/dollar rate is inconsequential for *all* EA countries, nor does it imply that the electronics cycle exerts the same effect on all countries. As the estimated coefficients of the real exchange rate variables in Table 4.4 are at least of the expected sign, there is a possibility that changes in the nominal yen/dollar exchange rate have some moderate impact on one or a few countries whose product mix is particularly close to that of Japan. In Figure 4.1, we also saw that the share of electronics in aggregate exports varies substantially across the eight countries. For example, its share remains quite small in Indonesia, suggesting that the direct impact of the electronics cycle on its economy is limited. Table 4.5 shows pairwise business cycle correlations for the EA countries and Japan, as well as the correlations of each country's business cycle with the electronics cycle, computed with semiannual data for the past 13 years (see the Appendix). In the rightmost column, we notice that the relationship between the national business cycle and the electronics cycle indeed reveals significant cross-country variation. Not surprisingly, the correlation is strongest in countries that depend heavily on the electronics industry, such as Malaysia, Singapore, and Taiwan.[12] By inspecting the other columns, we also notice that the correlation of national business cycles also varies significantly from one pair of countries to another. In general, output seems synchronized relatively strongly among countries that depend heavily on electronics, and also between countries that are geographically close to each other and engage in substantial bilateral trade. In the Appendix, we examine more closely factors underlying the business cycles of individual countries.

Table 4.5 Correlation of EA business cycles and world electronics cycle (semiannual basis, 1992: S1–2004: S2)

	Indonesia	Korea	Malaysia	Philippines	Singapore	Thailand	Taiwan	Japan	Δelc
Hong Kong	0.632	0.630	0.782	0.580	0.663	0.552	0.631	0.524	0.579
	(0.099)	(0.392)	(0.622)	(0.325)	(0.585)	(0.688)	(0.196)	(0.395)	(0.584)
Indonesia		0.764	0.837	0.556	0.484	0.252	0.837	0.309	0.294
		(0.203)	(0.255)	(0.010)	(0.162)	(0.344)	(0.526)	(−0.013)	(0.196)
Korea			0.797	0.534	0.542	0.348	0.789	0.331	0.410
			(0.556)	(0.224)	(0.415)	(0.508)	(0.351)	(0.065)	(0.413)
Malaysia				0.660	0.741	0.545	0.776	0.475	0.542
				(0.357)	(0.745)	(0.830)	(0.420)	(0.454)	(0.673)
Philippines					0.456	0.295	0.401	0.521	0.382
					(0.258)	(0.281)	(−0.159)	(0.471)	(0.311)
Singapore						0.762	0.445	0.379	0.736
						(0.795)	(0.202)	(0.309)	(0.739)
Thailand							0.281	0.278	0.702
							(0.398)	(0.301)	(0.719)
Taiwan								0.234	0.420
								(−0.234)	(0.384)
Japan									0.363
									(0.302)

Notes: Values in parentheses are correlation coefficients computed excluding the period of the financial crisis (1997: S2–1999: S1). Values larger than 0.5 are highlighted.
Source: See Table 4.1.

4.3   Global electronics cycle, the yen/dollar exchange rate, and East Asia's export performance

As we noted in Section 4.1, the yen depreciated against the dollar continuously from mid-1995 through the onset of the Asian crisis, during which the growth rates of most EA countries' export earnings fell sharply. Moreover, although there is evidence that the EA countries' exchange rate policies have been more pragmatic than commonly believed, most regional currencies remained unusually stable vis-à-vis the dollar during this particular period (see Section 4.4). This simultaneous unfolding of the yen depreciation and the regional export stagnation, against the background of the conspicuous stability of many EA currencies, has led to the perception that the yen/dollar exchange rate was the proximate cause of the Asian crisis (Ito et al. 1998; McKinnon 2005). As we saw in Figure 4.2, however, EA's export earnings are highly correlated with the global electronics cycle. Moreover, available data shows that the growth rate of world semiconductor shipments decelerated sharply in the second half of 1995, suggesting that an entirely different explanation is possible for the behavior of EA's exports during this critical period.[13]

Table 4.6 shows the year-on-year growth rates of ten East Asian countries' merchandise exports during the past decade. The effect of the world electronics cycle is evident in most countries, including Japan. If the yen depreciation had been the main factor behind EA's 1996 export slowdown, Japan should have experienced a major export boom in this year. This was, however, clearly not the case; the cyclical behavior of exports during the past ten years looks quite similar between Japan and most other countries.

The foregoing observation, however, does not necessarily rule out the possibility that the yen depreciation played some role in EA's export slump. Even if its main cause was the deceleration in global electronics activity, it is not inconceivable that the weak yen had some additional impact on some countries. Table 4.6 also indicates that in 1996 EA's export performance deteriorated across the board, including in such countries as Indonesia where electronics account for only a small proportion of exports (Figure 4.1). To the extent that its export slump reflected negative repercussions from other countries, it is difficult to judge from Table 4.6 alone the relative impact of the world electronics recession and other factors. In this section, therefore, we make efforts to isolate their relative importance using a modified version of the standard dynamic shift share analysis (DSSA). While DSSA is typically used to assess the medium- to long-term evolution of a country's comparative advantage, it is also useful for our present purpose.

To this end, let us first define $X_{i,t}^k$ as country i's exports of good k in year t, measured in terms of US dollars. Using this expression, we define the following two variables:

$$X_{i,t} \equiv \sum_k X_{i,t}^k \qquad X_t^k \equiv \sum_i X_{i,t}^k$$

Table 4.6 Annual growth rates of merchandise exports (in US dollar terms, %)

	1993	1994	1995	1996	1997	1998	1999	2000	2001	2002
Year-on-year growth rate of goods exports										
Hong Kong	-4.7	-0.3	4.2	-8.3	-0.5	-11.0	-9.6	5.7	-15.3	-14.7
Indonesia	8.3	9.9	18.0	5.8	12.2	-10.5	1.7	27.6	-12.3	2.5
Korea	7.7	15.7	31.2	4.3	6.7	-4.7	9.9	21.2	-14.0	7.5
Malaysia	16.1	23.1	26.1	7.3	0.7	-7.3	17.0	17.0	-10.6	6.1
Philippines	15.8	18.5	29.4	17.7	22.8	16.9	16.0	9.0	-16.2	10.1
Singapore	14.4	24.3	19.8	5.9	-1.1	-12.7	8.5	14.8	-16.3	0.8
Taiwan	4.4	9.4	20.0	3.8	5.3	-9.4	10.0	22.0	-17.2	6.3
Thailand	13.4	22.2	24.7	-1.9	4.1	-6.9	7.6	19.6	-6.9	5.7
Japan	6.0	9.4	11.2	-6.6	2.2	-8.6	7.9	13.8	-16.5	3.1
China	8.8	35.6	24.9	17.9	20.9	0.5	6.1	27.9	6.8	22.4
Year-on-year growth rate – average annual growth rate for 1993–2002										
Hong Kong	0.8	5.2	9.7	-2.9	5.0	-5.6	-4.2	11.2	-9.9	-9.3
Indonesia	2.0	3.6	11.7	-0.5	5.9	-16.8	-4.6	21.3	-18.6	-3.8
Korea	-0.9	7.2	22.7	-4.3	-1.9	-13.3	1.4	12.7	-22.6	-1.1
Malaysia	6.6	13.6	16.6	-2.3	-8.9	-16.9	7.5	7.5	-20.2	-3.5
Philippines	1.8	4.5	15.4	3.7	8.8	2.9	2.0	-5.0	-30.2	-3.9
Singapore	8.6	18.5	14.0	0.1	-6.9	-18.5	2.7	9.0	-22.1	-5.0
Taiwan	-1.1	3.9	14.5	-1.7	-0.2	-14.9	4.5	16.5	-22.7	0.8
Thailand	5.2	14.0	16.5	-10.1	-4.1	-15.1	-0.6	11.4	-15.1	-2.5
Japan	3.8	7.2	9.0	-8.8	0.0	-10.8	5.7	11.6	-18.7	0.9
China	-8.4	18.4	7.7	0.7	3.7	-16.7	-11.1	10.7	-10.4	5.2
Nominal yen/dollar exchange rate										
End of period	-12.2	-8.1	-8.0	15.6	11.2	8.2	-13.0	-5.4	12.8	3.2
Period average	-10.3	-10.8	3.1	12.8	12.0	-11.0	-11.6	12.4	14.7	-9.0

Note: Shading indicates years in which the world shipment of semiconductors fell below the level of the preceding year. Exports of Hong Kong and Singapore exclude reexports. For the yen/dollar rate a positive value indicates the yen's depreciation.
Source: IMF IFS, CEIC database.

In the above, $X_{i,t}$ corresponds to the value of country i's aggregate exports, while X_t^k corresponds to the global exports (=imports) of good k. In addition, we write the annual growth rates of these three values as

$$r_{i,t}^k \equiv \Delta X_{i,t}^k / X_{i,t-1}^k \qquad r_{i,t} \equiv \Delta X_{i,t} / X_{i,t-1} \qquad r_t^k \equiv \Delta X_t^k / X_{t-1}^k$$

The change in country i's aggregate export earnings in each year ($\Delta X_{i,t}$) is the sum of changes in its exports of individual goods ($\Delta X_{i,t}^k$). We let A denote the set of electronic products and express $\Delta X_{i,t}$ as the sum of the following two components:

$$\begin{aligned} \Delta X_{i,t} &= \sum_{k \in A} \Delta X_{i,t}^k + \sum_{k \notin A} \Delta X_{i,t}^k \\ &= \sum_{k \in A} r_{i,t}^k X_{i,t-1}^k + \sum_{k \notin A} r_{i,t}^k X_{i,t-1}^k \end{aligned} \tag{4.3}$$

In Equation (4.3), the first term on the right-hand side corresponds to the change in the exports of electronics goods between $t-1$ and t, whereas the second term is the change in the exports of other products. We further rewrite Equation (4.3) as follows:

$$\begin{aligned} \Delta X_{i,t} &= \sum_{k \in A} \left[r_t^k + \left(r_{i,t}^k - r_t^k \right) \right] X_{i,t-1}^k + \sum_{k \notin A} \left[r_t^k + \left(r_{i,t}^k - r_t^k \right) \right] X_{i,t-1}^k \\ &= \sum_{k \in A} r_t^k X_{i,t-1}^k + \sum_{k \notin A} r_t^k X_{i,t-1}^k + \sum_{k} \left(r_{i,t}^k - r_t^k \right) X_{i,t-1}^k \end{aligned} \tag{4.4}$$

In Equation (4.4), $r_{i,t}^k - r_t^k$ corresponds to the difference between the growth rates of country i's exports of good k and of the world import demand for this product. Each component in the last summation takes on a positive value when country i increases its share in the world market for this particular good but is negative when it loses its market share. By dividing Equation (4.4) through by $X_{i,t-1}$, we obtain

$$r_{i,t} = d_{i,t}^A + d_{i,t}^{A-} + s_{i,t} \tag{4.5}$$

where

$$d_{i,t}^A \equiv \sum_{k \in A} r_t^k X_{i,t}^k / X_{i,t-1} \qquad d_{i,t}^{A-} \equiv \sum_{k \notin A} r_t^k X_{i,t}^k / X_{i,t-1}$$

$$s_{i,t} \equiv \sum_{k} \left(r_{i,t}^k - r_t^k \right) X_{i,t}^k / X_{i,t-1}$$

Equation (4.5) expresses the growth rate of country i's aggregate exports ($r_{i,t}$) as the sum of three components. The first term on the right-hand side ($d_{i,t}^A$) corresponds to what the exports of electronics goods should contribute to $r_{i,t}$ if country i's share in the international market remains the same between $t-1$ and t. Similarly, the second term $(d_{i,t}^{A-})$ is what nonelectronics exports should add to $r_{i,t}$ if the country maintains its market share for these products. The sum of these two terms can thus be regarded as the part of $r_{i,t}$ that is broadly attributable to demand factors. Meanwhile, the last term $s_{i,t}$ reflects changes in country i's market share for both electronic and nonelectronic products and can be considered as the change in aggregate exports due to supply-side factors. If exchange rate movement alters country i's competitive position in the international market, this effect should appear in this last term.

We next apply this framework to the EA countries. As competitiveness shocks are unlikely to matter much for primary products, we limit our attention to manufactures (SITC 5 through 8). We classify goods according the three-digit code of SITC revision 2, and define SITC 751, 752, 759, 764, 772, 776, and 778 as the elements of A. This set includes IT goods and their parts and components but excludes general consumer electronics such as television receivers and sound recorders, and is thus a relatively narrow definition of electronic goods. To put the 1996 regional export recession into a long-term perspective, we conduct our DSSA for each year since 1988.[14]

The result of our calculation is shown in Figure 4.3. The top eight panels show the results for individual EA countries, while the bottom two panels present the results for Japan (right) and the pooled exports of the eight EA countries (left).[15] By looking first at the bottom left panel, we notice that for the eight EA economies as a group, demand shocks have been responsible for the major part of year-on-year fluctuations in their aggregate exports throughout our observation period. In particular, at least in terms of our decomposition, the 1996 export recession is more than entirely explicable by negative demand shocks, of which roughly half have been related to electronics goods. We also observe that in recent years, the importance of the world electronics cycle has increased substantially as a factor behind EA's export dynamics.

Let us next examine the results for individual countries. As we can see, although the time-series profile of $r_{i,t}$ is broadly similar across the eight EA countries, this is not the case for the relative contribution of $d_{i,t}^{A}$, $d_{i,t}^{A-}$ and $s_{i,t}$. In Malaysia, the Philippines, and Singapore, fluctuations in $d_{i,t}^{A}$ have played an important role in yearly fluctuations in $r_{i,t}$, clearly reflecting their heavy reliance on electronic goods. In contrast, the contribution of $d_{i,t}^{A}$ has been fairly limited in Indonesia and Thailand, although in the latter country its influence seems to have risen recently. In all countries but Korea and Thailand, the value of the competitiveness term $s_{i,t}$ was negative in 1995 but became positive in 1996. For most EA countries, therefore, there is no evidence that competitiveness shocks played an important part in their 1996 export slowdown. Even in Korea and Thailand, the drop in $r_{i,t}$ in 1996 was due primarily to falls in the two demand components, with only modest contributions from $s_{i,t}$.[16] We also observe that in Malaysia and Singapore, the downturn in the

124

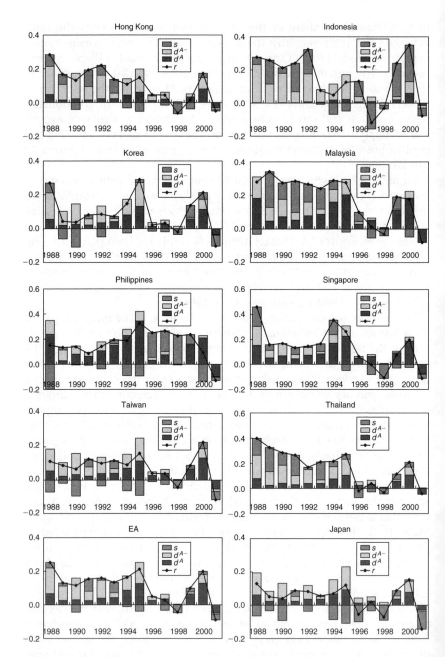

Figure 4.3   Factors underlying export growth (total exports)
Source: Author's calculation based on Statistics Canada WTD.

world electronics market was quite decisive in their export performance during this period.

Although the preceding observation seems largely to confirm the aggregate evidence in Table 4.6, there may be room for debate concerning its interpretation. First, although we have interpreted d_i^A and $d_{i,t}^{A-}$ as export fluctuations arising from demand factors and $s_{i,t}$ as those relating to supply-side factors, this neat distinction is in practice not as watertight as we would like it to be. In particular, since the geographical distribution of trade flows tends to entail a degree of stickiness, fluctuations in $s_{i,t}$ may reflect not just supply-side, competitiveness shocks but also what should conceptually be regarded as demand shocks. For example, suppose that country i depends heavily on country j as its export market. When the import demand of country j falls substantially because of, say, a home-grown recession, the growth rate of country i's aggregate exports is likely to fall by a larger proportion than that of the world average. Although the gap between the two tends to appear in $s_{i,t}$ in our DSSA, this is not what is normally considered as a supply-side effect. In Figure 4.3, we notice that in most EA countries the value of $s_{i,t}$ turned negative in 1997 and remained below 0 in 1998, even though the regional currency crisis should by then have improved the price competitiveness of several countries. While the negative $s_{i,t}$ in this period may have been partly due to temporary supply-side factors, we suspect that the severe contraction of intra-EA trade – which was an inevitable consequence of the crisis-induced regional recession – also played its part.

In our DSSA, moreover, $s_{i,t}$ does not distinguish changes in exports arising from domestic productivity shocks and those relating to other supply-side factors, such as multinational firms' cross-border reallocations of their assembly plants. During the first half of the 1990s when the yen progressively appreciated, the contribution of $s_{i,t}$ to national export growth was more noticeable in such countries as Malaysia and Thailand, which had received large amounts of FDI from Japan in the earlier years, than in Korea and Taiwan whose exporters should have competed more directly with those of Japan. On the other hand, $s_{i,t}$ contributed negatively to Japan's export performance in most years between 1988 and 2001, including periods of yen depreciation; this appears to reflect Japanese firms' outward shift of manufacturing activity.[17] In recent years, similar transfers of assembly operations have also become noticeable in EA's high-income countries, such as Hong Kong and Singapore. As a large fraction of the EA countries' outward FDI goes to the other countries in the region, and as FDI is known to generate substantial auxiliary trade in goods and services,[18] we need to be careful when making inferences about what was responsible for the computed time-series behavior of $s_{i,t}$.[19]

To address these complications, we next repeat the same decomposition using data for each country's exports to countries *outside the Asian region only*. By doing so, we should be able to mitigate the effects of the regional business cycle and FDI-induced regional trade on the computed value of $s_{i,t}$; this exercise should also help us assess more accurately the competitiveness effect of yen/dollar fluctuations on Japanese and EA exports to third countries. Data was compiled by subtracting from each country's aggregate exports those which went to EA, Japan and China. For the sake of comparison, this time we conduct the same decomposition also for China.

The result is shown in Figure 4.4. For the EA countries and Japan the result looks broadly similar to Figure 4.3, although the contribution of $s_{i,t}$ to $r_{i,t}$ now appears slightly larger in some countries. Similarly, while the value of $s_{i,t}$ for 1996 is a little smaller (or a little more negative) in many countries than in Figure 4.3, its contribution to the aggregate export slowdown is still eclipsed by those of $d_{i,t}^A$ and $d_{i,t}^{A-}$; in Japan, too, the value of $s_{i,t}$ for 1996 is negative and essentially the same as that for 1995. As in Figure 4.3, the importance of the external demand for electronics in aggregate export fluctuations varies considerably across countries and has been particularly important in Malaysia and Singapore.

Figure 4.4 also reveals interesting cross-country variation in the medium-term trend of $s_{i,t}$. In Japan and Taiwan, the contribution of this term to the aggregate export growth has generally remained negative throughout the past decade and a half. In Hong Kong, Malaysia, Singapore, and Thailand, although the contribution of $s_{i,t}$ to $r_{i,t}$ had been positive and numerically large until the mid-1990s, its role has diminished considerably during the subsequent period. In China, by contrast, the value of $s_{i,t}$ has remained positive every year since 1988, with its share in $r_{i,t}$ large and rising in recent years. These contrasting trends of the supply-side component seem to reflect rapid changes in FDI flows and associated redistributions of manufacturing activity within East Asia. As is widely documented, China replaced ASEAN countries by the mid-1990s as the region's leading recipient of FDI. Although inward FDI had in the past been the engine of industrialization and export growth in many ASEAN countries, this mechanism is no longer operative in some countries. In relatively high-wage countries like Malaysia and Singapore, both local firms and foreign multinationals are shifting labor-intensive operations to China and other low-wage countries; and the consequent transformation of regional production networks and trade dynamics seems to be altering the way in which the global electronics cycle influences individual EA economies (Monetary Authority of Singapore 2004).

4.4   Is East Asia a de facto dollar area?

As we noted in Section 4.1, the view that yen/dollar fluctuations constitute a primary threat to EA's macroeconomic stability rests on the assumption that most regional currencies are pegged to the dollar. McKinnon and Schnabl (2003) note: "(b)efore the Asian crisis of 1997–1998, all smaller East Asian countries pegged to the US dollar," and "contrary to the IMF's urging, by 2002 the East Asian countries other than Japan are returning – or have returned – to

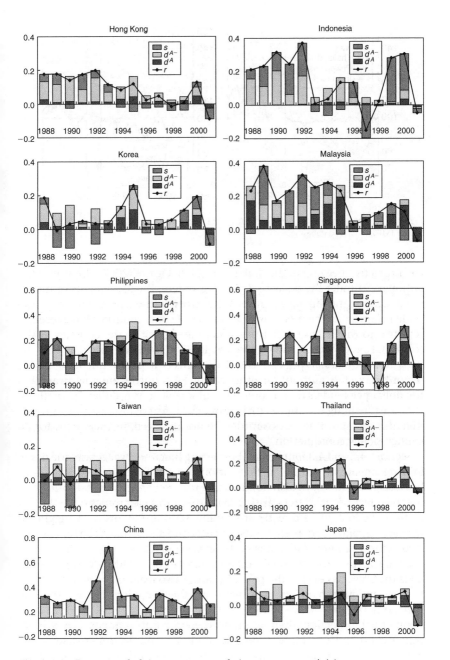

Figure 4.4 Factors underlying export growth (exports to non-Asia)
Source: See Figure 4.3.

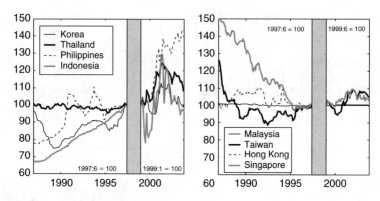

Figure 4.5   Exchange rates between EA currencies and the dollar
Source: IMF IFS, CEIC database.

their pre-crisis pegging to the dollar" (p. 1072). Ogawa (2002) also notes that although "(u)nder the de facto dollar peg system, the movements of the US dollar against the Japanese yen served to worsen (the East Asian countries') trade balances, ... the monetary authorities of some countries have recently returned to the *de facto* dollar peg system used prior to the currency crisis" (p. 182). Fukuda (2002) and Ogawa and Ito (2003) further speculate that the persistence of dollar pegs in East Asia reflects a policy dilemma of the region's monetary authorities: although the EA countries are now aware that the dollar peg renders their economies vulnerable to yen/dollar fluctuations, they are unwilling to "unpeg" their currency for fear of losing export competitiveness vis-à-vis other EA countries. Hence the need, in their view, for an explicit policy coordination.

Sections 4.2 and 4.3 found that the existing literature exaggerates the destabilizing impact of yen/dollar fluctuations on the EA economies, not least because it fails to distinguish nominal and real exchange rates and to account for the effect of real shocks arising from the world electronics cycle. In this section, we look more directly at the time-series behaviors of the eight EA currencies before and after the Asian crisis and show that the view of East Asia being a de facto dollar area is also exaggerated.

Figure 4.5 plots the bilateral exchange rates of the eight EA currencies vis-à-vis the US dollar during the past 15 years.[20] Two features are worth noting. First, the Indonesian rupiah, the Korean won, the Philippine peso, and the Thai baht have become markedly more volatile after the financial crisis. At least upon visual inspection, their recent movement hardly reminds us of a dollar peg. Second, in Hong Kong, Indonesia, and Thailand the dollar value of the home currencies remained within a narrow band or depreciated at a near-constant rate throughout the whole pre-crisis years, so we have no objection to calling their currency regime during this period a virtual dollar peg.[21]

Moreover, other currencies (except the Korean won) also remained conspic-
uously stable vis-à-vis the dollar between mid-1995 and the onset of the
Asian crisis. In the years before this period, however, these currencies appear
to have been substantially less stable.[22]

In the existing literature, that the EA countries have pegged and still peg
their currencies to the dollar is often "proved" by appealing to an empirical
method proposed by Frankel and Wei (1994).[23] To refute the (then) lingering
suspicion that a yen bloc was emerging in Asia, Frankel and Wei estimated
the following OLS model:

$$\Delta e_{i/k} = \alpha_0 + \alpha_1 \Delta e_{US/k}(t) + \alpha_2 \Delta e_{JP/k}(t) + \alpha_3 \Delta e_{EU/k}(t) + \cdots + u(t) \qquad (4.6)$$

where $e_{i/k}$ is the price of a unit of the currency of country i in terms of currency k, and EU stands for the ecu or the German mark before 1999 and the
euro after 1999. k is the numéraire in this equation and chosen from currencies that are floated against all other currencies in Equation (4.6). As developing countries' de facto exchange rate regimes often depart substantially from
their *de jure* policy,[24] k is normally chosen from the currencies of industrial
countries that are known to maintain floating exchange rates. Most authors
use the Swiss franc, following Frankel and Wei's original work.

Table 4.7 shows our own estimation of Equation (4.6), obtained by taking
the Swiss franc as k and using monthly average exchange rates. For the pre-
crisis period, we observe that the coefficient of $\Delta e_{US/k}(t)$ is highly significant
for all EA currencies, with its point estimates exceeding 0.8 for all but the
Singaporean dollar. In contrast, the coefficient on $\Delta e_{JP/k}(t)$ is either small or
statistically insignificant, even in countries like Korea and Taiwan whose
economies should presumably be vulnerable to yen/dollar fluctuations. Even
for the post-crisis period, Equation (4.6) generally exhibits a respectable
explanatory power, and the estimated coefficients on $\Delta e_{US/k}(t)$ still look large.
For example, in Thailand and the Philippines (which officially floated their
currencies in the wake of the financial crisis), the estimated coefficients on
$\Delta e_{US/k}(t)$ are 0.84 and 0.68 whereas those on $\Delta e_{JP/Ik}(t)$ remain negligible. For
some authors, these results are prima facie evidence of East Asia's collective
dollar pegs, not only before the crisis but even today (McKinnon 2005).

This conclusion is, however, premature. Although most authors seem to
believe that a large value of α_1 and small or statistically insignificant values
of α_2 and α_3, combined with a reasonable fit of the equation, are sufficient
evidence for a dollar peg, this is not necessarily the case. To see why, suppose
that the monetary authorities of country i conduct *high-frequency* (e.g. daily
or weekly) exchange rate smoothing, either to maintain liquidity in the local
foreign exchange market or for some other reasons. This short-run volatility
management is conducted in terms of the bilateral exchange rate with the
dollar, either by prespecifying the maximum range within which the
rate can change in each business day or week, or by resorting to more

Table 4.7 Frankel/Wei/McKinnon regression

	Constant		$\Delta e(US/k)$		$\Delta e(JP/k)$		$\Delta e(EU/k)$		R^2 (adj.)	D.W.
Pre-crisis (1988: 1–1997: 6)										
Hong Kong	0.000	(0.000)	1.000***	(0.004)	0.000	(0.003)	0.003	(0.009)	0.999	1.876
Indonesia	0.003***	(0.000)	0.963***	(0.023)	0.018	(0.016)	0.071	(0.042)	0.985	1.621
Korea	0.001	(0.001)	0.925***	(0.036)	0.112**	(0.035)	−0.028	(0.066)	0.933	0.656
Malaysia	0.000	(0.000)	0.837***	(0.038)	0.069*	(0.036)	0.221**	(0.091)	0.893	1.158
Philippines	0.000	(0.002)	0.997***	(0.115)	−0.087	(0.083)	0.305*	(0.162)	0.795	1.316
Singapore	−0.003***	(0.001)	0.674***	(0.029)	0.134***	(0.018)	0.230***	(0.056)	0.950	1.862
Taiwan	0.000	(0.001)	0.876***	(0.057)	0.087	(0.060)	0.180*	(0.096)	0.896	1.338
Thailand	0.000	(0.000)	0.804***	(0.014)	0.151***	(0.036)	0.047	(0.033)	0.975	0.904
Post-crisis (1999: 7–2003: 6)										
Hong Kong	0.000	(0.000)	1.000***	(0.002)	−0.002**	(0.001)	0.001	(0.005)	1.000	1.066
Indonesia	0.004	(0.007)	0.433	(0.452)	0.114	(0.408)	2.313	(0.525)	0.097	1.658
Korea	0.000	(0.003)	0.572***	(0.178)	0.546***	(0.185)	0.249	(0.199)	0.723	1.040
Malaysia	0.000	(0.000)	1.000***	(0.000)	0.000	(0.000)	0.000	(0.000)	1.000	2.138
Philippines	0.007***	(0.003)	0.843***	(0.139)	0.100	(0.132)	0.528	(0.341)	0.618	1.648
Singapore	0.001	(0.001)	0.596***	(0.080)	0.192***	(0.055)	0.271*	(0.149)	0.820	1.954
Taiwan	0.001	(0.002)	0.766***	(0.078)	0.175***	(0.052)	0.311	(0.186)	0.844	1.171
Thailand	0.003	(0.003)	0.679***	(0.151)	0.062	(0.166)	0.523**	(0.225)	0.581	1.276

Notes: Figures in parentheses are Newy-West standard errors. (*), (**), and (***) denote significance at 10, 5 and 1% levels. For the pre-crisis period, $\Delta e(EU/k)$ refers to the ecu/Swiss franc exchange rate; for the post-crisis period it is the euro/Swiss franc rate.
Source: CEIC database.

discretionary market intervention. Meanwhile, over relatively long time horizons (e.g. half a year or longer), the monetary authorities are *not* specifically interested in the stability of the bilateral exchange rate with the dollar. They may instead wish to keep the stability of the home currency's (real or nominal) *effective* exchange rate, or they may seek the stability of both exchange rates and other aggregate variables. Needless to say, such a policy is not a dollar peg, notwithstanding the presence of high-frequency smoothing operations.[25]

When the foregoing policy is in place, estimating Equation (4.6) with monthly exchange rates is bound to find a large value of α_1 even if the monetary authorities do not mechanically peg the home currency to the dollar at the monthly frequency. Similarly, since the monetary authorities do not systematically respond to daily and weekly movements of the yen/dollar and euro/dollar exchange rates, the estimated equation may give us an impression that they pay no attention to their movements over longer time horizons as well. Although one may think that this problem can be resolved by estimating Equation (4.6) with lower-frequency data, such a regression would need data that spans an inordinate length of time during which the monetary authorities may change their policy. As most existing studies use either daily or weekly data to ensure sufficient degrees of freedom, their results have little to say, at least by themselves, about the policy pursued over the time horizon that matters for the real economy.[26]

We next conduct a simple numerical experiment to show that what we have mentioned above is more than a theoretical possibility. Specifically, we consider two hypothetical exchange rate regimes as alternatives to a dollar peg, and simulate the exchange rate movements of the EA currencies that would have taken place if such policies had been adopted. We note that the aim of this exercise is *not* to rigorously identify individual countries' currency regimes; our purpose is merely to illustrate that looking at the past behavior of their currencies at an appropriately low frequency makes it difficult to believe that all countries have been solely concerned about the dollar value of their currencies.

Our first hypothetical regime is nominal effective exchange rate (NEER) targeting. For computational simplicity, we assume that each EA country trades only with the United States, Japan, Europe, other EA countries, and China. With this assumption, we can write the rate of change in currency i's NEER, defined in the standard manner, as

$$\Delta e_i(t) \equiv \alpha_{US}^* \Delta e_{i/US}(t) + \alpha_{JP}^* \Delta e_{i/JP}(t) + \alpha_{EU}^* \Delta e_{i/EU}(t) + \sum_{j \neq i} \alpha_j^* \Delta e_{i/j}(t) \qquad (4.7)$$

where $j = 1, 2, ..., 8$ corresponds to seven EA countries and China. The coefficient on the first term on the right-hand side, α_{US}^*, is the share of the United States in country i's total imports plus exports, and all other coefficients are defined analogously. Fixing the NEER means that the monetary authorities maintain the following equality relation:

$$0 \equiv \alpha_{US}^* \Delta e_{i/US}(t) + \alpha_{JP}^* \Delta e_{i/JP}(t) + \alpha_{EU}^* \Delta e_{i/EU}(t) + \sum_{j \neq i} \alpha_j^* \Delta e_{i/j}(t) \quad (4.8)$$

Rewriting Equation (4.8) in terms of exchange rates with the US dollar and rearranging, we find

$$\Delta e_{i/US}^*(t) = \alpha_{JP}^* \Delta e_{JP/US}(t) + \alpha_{EU}^* \Delta e_{EU/US}(t) + \sum_{j \neq i} \alpha_j^* \Delta e_{j/EU}(t) \quad (4.9)$$

As only the left-hand variable involves currency i, we can interpret this equation as the monetary authorities' reaction function. $\Delta e_{i/US}^*(t)$ corresponds to the *adjustment of currency i's bilateral exchange rate with the US dollar that is necessary to keep the former's NEER.*

Our second hypothetical regime is a common basket peg (CBP). As noted in Section 4.1, a number of authors recommend the EA countries to peg their currencies to a basket of the dollar, the yen and the euro, so as to ameliorate the effect of exchange rate movements among these currencies on their economies. It is thus interesting to see how each EA currency would have behaved if such a policy had been adopted in the past. CBP requires all EA monetary authorities to maintain the following relation:

$$0 = \hat{\alpha}_{US} \Delta e_{i/US}(t) + \hat{\alpha}_{JP} \Delta e_{i/JP}(t) + \hat{\alpha}_{EU} \Delta e_{i/EU}(t) \quad (4.10)$$

where $\hat{\alpha}_{US}$, $\hat{\alpha}_{JP}$, and $\hat{\alpha}_{EU}$ correspond to the weights attached to the dollar, the yen and the euro, which sums to one. Again by rewriting all terms as dollar exchange rates, we obtain

$$\Delta \hat{e}_{i/US}(t) = \hat{\alpha}_{JP} \Delta e_{JP/US}(t) + \hat{\alpha}_{EU} \Delta e_{EU/US}(t) \quad (4.11)$$

As in the previous case, Equation (4.11) can be regarded as the monetary authorities' reaction function. For simplicity, we set the values of $\hat{\alpha}_{JP}$ and $\hat{\alpha}_{EU}$ according to the following formulae:

$$\hat{\alpha}_{JP} \equiv \frac{\alpha_{JP}}{\alpha_{US} + \alpha_{JP} + \alpha_{EU}} \qquad \hat{\alpha}_{EU} \equiv \frac{\alpha_{EU}}{\alpha_{US} + \alpha_{JP} + \alpha_{EU}} \quad (4.12)$$

where α_{US}, α_{JP}, and α_{EU} are, respectively, the shares of trade with the United States, Japan, and Europe in the eight EA countries' aggregate imports plus exports.[27]

We let α_{JP}^*, α_{EU}^*, α_j^*, $\hat{\alpha}_{JP}$, and $\hat{\alpha}_{EU}$ in Equations (4.9) and (4.11) vary over time and compute their values in each period as a weighted average of the previous three years.[28] Although the coefficients for the NEER regime differ substantially across countries and time, those for the CBP regime (which are by definition identical for all countries) are fairly stable over time. Throughout the past 15 years the weights of the three major currencies remain roughly in the neighborhood of $\hat{\alpha}_{US} : \hat{\alpha}_{JP} : \hat{\alpha}_{EU}$; 0.40 : 0.35 : 0.25, which are close to those recommended by Williamson (2000) and Kawai and Akiyama (2000). Once these coefficients are determined, it is straightforward to calculate the time series of $\Delta\hat{e}^*_{i/US}$ (t) and $\Delta\hat{e}_{i/US}$ (t). To repeat, however, the point of this exercise is to compute their values at a sufficiently low frequency that is directly relevant to the real economy. We thus set the time unit *t* at six months.

Figure 4.6 plots the calculated exchange rate movements. Two general features stand out. First, except for the few currencies for which mechanical dollar pegs were apparent in Figure 4.5, there is little evidence that the EA currencies have been more stable against the dollar than would have been the case under an explicit NEER targeting. For example, the actual movement of the dollar/Philippine peso exchange rate has been consistently more volatile than those of the simulated paths, except for a brief period before the Asian crisis. After the crisis, moreover, the Indonesian rupiah, the Korean won, the Philippine peso, and the Thai baht have remained substantially more variable vis-à-vis the dollar than the simulated values. This visual impression is borne out in Table 4.8, which compares the standard deviations of the actual bilateral US dollar exchange rates with those of the simulated values.

Second, and again except for the few currencies officially pegged to the dollar, the time series of the actual exchange rate, $\Delta e_{i/US}$ (t), does not appear to be independent of the two simulated series. As correlation does not necessarily imply causation, it is not immediately clear how much of the observed correlations has been the result of the monetary authorities' conscious exchange rate targeting and how much has been due to market forces.[29] As we noted previously, however, many EA countries had until the Asian crisis officially maintained a policy of monitoring the medium-term movement of the effective – not dollar – value of their currencies. At least for Singapore and Taiwan, the paths of $\Delta e_{i/US}$ (t) and $\Delta e^*_{i/US}$ (t) are correlated to each other sufficiently tightly that it seems unlikely that these countries have merely pursued a dollar peg.[30]

A few important points follow from the preceding observations. First, there is now doubt about the sweeping claim by Ogawa (2002) and McKinnon (2005) that East Asia constitutes a virtual dollar zone. Even before the crisis, few EA currencies were linked to the dollar sufficiently tightly as to let yen/dollar fluctuations be translated directly into their effective values. As we discussed elsewhere, there is also evidence that the currencies of a few EA countries had a clear tendency to slide against the dollar in times of a marked deterioration in their export performance (Kumakura 2005a). After the Asian crisis, moreover, the medium-term movement of *all* crisis-hit currencies except the Malaysian ringgit has become so much more variable – relative to both their own movement in the pre-crisis period and what should have been necessary to keep their NEER stable – that it is incredible that their monetary authorities are now back to their pre-crisis policies.

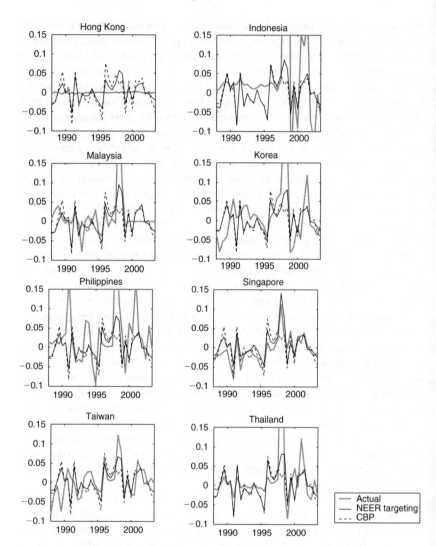

Figure 4.6   Actual and simulated movements of US dollar exchange rates
Source: Author's calculation based on IMF IFS, CEIC and Statistics Canada WTD.

Second, the preceding observations throw doubt over the assumptions under-lying the recent proposals for regional exchange rate targeting. For example, the fundamental premise of the CBP proposal is that the EA countries still target their currencies to the dollar sufficiently rigidly as to make their effec-tive value unnecessarily unstable. As far as we can see in Figure 4.6, however, if the EA countries adopted the CBP today, that would *strengthen* – not weaken – several currencies' medium-term links to the dollar. McKinnon and Schnabl's

Table 4.8 Standard deviation of the nominal exchange rate with the US dollar under alternative currency regimes (semiannual basis)

	Hong Kong	Indonesia	Korea	Malaysia	Philippines	Singapore	Thailand	Taiwan
Pre-crisis (1988: S1–1995: S1)								
Actual	0.002	0.007	0.038	0.030	0.066	0.026	0.013	0.031
NEER targeting	0.025	0.039	0.030	0.028	0.026	0.023	0.035	0.027
CBP	0.038	0.038	0.038	0.038	0.038	0.038	0.038	0.038
Pre-crisis (1990: S1–1997: S1)								
Actual	0.001	0.008	0.030	0.028	0.066	0.031	0.014	0.029
NEER targeting	0.027	0.044	0.034	0.034	0.031	0.027	0.040	0.030
CBP	0.045	0.045	0.045	0.045	0.045	0.045	0.045	0.045
Post-crisis (1999: S1–2003: S1)								
Actual	0.001	0.120	0.056	0.000	0.068	0.025	0.049	0.030
NEER targeting	0.017	0.030	0.024	0.026	0.025	0.021	0.028	0.023
CBP	0.032	0.032	0.032	0.032	0.032	0.032	0.032	0.032

Source: See Table 4.1.

(2003) formal EA dollar bloc proposal, predicated on the presumption that all EA countries but Japan have an innate penchant for a dollar peg, seems similarly unconvincing.

Third, Figure 4.6 illustrates that the Frankel–Wei regression can be highly misleading when the monetary authorities do not pursue the same policy over different time horizons. For example, at least since the early 1990s the actual movement of the US dollar/New Taiwan dollar exchange rate has remained fairly close to its hypothetical paths under the NEER targeting and CBP regimes. As noted previously, the basket weights used to simulate the CBP path were, while time-varying, roughly in the neighborhood of dollar : yen : euro = 0.40 : 0.35 : 0.25. In Table 4.7, however, the estimated "weights" of the three currencies were 0.88 : 0.09 : 0.18 (pre-crisis period) and 0.77 : 0.18 : 0.31 (post-crisis period).[31] Similarly, if the estimates in Table 4.7 were accurate, adopting the CBP today would require the Philippines and Thailand to cut the weights of the dollar roughly by half and raise that of the yen by two to three times. This is, however, clearly not what we find in Figure 4.6.

4.5   Conclusion

The recent calls for a regional exchange rate regime in East Asia are often motivated by concern about the instability of the yen/dollar exchange rate. The widespread view of yen/dollar fluctuations being the principal threat to EA's exports and income rests on two assumptions: (1) the EA countries peg their currencies to the dollar sufficiently tightly and routinely that changes in the yen/dollar exchange rate directly threaten their export competitiveness vis-à-vis Japan; (2) competitiveness shocks dominate other factors as a determinant of EA's exports and output. This chapter has found that these assumptions are largely unfounded.

First, the widely held view that most EA countries constitute a virtual US dollar bloc is exaggerated. Even before the crisis, the dollar exchange rates of many EA currencies were at least as flexible (or unstable) in the medium term as would have been the case if these countries had targeted the effective value of their currencies. After the crisis, moreover, the dollar values of most crisis-affected currencies have become substantially more volatile so that we can safely dismiss the view that the "East Asian dollar standard" has been revived recently (McKinnon 2005). As shown in Section 4.4, the gap between the empirical behavior of the EA currencies and that which is depicted in the literature is due partly to the latter's uncritical application of the Frankel/Wei regression model and its failure to properly distinguish short-run exchange rate smoothing and a longer-term peg.

Second, at least for the EA economies as a whole, the global electronics cycle – not the yen/dollar rate – has been the principal driver of medium-term fluctuations in their exports and output. Even between 1995 and 1997 when most EA currencies remained largely fixed to the dollar while the latter strengthened sharply against the yen, the EA countries' export stagnation was due almost entirely to a cyclical downturn in the global electronics industry, with little measurable impact from the yen depreciation. It seems inappropriate, therefore, to blame the yen for the subsequent Asian crisis, although this is what is often done in the literature.

The foregoing does not mean, however, that the EA economies are a homogeneous entity that responds to external shocks in an identical manner. Although many EA countries share broadly similar patterns of output and export dynamics, this aggregate observation is somewhat deceptive. As we saw in Sections 4.2 and 4.3, the exports and output cycles of some countries are not as strongly correlated as those among other countries, and the global electronics cycle also exerts varying impacts on individual economies. Evidence further suggests that many of the regional economies are currently undergoing substantial structural change, thanks in part to China's rise as a major international manufacturing base. These changes in the real economy are likely in the future to alter the ways in which the electronics cycle affects individual economies and in which such effects are propagated to other countries.

What we have seen in this chapter raises questions for recent proposals for a regional exchange rate regime. For example, the East Asian CBP proposal is predicated on the presumptions that most Asian countries still maintain clandestine dollar pegs and that yen/dollar fluctuations destabilize their economies. Nevertheless, the currencies of most crisis-affected countries have in fact been much more variable against the dollar in recent years than would have been permitted under a mechanical CBP; our computation in Section 4.4 suggests that adopting the CBP might have a perverse effect of strengthening these currencies' medium-term link to the dollar.

Similarly, although McKinnon and Schnabl (2003) recommend an explicit pan-Asia dollar peg under the assumption that most countries' "revealed preference" is to peg to the dollar, what we have seen in Section 4.4 suggests otherwise. With the exception of Hong Kong and Malaysia, the current policies of the EA monetary authorities seem more pragmatic than suggested by these authors. Even in Hong Kong and Malaysia, it is unlikely that their genuine preference is to defend their dollar pegs at all costs.[32] In Hong Kong, although the monetary authorities still officially pledge to maintain its dollar peg, a careful reading of their recent statements suggests that this depends very much on what China will do about its exchange rate policy (Yam 2003). Given Hong Kong's increasing integration into the Chinese economy, it seems hard to believe that the former will leave its current regime untouched once the Chinese renminbi starts to fluctuate against other currencies substantially.

Admittedly, concern about yen/dollar fluctuations is only one of many reasons behind the recent clamor for a regional exchange rate regime. As we noted in the Introduction, its proponents also speculate that coordinated exchange rate policies promote intraregional trade and investment and accelerate integration of the East Asian economies. While this claim may have some merits, recent cross-country studies suggest that reductions of exchange rate volatility per se have little influence on the volume of trade (Parsley and Wei 2002; Clark et al. 2004). Moreover, the economies of EA countries are not as homogeneous as often presumed, nor is the way in which each economy is linked to the rest of the world identical. For example, although this chapter has focused on the production and trade of physical goods, the importance of the service sector varies considerably across countries. As has been brought home by the 2002 terrorist attack in Indonesia and by the spread of the severe acute respiratory syndrome (SARS) in 2003, tourism and business-service trade are quite vulnerable to events that are outside the control of individual countries, although their monetary authorities do have to respond swiftly to such contingencies to safeguard their economies. It thus seems an open question whether the benefit of a regional exchange rate arrangement – which would inevitably constrain each country's monetary policy – really outweighs its potential costs.

Appendix 4A   System estimation of EA business cycles, 1992–2004

In Section 4.2, we adopted the empirical model of Kwan (2001) and McKinnon and Schnabl (2003) and investigated factors underlying the collective business cycle of the eight EA countries using annual data for 1980–2004. There are, however, a few reasons to suspect that this empirical framework is not the most desirable one. First, given the far-reaching transformation of the EA economies during the past few decades, there are questions about using data that spans such a long period of time. Second, annual statistics are generally not suitable for business-cycle regression, as data recorded at a low frequency can miss important information concerning the causal relationship among relevant variables. Third and as we stressed in the preceding sections, the eight EA economies are by no means homogeneous, with the business cycles of some countries (e.g. the Philippines) being correlated relatively weakly with those of the others (Table 4.1). This Appendix addresses these issues by estimating a system of simple structural equations for the eight EA economies' GDP cycles.

Now for each EA country $i = 1, 2, ..., 8$, consider the following general model

$$\Delta y_{i,t} = \alpha + \sum_{j=0} \beta_j \Delta x_{i,t-j} + \sum_{k=0} \gamma_k \Delta s_{i,t-k} + \sum_{l=0} \lambda_l \Delta elc_{t-l} + u_{i,t} \qquad i = 1, 2, ..., 8$$

$$(4A.1)$$

where $y_{i,t}$ stands for country i's real GDP in period t, $x_{i,t-j}$ is the external demand for country i's exports in period $x - j$, $s_{i,t-k}$ is an index of country i's external price competitiveness, elc_{t-l} is the condition of the world electronics market in $x - l$, and $u_{i,t}$ is a disturbance term (all in natural logarithms except for $u_{i,t}$).

As in Section 4.2, we generate $\Delta x_{i,t-j}$ by computing the weighted average of the real GDP growth rates of United States, Japan, EU, and China, where weights are computed by their shares in country i's exports. As for $s_{i,t-k}$, we consider both the nominal yen/dollar exchange rate and the PPI-based real exchange rate between the yen and currency i.

Although it is possible to estimate the eight equations in Equation (4A.1) independently, we choose to treat these equations as a system and estimate them with the seemingly unrelated regression (SUR) method. In contrast to OLS, SUR allows for cross-equation correlations among the error terms, which may prove useful for our purposes. As we saw in Section 4.2, although the EA countries' business cycles are generally correlated fairly strongly, the degree of their synchronization varies from one pair of countries to another. Moreover, as some countries are related more closely to one another through trade and investment than are others, it is unlikely that a shock that occurs in one country is propagated to other countries with equal strength. To the extent that individual economies share some of these shocks but respond to these shocks differently, the SUR method may permit more efficient estimation than does OLS.[33]

By the early 1990s, quarterly GDP and price data became available in all EA countries. If we estimate Equation (4A.1) with quarterly data, however, we have to examine numerous possibilities concerning the lag length of each explanatory variable, which may well differ from one country to another. Moreover, as SUR permits only contemporaneous correlation among the error terms, we would like to keep the time unit reasonably long so as to best exploit the merit of this estimation method. We thus set the time unit at six months as in Section 4.4 and built a semiannual dataset for 1992: S1–2004: S2.[34]

Before moving to the estimation result, a brief explanation is in order concerning time dummy variables. Our dataset includes periods in which there are strong a priori reasons to believe that a particular country (or a group of countries) was subject to major idiosyncratic shocks. While the most obvious example of such shocks is the Asian financial crisis in 1997–98, there are other occasions on which one or more countries are believed to have encountered an important one-time shock. For example, the Philippines experienced a major economic setback in the early 1990s with a string of natural disasters, political instability, and a near balance-of-payment crisis (Rodlauer et al. 2000). In Hong Kong and a few other countries, the spread of the SARS epidemic in early 2003 was a severe blow to their tourist revenue and business sentiment (ADB 2003). As ignoring these factors can bias the estimation result, we conducted extensive preliminary data analysis and chose a set of country-specific period dummies to be included on the right-hand side of Equation (4A.1). For each country, these dummy variables are fixed throughout the following estimation.

The general model of Equation (4A.1) nests both the Kwan/McKinnon/ Schnabl hypothesis and our hypothesis. As neither hypothesis necessarily rules

Table 4A.1 Seemingly unrelated regressions for EA business cycles (1992: S1–2004: S2)

Constant	Δx_i	$\Delta x_i(-1)$	$\Delta e_{Y/S}$	$\Delta e_{Y/S}(-1)$	Δelc	$[\Delta elc]^2$	$\Delta elc(-1)$	D.W.	R^2 (adj.)
Hong Kong (period dummies for 1998S1, 1998S2 and 2003S1)									
0.010 (0.026)	1.741* (1.000)							1.587	0.549
−0.041 (0.033)	2.126** (0.939)	1.612* (0.923)						1.559	0.599
0.002 (0.024)	1.980** (0.946)		−0.209** (0.086)					1.711	0.620
0.007 (0.026)	1.759* (1.031)		−0.198** (0.094)	−0.031 (0.103)				1.709	0.599
0.028 (0.024)	0.701 (0.968)				0.069*** (0.021)			1.820	0.656
0.027 (0.026)	0.703 (0.960)				0.071*** (0.023)	0.004 (0.068)		1.844	0.641
0.031 (0.023)	0.551 (0.953)				0.065*** (0.022)		0.012 (0.021)	1.750	0.641
Indonesia (period dummies for 1998S1 and 1998S2)									
0.066*** (0.012)	−0.621 (0.843)							2.225	0.841
0.060*** (0.015)	−0.519 (0.872)	0.346 (0.879)						2.242	0.834
0.064*** (0.012)	−0.487 (0.835)		−0.077 (0.088)					2.251	0.838
0.065*** (0.012)	−0.664 (0.851)		−0.044 (0.098)	−0.074 (0.100)				2.292	0.833
0.065*** (0.012)	−0.768 (0.883)				0.028 (0.022)			2.377	0.844
0.070*** (0.014)	−0.798 (0.880)				0.021 (0.024)	−0.045 (0.068)		2.439	0.839
0.072*** (0.011)	−1.530* (0.880)				0.019 (0.022)		0.036 (0.023)	2.513	0.848

Korea (period dummy for 1998S1)

0.054*** (0.017)	0.347 (0.907)							1.327	0.724
0.066*** (0.019)	0.771 (0.948)	−1.138 (0.908)						1.362	0.730
0.048*** (0.016)	0.600 (0.877)		−0.140 (0.085)					1.457	0.740
0.052*** (0.016)	0.369 (0.857)		−0.081 (0.089)					1.328	0.752
0.054*** (0.016)	0.083 (0.911)			−0.138 (0.087)	0.043** (0.021)			1.468	0.757
0.033** (0.016)	0.529 (0.813)				0.063*** (0.020)	0.139** (0.058)		1.273	0.789
0.055*** (0.016)	0.075 (0.916)				0.049** (0.022)		−0.012 (0.021)	1.485	0.749

Malaysia (period dummies for 1998S1 and 1998S2)

0.057*** (0.014)	0.910 (0.889)							1.066	0.695
0.050*** (0.016)	1.134 (0.964)	0.283 (0.975)						1.085	0.687
0.050*** (0.013)	1.255 (0.833)		−0.217** (0.085)					1.233	0.749
0.049*** (0.013)	1.318 (0.844)		−0.189** (0.094)					1.246	0.742
0.055*** (0.012)	0.368 (0.838)			−0.065 (0.096)	0.081*** (0.020)			1.443	0.807
0.063*** (0.014)	0.233 (0.821)				0.074*** (0.021)	−0.059 (0.059)		1.521	0.804
0.059*** (0.012)	0.003 (0.846)				0.079*** (0.021)		0.011 (0.021)	1.470	0.791

(Continued)

Table 4A.1 (Continued)

Constant	Δx_i	$\Delta x_i (-1)$	$\Delta e_{Y/S}$	$\Delta e_{Y/S} (-1)$	Δelc	$[\Delta elc]^2$	$\Delta elc (-1)$	D.W.	R^2 (adj.)
Philippines (period dummies for 1992S1, 1998S1 and 1998S2)									
0.028*** (0.008)	1.086** (0.557)							2.398	0.526
0.024** (0.010)	0.933 (0.590)	0.454 (0.596)						2.331	0.507
0.030*** (0.008)	0.991 (0.554)		0.003 (0.054)					2.368	0.471
0.030*** (0.009)	1.000* (0.564)		0.003 (0.060)	−0.001 (0.061)				2.368	0.471
0.027*** (0.008)	1.053* (0.601)				0.016 (0.013)			2.412	0.530
0.031*** (0.010)	0.985 (0.601)				0.012 (0.015)	−0.025 (0.042)		2.448	0.509
0.026*** (0.008)	1.246** (0.607)				0.021 (0.014)		−0.015 (0.014)	2.439	0.529
Singapore (period dummy for 1998S1)									
0.045* (0.026)	1.320 (1.667)							1.578	0.133
0.050* (0.030)	2.168 (1.794)	−1.255 (1.827)						1.566	0.127
0.044* (0.026)	1.323 (1.658)		−0.156 (0.162)					1.749	0.129
0.044** (0.023)	1.148 (1.488)		−0.004 (0.162)	−0.363** (0.161)				1.855	0.232
0.040** (0.020)	0.494 (1.370)				0.148*** (0.030)			1.599	0.541
0.053** (0.023)	0.158 (1.366)				0.137*** (0.032)	−0.090 (0.092)		1.581	0.535
0.044** (0.020)	0.149 (1.354)				0.144*** (0.032)		0.014 (0.031)	1.632	0.520

143

Taiwan (no period dummies)

0.039	0.688							1.489	0.026
(0.013)	(0.808)								
0.044***	1.444	−1.111						1.509	0.075
(0.014)	(0.912)	(0.937)							
0.036***	0.828		−0.184**					1.606	0.132
(0.012)	(0.776)		(0.090)						
0.033***	0.978		−0.172*	−0.026				1.605	0.103
(0.012)	(0.765)		(0.098)	(0.099)					
0.038***	0.118				0.086***			1.734	0.452
(0.010)	(0.690)				(0.018)				
0.050***	−0.127				0.075***	−0.091*		2.155	0.477
(0.012)	(0.658)				(0.019)	(0.054)			
0.038***	0.291				0.097***		−0.029	1.718	0.480
(0.009)	(0.626)				(0.018)		(0.018)		

Thailand (period dummies for 1997S1, 1997S2, 1998S1 and 1998S2)

0.090***	−1.986**							1.488	0.749
(0.013)	(0.884)								
0.094***	−1.406	−0.919						1.527	0.752
(0.016)	(0.928)	(0.941)							
0.075***	−1.203*		−0.321***					2.014	0.855
(0.011)	(0.719)		(0.071)						
0.075***	−1.266*		−0.303***	−0.045				2.049	0.848
(0.011)	(0.742)		(0.077)	(0.081)					
0.090***	−2.620***				0.072***			2.321	0.829
(0.011)	(0.815)				(0.018)				
0.091***	−2.615***				0.072***	−0.005		2.343	0.820
(0.013)	(0.818)				(0.021)	(0.059)			
0.094***	−2.949***				0.068***		0.015	2.308	0.819
(0.012)	(0.850)				(0.020)		(0.021)		

Source: Author's estimation based on data from IMF IFS, CEIC databases.

Notes: See Table 4.2. x_t = export demand from outside EA; $e_{y/\$}$ = nominal yen/dollar exchange rate; elc = world semiconductor shipment. See text for details.

out completely the mechanism underpinning the other hypothesis, we tried a number of specifications within this general model, in terms of both the included variables and their lag length. In each regression, however, we employed the same specification for all eight equations to facilitate cross-country comparison.

The result of the first round of our regressions is shown in Table 4A.1. In this set of regressions, we retained the general export demand variable $\Delta x_{i,t}$ throughout and compared the relative performance of the specifications that include the variables representing the nominal yen/dollar exchange rate and the electronics cycle, the latter proxied by the rate of change in world semiconductor shipments. The results in Table 4A.1 generally look similar to what we saw in Table 4.2, with both variables seemingly exerting considerable effect on the regressand.[35] As we noted previously, however, this result is not very informative since there exists a high empirical correlation between the yen/dollar rate and the world semiconductor shipments. It is telling, however, that in Malaysia, Singapore, and Taiwan, the specifications that include the electronics variables substantially outperform those with the yen/dollar variables. All specifications perform poorly for Indonesia, whose economy has experienced substantial setbacks after the Asian crisis.

In the next round of regressions, we consider specifications that include both the exchange-rate and the electronics variables. As the nominal yen/dollar exchange rate is highly correlated with the electronics cycle, this set of regressions adopts for $\Delta s_{i,t}$ the real exchange rate between the yen and each EA currency. In addition, we consider here an alternative proxy for the electronics cycle, as there is a possibility that our previous indicator may be influenced by the yen/dollar exchange rate (see Section 4.2). We create this alternative variable by taking the growth rate of the new orders for electronics goods in the United States, which constitutes by far the largest market for electronic products in the world.[36] In what follows, we write this value as $\Delta elc^*_{i,t}$, so as to distinguish it from the other indicator. Lastly, as the general demand variable $\Delta x_{i,t}$ seems to have only minor explanatory power in most countries, we now drop this term altogether.[37]

The result of our second-round estimation is shown in Tables 4A.2 and 4A.3. The impact of the world electronics cycle is again palpable in all countries but Indonesia, and this observation is generally robust to the choice of its proxy. In Tables 4A.2 and 4A.3, we also observe that the estimated impact of the electronics cycle is mostly limited to the contemporaneous period when the cycle is measured by world semiconductor sales, whereas its lagged effects appear slightly stronger when the cycle is proxied by the US electronics orders. This is just as expected, however, since the former is typically regarded as a *coincident* indicator of global electronics activity while the latter is used as its *leading* indicator (Ping et al. 2004). Our result therefore fits well with the hypothesis that cyclical fluctuations in global electronics markets constitute a major exogenous shock to the EA economies.

Table 4A.2 Seemingly unrelated regressions for EA business cycles (1992: S1–2004: S2)

Constant	Δs_{yfi}	$\Delta s_{yfi}(-1)$	Δelc	$|\Delta elc|^2$	$\Delta elc\,(-1)$	D.W.	$R^2\,(adj.)$
Hong Kong (period dummies for 1998S1, 1998S2 and 2003S1)							
0.044*** (0.006)			0.076*** (0.019)			1.758	0.660
0.043*** (0.009)			0.078*** (0.023)	0.005 (0.068)		1.791	0.645
0.044*** (0.006)			0.069*** (0.021)		0.014 (0.021)	1.695	0.649
0.046*** (0.006)	−0.117 (0.095)		0.060*** (0.023)			1.653	0.650
0.047*** (0.006)	−0.107 (0.095)	−0.052 (0.108)	0.053* (0.027)			1.643	0.623
0.045*** (0.009)	−0.123 (0.096)		0.060** (0.027)	−0.009 (0.070)		1.760	0.632
0.048*** (0.010)	−0.117 (0.096)	−0.045 (0.114)	0.050 (0.035)	−0.023 (0.073)		1.793	0.608
0.044*** (0.006)	−0.133 (0.093)	0.048 (0.114)	0.056** (0.027)		0.020 (0.023)	1.600	0.624
Indonesia (period dummies for 1998S1 and 1998S2)							
0.056*** (0.006)			0.022 (0.021)			2.399	0.847
0.060*** (0.009)			0.015 (0.024)	−0.041 (0.069)		2.441	0.841
0.054*** (0.006)			0.012 (0.023)		0.021 (0.023)	2.497	0.845
0.058*** (0.006)	−0.083 (0.061)		0.011 (0.022)			2.229	0.838
0.059*** (0.006)	−0.094 (0.066)	−0.010 (0.058)	0.009 (0.022)			2.229	0.827
0.061*** (0.009)	−0.078 (0.059)		0.006 (0.025)	−0.037 (0.069)		2.268	0.833
0.063*** (0.010)	−0.082 (0.065)	−0.013 (0.057)	0.003 (0.025)	−0.046 (0.070)		2.282	0.822
0.055*** (0.007)	−0.039 (0.064)	0.033 (0.057)	0.007 (0.024)		0.022 (0.025)	2.339	0.829

(*Continued*)

Table 4A.2   (Continued)

Constant	$\Delta s_{Y/i}$	$\Delta s_{Y/i}(-1)$	Δelc	$[\Delta elc]^2$	$\Delta elc(-1)$	D.W.	R^2 (adj.)
Korea (period dummy for 1998S1)							
0.055***			0.044**			1.478	0.768
(0.005)			(0.019)				
0.042***			0.066***	0.133**		1.338	0.799
(0.007)			(0.020)	(0.057)			
0.056***			0.049**		-0.012	1.493	0.761
(0.006)			(0.021)		(0.021)		
0.055***	-0.024		0.043**			1.447	0.757
(0.005)	(0.079)		(0.020)				
0.056***	-0.026	0.024	0.044**			1.451	0.748
(0.005)	(0.076)	-0.068	(0.020)				
0.041***	0.038		0.068***	0.139**		1.385	0.790
(0.008)	(0.066)		(0.020)	(0.058)			
0.040***	0.048	0.088	0.075***	0.151***		1.275	0.795
(0.007)	(0.062)	(0.054)	(0.020)	(0.057)			
0.056***	0.005	0.026	0.050**		-0.013	1.499	0.740
(0.005)	(0.076)	(0.068)	(0.022)		(0.021)		
Malaysia (period dummies for 1998S1 and 1998S2)							
0.060***			0.084***			1.439	0.810
(0.005)			(0.019)				
0.066***			0.075***	-0.061		1.522	0.810
(0.008)			(0.021)	(0.060)			
0.059***			0.079***		0.011	1.471	0.801
(0.005)			(0.021)		(0.020)		
0.060***	0.011		0.085***			1.435	0.801
(0.005)	(0.062)		(0.019)				
0.058***	0.013	0.122	0.098***			1.486	0.793
(0.006)	(0.062)	(0.078)	(0.021)				
0.066***	0.015		0.077***	-0.060		1.540	0.800
(0.008)	(0.059)		(0.021)	(0.060)			
0.061***	0.027	0.123	0.093***	-0.039		1.488	0.787
(0.009)	(0.059)	(0.078)	(0.024)	(0.063)			
0.055***	0.050	0.181**	0.099***		0.021	1.558	0.776
(0.006)	(0.059)	(0.077)	(0.022)		(0.020)		

Philippines (period dummies for 1992S1, 1998S1 and 1998S2)

0.040*** (0.004)				0.025* (0.013)	1.938	0.482
0.044*** (0.006)			−0.034 (0.045)	0.019 (0.015)	2.044	0.466
0.041*** (0.004)				0.028* (0.015)	1.897	0.461
0.040*** (0.004)	0.044 (0.044)	0.055 (0.049)		0.030** (0.014)	2.146	0.479
0.038*** (0.004)	0.060 (0.045)			0.038** (0.016)	2.187	0.484
0.043*** (0.006)	0.038 (0.044)		−0.035 (0.044)	0.024 (0.016)	2.233	0.462
0.041*** (0.006)	0.057 (0.045)	0.049 (0.049)	−0.028 (0.044)	0.033* (0.018)	2.275	0.460
0.038*** (0.004)	0.061 (0.046)	0.060 (0.054)		0.039 (0.016) −0.008 (0.015) / 0.000 (0.016)	2.204	0.455

Singapore (period dummy for 1998S1)

0.047*** (0.008)				0.151*** (0.029)	1.593	0.557
0.056*** (0.012)			−0.092 (0.091)	0.138*** (0.032)	1.583	0.555
0.046*** (0.008)				0.145*** (0.032) 0.015 (0.031)	1.631	0.540
0.045*** (0.008)	0.228* (0.129)	−0.060 (0.154)		0.168*** (0.030)	1.533	0.548
0.046*** (0.008)	0.228* (0.130)			0.158*** (0.034)	1.561	0.524
0.052*** (0.012)	0.243* (0.126)		−0.075 (0.090)	0.159*** (0.033)	1.549	0.537
0.055*** (0.012)	0.263** (0.127)	−0.109 (0.150)	−0.091 (0.091)	0.141*** (0.038)	1.628	0.510
0.046*** (0.008)	0.268** (0.130)	−0.047 (0.148)		0.163*** (0.037) −0.001 (0.032)	1.545	0.491

(Continued)

Table 4A.2 (Continued)

Constant	$\Delta s_{Y/i}$	$\Delta s_{Y/i}(-1)$	Δelc	$[\Delta elc]^2$	$\Delta elc(-1)$	D.W.	$R^2 (adj.)$
Taiwan (no period dummies)							
0.040*** (0.005)			0.087*** (0.017)			1.740	0.472
0.048*** (0.007)			0.074*** (0.018)	-0.090* (0.054)		2.139	0.502
0.041*** (0.005)			0.098*** (0.018)		-0.027 (0.018)	1.733	0.491
0.040*** (0.005)	0.005 (0.075)		0.087*** (0.018)			1.743	0.448
0.040*** (0.005)	-0.029 (0.074)	0.178** (0.083)	0.104*** (0.019)			1.791	0.461
0.048*** (0.005)	0.003 (0.070)		0.074*** (0.019)	-0.090* (0.054)		2.141	0.480
0.046*** (0.007)	-0.011 (0.068)	0.166** (0.078)	0.094*** (0.020)	-0.064 (0.054)		2.055	0.466
0.041*** (0.005)	0.029 (0.067)	0.167** (0.076)	0.117*** (0.020)		-0.026 (0.018)	1.755	0.470
Thailand (period dummies for 1997S1, 1997S2, 1998S1 and 1998S2)							
0.057*** (0.006)			0.052*** (0.019)			2.152	0.810
0.055*** (0.009)			0.055** (0.022)	0.014 (0.065)		2.134	0.800
0.057*** (0.009)			0.055*** (0.021)		-0.006 (0.021)	2.167	0.805
0.059*** (0.006)	-0.194** (0.078)		0.034* (0.019)			1.962	0.820
0.059*** (0.005)	-0.191** (0.079)	0.001 (0.076)	0.034 (0.021)			1.951	0.808
0.054*** (0.005)	-0.261*** (0.085)		0.032 (0.021)	0.030 (0.075)		1.751	0.731
0.055*** (0.010)	-0.260*** (0.086)	-0.019 (0.096)	0.029 (0.031)	0.023 (0.084)		1.689	0.711
0.057*** (0.011)	-0.248*** (0.086)	-0.023 (0.085)	0.021 (0.026)		0.006 (0.025)	1.789	0.719

Notes and Sources: See Table 4A.1. S_{ye} = real exchange between yen and the home currency.

148

Table 4.3 Seemingly unrelated regressions for EA business cycles (1992: S1–2004: S2)

Constant	Δs_{yfi}	$\Delta s_{yfi}(-1)$	Δelc^*	$[\Delta elc^*]^2$	$\Delta elc^*(-1)$	D.W.	$R^2(adj.)$
Hong Kong (period dummies for 1998S1, 1998S2 and 2003S1)							
0.047*** (0.005)			0.314*** (0.076)			1.930	0.677
0.052*** (0.008)			0.280*** (0.085)	−0.895 (0.979)		1.941	0.671
0.045*** (0.005)			0.195** (0.090)		0.187** (0.089)	1.710	0.704
0.047*** (0.005)	−0.133 (0.081)		0.265*** (0.079)			1.879	0.684
0.047*** (0.005)	−0.116 (0.085)	−0.023 (0.093)	0.260*** (0.087)			1.905	0.667
0.054*** (0.005)	−0.167** (0.081)		0.204** (0.089)	−1.206 (0.948)		1.925	0.685
0.054*** (0.008)	−0.165* (0.086)	−0.003 (0.091)	0.205** (0.095)	−1.174 (0.949)		1.930	0.668
0.045*** (0.005)	−0.177** (0.079)	0.040 (0.085)	0.129 (0.094)		0.214** (0.085)	1.769	0.708
Indonesia (period dummies for 1998S1 and 1998S2)							
0.056*** (0.006)			0.112 (0.082)			2.443	0.851
0.067*** (0.008)			0.029 (0.087)	−1.982** (0.994)		2.433	0.863
0.056*** (0.006)			0.145 (0.104)		−0.054 (0.103)	2.356	0.846
0.057*** (0.006)	−0.077 (0.060)		0.079 (0.086)			2.252	0.842
0.058*** (0.006)	−0.083 (0.066)	−0.007 (0.059)	0.076 (0.087)			2.246	0.833
0.066*** (0.008)	−0.031 (0.057)		0.026 (0.088)	−1.802* (1.028)		2.365	0.855
0.067*** (0.008)	−0.036 (0.063)	−0.010 (0.052)	0.022 (0.089)	−1.801* (1.031)		2.359	0.846
0.059*** (0.006)	−0.092 (0.067)	−0.032 (0.063)	0.173 (0.110)		−0.158 (0.125)	2.049	0.835

(Continued)

Table 4A.3 (Continued)

Constant	Δs_{Yit}	$\Delta s_{Yit}(-1)$	Δelc^*	$[\Delta elc^*]^2$	$\Delta elc^*(-1)$	D.W.	R^2 (adj.)
Korea (period dummy for 1998S1)							
0.056***			0.174**			1.335	0.767
(0.005)			(0.077)				
0.050***			0.218***	1.168		1.534	0.767
(0.007)			(0.084)	(0.957)			
0.057***			0.219**		−0.074	1.285	0.762
(0.005)			(0.096)		(0.096)		
0.057***	−0.021		0.168**			1.318	0.755
(0.005)	(0.082)		(0.080)				
0.057***	−0.039	0.022	0.165**			1.284	0.741
(0.005)	(0.078)	(0.066)	(0.080)				
0.048***	0.062		0.244***	1.402		1.660	0.760
(0.007)	(0.078)		(0.089)	(0.992)			
0.048***	0.043	0.051	0.244***	1.391		1.592	0.749
(0.007)	(0.075)	(0.060)	(0.089)	(0.988)			
0.057***	−0.024	−0.015	0.213*		−0.078	1.266	0.735
(0.005)	(0.077)	(0.067)	(0.098)		(0.098)		
Malaysia (period dummies for 1998S1 and 1998S2)							
0.062***			0.358***			2.160	0.825
(0.005)			(0.072)				
0.070***			0.296***	−1.508*		2.024	0.838
(0.007)			(0.075)	(0.861)			
0.061***			0.267***		0.142*	2.017	0.835
(0.007)			(0.086)		(0.086)		
0.062***	0.001		0.358***			2.160	0.817
(0.005)	(0.060)		(0.074)				
0.060***	−0.002	0.117	0.404***			2.098	0.807
(0.005)	(0.059)	(0.073)	(0.079)				
0.070***	−0.006		0.296***	−1.499*		2.024	0.830
(0.005)	(0.056)		(0.079)	(0.869)			
0.067***	−0.005	0.123*	0.354***	−1.263		1.904	0.813
(0.007)	(0.056)	(0.068)	(0.085)	(0.878)			
0.058***	0.008	0.132**	0.320***		0.148*	1.989	0.816
(0.005)	(0.054)	(0.065)	(0.089)		(0.085)		

Philippines (period dummies for 1992S1, 1998S1 and 1998S2)

(1)	(2)	(3)	(4)	(5)	(6)	(7)	(8)
0.041*** (0.004)	0.036 (0.042)		0.073 (0.055)			2.041	0.449
0.044*** (0.005)	0.039 (0.043)		0.056 (0.062)	−0.432 (0.706)		2.113	0.429
0.041*** (0.004)		0.029 (0.049)	0.058 (0.071)		0.023	1.992	0.422
0.041*** (0.004)	0.034 (0.042)		0.085 (0.057)		−0.069	2.218	0.427
0.041*** (0.004)		0.025 (0.049)	0.099 (0.061)			2.245	0.410
0.043*** (0.005)	0.038 (0.043)		0.068 (0.063)	−0.425 (0.701)		2.290	0.406
0.043*** (0.005)	0.034 (0.043)		0.080 (0.066)	−0.046 (0.694)		2.336	0.387
0.040*** (0.004)		0.035 (0.049)	0.079 (0.073)		0.032 (0.069)	2.167	0.382

Singapore (period dummy for 1998S1)

(1)	(2)	(3)	(4)	(5)	(6)	(7)	(8)
0.052*** (0.008)	0.136 (0.135)		0.562*** (0.122)			2.181	0.492
0.063*** (0.011)	0.168 (0.134)		0.483*** (0.130)	−2.060 (1.486)		2.076	0.507
0.050*** (0.008)		−0.135 (0.153)	0.436*** (0.147)		0.207 (0.147)	2.285	0.506
0.051*** (0.008)	0.103 (0.132)		0.590*** (0.125)			2.195	0.464
0.052*** (0.008)		−0.148 (0.145)	0.542*** (0.135)			2.278	0.455
0.061*** (0.011)	0.142 (0.130)		0.512*** (0.135)	−1.855 (1.507)		2.092	0.475
0.063*** (0.011)	0.197 (0.128)		0.456*** (0.145)	−1.947 (1.479)		2.203	0.469
0.050*** (0.008)		−0.132 (0.146)	0.423*** (0.159)		0.208 (0.145)	2.324	0.463

(Continued)

152

Table 4A.3 (Continued)

Constant	$\Delta s_{Y/I}$	$\Delta s_{Y/I}(-1)$	Δelc^*	$[\Delta elc^*]^P$	$\Delta elc^*(-1)$	D.W.	R^2 (adj.)
Taiwan (no period dummies)							
0.042*** (0.005)			0.347*** (0.071)			2.629	0.454
0.050*** (0.006)			0.288*** (0.075)	-1.531* (0.852)		2.596	0.494
0.041*** (0.005)			0.328*** (0.090)		0.031 (0.090)	2.585	0.433
0.041*** (0.005)	-0.031 (0.077)		0.342*** (0.072)			2.592	0.434
0.041*** (0.005)	-0.077 (0.075)	0.174** (0.085)	0.407*** (0.077)			2.529	0.442
0.050*** (0.006)	-0.045 (0.076)		0.277*** (0.076)	-1.627* (0.856)		2.537	0.482
0.049*** (0.006)	-0.083 (0.072)	0.173** (0.082)	0.352*** (0.083)	-1.390 (0.845)		2.388	0.472
0.041*** (0.005)	-0.057 (0.074)	0.180** (0.086)	0.407*** (0.096)		0.009 (0.087)	2.510	0.414
Thailand (period dummies for 1997S1, 1997S2, 1998S1 and 1998S2)							
0.059*** (0.005)			0.220*** (0.074)			2.237	0.821
0.057*** (0.007)			0.229*** (0.084)	0.166 (0.958)		2.240	0.813
0.059*** (0.005)			0.276*** (0.093)		-0.084 (0.092)	2.300	0.820
0.060*** (0.005)	-0.196** (0.077)		0.151** (0.075)			1.995	0.829
0.060*** (0.005)	-0.196** (0.078)	0.010 (0.076)	0.153* (0.079)			1.977	0.818
0.064*** (0.009)	-0.270*** (0.088)		0.047 (0.106)	-1.007 (1.162)		1.711	0.737
0.065*** (0.009)	-0.267*** (0.087)	-0.056 (0.084)	0.023 (0.109)	-1.094 (1.156)		1.619	0.719
0.060*** (0.006)	-0.264*** (0.084)	-0.094 (0.085)	0.139 (0.112)		-0.131 (0.114)	1.607	0.723

Notes and Sources: See Table 4A.1. elc* = US electronics new orders.

In regressions that include both the exchange rate and electronics variables, the coefficients of the former are either statistically insignificant or have the wrong sign in all countries but Thailand. In contrast, the electronics variables remain significant in most countries, and their values are largely insensitive to the inclusion of the exchange rate variables. In many countries, furthermore, the estimated coefficients of the electronics variables are very large; with the standard deviations of Δelc_t and Δelc_t^* being 0.26 and 0.06, Tables 4A.2 and 4A.3 suggest that a change in these variables by one standard deviation alters the contemporaneous real GDP of, for example, Malaysia and Taiwan by some 2.0–2.5 percent.

In Korea and Taiwan, two countries that should compete most directly with Japan in export markets, the coefficients of the contemporaneous exchange rate variable do have the expected sign, although their numerical values are not large and estimated imprecisely. The Kwan/McKinnon/Schnabl thesis therefore might have a grain of truth in these countries. Even in these countries, however, the lagged exchange rate variables are of the wrong sign, and any impact of exchange rate shocks is dwarfed by that of the electronics cycle.[38]

All in all, the exercise of this Appendix reinforces our hypothesis that cyclical fluctuations of global electronics activity exert a large and immediate impact on most EA economies. Although this does not necessarily mean that exchange rates are inconsequential for their business cycles, it seems likely that any effect of exchange rate-induced competitiveness shocks are washed off when world electronics markets are undergoing major cyclical fluctuations. Our estimation also suggests, however, that the quantitative impact of electronics shocks differs considerably across countries, highlighting the danger of discussing exchange rate policy coordination among these countries without recognizing the substantial heterogeneity of their economies.

Notes

1   The author wishes to thank two anonymous referees for their helpful comments on an earlier version of this chapter.
2   The weights are computed by the relative share of each country (region) in EA's collective trade.
3   While a single-equation OLS model like (4.1) is increasingly disfavored in time-series econometrics, a number of studies assess the impact of yen/dollar fluctuations on the EA economies by employing technically more sophisticated but conceptually similar methodologies. For example, Ito et al. (1998) regress the export volume of individual EA countries on the real GDP growth rates of the United States and Japan and on the real exchange rates of their currencies vis-à-vis the dollar and the yen. They argue that their regression produces "a reasonable result" in the sense that the yen's appreciation has a statistically significant negative effect on EA's export performance (Ito et al. 1998: 297). In Section 4.3, however, we show that their result is suspect; see also Kumakura (2005a).
4   To their credit, both Kwan (2001) and McKinnon and Schnabl (2003) refer to other channels through which changes in the yen/dollar exchange rate might affect the

EA economies, such as Japan's outward foreign direct investment and the price of goods imported from Japan. However, it is clear from the preceding statements that they consider such effects as comparatively minor.

5   This observation also raises the question of the causality between the yen/dollar exchange rate and the cycle of the world electronics market. As Japan exports a substantial amount of electronic goods (Figure 4.1), it is not surprising that a major downturn in the world electronics market put pressures on the value of the yen by reducing Japan's net exports. However, the fact that Japan is a leading exporter of semiconductors and consumer electronics also raises the possibility that a weak yen helps Japanese manufacturers undercut their foreign rivals and depress their prices on the international market. Although there may thus be an element of mutual dependence between the two variables, the preceding Kwan/McKinnon/Schnabl regression should be biased unless the electronics cycle is generated *entirely* by yen/dollar fluctuations. This is unlikely, however, since the cycle of the global electronics industry tends to reflect not just the demand–supply gap but also technical shocks and changes in leading end-user products in the market. While we performed the standard Granger and Sims tests using monthly series of the yen/dollar exchange rate and world semiconductor shipments, the result did not speak loudly about the presence of causality, suggesting that both series contain substantial idiosyncratic elements.

6   While it is possible to measure the growth rate in terms of sales volume, we judge this to be undesirable as changes in the sales price should also affect the profitability of producers. In Appendix 4A, we consider an alternative proxy for the electronics cycle to check the robustness of our estimation.

7   Whereas using the export price index is an option, export prices are not exogenous to exchange rates, particularly in countries whose exports are priced in foreign currencies. We used the wholesale price index (WPI) for domestically sold products and exported goods for countries where an appropriate PPI was unavailable.

8   See Chapter 6 of this volume for a detailed discussion on this point.

9   We use the lagged GDP to ensure that the weight is not influenced by contemporaneous exchange rate movements.

10   See Kumakura (2005a).

11   For our estimation period the coefficient of correlation for Δelc (t) and $\Delta e_{Y/\$}$ (t) is -0.421, whereas that for Δelc (t) and $\Delta s_{Y/EA}$ (t) is only -0.061.

12   The Philippines' business cycle bears little relation with the electronics cycle despite the fact that the share of electronics in its total exports is highest among the eight countries. This seems to be due in part to the fact that the bulk of its electronics exports is accounted for by foreign multinationals with an unusually high proportion of imported intermediate inputs, and partly to the fact that its economy has been exposed to a number of serious country-specific shocks during the 1980s and 1990s (ADB 2001; Rodlauer et al. 2000).

13   The large fall in semiconductor shipments during this period reflected a severe glut in world production capacity and an associated collapse of the price of 16 megabyte DRAM chips, as well as weakening demand from major importer countries (World Bank 2000).

14   Requisite data is gathered from Statistics Canada's World Trade database, which is based on the United Nation's COMTRADE database but also provides data for Taiwan. The most recent version of WTD provides data for up to 2001.

15   The pooled exports include trade among the EA economies; see also Figure 4.4.

16   The Korean won depreciated against the dollar by some 18 percent for two years before the regional currency crisis (see Section 4.4). In Korea, therefore, exchange

rate-induced competitiveness shocks during this period should have been comparatively moderate.

17 Until the 1990s, a large cyclical depreciation of the yen tended to accelerate Japanese manufacturers' transfers of their production plants to Southeast Asian countries, and the relocated plants started production and started contributing to the host countries' export performance after a year or two. In countries such as Thailand, therefore, changes in $s_{i,t}$ may reflect not only the contemporaneous competitiveness effect of yen/dollar fluctuations but also their lagged impact through FDI. Although this makes it less straightforward to interpret yearly fluctuations in $s_{i,t}$, the fact that its size was small in 1996 even in Korea – which had received little manufacturing FDI from Japan and should have competed most directly with Japan – suggests limited effects of the yen/dollar exchange rate on EA's pre-crisis export performance.

18 See Urata (2001).

19 Another limitation of DSSA is that this decomposition scheme does not distinguish the effects of changes in export price and quantity. As we noted previously, part of the pre-crisis decelerations in EA's export earnings were due to the collapse of the prices of its leading export goods, particularly semiconductors and other related electronics components.

20 All series are in terms of the monthly average. To facilitate visual inspection, we concealed the plots during the period of the Asian crisis and rescaled all series before (after) the crisis so that their June 1996 (January 1999) values equal 100. An upward movement indicates the EA currencies' depreciation.

21 Strictly speaking, there is evidence of some minor adjustment in the exchange rate policies of some of these countries toward the end of the pre-crisis period (Kumakura 2005b).

22 This observation raises the question of why most EA currencies became simultaneously stable vis-à-vis the dollar in mid-1995. While space does not permit us to have a full discussion of this issue (see Kumakura 2005a), as long as the region's monetary authorities monitor the relative value of their currencies, it is not surprising that one or two countries' switch to a strict dollar peg stabilizes the dollar value of other currencies. At least in the Philippines, there was a clear policy change in this period (Rodlauer et al. 2000; de Dios and Hutchcroft 2003).

23 Examples include Kawai and Takagi (2000), McKinnon (2001), and Fukuda (2002).

24 See Rogoff et al. (2004) and Chapter 1 of this volume.

25 This hypothetical currency regime is in fact not very dissimilar to the official policies of many EA countries. Prior to the crisis, most regional monetary authorities made high-frequency smoothing an integral part of their exchange rate management while monitoring the medium-term movement of the effective – not dollar – value of their currencies (Kumakura 2005a). Even today, many countries officially maintain measures for moderating short-run exchange rate volatility, while some other countries conduct such operations on a more discretionary basis (see, for example, Park et al. 2001).

26 While estimating Equation (4.4) with data of different frequencies and comparing their results can help us make inferences about differences in the monetary authorities' short- and longer-term policy objectives, such an exercise in fact gives rise to its own problems (Kumakura 2005b).

27 As noted in Section 4.1, some authors recommend a basket with a large weight of the yen, on the grounds that the EA countries' trade balance is much more sensitive to the yen value of their currencies than to their exchange rates with the dollar

and the euro. Ito et al. (1998), for example, estimate the weight of the yen that minimizes the volatility of some countries' exports to be well over 0.5. Their estimation, however, does not recognize the effect of the world electronics cycle and other real shocks and cannot be taken at face value.

28 For the coefficients for Equation (4.9), we included China only after 1994 due to problems associated with the country's dual exchange rate system in the preceding years.

29 In Figure 4.6, sharp upward spikes in $\Delta e_i^*(t)$ and $\Delta \hat{e}_i(t)$ tend to reflect the yen's depreciation against the dollar, as Japan is EA's important trading partner. However, we saw in Section 4.2 that the yen had the tendency of weakening against the dollar in times of a downturn in the world electronics market. This implies that, even if the EA monetary authorities merely let the home currency slide when export demand was weak, the bilateral dollar exchange rate should have behaved in a manner that stabilized the home currency's effective value.

30 According to its official explanation, the Monetary Authority of Singapore (MAS) had since 1981 maintained the policy of targeting the home currency to an undisclosed basket of foreign currencies. The target exchange rate has been adjusted continuously toward the Singaporean dollar's appreciation so as to accommodate MAS's preference for low inflation rates, which explains why the actual path of the Singapore/US dollar exchange rate in Figure 4.6 stayed below those of $\Delta e_i^*(t)$ and $\Delta \hat{e}_i(t)$ during most of the pre-crisis period. Nevertheless, MAS also states that its target exchange rate is reviewed regularly and adjusted when doing so is judged to be desirable. In recent years, such adjustments have taken place in the wake of the Asian crisis and in 2002 when the Singaporean economy was hit hard by a global electronics recession (Jin 2000; MAS 2003).

31 Using weekly data, McKinnon and Schnabl (2004) estimate that the yen's weight in the New Taiwan dollar's basket was 0.03 in both pre- and post-crisis years.

32 Malaysia officially abandoned its dollar peg in July 2005.

33 Potential endogeneity of individual countries' business cycles can be addressed more fully by a full-blown VAR model, although we then have to deal with the "curse of dimensionality" inherent in this framework (see Chapter 5 of this volume). The primary purpose of Appendix 4A is to provide further evidence in support of our previous argument without completely discarding the framework of Kwan (2001) and McKinnon and Schnabl (2003).

34 With the exception of nominal exchange rates, all data used in this Appendix was first compiled at the quarterly frequency and seasonally adjusted before being converted to the semiannual frequency. In Indonesia and Thailand, quarterly GDP data became available only in 1993. For these countries, the real GDP growth rates for 1992: S1–1993: S1 were interpolated from annual data. When measured at the quarterly frequency, all variables used in Appendix 4A pass the standard ADF stationarity test with flying colors.

35 Although the reported specifications include lagged explanatory variables of one period only, we experimented with lags of up to three semesters for all explanatory variables. Most lagged values of more than one semester were insignificant, however.

36 The US electronics new orders are computed as the sum of those for electronic computers, nondefense communication equipment, and other electronic components in NAICS-based industrial statistics compiled by the US Census Bureau and do not include semiconductors.

37 As the electronic industry is important not only for EA countries but also increasingly for the United States, the time series of $\Delta x_{i,t}$ and Δelc_t are correlated fairly

strongly in such countries as Hong Kong and Taiwan, whose export sectors depend heavily on the US market. In these countries, the relatively large estimates of the coefficient of $\Delta x_{i,t}$ in Table 4A.1 may represent the effect of the electronic cycle.

38 In Korea, for example, the standard deviation of the real yen/won exchange rate during our sample period is about 0.06; and a one standard deviation change in its value alters the country's GDP by no more than 0.2 percent.

References

Asian Development Bank, 2001, *Asian Recovery Report*, March.

Asian Development Bank, 2003, *Asian Economic Monitor*, December.

Clark, P. B., N. Tamirisa and S.-J. Wei, 2004, "A New Look at Exchange Rate Volatility and Trade Flows," IMF Occasional Paper No. 235.

de Dios, E. S. and P. D. Hutchcroft, 2003, "Political Economy," in A. M. Balisacan and H. Hill (eds), *The Philippine Economy: Development, Politics, and Challenges*, New York: Oxford University Press.

Doraisami, A., 2004, "Trade Causes of the Asian Crisis: the Malaysian Experience," *The World Economy*, 27: 715–25.

Frankel, J. and S. J. Wei, 1994, "Yen Bloc or Dollar Block? Exchange Rate Policies of the East Asian Countries," in T. Ito and A. Kruger (eds), *Macroeconomic Linkages: Savings, Exchange Rates, and Capital Flows*, Chicago: University of Chicago Press.

Fukuda, S., 2002, "Post-crisis Exchange Rate Regimes in Asia," University of Tokyo Center for International Research on the Japanese Economy Discussion Paper No. 2002-CF-181.

Ito, T., E. Ogawa, and Y. N. Sasaki, 1998, "How did the Dollar Peg Fail in East Asia?" *Journal of the Japanese and International Economies*, 12: 256–304.

Jin, N. K., 2000, "Coping with the Asian Financial Crisis: the Singaporean Experience," ISEAS Visiting Researchers Series No. 8, National University of Singapore.

Kawai, M. and S. Akiyama, 2000, "Implications of the Currency Crisis for Exchange Rate Arrangements in Emerging East Asia," World Bank Policy Research Paper No. 2502.

Kawai, M. and S. Takagi, 2000, "Proposed Strategy for a Regional Exchange Rate Arrangement in Post-crisis East Asia," World Bank Policy Research Working Paper No. 2503.

Kumakura, M., 2005a, "Is the Yen/Dollar Exchange Rate Really Responsible for East Asia's Export and Business Cycles? A Commentary on McKinnon and Schnabl (2003)," *The World Economy*, 28: 1509–37.

Kumakura, M., 2005b, "Exchange Rate Regimes in Asia: Dispelling the Myth of Soft Dollar Pegs," *Journal of the Asia Pacific Economy*, 10: 70–95.

Kwan, C. H., 2001, *Yen Bloc: Toward Economic Integration in Asia*, Washington, DC: Brookings Institution.

McKinnon, R., 2001, "After the Crisis, the East Asian Dollar Standard Resurrected," in J. Stiglitz and Y. Y. Shahid (eds), *Rethinking the East Asian Miracle*, New York: Oxford University Press, pp. 197–246.

McKinnon, R., 2005, *Exchange Rates under the East Asian Dollar Standard*, Cambridge, Mass.: MIT Press.

McKinnon, R. and G. Schnabl, 2003, "Synchronized Business Cycles in East Asia and Fluctuations in the Yen/Dollar Exchange Rate," *The World Economy*, 26: 1067–88.

McKinnon, R. and G. Schnabl, 2004, "The East Asian Dollar Standard, Fear of Floating, and Original Sin," *Review of Development Economics*, 8: 331–60.

MAS (Monetary Authority of Singapore), *Macroeconomic Review* (various issues).

Ogawa, E., 2002, "Should East Asian Countries Return to a Dollar Peg Again?" in P. Drysdale and K. Ishigaki (eds), *East Asian Trade and Financial Integration: New Issues*, Canberra: Asia Pacific Press, pp. 159–96.

Ogawa, E. and T. Ito, 2003, "On the Desirability of a Regional Basket Currency Arrangement," *Journal of the Japanese and International Economies*, 16: 317–34.

Park, Y. C., C. S. Chung, and Y. J. Wang, 2001, "Fear of Floating: Korea's Exchange Rate Policy after the Crisis," *Journal of the Japanese and International Economies*, 15: 225–51.

Parsley, D. and S.-J. Wei, 2002, "Currency Arrangements and Goods Market Integration: a Price Based Approach." (Downloadable at: http://mba.vanderbilt.edu/faculty/dparsley.cfm.)

Ping, N. Y., T. S. Ping, and E. Robinson, 2004, "Using Leading Indicators to Forecast the Singapore Electronics Industry," Monetary Authority of Singapore Staff Paper No. 30.

Rodlauer, M., P. Loungani, V. Arora, C. Christofides, E. G. de la Piedra, P. Kongsamut, K. Kostial, V. Summers, and A. Vamvakidis, 2000, "Philippines: toward Sustainable and Rapid Growth: Recent Developments and the Agenda Ahead," IMF Occasional Paper No. 187.

Rogoff, K., A. Husain, A. Mody, R. Brooks, and N. Oomes, 2004, "Evolution and Performance of Exchange Rate Regimes," IMF Occasional Paper No. 229.

Urata, S., 2001, "Emergence of an FDI-trade Nexus and Economic Growth in East Asia," in J. Stiglitz and Y. Y. Shahid (eds), *Rethinking the East Asian Miracle*, New York: Oxford University Press, pp. 409–59.

Williamson, J., 2000, *Exchange Rate Regimes for Emerging Markets: Reviving the Intermediate Option*, Washington, DC: Institute for International Economics.

World Bank, 2000, *East Asia: Recovery and Beyond*, Washington, DC: World Bank.

Yam. J., 2003, "The Link: 20 Years on." Speech at the Open University of Hong Kong (available at: http://www.info.gov.hk/hkma/eng/speeches/index.htm).

5
East Asian Monetary Integration: an Empirical Assessment of the Optimum Currency Area Criteria

Kiyotaka Sato

5.1 Introduction

East Asian economies have exhibited high economic growth over the last several decades, while economic interdependence among them has grown substantially through trade and investment. The recent surge in free trade agreements (FTAs) in the East Asian region is further evidence of growing economic linkage. A natural question is, therefore, whether monetary arrangement is feasible in the East Asian region on the basis of this deepening interdependence. Whereas it is generally reckoned that most East Asian economies adopted the de facto US dollar pegged exchange rate system, the Asian currency crisis in 1997/98 focused renewed attention on regional exchange rate arrangements. It is currently a matter of much interest which exchange rate arrangement is most suitable for East Asian economies – independent floating, a basket pegged exchange rate, or a common currency.[1] Before answering this question, we first need to explore whether East Asian economies meet the necessary preconditions for adopting a fixed exchange rate regime.

The theory of an optimum currency area (OCA) provides us with useful criteria to evaluate whether a fixed exchange rate or a common currency is feasible for the economies in question. Among the OCA criteria, the literature typically places particular emphasis on business cycle synchronization and/or symmetry in structural shocks between the economies concerned as major preconditions for forming a currency area. A large number of studies have applied the above OCA criterion to the European region,[2] and there is recently a growing literature focusing on the East Asian region.[3]

More specifically, these studies employ the structural vector autoregression (VAR) technique to identify fundamental shocks and then conduct a correlation analysis of shocks to assess which economies can form a currency area. Due to the problem in data availability for East Asian economies, however, most studies use annual data on output and prices with a relatively shorter sample period for the structural VAR analysis, which precludes us from taking into account possible changes in shock symmetry over time. In contrast, although using a conventional two-variable VAR model, we use the quarterly series of real outputs and prices over a longer sample period of 1975Q1–2003Q4. By dividing the whole sample into subsamples and then identifying the shocks for each subperiod, we examine whether the symmetry in shocks has changed over the last three decades.

In addition, we attempt to investigate the costs involved in forming a currency area. If countries start to fix their currency values relative to each other or adopt a common currency, they typically abandon national autonomy in monetary policy and instead follow common stabilization policies within the currency area. Accordingly, the costs of forming a currency area either with fixed exchange rates or a common currency will be quite large if each economy encounters idiosyncratic shocks. By employing the output loss function analysis proposed by Ghosh and Wolf (1994), we compare the costs of renouncing autonomous monetary policy between several groups of economies that are suggested as possible candidates for forming a currency area using our analysis of shock correlation.

The remainder of this chapter is organized as follows. Section 5.2 reviews the theory of OCA. Section 5.3 makes a preliminary analysis of whether East Asian economies meet the OCA criteria. Section 5.4 discusses the analytical model and presents the results of empirical research. Finally, Section 5.5 concludes the chapter.

5.2   The theory of the optimum currency area

An optimum currency area (OCA) can be defined as "the 'optimum' geographical domain having as a general means of payments either a single common currency or several currencies whose exchange values are immutably pegged to one another with unlimited convertibility for both current and capital transactions" (Kawai 1987: 740). A key assumption of OCA theory is that of downward rigidity in nominal prices and wages. If a country suffers from price and wage rigidities, it would be more beneficial to adopt flexible exchange rates, because any policy implemented to correct a current account imbalance would lead to unemployment or inflation under fixed exchange rates. However, if a country is highly integrated with the outside world in trade and financial transactions, factor mobility, etc., fixed exchange rates may reconcile internal and external balances more efficiently than flexible exchange rates.

To form a currency area, which conditions does the OCA theory suggest countries meet? Existing studies commonly propose the following as the qualifying OCA criteria:[4]

- Openness and goods market integration
- Factor market integration
- Business cycle synchronization and symmetry in shocks

- Financial market integration
- Policy coordination

5.2.1 Openness and goods market integration

A currency area must exhibit highly developed regional adjustment mechanisms. A large volume of intraregional trading, so-called "internal openness", is one of the keys to such mechanisms (McKinnon 1963). Internal openness is typically measured as the ratio of exports (or exports plus imports) to GDP. For a small economy with a high degree of openness, for example, tradable goods will account for a large share of the goods produced and consumed domestically. Exchange rate fluctuations will induce corresponding changes in the pricing of tradable goods in the country concerned, which will likely lead to changes in nominal wages and nontradable goods prices and, hence, to an unstable general price level. However, if the trade of the country in question has a high dependence on another specified country, it may be desirable for the former to peg its currency to the latter country's currency so that the former can mitigate the degree of instability in its domestic price level. The domestic price level of the former country will be more stable if the latter keeps its general price level stable.

The ratio of exports (plus imports) to GDP is often used as a measure of economic openness in the OCA literature. Recently, however, Kumakura (2004) has reconsidered the conventional openness indices and proposed alternative measures of openness to evaluate the regional adjustment mechanism more appropriately. Shin and Wang (2004) make a distinction between inter-industry trade and intra-industry trade, and find that the latter is the more important determinant of regional trade integration and, hence, regional business cycle synchronization.

5.2.2 Factor market integration

Mundell (1961) argues that the factors of production need to be fully mobile inside a currency area. If markets for factors of production are well integrated between the countries concerned, it is possible to adjust smoothly to shocks originating from a member country because labor and capital can be moved flexibly within the area. In this case, there is no need for exchange rate variation between the member countries and, hence, it is desirable for the countries to form a currency area. There have been only a few empirical studies that focus on such factor market integration (see De Grauwe and Vanhaverbeke 1993), and further empirical investigation of this criterion will be necessary.

5.2.3 Business cycle synchronization and symmetry in shocks

If business cycles between the member countries in the area are synchronized or if they exhibit symmetric disturbances, their governments or monetary authorities can use common macroeconomic policy to accommodate disturbances that cause unemployment or inflation. In addition, if the member countries have similar economic structures, disturbances are transmitted to the countries in a similar way and, hence, adjustments to disturbances can be made without exchange rate adjustment. As long as these conditions are met, therefore, the countries can adopt fixed exchange rates or a common currency rather than floating exchange rates.

There have so far been a large number of empirical studies on this issue. Bayoumi and Eichengreen (1993, 1994) go beyond a correlation analysis of observable macroeconomic variables[5] and first attempt to apply the structural VAR technique to an analysis of OCA in order to identify fundamental shocks. Currently, many studies employ the structural VAR approach to analyze an OCA in the East Asian region. While Bayoumi and Eichengreen estimate a two-variable VAR, recent studies, such as Chow and Kim (2003), Sato et al. (2003), and Zhang et al. (2004) employ three- and/or five-variable VAR for more rigorous examination of shock correlation among the East Asian economies. Although using a conventional two-variable VAR in this chapter, we attempt to identify fundamental shocks for three different subperiods and to check whether the correlation in shocks has changed over time.[6]

5.2.4   Financial market integration

If a currency area is tightly integrated through financial transactions, it will be easier to finance regional payments imbalances and, hence, to facilitate the smooth functioning of the adjustment process within the area. When, for example, an intra-area payments deficit is caused by transitory and reversible disturbances, sufficiently large financial flows within the area will be available to finance the payments deficit and reduce the need for real adjustment. There will consequently be less need for variation in the intra-area exchange rate. When an intra-area payments deficit is caused by permanent disturbances, financial flows alone cannot provide a permanent solution and real adjustment will be necessary. Even in this case, financial integration will lessen the cost of real adjustment and will help to enhance the real adjustment process. Accordingly, changes in the intra-area exchange rate will become less important or even unnecessary in the face of intra-area payments imbalance as financial integration deepens substantially.

The degree of financial integration is typically analyzed by applying interest rate parity checks. Owing to the problem in data availability, however, covered interest rate parity cannot be tested for all East Asian economies. Uncovered interest rate parity is generally rejected in the literature, even for developed countries.[7] Recent studies have tested the real interest rate parity condition to analyze whether the real interest rates of East Asian economies are linked with US and/or Japanese rates. Glick and Hutchison (1990), for example, analyzed real interest rate equalization between six Pacific Basin economies and the United States, and found strong real interest rate linkages between them. Chinn and Frankel (1995) and Phylaktis (1997) applied the cointegration technique and the error-correction model to the real interest rate parity test in the Pacific Basin region and found growing linkages between the Pacific Basin economies and Japan. Whereas these studies show that East Asian economies have increased their linkages with Japan, it is still unclear whether Japan's financial influence exceeds that of the US in the East Asian region.[8]

5.2.5 Policy coordination

Finally, policy coordination is important in determining the feasibility of a currency area. For example, in the absence of monetary policy coordination, fixed exchange rates or a common currency are not sustainable. In particular, it is political coordination that allows member countries to renounce monetary policy autonomy. Fiscal policy coordination is another key condition for forming a currency area. Moreover, if a fiscal transfer mechanism is established between the countries, the currency area will be further strengthened.

5.3 Preliminary analysis of the OCA criteria

Based on the theoretical consideration of OCA, this section investigates whether East Asian economies meet the OCA criteria. Among the criteria, we pay particular attention to macroeconomic linkages, i.e. trade integration, business cycle synchronization and financial integration, between East Asian economies. We also consider the linkages between East Asian economies and the Unites States as well as Japan. While factor market integration and policy coordination are undoubtedly important conditions for forming a currency area, they are beyond the scope of this section.

Before moving on to an analysis of the OCA criteria, let us briefly investigate the recent exchange rate movements of East Asian economies. Table 5.1

Table 5.1 The volatility of nominal exchange rates vis-à-vis the US dollar

	1990M1– 92M12	1993M1– 95M12	1996M1– 98M12	1999M1– 01M12	2002M1– 04M8
Japanese yen	0.0680	0.0639	0.0743	0.0498	0.0546
Korean won	0.0476	0.0250	0.4197	0.1039	0.0737
NT dollar	0.0352	0.0200	0.1083	0.0504	0.0227
HK dollar	0.0033	0.0009	0.0008	0.0025	0.0018
Singapore dollar	0.0469	0.0469	0.0656	0.0258	0.0224
Malaysian ringgit	0.0351	0.0266	0.2494	0.0000	0.0000
Indonesian rupiah	0.0449	0.0396	2.0870	0.7139	0.2855
Thai baht	0.0095	0.0095	0.3165	0.1236	0.0593
Philippine peso	0.0805	0.0539	0.3050	0.2412	0.0882
Chinese yuan	0.0705	0.2770	0.0035	0.0002	0.0000

Notes: Monthly and period average series of bilateral exchange rates are used. Standard deviations of the exchange rate series are used as a measure of volatility.
Source: IMF, *International Financial Statistics*, online version, and author's calculation.

shows the volatility of bilateral nominal exchange rates vis-à-vis the US dollar for each subperiod. It is often pointed out that most East Asian economies adopted de facto US dollar pegs until the currency crisis in 1997/98. Indeed, Hong Kong and Thailand's exchange rates against the dollar exhibited very low volatility during the first two subperiods, while that of Japan showed high volatility. However, the Philippines experienced much higher volatility than Japan for the first two subperiods and even other economies such as Korea and Indonesia display a high degree of volatility when compared to Hong Kong and Thailand.[9] Subsequently, the crisis-hit economies, i.e. Korea, Malaysia, Indonesia, Thailand, and the Philippines, showed a substantial increase in the volatility of nominal exchange rates during 1996–98. Although the extent of exchange rate volatility for the above economies declined from 1999, Korea, Indonesia, Thailand, and the Philippines still remained more volatile than Japan for the last two subperiods. Overall, whereas the crisis-hit economies saw a considerable decline in exchange rate volatility vis-à-vis the US dollar and US financial influence has likely been recovering in recent years, it is still unclear whether they have returned to the pre-crisis exchange rate policy.[10]

5.3.1   Trade integration

Let us now turn to an analysis of macroeconomic linkages among East Asian economies. The following openness indices are widely used in the literature:

$$X = \frac{EX}{GDP} \tag{5.1}$$

or

$$Z = \frac{(EX + IM)}{GDP} \tag{5.2}$$

where *EX* and *IM* denote total exports and imports of the country concerned, respectively, and nominal GDP is used in the denominator of both Equations (5.1) and (5.2).[11] Table 5.2 indicates that East Asian economies are generally very open, especially Singapore, Malaysia, Taiwan, and Hong Kong, in terms of both openness indices, *X* and *Z*. The openness index for Japan and the United States is far lower than that of East Asian economies, pointing to the relatively closed nature of the two countries. Moreover, East Asian economies are more open than other developed (mainly European) countries. It is thereby confirmed that East Asian economies are quite open in terms of the conventional openness index.

Tables 5.3 and 5.4 show export destinations and import sources for Japan and the East Asian economies. Although the United States was the most important destination for East Asian exports in the 1980s, the level of exports bound for the East Asian region itself increased, starting in the late 1980s. As of 2002, 31–50 percent of East Asian exports are accounted for by

Table 5.2 Openness indices: eight East Asian economies and developed countries

	X	Rank	Z	Rank
(a) Eight East Asian economies, Japan and the US				
Singapore	0.953	1	2.281	2
Malaysia	0.763	2	1.477	3
Taiwan	0.439	3	0.755	4
Hong Kong	0.369	4	2.599	1
China	0.311	5	0.499	6
Philippines	0.231	6	0.514	5
Korea	0.214	7	0.426	7
Indonesia	0.144	8	0.315	8
Japan	0.087	9	0.132	10
United States	0.072	10	0.163	9
(b) Other developed countries				
Ireland	0.555	1	0.964	1
Netherlands	0.336	2	0.658	2
Sweden	0.282	3	0.502	3
Finland	0.279	4	0.470	5
Canada	0.252	5	0.495	4
Austria	0.210	6	0.467	6
Denmark	0.206	7	0.406	8
Portugal	0.182	8	0.443	7
United Kingdom	0.171	9	0.379	9
Italy	0.167	10	0.306	10

Note: See text for the definition of each openness index (X and Z).
Source: Adapted from Kumakura (2004, Table 1).

intraregional trade (Table 5.3). The scale of intraregional imports also increased from the 1980s. On the import side, Japan is a more important source for East Asia than the United States. If we include Japan in the East Asian region, the share of intraregional trade becomes far larger. Overall, we note that East Asian intraregional trade has shown clear growth from the 1980s to the present.

5.3.2 Business cycle synchronization: comovements of output and prices

An analysis of the correlation between GDP growth rates and inflation rates is often conducted in the literature. Table 5.5 shows the correlation in real GDP growth rates for three subperiods. Interestingly, there is no evidence of high correlation in real GDP growth rates among the East Asian economies in 1975Q1–1984Q4 and 1985Q1–1994Q4. Correlations are even negative between Asian NIEs and ASEAN in 1985Q1–1994Q4. While some East Asian economies show positive and significant correlation with the United States and Japan for 1975Q1–1984Q4, such correlation deteriorated over the period 1985Q1–1994Q4. However, correlation in real GDP growth rates increased

Table 5.3   Exports of Japan and the East Asian economies (% share)

Exporters	Year	Importers							
		Japan	East Asia	NIEs4	ASEAN4	China	USA	Europe	Others
Japan	1985	–	24.1	12.8	4.2	7.1	37.6	14.2	24.2
	1995	–	42.1	25.0	12.1	5.0	27.5	16.7	13.7
	2002	–	41.5	22.7	9.3	9.6	28.9	15.3	14.3
Korea	1985	15.0	10.8	7.4	3.4	0.0	35.6	13.8	24.7
	1995	13.6	32.2	17.0	7.9	7.3	19.5	13.8	20.9
	2002	9.4	34.6	12.9	7.2	14.5	20.4	13.9	21.7
Taiwan	1985	11.3	15.1	12.0	3.1	0.0	48.1	9.7	15.9
	1995	11.8	38.5	29.6	8.5	0.3	23.7	13.5	12.6
	2002	9.2	44.3	29.9	6.8	7.6	20.5	12.8	13.2
Hong Kong	1985	4.2	36.6	7.0	3.6	26.0	30.8	14.9	13.5
	1995	6.1	44.0	7.1	3.6	33.3	21.8	15.8	12.3
	2002	5.4	49.2	6.4	3.7	39.1	21.2	14.1	10.2
Singapore	1985	9.1	33.8	9.0	23.4	1.4	20.4	11.1	25.6
	1995	7.6	45.4	15.1	28.0	2.3	17.9	13.6	15.5
	2002	6.9	49.8	17.7	26.8	5.3	14.2	13.1	15.9
Malaysia	1985	23.8	36.5	29.1	6.3	1.1	13.0	15.0	11.8
	1995	12.7	40.4	31.6	6.2	2.7	20.7	14.4	11.8
	2002	11.1	42.8	29.6	7.7	5.5	20.9	12.5	12.7
Indonesia	1985	46.2	18.4	16.1	1.9	0.5	21.7	6.4	7.2
	1995	27.1	31.1	22.3	5.0	3.8	13.9	15.1	12.8
	2002	21.1	34.5	22.3	7.1	5.1	13.2	14.0	17.2
Thailand	1985	13.4	25.6	15.4	6.3	3.8	19.7	20.9	20.5
	1995	16.8	30.9	23.0	4.9	2.9	17.9	16.1	18.4
	2002	14.5	31.9	18.3	8.4	5.2	19.6	15.6	4.9
Philippines	1985	18.9	20.6	12.9	6.1	1.6	35.9	16.9	7.6
	1995	15.7	24.6	16.2	7.1	1.2	35.8	17.8	6.1
	2002	14.9	36.1	24.0	8.3	3.7	25.4	18.2	5.3
China	1985	22.3	36.4	33.7	2.7	–	8.5	9.3	23.4
	1995	19.1	36.8	33.1	3.7	–	16.6	13.3	14.1
	2002	14.8	31.1	27.0	4.1	–	21.5	15.1	17.4

Source: International Centre for the Study of East Asian Development, *East Asian Economic Perspectives: Recent Trends and Prospects for Major Asian Economies*, Vol. 15, Special Issue, 2004, Tables 2.4, 3.4, 4.4, 5.4, 6.4, 7.4, 8.4, 9.4, 10.4, 11.4.

substantially among the East Asian economies in 1995Q1–2003Q4. A possible reason is that several economies suffered from a severe economic downturn during the currency crisis in 1997/98, which induced a high level of measured correlation among the economies. Accordingly, it is unclear whether real output growth is becoming more correlated among the economies after controlling for the effects of the currency crisis.

Table 5.6 shows the correlation in consumer price index (CPI) inflation rates. In 1975Q1–1984Q4 and 1985Q1–1994Q4 we can observe high and significant correlation in CPI inflation rates between several East Asian economies, the

Table 5.4   Imports of Japan and the East Asian economies (% share)

Importers	Year	Exporters							
		Japan	East Asia	NIEs4	ASEAN4	China	USA	Europe	Others
Japan	1985	–	25.5	7.6	12.9	5.0	20.0	9.5	45.0
	1995	–	34.4	12.3	11.4	10.7	22.6	16.1	26.9
	2002	–	41.4	10.5	12.6	18.3	17.4	14.3	26.9
Korea	1985	24.3	10.6	3.5	7.1	0.0	20.8	12.7	31.6
	1995	24.1	15.1	4.1	5.5	5.5	22.5	14.7	23.6
	2002	19.6	26.1	6.5	8.1	11.4	15.1	12.3	26.9
Taiwan	1985	27.6	9.6	3.9	5.7	0.0	23.6	12.2	27.0
	1995	29.2	18.8	8.8	7.0	3.0	20.1	15.8	16.1
	2002	24.2	29.8	11.5	11.2	7.1	16.1	11.6	18.4
Hong Kong	1985	23.0	45.7	17.5	2.8	25.5	9.1	13.9	8.2
	1995	14.6	59.0	18.9	4.6	35.6	7.9	12.1	6.4
	2002	11.3	67.1	16.5	6.3	44.2	5.7	10.0	5.9
Singapore	1985	16.1	36.5	6.4	21.9	8.1	14.3	12.5	20.6
	1995	20.5	38.4	11.4	23.8	3.2	14.6	14.4	12.1
	2002	12.0	45.8	10.2	28.3	7.3	13.5	13.2	15.5
Malaysia	1985	23.0	31.0	22.4	6.5	2.0	15.2	17.3	13.5
	1995	27.5	31.0	23.9	4.8	2.2	16.3	17.4	7.8
	2002	17.9	43.7	25.7	10.4	7.5	16.7	12.4	9.4
Indonesia	1985	25.8	17.1	13.5	1.2	2.4	16.8	19.8	20.5
	1995	21.1	22.9	15.9	3.6	3.4	10.9	19.9	18.3
	2002	11.2	29.9	17.8	5.9	6.2	6.7	10.4	21.2
Thailand	1985	26.5	23.4	13.8	7.2	2.4	11.4	17.9	20.8
	1995	30.5	24.6	15.3	6.3	3.0	12.0	17.7	15.2
	2002	23.0	31.6	14.3	9.7	7.6	9.6	12.0	3.3
Philippines	1985	14.4	30.6	13.7	11.5	5.4	25.3	10.1	19.7
	1995	22.1	29.2	21.0	5.9	2.3	18.9	11.3	18.4
	2002	20.2	36.1	24.1	8.7	3.3	21.2	8.3	14.3
China	1985	35.7	13.9	11.8	2.1	–	12.2	16.7	21.5
	1995	22.0	32.6	28.1	4.5	–	12.2	17.0	16.2
	2002	18.2	36.0	28.4	7.5	–	9.2	14.2	22.4

Source: See Table 5.3.

United States, and Japan. However, the East Asian economies' correlation with Japan and the United States fell during 1995Q1–2003Q4. In addition, CPI inflation became less correlated even between the East Asian economies during that period, although some economies showed a trend to higher correlation with China.

In summary, real output growth appears to improve substantially among East Asian economies and Japan from the mid-1990s, but such improvement was at least partly affected by the currency crisis and a further investigation is necessary. In contrast, CPI inflation became less correlated between the East Asian economies, the United States, and Japan from the mid-1990s. In the next section, we employ structural VAR techniques to make more rigorous examination of real output comovements and shock symmetry.

Table 5.5 Correlation of real GDP growth rates

	USA	JP	KR	TW	HK	SI	ML	ID	TH	PH	CH
Panel A: 1975Q1–1984Q4											
USA	1.00										
Japan	0.15	1.00									
Korea	0.24	−0.14	1.00								
Taiwan	**0.33**	**0.34**	0.09	1.00							
Hong Kong	0.03	−0.19	0.28	0.10	1.00						
Singapore	0.06	0.12	−0.15	0.22	0.06	1.00					
Malaysia	**0.45**	0.23	0.10	0.20	−0.16	0.17	1.00				
Indonesia	0.18	0.26	−0.21	0.31	0.17	0.23	0.23	1.00			
Thailand	0.10	0.26	−0.12	0.29	0.04	0.13	0.00	0.24	1.00		
Philippines	−0.08	0.15	0.00	0.11	0.19	−0.06	0.12	0.21	0.20	1.00	
China	−0.02	−0.16	−0.22	0.10	−0.15	−0.15	−0.30	−0.23	−0.13	−0.45	1.00
Panel B: 1985Q1–1994Q4											
USA	1.00										
Japan	−0.03	1.00									
Korea	−0.25	0.09	1.00								
Taiwan	−0.06	−0.23	0.16	1.00							
Hong Kong	−0.04	0.06	0.12	0.36	1.00						
Singapore	0.01	−0.35	−0.17	0.16	0.22	1.00					
Malaysia	−0.13	−0.09	−0.03	−0.04	−0.07	**0.43**	1.00				
Indonesia	0.14	−0.04	−0.07	−0.05	−0.05	0.08	0.16	1.00			
Thailand	0.23	−0.12	0.12	−0.09	−0.05	**0.35**	0.24	0.16	1.00		
Philippines	0.00	0.01	0.07	0.20	0.25	0.25	0.12	−0.18	−0.05	1.00	
China	0.10	−0.05	−0.15	−0.16	0.13	−0.05	−0.24	−0.18	−0.37	0.02	1.00
Panel C: 1995Q1–2003Q4											
USA	1.00										
Japan	0.08	1.00									
Korea	0.04	0.22	1.00								
Taiwan	**0.44**	0.31	0.29	1.00							
Hong Kong	0.19	**0.45**	**0.53**	**0.65**	1.00						
Singapore	0.01	**0.51**	**0.37**	**0.39**	**0.50**	1.00					
Malaysia	0.08	**0.41**	**0.81**	**0.37**	**0.61**	**0.35**	1.00				
Indonesia	−0.01	**0.36**	**0.62**	0.07	**0.41**	0.26	**0.78**	1.00			
Thailand	0.08	0.19	**0.59**	−0.02	**0.42**	0.12	**0.57**	**0.65**	1.00		
Philippines	−0.01	0.23	**0.56**	0.16	**0.42**	0.23	**0.52**	**0.64**	**0.50**	1.00	
China	0.17	0.17	0.08	0.24	0.25	0.15	−0.02	−0.05	0.09	−0.19	1.00

Notes: Real GDP growth rates are computed by taking the first difference of the natural log of real GDP. Bold and shaded figures denote positive and significant at the 2.5 and 5% levels, respectively (one-tailed test). Significance levels for correlation coefficients are assessed using the Fisher's variance-stabilizing transformation (see Rodriguez 1982).

Source: Abeysinghe and Lee (1998), Abeysinghe and Gulasekaran (2004), National Bureau of Statistics of China, Hong Kong Census & Statistics Department, Bank Indonesia, Economic and Social Research Institute, Cabinet Office, Government of Japan, Bank of Korea, Bank Negara Malaysia, Central Bank of the Philippines, NUS ESU Databank, Singapore Department of Statistics, *Economic Survey of Singapore*, (Ministry of Trade and Industry, Government of Singapore), Taiwan Economic Data Center, Directorate General of Budget, Accounting and Statistics, Executive Yuan, R.O.C., Bank of Thailand, Bureau of Economic Analysis, Department of Commerce, United States.

Table 5.6 Correlation of CPI inflation rates

	USA	JP	KR	TW	HK	SI	ML	ID	TH	PH	CH
Panel A: 1975Q1–1984Q4											
United States	1.00										
Japan	0.37	1.00									
Korea	0.73	0.50	1.00								
Taiwan	0.71	0.33	0.65	1.00							
Hong Kong	0.46	−0.02	0.30	0.44	1.00						
Singapore	0.56	0.03	0.35	0.45	0.52	1.00					
Malaysia	0.40	0.12	0.19	0.48	0.47	0.65	1.00				
Indonesia	0.21	0.36	0.27	0.25	0.10	−0.03	−0.03	1.00			
Thailand	0.77	0.39	0.53	0.70	0.40	0.65	0.43	0.26	1.00		
Philippines	0.03	−0.16	−0.18	−0.08	0.04	0.08	0.03	−0.09	−0.17	1.00	
China	–	–	–	–	–	–	–	–	–	–	–
Panel B: 1985Q1–1994Q4											
USA	1.00										
Japan	0.43	1.00									
Korea	0.28	0.37	1.00								
Taiwan	0.17	0.05	0.43	1.00							
Hong Kong	0.39	0.27	0.50	0.42	1.00						
Singapore	0.47	0.52	0.43	0.24	0.70	1.00					
Malaysia	−0.03	0.32	0.31	0.13	0.47	0.53	1.00				
Indonesia	0.17	0.03	0.05	0.26	0.22	0.26	0.14	1.00			
Thailand	0.25	0.36	0.32	0.05	0.42	0.57	0.31	−0.02	1.00		
Philippines	0.33	0.45	0.53	0.09	0.42	0.63	0.28	−0.16	0.53	1.00	
China	0.00	−0.15	−0.09	0.03	0.01	0.05	0.27	0.09	−0.02	−0.12	1.00
Panel C: 1995Q1–2003Q4											
USA	1.00										
Japan	−0.07	1.00									
Korea	0.01	0.21	1.00								
Taiwan	0.04	0.22	0.39	1.00							
Hong Kong	0.03	0.20	0.43	0.28	1.00						
Singapore	0.59	0.27	−0.03	−0.06	0.30	1.00					
Malaysia	−0.23	0.08	0.50	0.43	0.39	−0.31	1.00				
Indonesia	−0.33	−0.10	0.25	0.21	0.09	−0.56	0.66	1.00			
Thailand	−0.01	0.17	0.55	0.24	0.71	0.16	0.62	0.35	1.00		
Philippines	−0.06	0.20	0.20	0.30	0.45	−0.07	0.68	0.54	0.58	1.00	
China	0.31	0.16	0.19	0.39	0.60	0.38	0.08	−0.30	0.34	0.27	1.00

Notes: CPI inflation rates are computed by taking the first difference of the natural log of CPI. Bold and shaded figures denote positive and significant at the 2.5 and 5% levels, respectively (one-tailed test). Significance levels for correlation coefficients are assessed using the Fisher's variance-stabilizing transformation (see Rodriguez 1982).
Source: China Monthly Statistics, China Economic Monitoring & Analysis Center, National Bureau of Statistics of China, *Hong Kong Monthly Digest of Statistics*, Census and Statistics Department, *International Financial Statistics*, CD-ROM, IMF, Taiwan Economic Data Center, Directorate General of Budget, Accounting and Statistics, Executive Yuan, R.O.C.

5.3.3   Financial integration

Financial linkage among the East Asian economies has not yet been fully investigated in the previous literature. Financial linkage or integration is typically analyzed by testing interest rate parity conditions. Among the parity conditions, we test real interest rate parity to investigate real interest rate linkages between East Asian economies and two financial markets, the United States and Japan. We use the following form of a regression to test the *ex ante* real interest rate parity:[12]

$$(i_t^m - \pi_{t,t+k}^{em}) = \alpha + \beta (i_t^n - \pi_{t,t+k}^{en}) + \varepsilon_t \tag{5.3}$$

where i_t is the nominal k period interest rate, $\pi_{t,t+k}^e$ denotes the expectation at time t of the inflation rate from t to $t + k$, superscripts denote country m and n, respectively, and ε_t is an error term. The *ex ante* real interest parity (RIP) is supported when the joint hypothesis that $\alpha = 0$ and $\beta = 1$ is not rejected. However, because of the existence of some market imperfections such as transaction costs, $\alpha = 0$ does not necessarily hold.[13] So, our major interest is in testing the hypothesis of $\beta = 1$.

The test results are reported in Table 5.7. We tested real interest rate parity with respect to both the United States and Japan for 1981Q1–1996Q4 as well as 1981Q1–2003Q4, because the Asian currency crisis may affect the linkages between the countries. It is found that Asian NIEs and Thailand show strong real interest rate linkages with respect to both the United States and Japan before the currency crisis (Table 5.7a). However, including the post-crisis period in the sample, the strength of the link between Hong Kong and the United States as well as Japan falls (Table 5.7b). Singapore also shows a decline in linkage with respect to Japan.

Although the linkages deteriorated after the currency crisis, Asian NIEs and Thailand exhibit strong linkages with both the United States and Japan. Because real interest rate parity implies the joint hypothesis of uncovered interest rate parity and *ex ante* purchasing power parity and, hence, conditions of both financial market and goods market integration, the above findings indicate that Asian NIEs and Thailand exhibit strong financial and real linkage with both the United States and Japan.

5.4   Empirical analysis

5.4.1   Model

Business cycle synchronization and/or symmetry in shocks, one of the OCA criteria, are often analyzed in the literature. The aim of this section is to employ the structural VAR methodology and also an analysis of output losses in order to assess the viability of monetary arrangements in the East Asian region.

5.4.1(a)   *Structural VAR analysis*

We employ the conventional two-variable VAR with the log of home output (y) and home price level (p) to identify fundamental supply and demand

Table 5.7(a) The results of the real interest parity tests with realized inflation series: 1981Q1–1996Q4

Country	Panel A: Comparisons with the United States					Panel B: Comparisons with Japan				
	α	β	$\beta = 1$	$\alpha = 0$ and $\beta = 1$	$Adj.R^2$	α	β	$\beta = 1$	$\alpha = 0$ and $\beta = 1$	$Adj.R^2$
Korea 1981Q1–1996Q4	0.066** (0.011)	0.767* (0.348)	0.45	121.83**	0.25	0.056** (0.012)	1.049** (0.360)	0.02	103.18**	0.16
Taiwan 1981Q1–1996Q4	0.008 (0.018)	1.414* (0.542)	0.58	6.09*	0.15	0.000 (0.019)	1.600** (0.567)	1.13	5.30#	0.04
Hong Kong 1982Q1–1996Q4	−0.047** (0.011)	1.590** (0.363)	2.64	35.00**	0.24	−0.037** (0.013)	1.124** (0.394)	0.10	27.31**	−0.07
Singapore 1981Q1–1996Q4	0.004 (0.007)	0.898** (0.222)	0.21	0.31	0.25	0.006 (0.008)	0.778** (0.224)	0.98	1.00	0.19
Malaysia 1981Q1–1996Q4	0.032** (0.008)	−0.001 (0.246)	16.53**	17.25**	−0.02	0.028** (0.009)	0.131 (0.237)	13.46**	13.68**	0.01
Indonesia 1985Q1–1996Q4	0.023 (0.019)	1.035 (0.842)	0.00	8.37*	0.03	0.034* (0.016)	0.393 (0.534)	1.29	5.64#	−0.05
Thailand 1981Q1–1996Q4	0.018 (0.011)	1.503** (0.352)	2.05	36.82**	0.19	0.011 (0.013)	1.653** (0.395)	2.73#	26.73**	−0.07
Philippines 1981Q1–1996Q4	0.097** (0.034)	−1.781# (1.041)	7.14**	8.26*	−0.02	0.071* (0.035)	−0.829 (1.033)	3.13#	4.05	−0.06

Notes: Panels A and B report the results of the two-stage least squares estimation of Equation (5.3) in the text. The instruments are a constant, a time trend, the nominal interest of the United States or Japan, and the inflation rates of the United States or Japan lagged by 1 through 3. The fourth and fifth columns as well as the ninth and tenth report the Wald test statistics for the null hypothesis indicated in the second row. Double asterisk (**), single asterisk (*), and sharp (#) denote statistical significance at 1, 5, and 10% levels, respectively. Standard errors are reported in parentheses.
Source: Adapted from Sato (2004: Table 1).

Table 5.7(b) The results of the real interest parity tests with realized inflation series: 1981Q1–2003Q4

Country	Panel A: Comparisons with the United States					Panel B: Comparisons with Japan				
	α	β	$\beta = 1$	$\alpha = 0$ and $\beta = 1$	Adj.R²	α	β	$\beta = 1$	$\alpha = 0$ and $\beta = 1$	Adj.R²
Korea 1981Q1–2003Q4	0.048** (0.009)	1.228** (0.288)	0.63	145.84**	0.31	0.058** (0.008)	0.955** (0.280)	0.03	121.16**	0.07
Taiwan 1981Q1–2003Q4	0.015 (0.012)	1.190** (0.420)	0.21	9.46**	0.10	0.022* (0.010)	1.059** (0.345)	0.03	12.72**	0.13
Hong Kong 1982Q1–2003Q4	0.011 (0.012)	0.217 (0.436)	3.22#	4.63#	0.04	0.029** (0.010)	−0.624# (0.368)	19.51**	20.13**	−0.04
Singapore 1981Q1–2003Q4	0.010# (0.005)	0.691** (0.185)	2.79#	3.25	0.24	0.015** (0.005)	0.530** (0.165)	8.07**	10.72**	0.13
Malaysia 1981Q1–2003Q4	0.025** (0.006)	0.121 (0.199)	19.52**	20.57**	0.00	0.022** (0.005)	0.277 (0.167)	18.66**	22.65**	−0.01
Indonesia 1985Q1–2003Q4	0.032 (0.028)	0.570 (1.260)	0.12	2.67	−0.02	0.031 (0.021)	0.641 (0.861)	0.17	2.97	−0.03
Thailand 1981Q1–2003Q4	0.012 (0.009)	1.565** (0.303)	3.47#	34.31**	0.23	0.019* (0.009)	1.483** (0.298)	2.62	30.27**	−0.07
Philippines 1981Q1–2003Q3	0.071** (0.021)	−1.051 (0.728)	7.94**	10.98**	−0.01	0.049** (0.017)	−0.219 (0.610)	4.00*	8.02*	−0.02

Notes: Panels A and B report the results of the two-stage least squares estimation of Equation (5.3) in the text. The instruments are a constant, a time trend, the nominal interest of the United States or Japan, and the inflation rates of the United States or Japan lagged by 1 through 3. The fourth and fifth columns as well as the ninth and tenth report the Wald test statistics for the null hypothesis indicated in the second row. Double asterisk (**), single asterisk (*), and sharp (#) denote statistical significance at 1, 5, and 10% levels, respectively. Standard errors are reported in parentheses.
Source: Adapted from Sato (2004: Table 2).

shocks. Let $\Delta x_t = [\Delta y_t, \Delta p_t]'$ and $\varepsilon_t = [\varepsilon_{st}, \varepsilon_{dt}]'$ where Δ represents the first-order difference operator and ε_{st} and ε_{dt} denote supply and demand shocks, respectively. The structural model can be compactly written as

$$\Delta x_t = A_0\varepsilon_t + A_1\varepsilon_{t-1} + A_2\varepsilon_{t-2} + \cdots = A(L)\varepsilon_t \qquad (5.4)$$

or

$$\begin{bmatrix} \Delta y_t \\ \Delta p_t \end{bmatrix} = \begin{bmatrix} A_{11}(L) & A_{12}(L) \\ A_{21}(L) & A_{22}(L) \end{bmatrix} \begin{bmatrix} \varepsilon_{st} \\ \varepsilon_{dt} \end{bmatrix} \qquad (5.5)$$

where $A_{ij}(L) = a_{ij}^0 + a_{ij}^1 L + a_{ij}^2 L + \cdots$ is a polynomial function of the lag operator, L. We assume that the structural shocks are serially uncorrelated and have a covariance matrix normalized to the identity matrix.

In order to identify the structural A_i matrices, we follow the method developed by Blanchard and Quah (1989). We impose the following long-run restrictions based on standard macroeconomic theory: only supply shocks affect output in the long run, but both supply and demand shocks have a long-run impact on prices. Thus, the restrictions require $A_{12}(1) = 0$ which is sufficient to identify the structural A_i matrices and, hence, the time series of structural shocks (see Appendix 5A for further explanation of the structural VAR estimation). Once structural shocks are identified, we conduct a correlation analysis of the shocks to investigate the degree of shock symmetry.

5.4.1(b)   Analysis of output losses

The analysis of output losses is another useful approach to assess the viability of a currency area. In forming a currency area, countries typically renounce monetary policy autonomy in favor of an area-wide common policy. However, such a common monetary policy cannot work well in the face of country-specific shocks. Consequently, to the extent that each economy faces idiosyncratic shocks, the cost of forming a currency area may be quite large.

Ghosh and Wolf (1994) set up a simple macroeconomic model in which downward rigidity in nominal wages is assumed, and derive the following loss function to evaluate the country's output loss, in percentage terms, of relinquishing monetary policy autonomy and pursuing a common monetary policy:

$$L_t = 1 - \exp[(\varepsilon_t - \varepsilon_t^c)\alpha /(1 - \alpha)] \qquad \text{if } \varepsilon_t < \varepsilon_t^c \qquad (5.6)$$

where ε_t denotes the productivity shock to the individual country, ε_t^c the shock to the currency area, and α the labor share. Although highly simplified, Equation (5.6) enables us to evaluate the cost of forming a currency area (see Appendix 5B for the details of the model).

5.4.2 Data

Real GDP and the consumer price index (CPI) are used as proxies for real output and prices, respectively. All data is quarterly, expressed in natural logarithms and seasonally adjusted.[14] The sample period covers 1975Q1–2003Q4 for all economies except Korea (1975Q1–2003Q3) and China (1978Q1–2003Q4).

The data for real GDP is obtained from the websites of the statistical authorities in each economy and the NUS ESU databank.[15] The data for CPI is collected from IMF, *International Financial Statistics*, online version, and the websites of the statistical authorities in China, Taiwan, and Hong Kong.

5.4.3 Results

5.4.3(a) Result of correlation analysis in shocks

We estimate a two-variable VAR with the first difference of real GDP (Δy_t) and CPI (Δp_t). The result of our preliminary unit root test shows that almost all variables are nonstationary in level and stationary in first differences for the whole sample of 1975Q1–2003Q4 and, hence, it is usual to proceed to cointegration test and error-correction models.[16] However, our primary interest is in analyzing the correlation between structural shocks for the East Asian economies. Moreover, we divide the whole sample period into three subsamples (1975Q1–1984Q4, 1985Q1–1994Q1, and 1995Q1–2003Q4) and perform structural VAR estimation to investigate changes in the correlation of shocks across the three subsamples.[17] As long as we estimate VAR for each subsample (ten years or less using the quarterly series), the sample size is insufficient for cointegration testing. Accordingly, we proceed to estimate VAR for first differences within each subsample and then identify structural shocks to conduct an analysis of correlation in shocks.

Tables 5.8 and 5.9 show the correlation pattern of supply and demand shocks, respectively. First, asymmetric supply shocks prevailed in the first two subperiods, 1975Q1–1984Q4 and 1985Q1–1994Q4 (Panels A and B of Table 5.8). Significant correlation is found for only three pairs in 1975Q1–1984Q4 and for two pairs in 1985Q1–1994Q4. Bayoumi and Eichengreen (1994) report that supply shocks are significantly correlated in 1972–89 for two subgroups in East Asia: one consists of Japan, Korea, and Taiwan, and the other is composed of Hong Kong, Indonesia, Malaysia, Singapore, and possibly Thailand.[18] Our result contrasts markedly with Bayoumi and Eichengreen's finding.

Second, demand shocks are correlated more than supply shocks in the first two subperiods (Panels A and B of Table 5.9). But about one-half of significant correlations are with respect to Japan and/or the United States, and only five correlations are significantly different from zero among the East Asian economies excluding Japan in the first two subperiods. Again, this result is quite different from that of Bayoumi and Eichengreen (1994) that shows that demand shocks are highly correlated among Asian NIEs and some ASEAN economies. Moreover, East Asian economies show a declining correlation in

Table 5.8   Correlation of supply shocks

	USA	JP	KR	TW	HK	SI	ML	ID	TH	PH	CH
Panel A: 1975Q1–1984Q4											
United States	1.00										
Japan	−0.19	1.00									
Korea	**0.46**	−0.22	1.00								
Taiwan	−0.06	0.10	0.20	1.00							
Hong Kong	0.27	−0.12	**0.40**	0.02	1.00						
Singapore	−0.13	0.21	−0.16	0.16	0.11	1.00					
Malaysia	−0.06	0.11	−0.03	0.09	−0.18	−0.07	1.00				
Indonesia	−0.26	0.11	−0.25	0.22	0.15	0.27	0.27	1.00			
Thailand	0.13	0.14	−0.04	0.17	0.04	0.14	−0.13	0.09	1.00		
Philippines	0.08	−0.07	0.06	−0.01	0.12	−0.16	0.13	0.24	0.11	1.00	
China	−	−	−	−	−	−	−	−	−	−	−
Panel B: 1985Q1–1994Q4											
USA	1.00										
Japan	−0.18	1.00									
Korea	−0.16	0.12	1.00								
Taiwan	−0.23	−0.15	0.23	1.00							
Hong Kong	−0.09	−0.23	**0.37**	0.27	1.00						
Singapore	0.26	−0.24	−0.26	−0.10	0.05	1.00					
Malaysia	−0.18	0.04	0.00	−0.10	0.12	−0.01	1.00				
Indonesia	0.23	−0.14	−0.08	−0.18	−0.23	0.04	−0.13	1.00			
Thailand	0.28	−0.02	0.14	−0.09	0.03	0.10	0.00	0.11	1.00		
Philippines	−0.26	0.02	0.19	0.26	0.15	0.13	0.00	−0.07	0.00	1.00	
China	0.08	−0.17	−0.26	0.09	−0.04	0.25	−0.12	−0.04	−0.41	0.03	1.00
Panel C: 1995Q1–2003Q4											
USA	1.00										
Japan	−0.14	1.00									
Korea	−0.09	0.10	1.00								
Taiwan	0.22	**0.31**	0.11	1.00							
Hong Kong	0.12	0.10	0.33	**0.62**	1.00						
Singapore	−0.23	**0.47**	0.30	**0.41**	**0.55**	1.00					
Malaysia	−0.13	0.29	**0.76**	0.34	**0.52**	**0.44**	1.00				
Indonesia	−0.05	0.16	**0.72**	−0.06	0.23	0.34	**0.57**	1.00			
Thailand	0.17	0.03	0.21	0.03	0.19	−0.04	0.06	**0.30**	1.00		
Philippines	−0.03	0.22	**0.32**	0.15	0.14	0.28	0.20	**0.34**	0.28	1.00	
China	−0.03	0.14	0.02	0.08	0.26	0.18	0.18	**0.35**	0.02	−0.16	1.00

Notes: Bold and shaded figures denote positive and significant at the 2.5 and 5% levels, respectively (one-tailed test). Significance levels for correlation coefficients are assessed using the Fisher's variance-stabilizing transformation (see Rodriguez 1982).
Source: See Table 5.5.

demand shocks with Japan as well as among the regional economies in 1995Q1–2003Q4 (Panel C of Table 5.9). We cannot observe any clear pattern of demand shock correlation in East Asia.

Third, correlation in supply shocks increased significantly in 1995Q1–2003Q4 (Panel C of Table 5.8). The correlation coefficients are statistically significant and far higher between Korea, Malaysia, and Indonesia, which is

Table 5.9   Correlation of demand shocks

	USA	JP	KR	TW	HK	SI	ML	ID	TH	PH	CH
Panel A: 1975Q1–1984Q4											
United States	1.00										
Japan	0.30	1.00									
Korea	0.23	0.14	1.00								
Taiwan	0.60	0.47	0.21	1.00							
Hong Kong	0.09	0.36	0.20	0.38	1.00						
Singapore	−0.16	−0.02	0.11	−0.05	0.15	1.00					
Malaysia	0.30	0.37	0.26	0.32	0.33	0.11	1.00				
Indonesia	−0.11	−0.16	−0.05	0.08	0.03	−0.05	0.03	1.00			
Thailand	0.29	0.25	−0.09	0.42	0.11	0.23	0.10	0.13	1.00		
Philippines	0.22	0.27	−0.01	0.20	0.03	0.08	0.40	0.19	0.09	1.00	
China	−	−	−	−	−	−	−	−	−	−	−
Panel B: 1985Q1–1994Q4											
USA	1.00										
Japan	0.13	1.00									
Korea	0.00	0.28	1.00								
Taiwan	0.05	−0.02	0.17	1.00							
Hong Kong	0.08	0.11	0.20	0.12	1.00						
Singapore	0.08	0.50	0.09	0.07	0.13	1.00					
Malaysia	−0.24	0.30	0.11	−0.02	0.10	0.18	1.00				
Indonesia	0.14	−0.02	−0.03	0.29	−0.03	0.23	−0.20	1.00			
Thailand	−0.04	0.32	0.21	0.03	0.19	0.12	0.35	−0.07	1.00		
Philippines	−0.08	0.30	0.36	0.00	−0.08	0.25	0.21	0.04	0.28	1.00	
China	0.18	−0.04	0.03	−0.03	−0.13	−0.15	0.42	0.04	−0.01	−0.12	1.00
Panel C: 1995Q1–2003Q4											
USA	1.00										
Japan	0.05	1.00									
Korea	0.22	0.40	1.00								
Taiwan	0.05	0.12	0.18	1.00							
Hong Kong	0.39	−0.08	0.09	−0.09	1.00						
Singapore	0.12	0.23	0.18	0.00	0.03	1.00					
Malaysia	−0.03	0.07	0.15	0.47	−0.27	0.20	1.00				
Indonesia	0.18	−0.19	−0.13	0.04	0.30	0.26	0.14	1.00			
Thailand	0.17	0.19	0.20	0.25	0.03	0.39	0.17	−0.07	1.00		
Philippines	0.04	0.21	0.27	0.18	−0.06	0.20	0.10	0.04	0.30	1.00	
China	0.09	−0.15	0.06	0.07	0.17	0.11	0.12	0.11	0.28	0.12	1.00

Notes: Bold and shaded figures denote positive and significant at the 2.5 and 5% levels, respectively (one-tailed test). Significance levels for correlation coefficients are assessed using the Fisher's variance-stabilizing transformation (see Rodriguez 1982).
Source: See Table 5.5.

largely due to the Asian currency crisis in 1997/98. As the crisis-hit economies experienced severe economic downturn during the crisis period, supply shocks became more correlated among the countries. More interestingly, Taiwan, Hong Kong, and Singapore that were less affected by the crisis also exhibit strong correlation in supply shocks, and the shocks for these economies are highly correlated with those for Malaysia as well. This strong correlation in supply shocks is likely due to the growing similarity in economic structure among the economies.

Table 5.10 shows that the real GDP growth rate of the above four economies declined to almost zero or even recorded negative growth in 2001, which reflects the cyclical downturn in the information technology (IT) industry. The IT sector has accounted for an increasing share of domestic production of these economies. As of 2000, for example, the share of IT production in GDP was 51 percent in Singapore and 49.7 percent in Malaysia.[19] Such similarity in industrial structure ensures that industry-specific shocks will be well transmitted between the economies, facilitating comovement in the business cycle.[20] One of the OCA criteria, therefore, appears to have been well satisfied among the economies in 1995Q1–2003Q4.

Our result shows that East Asian economies showed improving symmetry in supply shocks during 1995Q1–2003Q4, which is partly due to the financial crisis. In particular, because of growing similarity in industrial structure, supply shocks became strongly correlated between Hong Kong, Taiwan, and Singapore during the latest subperiod. Malaysia also has a high correlation in supply shocks with the above three economies. This implies that the four economies are possible candidates for a currency area.

5.4.3(b)   *Result of output loss analysis*

To support the above findings, we investigate the cost side of forming a currency area. We estimate output losses by Equation (5.6) using the identified supply shocks in the previous subsection.[21] The shocks to the currency area, ε_t^c, are defined as the GDP-weighted average of individual member country's shocks. We arbitrarily set the labor share parameter, α, to be 0.6 for calculation of output losses.[22]

Table 5.11 shows the estimates of output losses in percentages in 1996Q1–2003Q4 when a currency area is formed by Taiwan, Hong Kong, Singapore, and Malaysia.[23] This is the baseline case because the result of correlation analysis in supply shocks (Panel C of Table 5.8) indicates that the above four economies are candidates for forming a currency area. We also present the estimates of output losses when one more economy joins the above currency area, and compare the results of the baseline case with that of four plus one economies.

First, Table 5.11 shows that output losses are the smallest in the baseline case. When one more economy joins the currency area, output losses of the original member economies increase in all cases. This is particularly the case when Japan, China, or Korea becomes a member economy. Because the area-wide shock is defined as a GDP-weighted average of individual shocks, the estimates of output losses are more affected by a larger economy in terms of GDP.

Second, to check possible changes in costs of forming a currency area, we divide 1996Q1–2003Q4 into two periods (1996Q1–1999Q4 and 2000Q1–2003Q4) and then recalculate the average of output losses for each subperiod

Table 5.10 Economic growth of Japan and East Asian economies (% change of real GDP in domestic currency)

Economy	1990	1991	1992	1993	1994	1995	1996	1997	1998	1999	2000	2001	2002	2003est.
Japan	5.20	3.35	0.97	0.25	1.10	1.93	3.42	1.85	-1.13	0.06	2.84	0.43	-0.35	2.70
China	3.80	9.20	14.20	13.50	12.60	10.50	9.60	8.80	7.80	7.10	8.00	7.30	8.00	9.10
Hong Kong	3.72	5.61	6.64	6.36	5.46	3.95	4.27	5.12	-4.98	3.42	10.13	0.47	2.26	3.00
Korea	8.98	9.23	5.44	5.49	8.25	8.92	6.75	5.01	-6.69	10.89	9.33	3.10	6.30	2.80
Taiwan	5.39	7.55	7.49	7.01	7.11	6.42	6.10	6.68	4.57	5.42	5.86	-2.18	3.59	3.20
Indonesia	7.24	6.95	6.46	6.50	7.54	8.22	7.82	4.70	-13.13	0.79	4.92	3.44	3.66	4.20
Malaysia	9.01	9.55	8.89	9.89	9.21	9.83	10.00	7.32	-7.36	6.14	8.55	0.32	4.12	4.90
Philippines	3.04	-0.58	0.34	2.12	4.39	4.68	5.85	5.19	-0.58	3.40	5.97	2.96	4.43	4.20
Singapore	9.03	6.76	6.69	12.26	11.40	8.04	8.15	8.51	-0.86	6.42	9.41	-2.37	2.25	1.00
Thailand	11.17	8.56	8.08	8.25	8.99	9.24	5.90	-1.37	-10.51	4.45	4.76	2.14	5.41	6.50

Note: The growth rates for 2003 are estimated figures.
Source: International Centre for the Study of East Asian Development, *East Asian Economic Perspectives: Recent Trends and Prospects for Major Asian Economies*, Vol. 15, Special Issue, 2004, Table 1.1.

Table 5.11   The average output losses in percentages ($\beta = 0.6$): 1996Q1–2003Q4

	Tw	HK	Si	Ml	Average of four	Fifth economy
Baseline case						
Four economies	0.130	0.178	0.189	0.127	0.156	–
Four economies plus one						
Four plus China	0.208	0.200	0.230	0.141	0.195	0.134
Four plus Japan	0.182	0.322	0.200	0.247	0.238	0.047
Four plus Korea	0.185	0.215	0.226	0.155	0.195	0.130
Four plus Indonesia	0.140	0.183	0.198	0.142	0.166	0.144
Four plus Thailand	0.148	0.182	0.217	0.150	0.174	0.211
Four plus Philippines	0.132	0.182	0.190	0.135	0.160	0.211

Notes: The output losses in percentages are calculated based on supply shocks estimated from the Blanchard–Quah method. It is assumed that a currency union consists of four economies (baseline case) and then one more economy (fifth economy) becomes a member of the currency area. The monetary authorities in the currency area are assumed to accommodate the GDP-weighted average of the shocks to the member countries. β is assumed to be 0.6. "Average of four" denotes a simple average of output losses for four economies: Taiwan (Tw), Hong Kong (HK), Singapore (Si), and Malaysia (Ml). Each column denotes the output loss of the economy listed on the first row.
Source: See Table 5.5.

(Table 5.12). It can be seen that Singapore and Malaysia decrease the output losses in the latter subsample of 2000Q1–2003Q4 in almost all cases. Hong Kong's output losses decline in the latter subsample when a relatively small economy (Indonesia or the Philippines) becomes a member. Interestingly, Taiwan increases output losses no matter which country becomes a member. However, if comparing the output loss per se, the loss is smaller in the baseline case than the case that includes one more economy in the currency area.

5.5   Concluding remarks

To explore a suitable monetary arrangement for East Asian economies, we rely on the OCA theory and analyze whether East Asian economies meet the OCA criteria. A casual examination of each OCA criterion shows that the East Asian economies have increased regional interdependence. To conduct more rigorous examination, we particularly focus on the symmetry in structural shocks as one of the major conditions for forming a currency area.

We first identify the supply and demand shocks using structural VAR techniques and conduct an analysis of correlation in shocks. We find that supply shocks became highly correlated among the East Asian economies quite recently. Before the mid-1990s, asymmetric supply shocks prevailed among East Asian economies. Although such high correlation in supply shocks after

Table 5.12   The average output losses in percentages ($\beta = 0.6$) for two subperiods

	Tw	HK	Si	Ml	Average of four	Fifth economy
Baseline case (Four economies)						
1996–99	0.073	0.192	0.233	0.186	0.171	–
2000–03	0.187	0.164	0.144	0.067	0.141	–
Four plus China						
1996–99	0.113	0.179	0.278	0.173	0.186	0.188
2000–03	0.304	0.221	0.183	0.110	0.204	0.080
Four plus Japan						
1996–99	0.087	0.275	0.236	0.275	0.218	0.059
2000–03	0.277	0.369	0.164	0.220	0.258	0.036
Four plus Korea						
1996–99	0.120	0.211	0.222	0.212	0.191	0.137
2000–03	0.250	0.219	0.229	0.098	0.199	0.123
Four plus Indonesia						
1996–99	0.076	0.184	0.232	0.206	0.174	0.187
2000–03	0.205	0.182	0.163	0.078	0.157	0.101
Four plus Thailand						
1996–99	0.085	0.176	0.252	0.210	0.181	0.280
2000–03	0.212	0.189	0.182	0.089	0.168	0.141
Four plus Philippines						
1996–99	0.069	0.190	0.229	0.201	0.172	0.311
2000–03	0.194	0.174	0.151	0.069	0.147	0.111

Note and Source: See Table 5.11.

the mid-1990s is affected by the Asian currency crisis, Taiwan, Hong Kong, Singapore, and Malaysia, the first three of which were less affected by the crisis, show positive and significant correlation in supply shocks. This is likely due to the increasing similarity in industrial structure and, hence, the four economies are possible candidates for a currency area.

Our analysis of output losses also supports the above findings. The output losses are smallest in the baseline case where Taiwan, Hong Kong, Singapore, and Malaysia form a currency area. Interestingly, even when including one more economy in the currency area, Malaysia, Singapore and, to a lesser extent, Hong Kong show a decline in output losses over the period, underlining the deepening regional linkages. However, the output loss per se is smaller in the baseline case for each subperiod than the case of including one more economy in the currency area.

Overall, Taiwan, Hong Kong, Singapore, and Malaysia meet the condition for forming a regional currency area, as supply shocks are significantly correlated and the output loss is smaller. Other ASEAN economies appear to be candidates for joining the above group when focusing on the cost side of forming a currency area. However, an analysis of shock symmetry indicates that only Indonesia would be a candidate for joining the currency area. Japan, China, and Korea are less likely to become members.

Appendix 5A   Estimation of structural shocks

We first estimate a reduced-form VAR as

$$\Delta x_t = B(L)\Delta x_{t-1} + u_t \tag{5A.1}$$

where u_t is a vector reduced form disturbance and $B(L)$ is a 2×2 matrix of lag polynomials. An MA representation of Equation (5A.1) is given as

$$\Delta x_t = C(L)u_t \tag{5A.2}$$

where $C(L) = (1 - B(L)L)^{-1}$ and the lead matrix of $C(L)$ is, by construction, $C_0 = I$.

By comparing Equations (5.4) and (5A.2), we obtain the relationship between the structural and reduced form disturbances: $u_t = A_0\varepsilon_t$. As the shocks are mutually orthogonal and each shock has unit variance, $C(1)\Sigma C(1)' = A(1)A(1)'$ where $\Sigma = Eu_tu_t' = EA_0\varepsilon_t\varepsilon_t'A_0' = A_0A_0'$. Letting H denote the lower triangular Choleski decomposition of $C(1)\Sigma C(1)'$, we obtain $A(1) = H$ since our long-run restrictions imply that $A(1)$ is also lower triangular. Consequently, we obtain $A_0 = C(1)^{-1}A(1) = C(1)^{-1}H$. Given an estimate of A_0, we can recover the time series of structural shocks.

Appendix 5B   Analysis of output losses

Ghosh and Wolf (1994) set up a simple macroeconomic model and assume that nominal wages are rigid downward. Let a country's output at time t be given by

$$Q_t = e^{\theta_t}l_t^\beta \tag{5B.1}$$

where θ_t is a productivity shock, l_t is labor employed in period t, and $0 < \beta < 1$ is a labor share. The real wage is equal to the marginal product of labor. The nominal wage is assumed to be set based on information available at $t - 1$ to reach labor market equilibrium:

$$\log(w_t) = \log(E_{t-1}p_t) + \log(\beta) + E_{t-1}\theta_t + (\beta - 1)\log(\overline{l}) \tag{5B.2}$$

where p_t is the price level, E_{t-1} is the expectations operator based on information available at $t - 1$, and $\overline{l}$ is the equilibrium employment level.

As nominal wages are downward sticky, the *ex post* labor demand is conditional on whether the unexpected productivity shock ε_t ($\equiv \theta_t - E_{t-1}\theta_t$) is positive or negative. If the unexpected productivity shock is positive, nominal wages are assumed to adjust so that full employment can prevail. If the unexpected productivity shock is negative, however, nominal wages do not go down and the *ex post* labor demand, l_t, is given by

$$\log(p_t) + \log(\beta) + \theta_t + (\beta - 1)\log(l_t) = \log(w_t) \qquad (5B.3)$$

If the country is not a member of a currency union, it conducts discretionary monetary policy to offset an adverse shock and set the price at the following level to restore labor market equilibrium:

$$\log(p_t) - \log(E_{t-1}p_t) = -\varepsilon_t \qquad (5B.4)$$

From Equations (5B.2) and (5B.3),

$$\begin{aligned}
\log(p_t) + \log(\beta) + \theta_t + (\beta - 1)\log(l_t) &= \log(w_t) \\
&= \log(E_{t-1}p_t) + \log(\beta) + E_{t-1}\theta_t + (\beta - 1)\log(\bar{l})
\end{aligned} \qquad (5B.5)$$

Suppose, instead, that the country forms a currency union with another country. Let the productivity shock to the currency union be ε_t^c, a weighted average shock to the two member countries. It is also assumed that the monetary authorities in the currency union pursue a stabilization policy similar to Equation (5B.4) and, hence, the price level (p_t^c) in the currency union is set based on

$$\log(p_t^c) - \log(E_{t-1}p_t^c) = -\varepsilon_t^c \qquad (5B.6)$$

Then, the *ex post* labor demand when forming the currency union is given by

$$l_t/\bar{l} = \exp[(\varepsilon_t - \varepsilon_t^c)/(1 - \beta)] \qquad (5B.7)$$

and output, Q_t^c, is given by

$$Q_t^c/Q_t = (e^{\theta_t}l_t^\beta)/(e^{\theta_t}\bar{l}^\beta) = \exp[(\varepsilon_t - \varepsilon_t^c)\beta/(1 - \beta)] \qquad (5B.8)$$

Accordingly, when $\varepsilon_t < \varepsilon_t^c$, the stabilization policy (5B.6) does not lead to full employment for the member country concerned, and the country's output loss in percentage terms is given by

$$L_t = 1 - \exp[(\varepsilon_t - \varepsilon_t^c)\beta/(1 - \beta)] \qquad \text{if } \varepsilon_t < \varepsilon_t^c \qquad (5B.9)$$

Notes

1 Recently, a large number of papers have been published on this issue. See, for example, papers contained in the following books: de Brouwer and Kawai (2004) and Asian Development Bank (2004).

2 See, for example, Bayoumi and Eichengreen (1993), Demertzis et al. (2000), etc.

3 See Bayoumi and Eichengreen (1994), Bayoumi et al. (2000), Chow and Kim (2003), and Zhang et al. (2004).

4 For a good survey of the OCA theory, see, for example, Kawai (1987), Tavlas (1993), and De Grauwe (2000). This section mainly relies on Kawai (1987).

5 See, for example, Taguchi (1994) and Kwan (1998) for a simple correlation analysis of observable macroeconomic variables.

6 Zhang and Sato (2004) employ the Kalman filter technique to analyze a time-varying correlation of shocks among the East Asian economies. Cheung and Yuen (2005) use the cointegration technique to investigate business cycle synchronization in some East Asian economies.

7 See de Brouwer (1999) for the result of uncovered interest parity tests for East Asian economies with respect to the US rate.

8 Phylaktis (1999) shows that Japan's financial influence has overtaken that of the US based on the impulse response function analysis. In contrast, Sato (2004) argues that East Asian economies are financially integrated more with the US than with Japan based on the result of time-varying parameter estimation.

9 Our casual observation implies that the East Asian economies stabilized their currencies more loosely to the US dollar than suggested by the "de facto US dollar pegged system" even before the currency crisis. See Chapter 1 in this book for a rigorous discussion on this issue.

10 McKinnon and Schnabl (2004) argue that East Asian economies are returning to the "soft dollar pegs."

11 It is assumed that exports, imports and nominal GDP are measured in terms of a single currency (e.g. US dollars). See also Sato (2004) for the details of the *ex ante* real interest parity test.

12 See Cumby and Mishkin (1986), Glick and Hutchison (1990), and Fujii and Chinn (2000).

13 See Phylaktis (1997, 1999).

14 We use *EViews 5* for empirical analysis. Seasonality is adjusted using Census X-12.

15 We are grateful to Tilak Abeysinghe for providing us with the real GDP series for some East Asian economies. See Table 5.5 for the details.

16 The result of the augmented Dickey-Fuller test (not reported in this chapter) shows that all variables are nonstationary in level except for the Japanese CPI.

17 Although it is a somewhat arbitrary division, our approach can reveal whether the correlation of shocks has changed over the last three decades.

18 Bayoumi and Eichengreen (1994) use the annual observations from 1972–89 for their structural VAR estimation.

19 See Table 1 of Van Assche et al. (2004) in which IT trade is defined as encompassing SITC 75, 76 and 776. The share of IT production in GDP for Taiwan is not reported in the paper due to the problem in data availability.

20 See also Zhang and Sato (2004) for increasing economic linkages between Taiwan and Hong Kong.

21 Cheung and Yuen (2005) also applied this output loss analysis to a Greater China currency area consisting of mainland China, Hong Kong and Taiwan.

22   We attempted to calculate output losses with α ranging from 0.3 to 0.7, but our conclusion did not change.
23   We first estimate output losses for each quarter and then calculate the average of the series of estimated output for 1996Q1–2003Q4, which is reported in Table 5.11.

References

Abeysinghe, T. and R. Gulasekaran, 2004, "Quarterly Real GDP Estimates for China and ASEAN4 with a Forecast Evaluation," *Journal of Forecasting* 23: 431–47.

Abeysinghe, T. and C. Lee, 1998, "Best Linear Unbiased Disaggregation of Annual GDP to Quarterly Figures: the Case of Malaysia," *Journal of Forecasting* 17: 527–37.

Asian Development Bank (ed.), 2004, *Monetary and Financial Integration in East Asia: the Way Ahead*, Vols 1 and 2, Basingstoke and New York: Palgrave Macmillan.

Bayoumi, T. and B. Eichengreen, 1993, "Shocking Aspects of European Monetary Integration," in F. Torres and F. Giavazzi (eds), *Adjustment and Growth in the European Monetary Union*, Cambridge: Cambridge University Press, pp. 193–229.

Bayoumi, T. and B. Eichengreen, 1994, "One Money or Many? Analyzing the Prospects for Monetary Unification in Various Parts of the World," *Princeton Studies in International Finance*, No. 16.

Bayoumi, T., B. Eichengreen, and P. Mauro, 2000, "On Regional Monetary Arrangements for ASEAN," *Journal of the Japanese and International Economies*, 14: 121–48.

Blanchard, O.J. and D. Quah, 1989, "The Dynamic Effects of Aggregate Demand and Supply Disturbances," *American Economic Review*, 79: 655–73.

Cheung, Y.-W. and J. Yuen, 2005, "The Suitability of a Greater China Currency Union," *Pacific Economic Review* 10(1): 83–103.

Chinn, M.D. and J.A. Frankel, 1995, "Who Drives Real Interest Rates around the Pacific Rim: the USA or Japan?" *Journal of International Money and Finance*, 14(6): 801–21.

Chow, H.K. and Y. Kim, 2003, "A Common Currency Peg in East Asia? Perspectives from Western Europe," *Journal of Macroeconomics*, 25: 331–50.

Cumby, R.E. and M.S. Mishkin, 1986, "The International Linkage of Real Interest Rates: the European–US Connection," *Journal of International Money and Finance*, 5: 5–23.

de Brouwer, G., 1999, *Financial Integration in East Asia*, Cambridge: Cambridge University Press.

de Brouwer, G. and M. Kawai (eds), 2004, *Exchange Rate Regimes in East Asia*, RoutledgeCurzon: London.

De Grauwe, P., 2000, *Economics of Monetary Union*, 4th edn, Oxford and New York: Oxford University Press.

De Grauwe, P. and W. Vanhaverbeke, 1993, "Is Europe an Optimum Currency Area?: Evidence from Regional Data," in P.R. Masson and M.P. Taylor (eds), *Policy Issues in the Operation of Currency Unions*, Cambridge: Cambridge University Press, pp. 111–29.

Demertzis, M., A.H. Hallett, and O. Rummel, 2000. "Is the European Union a National Currency Area, or Is It Held Together by Policy Makers?" *Weltwirtschaftliches Archiv*, 136 (4): 657–79.

Fujii, E. and M.D. Chinn, 2000, "*Fin de Siècle* Real Interest Parity," NBER Working Paper 7880.

Ghosh, A.R. and H.C. Wolf, 1994, "How Many Monies? A Genetic Approach to Finding Optimum Currency Areas," NBER Working Paper No. 4805.

Glick, R. and M. Hutchison, 1990, "Financial Liberalization in the Pacific Basin: Implications for Real Interest Rate Linkages," *Journal of the Japanese and International Economies*, 4: 36–48.

Kawai, M., 1987, "Optimum Currency Areas," in J. Eatwell, M. Milgate, and P. Newman (eds), *The New Palgrave: a Dictionary of Economics*, London: Macmillan Press, Ltd, pp. 740–3.

Kumakura, M., 2004, "Optimum Currency Area and Openness," in H. Mitsuo (ed.), *Exchange Rate Regimes in Developing Countries*, Institute of Developing Economies, JETRO, pp. 55–90, March.

Kwan C.H., 1998, "The Theory of Optimum Currency Areas and the Possibility of Forming a Yen Bloc in Asia," *Journal of Asian Economics*, 9(4): 555–80.

McKinnon, R.I., 1963, "Optimum Currency Areas," *American Economic Review*, 53: 717–25.

McKinnon, R.I. and G. Schnabl, 2004, "The Return to Soft Dollar Pegging in East Asia: Mitigating Conflicted Virtue," *International Finance*, 7(2): 169–201.

Mundell, R.A., 1961, "A Theory of Optimum Currency Areas," *American Economic Review*, 51: 657–65.

Phylaktis, K., 1997, "Capital Market Integration in the Pacific-Basin Region: an Analysis of Real Interest Rate Linkages," *Pacific-Basin Finance Journal*, 5: 195–213.

Phylaktis, K., 1999, "Capital Market Integration in the Pacific-Basin Region: an Impulse Response Analysis," *Journal of International Money and Finance*, 18: 267–87.

Rodriguez, R.N., 1982, "Correlation," in S. Kotz and N.L. Johnson (eds), *Encyclopedia of Statistical Sciences*, Vol. 2, John Wiley & Sons, pp. 193–204.

Sato, K., 2004, "Real Interest Rate Linkages in the Asian-Pacific Region: a Time-Varying Parameter Approach", CNAEC Research Series 04-03, Korea Institute for International Economic Policy.

Sato, K., Z.Y. Zhang, and M. McAleer, 2003, "Shocking Aspects of East Asian Monetary Integration: an Optimum Currency Area Approach," CITS Working Paper 2003-01, Center for International Trade Studies, Faculty of Economics, Yokohama National University.

Shin, Kwanho and Yunjong Wang, 2004, "Trade Integration and Business Cycle Co-movements: the Case of Korea with Other Asian Countries", *Japan and the World Economy*, pp. 213–30.

Taguchi, H., 1994, "On the Internationalization of the Japanese Yen," in T. Ito and A.O. Krueger (eds), *Macroeconomic Linkage*, Chicago: University of Chicago Press, pp. 335–55.

Tavlas, G.S., 1993, "The 'New' Theory of Optimum Currency Areas," *The World Economy*, 16(6): 663–85.

Van Assche, A., B. Gangnes, and C. Bonham, 2004, "The Determinants of Asia's Information Technology Trade," paper presented at the Western Economic Association International 79th Annual Conference, Vancouver, BC, June 29–July 3, 2004.

Zhang, Z.Y. and K. Sato, 2004, "Whither Currency Union in Greater China?" paper presented at the 9th International Convention of the East Asian Economic Association, Hong Kong, November 12–14.

Zhang, Z.Y., K. Sato, and M. McAleer, 2004, "Is a Monetary Union Feasible for East Asia?" *Applied Economics*, 36: 1031–43.

6
Trade Competition and Real Exchange Rates[1]

Masanaga Kumakura

6.1 Introduction

The formation of the European Monetary Union (EMU) in 1999 was hailed as a milestone in the history of international monetary affairs. While the traditional theory of optimum currency areas (OCA) focuses on static efficiency gains as the benefit of monetary union, recent studies stress the possibility that currency union boosts trade among member countries and helps synchronize their business cycles, thus obviating the need for national monetary policy (Frankel and Rose 1998). Such dynamic effects of monetary unification should presumably be more substantial when member countries share a similar industrial structure and engage in extensive intra-industry trade (Baldwin 1989; Allen et al. 1998). Moreover, although the general public often attaches a sentimental value to the national legal tender, this psychological barrier to currency union may be more easily overcome if firms in each country have a large number of competitors in other prospective member countries and if people feel that unstable exchange rates can threaten their job security. Other things being equal, therefore, monetary union is more likely to prove successful – both economically and politically – among countries that trade a wide range of similar products with one another.

Although the degree of trade competition among two or more countries is often measured by their gross trade volume and/or similarity of their export products, the quality of information contained in these indicators is not clear. This chapter proposes a set of new indices for international trade competition and estimates their values for a group of East Asian countries.[2] In recent years, interest in a regional exchange rate regime has been growing in East Asia,[3] as in many other parts of the world. Whereas the recent discussion about exchange rate policy coordination in East Asia has its roots in the contagious currency crises that swept the region in 1997–98, it also seems to reflect a perception that the industrial and export structures of the regional economies are now sufficiently competitive as to call for an explicit mechanism with which to prevent currency manipulation and competitive devaluation. Using our new trade competition indices as a guide, we examine how the East Asian countries' external competitive relationship has evolved during the past decade and what this evolution implies for their exchange rate policies. As part of this discussion, we also develop a set of real effective exchange rate indices that embed our competitiveness indicators.

The rest of this chapter is organized as follows. In the next section, we briefly survey the existing indicators of international trade competitiveness and define a set of alternative indices. Section 6.3 estimates our competition indices for ten East Asian countries and documents recent changes in the competitive structure of individual countries. While our indices are closely related to the notion of intra-industry trade, growing international production sharing and intra-firm trade complicate the relationship between intra-industry trade and international competitiveness. In Section 6.4, we thus look more closely at what lies behind the observed cross-country and time-series variation in our competition indices, focusing in particular on evidence from Japan. Section 6.5 develops a series of real effective exchange rate indices that embed our competition indices and examines the past movement of the external values of the East Asian currencies. Section 6.6 summarizes the findings of this chapter.

6.2   Measuring international trade competition

This chapter considers a situation in which goods produced in the home country i compete for customers with goods produced in foreign countries $j = 1$, $2, ..., n$ in their own markets and/or some third countries, and develop a series of indices that measure the relative importance of countries $j = 1, 2, ..., n$ as the home country's competitors.[4] Such indices are useful for describing compactly a country's external competitive relationship and can be used as an input to discussion over exchange rate policy. Although the existing literature offers a number of such indices, they are not without their shortcomings. Perhaps the most straightforward measure is the share of each foreign country j in the home country's aggregate trade, i.e.

$$w_j \equiv \frac{X_i^j + X_j^i}{\sum_j (X_i^j + X_j^i)} \tag{6.1}$$

where X_i^j denotes the value of exports from country i to country j. As this index satisfies the following equality

$$\sum_j w_i = 1 \tag{6.2}$$

it is used frequently as the weight of country j's currency when computing the effective value of the home currency.

The foregoing index, however, possesses a number of shortcomings as a measure of trade competitiveness. First of all, a pair of countries generally engages in both inter- and intra-industry trade, of which the former is less relevant to the notion of trade competition. The relative importance of inter- and intra-industry trade in bilateral trade is often measured by the well-known Grubel–Lloyd (GL) index:

$$w_j \equiv 1 - \frac{\sum_k |X_i^j(k) - X_j^i(k)|}{X_i^j + X_j^i} = 2 \times \frac{\sum_k \min[X_i^j(k), X_j^i(k)]}{X_i^j + X_j^i} \qquad (6.3)$$

where $X_i^j(k)$ denotes exports of good k from country i to j. This index ranges between 0 and 1, with a larger value indicating more intra-industry trade. When used in conjunction with the index in Equation (6.1), this index can provide useful information regarding the importance of country j as the home country's trade competitor.

The foregoing two indices, however, refer solely to bilateral trade and do not reflect the two countries' potential competition in third countries. An example of indicators that take account of the latter would be

$$w_j \equiv \frac{\sum_l x_i^l s_j^l}{\sum_l x_i^l (1 - s_i^l)} \qquad (6.4)$$

where

$$x_i^l \equiv \frac{X_i^l}{\sum_h X_i^h} \qquad s_i^l \equiv \frac{X_i^l}{\sum_i X_i^l} \qquad (6.5)$$

Assuming the CES utility function and some additional conditions, the competitiveness indices $\{w_1, w_2, \ldots, w_n\}$ in Equation (6.4) turn out to be proportional to the elasticities of the demand for domestic goods with respect to the relative price between domestic goods and those of countries $j = 1, 2, \ldots$ (Armington 1969). This index therefore possesses a desirable property as an indicator of the home country's competitiveness vis-à-vis countries $j = 1, 2, \ldots$ It also makes sense to use this index as the weight of the currency of each foreign currency when computing the home currency's effective value.[5] Nevertheless, the assumptions underlying this property come more from their theoretical expediency than from their empirical plausibility; evidence is in fact not in favor of these assumptions for, *inter alia*, countries with significantly different income levels (Spilimbergo and Vamvakidis 2000). Moreover, this index makes no use of information about the product composition of multilateral trade flows.[6]

With the preceding observation in mind, this chapter starts by considering the following indicator of bilateral trade competition:

$$w_j^1 \equiv \frac{\sum_k \min[X_i^j(k), X_j^i(k)]}{\sum_j \sum_k \min[X_i^j(k), X_j^i(k)]} \qquad (6.6)$$

This index measures the share of country j in the home country's intra-industry trade with $j = 1, 2, ..., n$. While this index may be regarded as a hybrid of the indicators in Equations (6.1) and (6.3), an alternative interpretation is available. If we define $I^j(k)$ as

$$I^j(k) \equiv \begin{cases} X_j^i(k)/X_i^j(k) & \text{if } X_i^j(k) \geq X_j^i(k) \\ 1 & \text{otherwise} \end{cases}$$

we can rewrite Equation (6.6) as

$$w_j^1 \equiv \frac{\sum_k I^j(k) X_i^j(k)}{\sum_j \sum_k I^j(k) X_i^j(k)} \tag{6.7}$$

Thus, w_j^1 can also be interpreted as the share of exports to country j in the home country's total exports, with export values adjusted differently for each good and destination country.

While the adjustment factor $I_j(k)$ is a kinked function of $X_{ij}(k)$, this property is not desirable when there is a large variation in the home country's bilateral trade balance with each foreign currency. To see why, suppose that the home country exports the same amount of good k to countries 1 and 2. Suppose also that the home country's trade in this good is roughly balanced with country 1 but registers a large deficit with country 2, i.e. $X_1^1(k) = X_i^2(k) \cong X_1^i(k) \ll X_2^i(k)$. In such circumstances, although trade in good k should add roughly the same value to the numerators of w_1^1 and w_2^1, producers of this good in the home country may not feel the same competitive pressure from firms in countries 1 and 2. To the extent that the producers of country 2 possess a substantially larger market share in the home country than do those of country 1, the former may be better positioned to expand their output and boost their sales when the home producers lose their price competitiveness. Taking these considerations into account, we also consider the following index:

$$w_j^2 \equiv \frac{\sum_k \sqrt{X_i^j(k)\, X_j^i(k)}}{\sum_j \sum_k \sqrt{X_i^j(k)\, X_j^i(k)}} \tag{6.8}$$

where the numerator on the right-hand side is now a geometric average of bilateral imports and exports of individual products. If we define $\bar{I}^j(k)$ as

$$\bar{I}^j(k) \equiv \sqrt{X_j^i(k) / X_i^j(k)}$$

Equation (6.8) can also be rewritten as

$$w_j^2 \equiv \frac{\sum_k \bar{I}^j(k) X_i^j(k)}{\sum_j \sum_k \bar{I}^j(k) X_i^j(k)} \qquad (6.9)$$

The preceding two indices are based solely on bilateral trade between the home country and countries $j = 1, 2, ..., n$ and do not take account of competition in third countries. To measure the latter, we next define the following two indices:

$$z_j^1 \equiv \frac{\sum_{l \neq j} \sum_k \min[X_i^l(k), X_j^l(k)]}{\sum_j \left[\sum_{l \neq j} \sum_k \min[X_i^l(k), X_j^l(k)] \right]} \qquad (6.10)$$

$$z_j^2 \equiv \frac{\sum_{l \neq j} \sum_k \sqrt{X_i^l(k) X_j^l(k)}}{\sum_j \left[\sum_{l \neq j} \sum_k \sqrt{X_i^l(k) X_j^l(k)} \right]} \qquad (6.11)$$

where $l = 1, 2, ...$ are countries that constitute important markets for home products, which may or may not coincide with $j = 1, 2, ..., n$. Equations (6.10) and (6.11) can be interpreted analogously as Equations (6.6) and (6.8).

Lastly, we define the following indices that combine the previous two sets of indicators:

$$v_j^1 \equiv \theta w_j^1 + (1 - \theta) z_j^1 \qquad (6.12)$$

$$v_j^2 \equiv \theta w_j^2 + (1 - \theta) z_j^2 \qquad (6.13)$$

where θ is the weight defined as

$$\theta \equiv \frac{\sum_j (X_i^j + X_j^i)}{\sum_j (X_i^j + X_j^i) + \sum_j X_i^j} \qquad (6.14)$$

Although the weight in Equation (6.14) is not grounded on an explicit theory, its construction draws loosely on the following consideration. When home producers gain or lose price competitiveness vis-à-vis those of a particular foreign country j, this will in general affect their sales in all of the home country, country j, and other countries in which they compete with the producers of country j. In Equations (6.12) and (6.13), w_j^1 and w_j^2 aim to measure (the cross-country variation in) its effect in the first two markets, whereas z_j^1 and z_j^2 evaluate (the cross-country variation in) its effect in the third markets. The formula in Equation (6.14) weighs the two sets of indices by considering the relative importance of these two effects. It implicitly uses the home country's import value from country j as a proxy for domestic producers' potential market loss in the home country.

Before proceeding, we note that w_j^1, w_j^2, z_j^1, and z_j^2 are not merely the components of the overall competition indices v_j^1 and v_j^2 but can be informative in their own right. In practice, bilateral trade tends to dominate popular discourse about international competitiveness while competition in third countries is often neglected. As we will see in the next section, however, the values of w_j^1 and w_j^2 often depart considerably from the corresponding values of z_j^1 and z_j^2 and hence also from those of v_j^1 and v_j^2. To the extent that domestic producers and policy-makers pay more attention to bilateral trade competition, the discrepancies between w_j^1 (w_j^2) and v_j^1 (v_j^2) might help us predict the direction of potential political bias in the home country's trade and exchange rate policies; divergent movements of w_j^1 (w_j^2) and z_j^1 (z_j^2) can also help us identify the reasons behind the observed changes in the overall indicators v_j^1 and v_j^2.

6.3   Application to East Asian countries

This section estimates the trade competition indices defined in Section 6.2 for ten East Asian countries. Although our indices can be computed only with trade statistics, we need reliable data on disaggregated bilateral trade flows to make our exercise meaningful. While the United Nations' COMTRADE database is a standard source of detailed bilateral trade data, this database has several undesirable properties for our purpose. First, COMTRADE lacks data for Taiwan and its commodity classification system varies over time and across countries. Second, although COMTRADE includes statistics reported by both importing and exporting countries, the two sets of statistics often exhibit substantial discrepancies. Considering these difficulties, this section adopts Statistics Canada's World Trade Database (WTD) as the main source of information. Although WTD is in principle based on COMTRADE's importer-country statistics, it makes a number of adjustments to the latter using exporter data.[7] It includes data for Taiwan, using both Taiwanese statistics and those of its trading partners.

WTD has its own shortcomings, however, of which the most important for our purpose is its relatively coarse commodity classification. In WTD, the COMTRADE data is reclassified according to (a modified version of) the Standard International Trade Classification (SITC) Revision 2. While WTD employs SITC's four-digit product code as its basic classification system, many of the original four-digit codes are aggregated further to ensure its consistency as a three-dimensional dataset. Therefore, WTD's most detailed commodity classification is effectively a mixture of the SITC three- and four-digit codes. As the GL index in Equation (6.3) is often found sensitive to the level of product aggregation,[8] there is a possibility that the results presented below also entail some bias. We will return to this issue in Section 6.4.

As practical discussion over international competitiveness tends to focus on manufacturing industries, we compute our indices using data only for

SITC industries 5–8. For home country i, we consider the ten East Asian countries of Japan, China, Hong Kong, Indonesia, Korea, Malaysia, the Philippines, Singapore, Taiwan, and Thailand. However, Hong Kong's trade includes substantial reexports to and from China, and even those classified specifically as "domestic" exports in the original Hong Kong statistics contain goods for which a substantial part of manufacturing activity is conducted on the mainland. Although WTD does make adjustment for entrepôt trade, this adjustment does not resolve distortions due to this special relationship between China and Hong Kong (Feenstra et al. 1999). To avoid this problem, we treat China and Hong Kong as a single economic entity and refer to this area as "greater China." Thus we have nine "countries" for which to calculate our competition indices.[9]

To compute our competition indices, we need to decide the sets of competitor countries $j = 1, 2, ...$ and export market countries $l = 1, 2, ...$ For ease of comparison, we use the same set for both $j = 1, 2, ...$ and $l = 1, 2, ...$ and fix this set for all nine East Asian countries (excluding themselves). We chose this set of countries using the following two-stage procedure. We first pooled the manufacturing exports of the nine Asian countries and computed the average share of each importer country for 1988–94, 1995–2001 and 1988–2001. Those countries for which the computed share exceeded 1 percent in any of these three periods were judged to be important markets for the East Asian countries and were included in the set of competitor/market countries. This first extraction process picked up all nine East Asian countries themselves and the following eight countries: Canada, the United States, France, Germany, Italy, the Netherlands, the United Kingdom, and Australia. Second, considering the possibility that exports of the Asian countries compete in these countries with those coming from third countries, we next pooled the imports of these 17 (9 + 8) countries and computed the shares of each source country for 1988–94, 1995–2001 and 1988–2001. We then picked up and added to the previous list all countries whose export shares exceeded 1 percent in any these periods. This second-round extraction identified the following seven countries: Mexico, Belgium,[10] Ireland, Spain, Austria, Sweden, and Switzerland. For each of the nine East Asian countries (i), therefore, the number of competitors (j) totals 23 (= 9 + 8 + 7 − 1, where the last one is itself).

We computed our competition indices for all years between 1985 and 2001, the entire period for which the most recent version of WTD provides requisite data. For the sake of comparison, we also calculated the gross trade share defined in Equation (6.1). Tables 6.1–6.9 show the results for 1990 and 2000.[11] Each table takes a specific East Asian country as the home country and lists the values of w_j, w_j^1, w_j^2, z_j^1, z_j^2, v_j^1, and v_j^2 for the 23 competitor countries in each column.[12] Apart from the values for individual countries, we also show the subtotals for six country groups to facilitate inspection. These groups are: NAFTA (Canada, the United States, and Mexico); euro area (Austria, Belgium, France, Germany, Ireland, Italy, the Netherlands, and Spain); EU (euro area

Table 6.1 Trade competition indices (Japan)

Competitor (j)	1990 w_j	w_j^1	w_j^2	z_j^1	z_j^2	v_j^1	v_j^2	2000 w_j	w_j^1	w_j^2	z_j^1	z_j^2	v_j^1	v_j^2
Australia	4.3	0.7	1.2	0.6	1.5	0.7	1.3	3.0	0.5	0.8	0.7	1.5	0.6	1.1
Austria	0.6	0.3	0.4	2.0	2.6	1.0	1.3	0.3	0.3	0.3	1.5	2.2	0.8	1.1
Belgium (inc. Lux.)	0.9	0.6	0.8	4.3	4.5	2.2	2.3	1.1	0.7	0.9	3.4	3.9	1.8	2.1
Canada	3.7	0.7	1.3	7.7	6.0	3.6	3.3	2.2	0.6	1.0	6.8	5.4	3.1	2.8
Greater China	8.4	6.0	7.2	5.9	6.0	6.0	6.7	16.7	16.1	16.3	9.2	8.1	13.3	13.0
France	2.8	2.7	2.8	7.1	6.8	4.5	4.5	2.2	1.8	2.0	5.3	5.5	3.2	3.4
Germany	6.8	13.9	10.5	11.7	10.9	13.0	10.6	4.9	6.8	6.2	9.1	8.8	7.7	7.3
Indonesia	3.8	0.6	0.8	0.5	0.8	0.5	0.8	2.8	0.9	1.1	0.9	1.6	0.9	1.3
Ireland	0.3	0.3	0.3	1.6	1.8	0.9	0.9	0.7	0.8	0.7	2.0	2.4	1.3	1.4
Italy	1.8	1.8	1.9	6.1	6.1	3.6	3.7	1.5	1.3	1.4	4.2	4.7	2.4	2.7
Korea	7.4	10.4	9.1	4.6	4.9	7.9	7.4	6.8	8.2	7.7	6.4	5.8	7.5	7.0
Malaysia	2.6	1.4	1.6	1.9	2.2	1.6	1.9	3.8	3.6	3.6	3.8	3.6	3.7	3.6
Mexico	0.7	0.1	0.2	1.6	2.2	0.8	1.0	1.0	0.3	0.5	5.5	4.5	2.3	2.1
Netherlands	1.2	0.8	0.9	4.2	4.3	2.2	2.4	1.4	1.0	1.2	3.4	3.9	1.9	2.3
Philippines	1.0	0.4	0.4	0.4	0.8	0.4	0.6	1.8	2.5	2.0	1.7	2.0	2.2	2.0
Singapore	3.6	3.3	3.7	4.3	4.2	3.7	3.9	4.2	5.2	5.0	5.0	4.4	5.1	4.7
Spain	0.9	0.3	0.5	2.6	2.9	1.3	1.5	0.8	0.4	0.6	2.3	2.7	1.2	1.4
Sweden	0.8	1.1	1.1	3.0	3.9	1.9	2.2	0.6	0.6	0.6	1.9	2.7	1.1	1.5
Switzerland	1.3	1.3	1.2	3.3	3.5	2.1	2.2	0.8	0.7	0.7	2.2	2.8	1.3	1.6
Taiwan	6.1	7.7	7.5	5.9	5.5	6.9	6.7	6.8	8.3	7.8	6.8	5.6	7.7	6.9
Thailand	3.1	1.8	2.0	1.1	1.9	1.5	2.0	3.4	3.4	3.4	2.1	2.8	2.8	3.2
United Kingdom	3.7	4.3	4.5	7.7	7.3	5.7	5.7	3.0	3.2	3.5	6.1	6.2	4.4	4.5
United States	34.1	39.6	40.1	11.8	9.3	27.8	27.1	30.1	33.0	32.5	9.8	8.7	23.7	23.0
NAFTA	38.4	40.4	41.6	21.2	17.6	32.3	31.4	33.3	33.8	34.0	22.1	18.7	29.1	27.9
Euro area	15.3	20.7	18.0	39.6	39.9	28.7	27.2	12.9	13.0	13.3	31.2	34.2	20.3	21.7
EU	19.9	26.1	23.6	50.3	51.0	36.3	35.2	16.5	16.8	17.4	39.2	43.0	25.8	27.7
ANIES	17.2	21.4	20.4	14.7	14.6	18.6	17.9	17.9	21.7	20.5	18.2	15.8	20.3	18.6
ASEAN	10.5	4.2	4.8	3.9	5.8	4.1	5.2	11.8	10.4	10.2	8.5	10.0	9.6	10.2
East Asia	36.1	31.6	32.4	24.6	26.4	28.6	29.9	46.4	48.2	47.0	35.9	33.9	43.2	41.8

Source: Author's calculation based on Statistics Canada World Trade Database.

Table 6.2 Trade competition indices (Greater China)

Competitor (i)	1990							2000						
	w_j	w_j^1	w_j^2	z_j^1	z_j^2	v_j^1	v_j^2	w_j	w_j^1	w_j^2	z_j^1	z_j^2	v_j^1	v_j^2
Australia	2.5	1.4	1.5	1.0	1.3	1.2	1.5	2.1	1.1	1.4	0.8	1.4	1.0	1.4
Austria	0.6	0.3	0.4	2.3	2.5	1.0	1.1	0.3	0.2	0.3	1.6	2.1	0.7	0.9
Belgium (inc. Lux.)	1.2	1.6	1.5	3.5	3.7	2.3	2.2	1.2	1.5	1.3	3.5	3.6	2.2	2.1
Canada	2.5	0.9	1.1	3.2	3.5	1.7	1.9	1.8	0.9	1.0	4.6	4.4	2.2	2.2
France	2.9	3.4	3.1	6.1	6.1	4.3	4.1	2.7	2.8	2.9	5.4	5.5	3.7	3.8
Germany	7.0	6.2	6.9	7.3	8.1	6.6	7.3	5.9	5.8	6.0	6.7	7.0	6.1	6.3
Indonesia	2.6	3.0	2.7	1.8	2.2	2.6	2.6	1.4	0.9	0.9	2.1	2.9	1.4	1.6
Ireland	0.1	0.1	0.1	1.8	1.9	0.7	0.7	0.3	0.4	0.4	2.5	2.7	1.1	1.2
Italy	2.7	3.5	3.2	7.3	6.9	4.8	4.4	2.2	2.5	2.5	5.7	5.6	3.6	3.6
Japan	21.5	17.1	20.2	8.8	9.7	14.3	16.7	20.6	21.6	21.1	8.9	8.0	17.1	16.5
Korea	4.6	7.2	6.3	8.8	6.7	7.8	6.4	8.2	9.3	9.0	5.9	5.3	8.1	7.7
Malaysia	1.7	1.6	1.6	2.8	2.8	2.0	2.0	2.4	3.5	3.0	4.8	4.2	3.9	3.4
Mexico	0.3	0.1	0.1	1.2	1.5	0.4	0.6	0.5	0.3	0.3	5.6	4.7	2.2	1.9
Netherlands	1.5	1.3	1.3	3.7	3.9	2.1	2.2	1.9	1.0	1.4	3.6	3.8	1.9	2.2
Philippines	0.9	0.8	0.7	1.0	1.5	0.9	1.0	1.1	1.2	1.2	2.4	2.8	1.6	1.7
Singapore	5.5	8.2	6.5	4.6	4.1	7.0	5.7	4.8	8.0	6.4	4.7	4.3	6.8	5.6
Spain	0.8	0.5	0.6	2.5	2.6	1.2	1.3	1.0	0.6	0.8	2.2	2.7	1.2	1.4
Sweden	0.7	0.6	0.6	2.4	2.4	1.2	1.2	0.8	0.7	0.7	1.9	2.3	1.1	1.3
Switzerland	1.7	2.3	2.2	4.0	3.9	2.9	2.8	1.0	1.0	1.0	2.8	3.1	1.7	1.8
Taiwan	8.0	11.1	10.4	9.5	7.2	10.6	9.3	8.9	8.9	9.7	7.1	5.9	8.3	8.4
Thailand	2.0	2.4	2.1	3.5	3.4	2.8	2.6	2.0	2.7	2.4	3.6	3.9	3.0	2.9
United Kingdom	4.4	4.8	5.1	6.1	6.2	5.3	5.5	4.1	4.3	4.4	5.7	5.7	4.7	4.9
United States	24.1	21.4	21.6	6.9	7.8	16.5	17.0	24.7	20.7	22.0	8.0	8.1	16.2	17.1
NAFTA	26.9	22.4	22.8	11.3	12.8	18.6	19.4	27.1	21.9	23.3	18.2	17.2	20.6	21.1
Euro area	16.9	17.0	17.1	34.5	35.8	22.9	23.4	15.6	15.0	15.5	31.1	33.0	20.7	21.7
EU	22.0	22.4	22.8	43.0	44.5	29.4	30.1	20.4	19.9	20.6	38.6	41.0	26.5	27.9
ANIES	18.1	26.6	23.2	22.8	17.9	25.3	21.4	21.8	26.2	25.1	17.7	15.5	23.2	21.7
ASEAN	7.1	7.8	7.2	9.1	10.0	8.2	8.2	6.9	8.3	7.5	13.0	13.9	10.0	9.7
East Asia	46.8	51.5	50.6	40.7	37.6	47.8	46.2	49.3	56.1	53.7	39.6	37.3	50.2	47.9

Source: See Table 6.1

Competitor (i)	1990							2000						
	w_i	w_i^1	w_i^2	z_i^1	z_i^2	v_i^1	v_i^2	w_i	w_i^1	w_i^2	z_i^1	z_i^2	v_i^1	v_i^2
Australia	3.4	1.7	1.8	1.7	1.6	1.7	1.7	4.6	3.6	3.8	1.5	1.4	2.8	2.9
Austria	0.3	0.0	0.0	2.6	2.4	0.8	0.7	0.3	0.1	0.1	2.0	1.8	0.8	0.8
Belgium (inc. Lux.)	0.8	0.2	0.3	3.4	3.4	1.2	1.2	1.4	0.7	0.8	3.3	3.3	1.7	1.8
Canada	1.1	0.2	0.4	2.8	3.2	1.0	1.2	1.1	0.3	0.4	3.4	3.9	1.5	1.7
Greater China	9.8	39.9	31.9	8.5	9.2	30.9	25.4	10.1	18.8	16.2	8.7	9.9	14.8	13.7
France	2.6	1.6	1.8	5.5	5.4	2.7	2.8	1.7	2.6	2.2	5.0	4.8	3.5	3.2
Germany	5.4	2.6	4.0	5.6	6.7	3.4	4.8	4.1	4.8	4.9	5.7	6.2	5.1	5.4
Ireland	0.1	0.0	0.0	1.3	1.3	0.4	0.4	0.2	0.1	0.1	2.0	2.0	0.8	0.8
Italy	1.7	1.1	1.4	6.9	7.4	2.8	3.1	1.5	1.2	1.5	5.5	5.1	2.9	2.9
Japan	36.3	22.7	25.3	4.6	7.3	17.5	20.2	25.3	24.2	25.3	5.4	7.5	16.8	18.3
Korea	5.6	6.8	6.1	8.1	7.4	7.2	6.5	9.2	6.9	7.2	6.5	5.8	6.8	6.6
Malaysia	1.8	2.5	2.3	3.8	3.3	2.9	2.6	4.4	6.9	6.5	5.6	4.6	6.4	5.7
Mexico	0.1	0.0	0.0	1.2	1.2	0.3	0.4	0.4	0.1	0.1	3.1	3.7	1.2	1.5
Netherlands	1.9	0.8	1.0	3.4	3.2	1.5	1.7	2.1	1.1	1.3	3.4	3.3	2.0	2.1
Philippines	0.5	0.2	0.4	2.6	2.0	0.9	0.8	1.3	1.4	1.3	3.4	2.7	2.2	1.8
Singapore	4.1	3.4	3.7	4.6	3.9	3.8	3.7	4.7	1.0	1.0	4.4	4.4	2.3	2.3
Spain	0.6	0.3	0.4	3.1	2.7	1.1	1.1	1.6	1.1	1.0	2.8	2.5	1.8	1.6
Sweden	0.5	0.1	0.1	1.8	1.8	0.6	0.6	0.4	0.3	0.3	2.6	2.2	1.2	1.1
Switzerland	0.6	0.3	0.4	2.8	2.8	1.0	1.1	0.3	0.3	0.3	2.3	2.3	1.1	1.1
Taiwan	4.8	5.3	5.6	8.5	8.1	6.2	6.3	4.4	5.3	5.1	6.5	6.1	5.8	5.5
Thailand	1.0	1.3	1.0	5.9	3.8	2.6	1.8	3.2	5.4	4.9	6.1	4.1	5.7	4.5
United Kingdom	2.4	1.4	1.9	5.4	5.1	2.5	2.8	2.7	2.0	2.5	5.0	4.7	3.2	3.4
United States	14.6	7.6	10.4	5.8	6.5	7.1	9.3	15.1	11.9	13.3	5.7	7.4	9.4	11.0
NAFTA	15.8	7.8	10.7	9.8	11.0	8.4	10.8	16.6	12.2	13.7	12.2	15.0	12.2	14.2
Euro area	13.4	6.6	8.9	31.9	32.6	13.8	15.7	12.7	11.7	11.9	29.7	29.1	18.8	18.6
EU	16.4	8.0	10.9	39.0	39.4	16.9	19.1	15.8	13.9	14.7	37.3	36.1	23.1	23.1
ANIES	14.5	15.6	15.3	21.2	19.4	17.2	16.5	18.3	13.3	13.3	17.5	16.3	14.9	14.5
ASEAN	3.3	4.0	3.7	12.3	9.2	6.4	5.3	8.8	13.7	12.7	15.2	11.4	14.3	12.2
East Asia	63.9	82.1	76.2	46.7	45.2	71.9	67.3	62.6	70.0	67.4	46.7	45.2	60.8	58.7

Source: See Table 6.1.

Table 6.4 Trade competition indices (Korea)

Competitor (i)	1990							2000						
	w_i	w_j^1	w_j^2	z_j^1	z_j^2	v_j^1	v_j^2	w_i	w_j^1	w_j^2	z_j^1	z_j^2	v_j^1	v_j^2
Australia	4.2	0.7	0.8	1.1	1.3	0.8	1.0	4.5	0.4	0.7	0.9	1.4	0.6	0.9
Austria	0.2	0.2	0.2	2.0	2.2	0.8	0.9	0.2	0.1	0.2	1.5	1.8	0.6	0.8
Belgium (inc. Lux.)	0.7	0.4	0.5	2.9	3.2	1.3	1.5	0.6	0.4	0.5	2.8	3.3	1.2	1.5
Canada	2.8	1.0	1.4	4.3	4.6	2.2	2.5	1.4	0.5	0.7	4.2	4.7	1.9	2.2
Greater China	5.4	8.8	8.5	9.2	7.2	8.9	8.0	13.3	18.3	19.1	7.4	7.0	14.2	14.6
France	2.1	1.3	1.9	5.4	5.7	2.8	3.3	1.9	1.6	1.7	4.5	5.0	2.6	2.9
Germany	5.3	3.3	4.4	6.8	8.1	4.6	5.7	4.0	2.9	3.8	6.5	7.4	4.2	5.1
Indonesia	2.6	0.6	0.7	1.8	1.9	1.1	1.1	4.1	0.7	0.9	2.0	2.2	1.2	1.4
Ireland	0.1	0.1	0.1	1.5	1.6	0.6	0.6	0.7	0.9	0.8	2.1	2.3	1.4	1.4
Italy	1.9	1.4	1.6	6.2	6.2	3.1	3.3	1.5	1.0	1.3	4.0	4.4	2.1	2.4
Japan	33.1	35.8	34.1	10.2	11.4	26.6	25.9	25.9	21.5	21.3	11.4	10.4	17.7	17.3
Malaysia	2.5	1.2	1.1	3.5	2.8	2.0	1.7	3.3	3.0	2.8	5.3	4.2	3.8	3.3
Mexico	0.2	0.0	0.1	1.9	1.9	0.7	0.7	0.2	0.3	0.6	4.2	4.1	1.8	1.9
Netherlands	0.7	0.5	0.6	3.2	3.5	1.5	1.6	0.9	0.7	1.0	2.9	3.4	1.5	1.9
Philippines	0.4	0.2	0.3	1.1	1.4	0.5	0.7	1.2	1.9	1.7	3.4	2.7	2.4	2.1
Singapore	2.0	2.7	3.1	5.5	4.3	3.7	3.5	4.1	5.6	4.8	6.1	4.8	5.8	4.8
Spain	0.4	0.2	0.3	2.4	2.6	1.0	1.1	0.3	0.3	0.4	2.0	2.4	0.9	1.1
Sweden	0.6	0.3	0.3	2.8	2.6	1.2	1.2	0.5	0.3	0.3	2.1	2.3	1.0	1.1
Switzerland	0.9	0.4	0.5	2.5	2.8	1.1	1.4	0.6	0.2	0.3	1.8	2.2	0.8	1.0
Taiwan	2.6	4.5	3.7	10.0	7.5	6.5	5.1	3.7	7.3	6.2	8.9	6.6	7.9	6.4
Thailand	0.7	0.7	0.7	3.3	3.1	1.6	1.6	1.3	1.4	1.4	3.7	3.5	2.3	2.1
United Kingdom	2.1	2.3	2.7	5.8	6.0	3.6	3.9	1.7	1.5	2.1	5.1	5.3	2.8	3.3
United States	28.5	33.3	32.4	6.7	8.0	23.7	23.7	24.0	29.2	27.7	7.5	8.3	21.2	20.5
NAFTA	31.5	34.4	33.9	12.8	14.4	26.6	26.9	25.6	30.1	28.9	16.0	17.1	24.8	24.5
Euro area	11.4	7.5	9.6	30.4	33.2	15.7	18.1	10.1	7.9	9.5	26.0	30.2	14.7	17.2
EU	14.0	10.1	12.6	39.0	41.8	20.5	23.1	12.2	9.7	11.9	33.2	37.8	18.5	21.5
ANIES	4.5	7.2	6.8	15.6	11.7	10.2	8.6	7.8	12.9	11.1	15.0	11.4	13.7	11.2
ASEAN	6.3	2.7	2.8	9.7	9.2	5.2	5.1	9.9	6.9	6.7	14.3	12.7	9.7	8.9
East Asia	49.4	54.5	52.2	44.7	39.6	50.9	47.7	57.0	59.5	58.2	48.1	41.4	55.3	52.0

Source: See Table 6.1

Table 6.5 Trade competition indices (Malaysia)

Competitor (j)	1990							2000						
	w_j	w_j^1	w_j^2	z_j^1	z_j^2	v_j^1	v_j^2	w_j	w_j^1	w_j^2	z_j^1	z_j^2	v_j^1	v_j^2
Australia	2.6	0.7	0.9	1.4	1.4	0.9	1.0	2.2	0.7	1.0	0.9	1.3	0.8	1.1
Austria	0.2	0.1	0.1	1.9	2.1	0.6	0.7	0.2	0.1	0.1	1.2	1.6	0.4	0.6
Belgium (inc. Lux.)	0.8	0.8	0.6	2.5	2.8	1.3	1.3	0.6	0.3	0.4	2.2	2.7	1.0	1.2
Canada	1.0	0.3	0.4	4.3	3.9	1.5	1.5	0.8	0.1	0.3	3.5	3.7	1.3	1.5
Greater China	5.1	3.7	4.9	7.3	7.0	4.8	5.5	8.1	8.2	8.5	8.9	8.1	8.4	8.4
France	1.6	1.2	1.3	4.7	5.4	2.2	2.5	1.7	1.9	1.7	3.9	4.5	2.6	2.7
Germany	4.2	4.3	4.1	5.8	7.1	4.7	5.0	3.2	3.3	3.2	5.0	6.0	3.9	4.2
Indonesia	1.5	0.4	0.6	2.2	2.0	0.9	1.0	2.0	0.8	1.1	2.6	2.6	1.4	1.6
Ireland	0.1	0.0	0.0	1.6	1.7	0.5	0.5	0.9	0.6	0.9	2.6	2.8	1.3	1.5
Italy	1.2	0.4	0.6	4.1	5.0	1.5	1.9	0.9	0.4	0.6	2.9	3.7	1.2	1.6
Japan	20.0	8.9	12.7	10.9	12.0	9.5	12.5	15.9	11.4	13.3	9.9	9.4	10.9	12.0
Korea	4.2	2.3	2.4	8.8	6.5	4.2	3.6	4.3	3.6	3.7	7.8	6.2	5.0	4.5
Mexico	0.1	0.0	0.0	1.1	1.2	0.3	0.3	0.4	0.1	0.2	3.6	4.0	1.3	1.5
Netherlands	1.5	0.2	0.4	3.3	3.6	1.1	1.3	1.7	0.5	0.9	2.7	3.3	1.3	1.8
Philippines	0.9	0.5	0.5	1.9	1.8	0.9	0.9	1.7	1.4	1.7	4.6	3.6	2.5	2.3
Singapore	24.7	37.2	34.0	7.0	4.8	28.4	25.4	23.1	34.6	29.6	7.3	5.4	25.2	21.3
Spain	0.4	0.0	0.1	1.9	2.1	0.6	0.7	0.4	0.1	0.2	1.4	1.9	0.5	0.8
Sweden	0.6	0.2	0.3	2.4	2.4	0.9	0.9	0.4	0.4	0.4	1.8	2.1	0.9	1.0
Switzerland	0.5	0.3	0.4	2.4	2.7	0.9	1.1	0.4	0.2	0.3	1.6	2.2	0.7	0.9
Taiwan	4.1	2.5	3.3	7.8	6.8	4.1	4.4	4.9	5.9	5.5	8.5	7.0	6.8	6.0
Thailand	2.9	1.6	1.5	4.5	3.5	2.4	2.1	3.6	4.3	3.7	4.9	4.1	4.5	3.8
United Kingdom	4.2	4.5	5.0	5.1	5.7	4.7	5.2	3.0	2.5	2.8	4.5	5.0	3.1	3.5
United States	17.6	29.7	25.7	6.9	8.5	23.0	20.6	19.6	18.8	20.2	7.9	8.8	15.0	16.3
NAFTA	18.6	30.0	26.1	12.3	13.6	24.8	22.5	20.8	19.0	20.7	14.9	16.5	17.6	19.2
Euro area	10.0	7.1	7.3	25.9	29.9	12.6	13.9	9.6	7.1	7.9	21.9	26.6	12.2	14.3
EU	14.8	11.8	12.6	33.4	38.0	18.1	20.1	13.0	10.0	11.1	28.2	33.6	16.2	18.8
ANIES	33.0	42.1	39.7	23.6	18.1	36.7	33.4	32.3	44.0	38.7	23.6	18.6	37.0	31.8
ASEAN	5.3	2.5	2.6	8.6	7.3	4.3	4.0	7.3	6.4	6.4	12.0	10.3	8.3	7.7
East Asia	63.5	57.2	60.0	50.5	44.4	55.3	55.4	63.7	70.1	66.9	54.3	46.4	64.7	59.9

Source: See Table 6.1.

Table 6.6 Trade competition indices (Philippines)

Competitor (i)	1990							2000						
	w_j	w_j^1	w_j^2	z_j^1	z_j^2	v_j^1	v_j^2	w_j	w_j^1	w_j^2	z_j^1	z_j^2	v_j^1	v_j^2
Australia	2.7	1.0	1.1	1.6	1.3	1.1	1.2	1.6	0.6	0.6	0.9	1.1	0.7	0.8
Austria	0.2	0.1	0.1	2.3	2.0	0.6	0.6	0.1	0.1	0.1	1.2	1.4	0.5	0.6
Belgium (inc. Lux.)	0.7	0.2	0.2	2.7	2.7	0.9	0.9	0.4	0.1	0.2	2.0	2.2	0.8	0.9
Canada	1.8	0.4	0.5	4.4	4.1	1.5	1.4	1.0	0.2	0.4	3.4	3.6	1.4	1.5
Greater China	8.2	12.7	12.5	7.6	9.1	11.3	11.6	8.8	7.6	8.9	8.4	9.8	7.9	9.2
France	2.0	2.1	2.1	5.3	4.8	3.0	2.8	1.1	0.9	1.0	4.0	4.3	2.1	2.2
Germany	5.5	6.3	5.2	5.6	6.3	6.1	5.5	3.6	2.6	3.0	4.6	5.2	3.3	3.8
Indonesia	1.3	0.3	0.6	3.9	2.6	1.2	1.1	1.4	0.5	0.6	2.7	2.4	1.3	1.2
Ireland	0.2	0.0	0.0	1.9	1.5	0.5	0.4	1.2	1.7	1.6	3.0	2.9	2.2	2.1
Italy	1.0	0.8	0.8	5.3	6.1	2.0	2.2	0.6	0.4	0.4	2.9	3.6	1.3	1.6
Japan	22.6	17.3	19.2	5.3	9.2	14.2	16.6	18.3	21.8	19.6	7.8	8.5	16.7	15.6
Korea	4.2	2.6	3.5	6.9	7.1	3.8	4.5	6.0	6.2	6.0	8.6	6.3	7.1	6.1
Malaysia	2.7	2.6	2.2	5.0	3.8	3.2	2.6	4.0	3.8	4.4	7.9	5.7	5.3	4.9
Mexico	0.1	0.0	0.0	2.1	1.6	0.6	0.4	0.4	0.0	0.1	3.4	4.1	1.2	1.6
Netherlands	1.8	1.3	1.4	3.1	3.0	1.8	1.8	3.9	0.6	1.8	2.5	3.0	1.3	2.2
Singapore	4.9	5.9	6.3	5.6	4.7	5.8	5.9	8.5	10.0	10.1	8.1	6.3	9.3	8.7
Spain	0.5	0.1	0.1	2.6	2.2	0.7	0.7	0.3	0.1	0.1	1.3	1.7	0.5	0.7
Sweden	0.4	0.1	0.1	2.4	2.0	0.7	0.6	0.2	0.1	0.1	1.4	1.7	0.6	0.7
Switzerland	0.5	0.2	0.2	2.7	2.4	0.8	0.8	0.3	0.1	0.1	1.6	2.0	0.6	0.8
Taiwan	4.0	3.4	4.3	7.6	7.7	4.5	5.2	7.0	6.0	7.2	8.3	7.0	6.8	7.2
Thailand	1.5	0.7	0.8	6.0	3.8	2.0	1.6	3.0	3.4	3.5	5.3	4.1	4.1	3.7
United Kingdom	3.4	3.0	2.9	5.4	5.0	3.6	3.5	3.1	1.4	2.3	4.0	4.6	2.3	3.1
United States	29.8	39.0	35.9	4.7	6.8	30.0	28.3	25.4	31.9	27.9	6.8	8.3	22.8	20.8
NAFTA	31.7	39.4	36.4	11.2	12.5	32.0	30.1	26.8	32.2	28.4	13.6	16.0	25.4	23.9
Euro area	11.9	10.8	10.0	28.9	28.7	15.5	14.8	11.1	6.5	8.2	21.5	24.4	11.9	14.0
EU	15.7	13.8	13.0	36.7	35.7	19.8	18.9	14.4	8.0	10.6	26.9	30.7	14.8	17.8
ANIES	13.0	12.0	14.1	20.0	19.6	14.1	15.5	21.4	22.2	23.4	25.0	19.6	23.2	22.0
ASEAN	5.5	3.6	3.5	14.8	10.2	6.5	5.3	8.5	7.6	8.4	15.9	12.2	10.6	9.8
East Asia	49.3	45.6	49.3	47.8	48.1	46.2	49.0	57.0	59.2	60.2	57.0	50.2	58.4	56.6

Source: See Table 6.1.

Competitor (j)	1990							2000						
	w_j	w_j^1	w_j^2	z_j^1	z_j^2	v_j^1	v_j^2	w_j	w_j^1	w_j^2	z_j^1	z_j^2	v_j^1	v_j^2
Australia	3.4	1.7	1.7	1.2	1.5	1.5	1.7	2.8	1.1	1.4	0.9	1.3	1.0	1.4
Austria	0.3	0.2	0.2	1.9	2.1	0.8	0.8	0.2	0.1	0.1	1.0	1.5	0.4	0.6
Belgium (inc. Lux.)	0.6	0.4	0.5	2.8	3.1	1.1	1.3	0.6	0.4	0.4	2.2	2.7	1.0	1.2
Canada	1.0	0.5	0.6	4.1	4.0	1.6	1.7	0.5	0.2	0.3	2.7	3.3	1.0	1.3
Greater China	9.9	9.9	9.2	7.2	6.8	9.1	8.4	12.1	13.3	12.7	8.6	8.3	11.7	11.2
France	2.4	1.7	2.0	5.3	5.5	2.8	3.1	2.1	1.6	1.8	4.0	4.6	2.4	2.7
Germany	4.3	4.3	4.4	6.7	7.8	5.0	5.4	3.6	2.9	3.3	5.2	6.2	3.7	4.3
Indonesia	1.9	0.3	0.5	1.4	1.3	0.6	0.7	1.6	0.1	0.1	1.7	2.2	0.6	0.8
Ireland	0.2	0.2	0.2	2.2	2.1	0.9	0.8	1.1	0.8	1.0	3.1	3.4	1.6	1.8
Italy	1.6	1.1	1.3	4.6	5.1	2.2	2.5	0.9	0.5	0.7	2.7	3.6	1.2	1.6
Japan	16.5	11.4	14.9	12.7	12.9	11.8	14.2	13.3	11.7	12.8	11.4	10.1	11.6	11.9
Korea	3.4	2.7	3.3	7.4	5.8	4.1	4.0	4.3	4.8	4.5	7.8	6.2	5.8	5.1
Malaysia	14.5	19.4	16.3	3.7	2.8	14.5	12.1	17.4	24.7	20.9	6.3	4.7	18.5	15.4
Mexico	0.1	0.0	0.0	1.1	1.3	0.4	0.4	0.7	0.4	0.6	3.1	3.3	1.3	1.5
Netherlands	1.4	1.0	1.2	3.6	3.8	1.8	2.0	2.0	0.6	1.2	2.9	3.5	1.4	2.0
Philippines	1.0	0.5	0.5	1.1	1.3	0.7	0.8	2.6	2.6	2.7	4.1	3.5	3.1	3.0
Spain	0.5	0.2	0.2	2.0	2.1	0.7	0.8	0.4	0.3	0.4	1.3	1.7	0.6	0.8
Sweden	0.5	0.3	0.3	2.7	2.7	1.0	1.1	0.3	0.1	0.1	1.6	2.0	0.6	0.8
Switzerland	0.8	0.4	0.6	2.6	3.1	1.1	1.4	0.7	0.2	0.3	1.9	2.5	0.8	1.1
Taiwan	5.6	7.3	6.4	8.7	6.7	7.7	6.5	5.7	7.9	6.9	9.0	7.0	8.2	6.9
Thailand	5.0	6.5	5.1	2.8	2.7	5.3	4.3	5.1	4.6	5.0	3.7	3.7	4.3	4.6
United Kingdom	3.8	4.0	4.3	6.3	6.4	4.7	5.0	2.9	2.2	2.7	4.9	5.3	3.1	3.6
United States	21.3	26.1	26.1	7.8	9.2	20.4	20.8	19.0	18.9	20.0	9.9	9.5	15.8	16.4
NAFTA	22.4	26.6	26.7	13.0	14.5	22.4	22.9	20.2	19.5	20.9	15.7	16.1	18.2	19.2
Euro area	11.2	9.0	10.1	29.2	31.7	15.3	16.8	10.9	7.2	8.8	22.4	27.1	12.4	15.0
EU	15.5	13.3	14.8	38.1	40.8	21.1	22.9	14.1	9.5	11.7	28.9	34.4	16.1	19.4
ANIES	9.0	10.0	9.7	16.1	12.5	11.9	10.5	9.9	12.7	11.4	16.8	13.2	14.1	12.0
ASEAN	22.4	26.6	22.4	9.0	8.1	21.1	17.9	26.8	32.0	28.8	15.8	14.1	26.5	23.8
East Asia	57.8	58.0	56.1	45.0	40.2	53.9	51.1	62.1	69.7	65.8	52.7	45.6	63.9	58.9

Source: See Table 6.1.

Table 6.8 Trade competition indices (Taiwan)

Competitor (j)	1990							2000						
	w_j	w_j^1	w_j^2	z_j^1	z_j^2	v_j^1	v_j^2	w_j	w_j^1	w_j^2	z_j^1	z_j^2	v_j^1	v_j^2
Australia	2.6	0.6	1.0	0.9	1.3	0.7	1.1	1.9	0.4	0.6	0.8	1.4	0.5	0.9
Austria	0.5	0.2	0.3	2.1	2.4	0.9	1.1	0.3	0.2	0.3	1.3	1.8	0.6	0.8
Belgium (inc. Lux.)	0.7	0.4	0.4	2.6	3.1	1.2	1.5	0.6	0.3	0.4	2.2	2.9	1.0	1.3
Canada	2.3	0.7	1.0	4.3	4.2	2.1	2.2	1.6	0.5	0.8	3.6	3.9	1.6	1.9
Greater China	11.4	13.8	13.4	10.3	8.6	12.5	11.5	19.7	17.1	19.6	11.8	10.4	15.1	16.2
France	2.4	2.0	2.2	5.5	5.6	3.3	3.5	1.8	1.7	1.7	4.1	4.6	2.6	2.8
Germany	5.3	4.5	5.2	7.1	8.0	5.5	6.3	4.3	4.0	4.1	5.7	6.5	4.6	4.9
Indonesia	1.8	0.5	0.6	1.6	1.8	0.9	1.1	1.3	0.5	0.6	1.8	2.2	1.0	1.2
Ireland	0.1	0.1	0.1	1.8	1.9	0.8	0.8	0.5	0.4	0.5	2.6	2.7	1.2	1.3
Italy	1.6	1.8	1.8	6.4	6.4	3.6	3.6	1.1	1.1	1.1	3.7	4.3	2.1	2.3
Japan	22.0	27.2	26.8	11.1	11.2	21.0	20.8	18.8	21.2	20.4	11.1	9.5	17.4	16.4
Korea	2.4	4.6	3.6	8.5	6.5	6.1	4.7	4.5	7.2	5.9	8.2	6.2	7.6	6.0
Malaysia	1.9	1.4	1.5	2.6	2.6	1.9	1.9	3.2	4.9	3.9	5.3	4.5	5.0	4.1
Mexico	0.0	0.0	0.0	1.3	1.6	0.5	0.6	1.1	0.2	0.2	3.9	3.9	1.6	1.6
Netherlands	1.3	1.1	1.2	3.3	3.6	1.9	2.1	2.0	1.1	1.4	2.9	3.4	1.8	2.1
Philippines	0.6	0.2	0.3	1.0	1.4	0.5	0.7	1.9	1.7	1.9	3.0	2.8	2.2	2.3
Singapore	4.5	7.5	5.8	5.5	4.4	6.8	5.3	5.0	9.0	7.0	6.5	5.1	8.1	6.3
Spain	0.8	0.2	0.4	2.4	2.6	1.0	1.2	0.5	0.3	0.4	1.6	2.1	0.8	1.0
Sweden	0.8	0.6	0.7	2.4	2.6	1.3	1.4	0.5	0.4	0.4	1.7	2.1	0.9	1.0
Switzerland	0.7	0.6	0.7	2.9	3.3	1.5	1.7	0.6	0.4	0.5	1.9	2.4	1.0	1.2
Thailand	1.7	1.1	1.2	2.9	3.0	1.8	1.9	2.0	2.2	2.0	3.5	3.6	2.7	2.6
United Kingdom	2.6	2.2	2.4	6.2	6.0	3.7	3.8	2.5	1.7	2.1	4.7	5.1	2.8	3.2
United States	31.9	28.6	29.7	7.4	7.8	20.5	21.3	24.4	23.8	24.2	8.0	8.4	17.9	18.4
NAFTA	34.3	29.3	30.7	13.0	13.6	23.1	24.1	27.0	24.4	25.2	15.5	16.3	21.1	21.9
Euro area	12.8	10.3	11.5	31.1	33.6	18.3	20.0	11.1	9.0	9.8	24.1	28.2	14.6	16.7
EU	16.1	13.1	14.6	39.7	42.3	23.3	25.2	14.1	11.1	12.4	30.5	35.4	18.3	20.9
ANIES	6.9	12.2	9.4	14.0	10.9	12.9	10.0	9.5	16.2	12.9	14.7	11.4	15.6	12.3
ASEAN	6.0	3.2	3.6	8.1	8.8	5.1	5.6	8.4	9.2	8.5	13.7	13.2	10.9	10.3
East Asia	46.3	56.4	53.1	43.6	39.6	51.5	47.9	56.5	63.7	61.4	51.3	44.5	59.1	55.1

Competitor (j)	1990							2000						
	w_j	w_j^1	w_j^2	z_j^1	z_j^2	v_j^1	v_j^2	w_j	w_j^1	w_j^2	z_j^1	z_j^2	v_j^1	v_j^2
Australia	2.0	0.9	1.1	1.3	1.3	1.0	1.1	2.5	0.8	1.1	1.2	1.3	1.0	1.2
Austria	0.4	0.1	0.2	2.3	2.3	0.7	0.7	0.2	0.1	0.1	1.6	1.7	0.6	0.7
Belgium (inc. Lux.)	1.7	3.2	2.7	2.9	3.2	3.1	2.8	1.5	1.4	1.2	2.6	3.0	1.8	1.8
Canada	1.5	0.2	0.3	3.4	3.4	1.1	1.2	1.0	0.3	0.3	3.4	3.6	1.3	1.5
Greater China	7.0	9.3	9.3	8.8	8.0	9.2	8.9	10.4	13.3	12.2	8.5	8.8	11.7	11.1
France	2.6	0.9	1.5	5.6	5.5	2.2	2.6	2.2	1.5	1.6	4.8	4.8	2.6	2.7
Germany	5.8	3.9	4.6	6.4	7.2	4.6	5.3	3.8	3.4	3.5	5.9	6.3	4.2	4.5
Indonesia	0.9	0.4	0.4	3.2	2.8	1.1	0.9	2.2	1.3	1.5	3.5	2.7	2.1	1.9
Ireland	0.1	0.0	0.0	1.8	1.8	0.5	0.5	0.3	0.3	0.3	2.8	2.5	1.2	1.1
Italy	1.8	0.8	1.1	5.9	6.5	2.2	2.6	1.3	0.9	1.0	4.3	4.5	2.0	2.2
Japan	27.9	19.7	24.3	6.1	9.6	16.0	20.3	21.7	21.8	23.1	7.0	8.5	16.7	18.1
Korea	3.2	2.1	2.4	7.8	6.7	3.7	3.6	3.2	3.5	3.3	7.0	6.0	4.7	4.2
Malaysia	3.4	2.6	2.3	4.3	3.3	3.1	2.6	5.5	8.8	6.7	6.3	4.9	7.9	6.1
Mexico	0.2	0.0	0.0	1.6	1.4	0.4	0.4	0.4	0.3	0.3	3.3	3.9	1.3	1.6
Netherlands	1.9	1.0	0.9	3.3	3.3	1.6	1.6	1.8	1.0	1.1	3.0	3.4	1.7	1.9
Philippines	0.6	0.2	0.2	2.2	1.7	0.7	0.6	1.9	2.5	2.4	3.9	3.0	3.0	2.6
Singapore	9.9	20.6	15.7	5.0	4.3	16.3	12.6	10.3	13.3	13.1	5.5	4.9	10.6	10.3
Spain	0.8	0.1	0.2	2.7	2.5	0.8	0.8	0.8	0.4	0.5	2.1	2.3	1.0	1.1
Sweden	0.8	0.2	0.4	2.3	2.2	0.8	0.8	0.5	0.3	0.3	2.1	2.1	0.9	0.9
Switzerland	1.4	2.2	1.9	3.3	3.2	2.5	2.3	1.0	1.1	0.9	2.2	2.3	1.4	1.4
Taiwan	4.2	3.4	4.2	8.1	7.5	4.7	5.1	4.6	5.5	5.3	7.3	6.5	6.1	5.7
United Kingdom	3.6	2.4	2.9	5.8	5.7	3.3	3.7	3.0	1.8	2.4	5.2	5.0	2.9	3.3
United States	18.2	25.7	23.4	5.6	7.5	20.3	19.1	19.9	16.6	17.7	6.5	8.0	13.2	14.4
NAFTA	19.8	26.0	23.8	10.6	12.3	21.8	20.6	21.3	17.2	18.4	13.2	15.5	15.8	17.4
Euro area	15.3	10.0	11.1	31.1	32.2	15.8	16.9	11.9	8.9	9.3	27.2	28.5	15.1	15.9
EU	19.7	12.6	14.4	39.3	40.1	19.9	21.4	15.4	10.9	12.1	34.5	35.5	18.9	20.1
ANIES	17.3	26.1	22.3	20.9	18.5	24.7	21.3	18.1	22.3	21.7	19.8	17.3	21.4	20.2
ASEAN	4.9	3.1	2.9	9.7	7.2	4.9	4.0	9.6	12.6	10.6	13.8	10.6	13.0	10.6
East Asia	57.1	58.3	58.8	45.5	43.2	54.8	54.6	59.7	70.0	67.6	49.0	45.3	62.8	60.0

Note and Source: See Table 6.1.

countries, Sweden, and the United Kingdom); ANIES (Korea, Singapore, and Taiwan); ASEAN (Indonesia, Malaysia, the Philippines, and Thailand), and East Asia (ANIES, ASEAN, Japan, and greater China).

By skimming through the nine tables, we first find that the values of our competitiveness indices often deviate substantially from the corresponding gross trade share. In particular, the values of our third-market competition indices, z_j^1 and $z_{j'}^2$ tend to depart significantly from the corresponding value of w_j, suggesting that the magnitude of bilateral trade is a poor indicator of the extent to which two countries compete in third markets.[13] On the other hand, the values of w_j^1 and z_j^1 are correlated fairly tightly with the corresponding values of w_j^2 and $z_{j'}^2$ and in consequence discrepancies between v_j^1 and v_j^2 are also generally modest.[14]

As is clear from Tables 6.1–6.9, the main trade competitors for the East Asian countries are the United States, the EU, and other Asian countries. Let us next examine how the relative importance of these three groups of countries has evolved during the past decade. In most Asian countries, the share of trade with the United States in their total trade, w_j, has either remained stagnant or fallen marginally between 1990 and 2000, despite the relatively robust growth of the US economy during this period. In all countries but Indonesia, the share of the United States measured by our bilateral trade indices, w_j^1 and $w_{j'}^2$ has fallen by even larger proportions.[15] This tendency is particularly salient in the relatively developing low-income ASEAN countries. In Malaysia and the Philippines, whereas the United States' w_j^1 and w_j^2 in 1990 were substantially larger than its value of w_j, this relationship has been reversed by the end of the decade. In most countries, meanwhile, the values of z_j^1 and z_j^2 for the United States are substantially smaller than the corresponding values of w_j^1 and $w_{j'}^2$,[16] and the former have remained relatively stable during the 1990s. In consequence, when measured by the overall competition indices of v_j^1 and $v_{j'}^2$ the relative importance of the United States among the 23 competitor countries has fallen in all countries but greater China and Indonesia.

In most East Asian countries, the gross trade share of the EU countries remained stable or declined marginally during the 1990s. In most countries, the corresponding values of w_j^1 and w_j^2 are generally smaller and have fallen at a faster pace. In contrast to the United States, however, the values of z_j^1 and z_j^2 for the EU countries are in general much larger relative to their values of w_j^1 and $w_{j'}^2$ apparently reflecting the fact that the exporters of the East Asian countries compete with those of the EU countries in the markets of other European countries. In most East Asian countries, however, the overall importance of the EU countries as trade competitors, measured in terms of our composite indices v_j^1 and $v_{j'}^2$ seems to be on a declining trend, as we can see in the group subtotal in each table.

Lastly, let us examine how the competitive relationship among the East Asian countries has changed over the past decade. As is clear from Tables 6.1–6.9, intra-regional trade constitutes an important part of each country's external transactions. In 2000, the sum of w_j for the East Asian countries is well above 50 percent in all countries but Japan and greater China. In many countries, moreover, the share of intra-regional trade has risen substantially during the 1990s. In Japan, Korea, and Taiwan the increase in intra-regional trade has been particularly noticeable, of which a substantial part is accounted for by their growing trade with China.

In most East Asian countries, the share of the other Asian countries measured by our competition indices is even larger than the corresponding gross trade share. Their collective shares measured by w_j^1 and w_j^2 exceed the corresponding value of w_j in all nine countries, and the difference is particularly salient in Malaysia and Taiwan. The share of the East Asian countries tends to be smaller when measured by z_j^1 and z_j^2 but is still generally quite significant.[17] Between 1990 and 2000, moreover, the aggregate sum of the Asian countries' z_j^1 and z_j^2 rose in all countries except China and Indonesia, and in some countries by significant margins. As a result, the shares of the East Asian countries measured by our composite indices have also risen in most countries and in 2000 exceed 50 percent in all countries but Japan. Even in Japan, the sums of the values of v_j^1 and v_j^2 for the other East Asian countries has risen from 28.6 and 29.9 percent in 1990 to 43.1 and 41.8 percent in 2000. By looking at values for individual competitors, we further note that: (1) the share of the ASEAN countries has risen particularly sharply, not only in Japan and the ANIES countries but also in the ASEAN countries themselves; (2) the rise in China's share is particularly significant in Japan, Korea, and Taiwan; and (3) the share of Japan has been either stable or fallen slightly in most countries.

One problem of our competition indices is that if we compute their values by treating two or more countries as a single competitor, just as we have done for China and Hong Kong, the results will change not only for these countries but also for all other countries.[18] More specifically, if we recalculate our competition indices treating a subset of foreign countries as if they were a single competitor, the values of w_j^1 and w_j^2 for the latter will become larger than the sum of the corresponding values for individual countries, while the converse is generally the case for z_j^1 and z_j^2.[19] As we noted previously, when measured by z_j^1 and z_j^2 the EU countries tend to seem more important competitors for the Asian countries than when measured in terms of the other indices, largely because the continental European economies are relatively small and trade heavily with one another. As these countries now form a customs union with free internal capital and labor movement, it might be more appropriate to treat them as a single trading partner/competitor. Furthermore, eight of the ten EU countries included in our list of competitor countries now share a single currency. As the next section applies our competition indices to the compilation of real exchange rate indices, we next recalculate our indices by treating the eight euro-member countries as a single economic region and check how doing so affects the results shown in Tables 6.1–6.9.

Tables 6.10 and 6.11 present the recomputed indices. As the EMU came into effect in 1999, the tables present only the results for 2000.[20] As expected, in all East Asian countries the computed values of w_j^1 and w_j^2 for the composite euro area are larger than the subtotal for its member countries in Tables 6.1–6.9, although their discrepancies are generally modest. On the other hand, the euro area's values of z_j^1 and z_j^2 are now markedly smaller than the corresponding sum in Tables 6.1–6.9, falling by as much as 50–60 percent except for Japan. As a result, the values of v_j^1 and v_j^2 for the euro region are also substantially smaller than the previous subtotals.

Before closing this section, we consider implications of what we have seen above for the exchange rate policies of the East Asian countries. Although it is not appropriate to discuss exchange rate policy solely in terms of its relationship with export performance, the relatively high dependence of the East Asian economies on exports suggests that a currency regime that invites wild fluctuations in external competitiveness is likely to meet domestic opposition.[21] As we noted previously, moreover, an increasing sense of export rivalry seems to be an important factor behind the recent calls for joint exchange rate management in East Asia. The following discussion is thus not so much about the optimal exchange rate regime as about how individual countries' concern about their external competitiveness is likely to constrain the range of options concerning regional policy coordination.

Although a sizable literature assesses the merits of monetary unification in East Asia, most authors admit this to be at best a long-term goal and instead recommend less ambitious arrangements.[22] An example of the latter that has a number of supporters in Japan and some other countries is the so-called common basket peg (CBP) regime. Under this arrangement, most or all of the East Asian countries *other than Japan* pledge to stabilize the value of their currencies in terms of a currency basket composed of the dollar, the yen, and the euro. Although there is debate concerning how to decide the weight of each of these three currencies, it is typically envisaged that all participating countries use the same set of weights to fix the relative value of their own currencies. Underlying this proposal is the view that most Asian monetary authorities still loosely peg their currencies to the dollar and that this soft dollar peg renders the effective value of their currencies unstable.[23] The proponents of the CBP arrangement also stress that, as we have just seen, most East Asian countries trade extensively with the United States and Europe but also increasingly with the other Asian countries. In their view, the CBP is useful not only to stabilize the effective value of the East Asian currencies but also to prevent member countries from manipulating exchange rates to boost their export competitiveness.[24]

There is little doubt that manufacturers of the East Asian countries compete more vigorously today than a decade ago, in terms of both the geographical distribution of their exports and the range of products they sell. To the extent that this is the case, the monetary authorities of the East Asian countries may find

... Trade compentnon muncs (2000, cuto area as a single country)

Competitor (j)	Japan				Greater China				Indonesia			
	w_j	w_j^1	z_j^1	v_j^1	w_j	w_j^1	z_j^1	v_j^1	w_j	w_j^1	z_j^1	v_j^1
Australia	3.0	0.5	0.8	0.6	2.1	1.1	1.0	1.1	4.6	3.4	2.0	2.8
Canada	2.2	0.6	8.5	3.7	1.8	0.9	5.9	2.6	1.1	0.3	4.4	1.9
Greater China	16.7	15.6	11.4	13.9	–	–	–	–	10.1	18.1	11.2	15.4
Indonesia	2.8	0.9	1.2	1.0	1.4	0.9	2.7	1.6	–	–	–	–
Japan	–	–	–	–	20.6	21.1	11.4	17.7	25.3	23.3	7.0	16.9
Korea	6.8	7.9	8.0	8.0	8.2	9.1	7.6	8.6	9.2	6.7	8.4	7.4
Malaysia	3.8	3.5	4.7	4.0	2.4	3.4	6.2	4.4	4.4	6.7	7.3	6.9
Mexico	1.0	0.3	6.8	2.9	0.5	0.3	7.2	2.7	0.4	0.1	4.0	1.6
Philippines	1.8	2.4	2.1	2.3	1.1	1.2	3.1	1.8	1.3	1.4	4.4	2.5
Singapore	4.2	5.0	6.3	5.5	4.8	7.8	6.1	7.2	4.7	1.0	5.7	2.8
Sweden	0.6	0.6	2.4	1.3	0.8	0.7	2.4	1.3	0.4	0.3	3.3	1.5
Switzerland	0.8	0.7	2.8	1.5	1.0	1.0	3.5	1.9	0.3	0.3	3.0	1.4
Taiwan	6.8	8.0	8.5	8.2	8.9	8.7	9.0	8.8	4.4	5.1	8.4	6.4
Thailand	3.4	3.2	2.6	3.0	2.0	2.7	4.6	3.4	3.2	5.2	7.9	6.3
United Kingdom	3.0	3.1	7.6	4.9	4.1	4.2	7.2	5.2	2.7	1.9	6.5	3.7
United States	30.1	31.9	12.2	24.0	24.7	20.3	10.2	16.7	15.1	11.4	7.4	9.8
Euro area	12.9	15.9	14.2	15.2	15.6	16.7	12.1	15.1	12.7	14.9	9.2	12.7

Competitor (j)	Korea				Malaysia				Philippines			
	w_j	w_j^1	z_j^1	v_j^1	w_j	w_j^1	z_j^1	v_j^1	w_j	w_j^1	z_j^1	v_j^1
Australia	4.5	0.4	1.1	0.7	2.2	0.7	1.1	0.8	1.6	0.5	1.1	0.7
Canada	1.4	0.5	5.1	2.2	0.8	0.1	4.1	1.5	1.0	0.2	3.9	1.5
Greater China	13.3	17.7	8.9	14.4	8.1	8.0	10.4	8.8	8.8	7.4	9.8	8.3
Indonesia	4.1	0.7	2.4	1.3	2.0	0.8	3.0	1.5	1.4	0.4	3.1	1.4
Japan	25.9	20.8	13.8	18.2	15.9	11.2	11.5	11.3	18.3	21.2	9.0	16.8
Korea	–	–	–	–	4.3	3.5	9.1	5.4	6.0	6.1	10.0	7.5
Malaysia	3.3	2.9	6.4	4.2	–	–	–	–	4.0	3.7	9.2	5.7
Mexico	0.2	0.3	5.1	2.1	0.4	0.1	4.2	1.5	0.4	0.0	3.9	1.4
Philippines	1.2	1.8	4.1	2.7	1.7	1.3	5.3	2.7	–	–	–	–

(Continued)

Table 6.10   (Continued)

Competitor (j)	Korea				Malaysia				Philippines			
	w_j	w_j^1	z_j^1	v_j^1	w_j	w_j^1	z_j^1	v_j^1	w_j	w_j^1	z_j^1	v_j^1
Singapore	4.1	5.4	7.4	6.2	23.1	33.8	8.5	25.1	8.5	9.8	9.4	9.6
Sweden	0.5	0.3	2.6	1.1	0.4	0.4	2.1	1.0	0.2	0.1	1.6	0.6
Switzerland	0.6	0.2	2.2	0.9	0.4	0.2	1.9	0.8	0.3	0.1	1.9	0.7
Taiwan	3.7	7.1	10.8	8.4	4.9	5.8	9.9	7.2	7.0	5.8	9.6	7.2
Thailand	1.3	1.4	4.5	2.5	3.6	4.2	5.7	4.7	3.0	3.3	6.2	4.3
United Kingdom	1.7	1.5	6.1	3.2	3.0	2.4	5.2	3.4	3.1	1.3	4.6	2.5
United States	24.0	28.4	9.1	21.2	19.6	18.4	9.2	15.2	25.4	31.1	7.9	22.7
Euro area	10.1	10.8	10.6	10.7	9.6	9.2	8.7	9.0	11.1	9.0	8.8	8.9

Competitor (j)	Singapore				Taiwan				Thailand			
	w_j	w_j^1	z_j^1	v_j^1	w_j	w_j^1	z_j^1	v_j^1	w_j	w_j^1	z_j^1	v_j^1
Australia	2.8	1.0	1.0	1.0	1.9	0.4	1.0	0.6	2.5	0.8	1.5	1.0
Canada	0.5	0.2	3.2	1.2	1.6	0.5	4.3	1.9	1.0	0.3	4.2	1.6
Greater China	12.1	13.1	10.2	12.1	19.7	16.7	14.1	15.8	10.4	13.0	10.6	12.2
Indonesia	1.6	0.1	2.0	0.8	1.3	0.5	2.2	1.1	2.2	1.3	4.4	2.4
Japan	13.3	11.5	13.4	12.1	18.8	20.8	13.2	18.0	21.7	21.2	8.7	16.9
Korea	4.3	4.7	9.2	6.2	4.5	7.0	9.8	8.0	3.2	3.4	8.7	5.2
Malaysia	17.4	24.2	7.5	18.5	3.2	4.8	6.3	5.3	5.5	8.6	7.8	8.3
Mexico	0.7	0.4	3.6	1.5	1.1	0.2	4.7	1.8	0.4	0.3	4.1	1.6
Philippines	2.6	2.5	4.8	3.3	1.9	1.7	3.5	2.4	1.9	2.5	4.9	3.3
Singapore	–	–	–	–	5.0	8.8	7.7	8.4	10.3	13.0	6.8	10.9
Sweden	0.3	0.1	1.9	0.7	0.5	0.4	2.0	1.0	0.5	0.3	2.6	1.1
Switzerland	0.7	0.2	2.2	0.9	0.6	0.4	2.2	1.1	1.0	1.0	2.7	1.6
Taiwan	5.7	7.7	10.6	8.7	–	–	–	–	4.6	5.3	9.1	6.6
Thailand	5.1	4.5	4.3	4.4	2.0	2.1	4.2	2.9	–	–	–	–
United Kingdom	2.9	2.2	5.7	3.4	2.5	1.7	5.6	3.1	3.0	1.7	6.4	3.3
United States	19.0	18.5	11.6	16.2	24.4	23.3	9.5	18.2	19.9	16.2	8.2	13.5
Euro area	10.9	9.0	8.6	8.9	11.1	10.8	9.8	10.4	11.9	11.2	9.3	10.5

Competitor (i)	Japan				Greater China				Indonesia			
	w_j	w_j^2	z_j^2	v_j^2	w_j	w_j^2	z_j^2	v_j^2	w_j	w_j^2	z_j^2	v_j^2
Australia	3.0	0.8	2.0	1.3	2.1	1.3	1.8	1.5	4.6	3.7	1.8	2.9
Canada	2.2	1.0	7.1	3.5	1.8	1.0	5.8	2.7	1.1	0.3	4.9	2.1
Greater China	16.7	15.9	10.7	13.8	–	–	–	–	10.1	15.6	12.6	14.4
Indonesia	2.8	1.1	2.1	1.5	1.4	0.9	3.8	2.0	–	–	–	–
Japan	–	–	–	–	20.6	20.7	10.5	17.1	25.3	24.3	9.5	18.5
Korea	6.8	7.5	7.6	7.6	8.2	8.8	7.0	8.2	9.2	6.9	7.4	7.1
Malaysia	3.8	3.6	4.7	4.0	2.4	2.9	5.6	3.9	4.4	6.3	5.8	6.1
Mexico	1.0	0.5	6.0	2.7	0.5	0.3	6.2	2.4	0.4	0.1	4.7	1.9
Philippines	1.8	2.0	2.7	2.3	1.1	1.2	3.6	2.0	1.3	1.2	3.4	2.1
Singapore	4.2	4.8	5.8	5.2	4.8	6.3	5.6	6.0	4.7	0.9	5.5	2.7
Sweden	0.6	0.6	3.6	1.8	0.8	0.7	3.0	1.5	0.4	0.3	2.8	1.3
Switzerland	0.8	0.7	3.7	1.9	1.0	1.0	4.1	2.1	0.3	0.3	2.9	1.3
Taiwan	6.8	7.6	7.4	7.5	8.9	9.5	7.8	8.9	4.4	4.9	7.8	6.0
Thailand	3.4	3.4	3.6	3.5	2.0	2.3	5.2	3.3	3.2	4.7	5.2	4.9
United Kingdom	3.0	3.4	8.1	5.3	4.1	4.3	7.5	5.4	2.7	2.4	6.0	3.8
United States	30.1	31.7	11.5	23.6	24.7	21.6	10.6	17.7	15.1	12.8	9.4	11.4
Euro area	12.9	15.4	13.2	14.5	15.6	17.1	11.9	15.3	12.7	15.3	10.3	13.3

Competitor (i)	Korea				Malaysia				Philippines			
	w_j	w_j^2	z_j^2	v_j^2	w_j	w_j^2	z_j^2	v_j^2	w_j	w_j^2	z_j^2	v_j^2
Australia	4.5	0.7	1.7	1.1	2.2	1.0	1.6	1.2	1.6	0.6	1.3	0.9
Canada	1.4	0.7	5.9	2.6	0.8	0.3	4.5	1.8	1.0	0.4	4.3	1.8
Greater China	13.3	18.7	8.8	15.0	8.1	8.4	10.0	8.9	8.8	8.6	11.8	9.8
Indonesia	4.1	0.9	2.8	1.6	2.0	1.1	3.1	1.8	1.4	0.5	2.9	1.4
Japan	25.9	20.8	13.2	18.0	15.9	13.1	11.6	12.6	18.3	19.0	10.3	15.9
Korea	–	–	–	–	4.3	3.6	7.6	5.0	6.0	5.8	7.6	6.5
Malaysia	3.3	2.7	5.4	3.7	–	–	–	–	4.0	4.3	6.8	5.2
Mexico	0.2	0.6	5.3	2.3	0.4	0.2	4.9	1.8	0.4	0.1	5.0	1.9
Philippines	1.2	1.7	3.4	2.3	1.7	1.6	4.4	2.6	–	–	–	–

(Continued)

Table 6.11 (Continued)

Competitor (j)	Korea				Malaysia				Philippines			
	w_j	w_j^2	z_j^2	v_j^2	w_j	w_j^2	z_j^2	v_j^2	w_j	w_j^2	z_j^2	v_j^2
Singapore	4.1	4.7	6.1	5.2	23.1	29.1	6.6	21.4	8.5	9.8	7.6	9.0
Sweden	0.5	0.3	2.9	1.3	0.4	0.4	2.5	1.1	0.2	0.1	2.0	0.8
Switzerland	0.6	0.3	2.8	1.2	0.4	0.3	2.7	1.1	0.3	0.1	2.4	1.0
Taiwan	3.7	6.1	8.3	6.9	4.9	5.4	8.5	6.5	7.0	7.0	8.4	7.5
Thailand	1.3	1.3	4.4	2.5	3.6	3.6	5.1	4.1	3.0	3.4	4.9	3.9
United Kingdom	1.7	2.0	6.8	3.8	3.0	2.7	6.1	3.9	3.1	2.2	5.5	3.4
United States	24.0	27.0	10.5	20.9	19.6	19.8	10.8	16.7	25.4	27.1	10.0	20.9
Euro area	10.1	11.6	11.5	11.5	9.6	9.4	9.8	9.6	11.1	10.9	9.0	10.2

Competitor (j)	Singapore				Taiwan				Thailand			
	w_j	w_j^2	z_j^2	v_j^2	w_j	w_j^2	z_j^2	v_j^2	w_j	w_j^2	z_j^2	v_j^2
Australia	2.8	1.4	1.6	1.5	1.9	0.6	1.4	1.2	2.5	1.1	1.7	1.3
Canada	0.5	0.3	4.0	1.6	1.6	0.7	1.3	2.8	1.0	0.3	4.5	1.8
China/Hong Kong	12.1	12.5	10.2	11.7	19.7	19.3	19.6	16.2	10.4	11.9	11.1	11.6
Greater China	1.6	0.1	2.7	1.0	1.3	0.6	1.1	1.7	2.2	1.4	3.4	2.1
Japan	13.3	12.6	12.5	12.6	18.8	20.1	19.3	16.0	21.7	22.6	10.7	18.5
Korea	4.3	4.5	7.6	5.5	4.5	5.8	5.0	6.8	3.2	3.2	7.5	4.7
Malaysia	17.4	20.6	5.8	15.6	3.2	3.9	3.5	4.7	5.5	6.6	6.1	6.4
Mexico	0.7	0.5	4.1	1.7	1.1	0.2	0.7	2.5	0.4	0.3	4.9	1.9
Philippines	2.6	2.7	4.3	3.2	1.9	1.9	1.9	2.7	1.9	2.3	3.8	2.8
Singapore	–	–	–	–	5.0	6.9	5.7	6.6	10.3	12.8	6.1	10.5
Sweden	0.3	0.1	2.5	0.9	0.5	0.4	0.4	1.5	0.5	0.3	2.6	1.1
Switzerland	0.7	0.3	3.1	1.3	0.6	0.5	0.6	1.8	1.0	0.9	2.9	1.6
Taiwan	5.7	6.8	8.6	7.4	–	–	–	–	4.6	5.1	8.2	6.2
Thailand	5.1	4.9	4.5	4.8	2.0	2.0	2.0	3.3	–	–	–	–
United Kingdom	2.9	2.7	6.5	4.0	2.5	2.1	2.4	4.2	3.0	2.4	6.2	3.7
United States	19.0	19.7	11.8	17.0	24.4	23.9	24.2	17.2	19.9	17.2	10.1	14.8
Euro area	10.9	10.2	10.2	10.2	11.1	11.1	11.1	10.8	11.9	11.5	10.3	11.1

appealing a mechanism that explicitly aims to stabilize the relative value of their currencies, although this appeal must be weighed against the cost of giving up monetary policy autonomy. In contrast to the pre-1999 European Exchange Rate Mechanism (ERM), however, the Asian CBP regime demands that the participating countries adopt the currencies of nonmember countries as the anchor for their monetary policy. As there is little evidence that the East Asian countries need an external monetary anchor to maintain long-term domestic price stability,[25] and the CBP arrangement is designed to stabilize the prospective member countries' overall external competitiveness, this regime would make little sense even as an intermediate arrangement unless the three external regions constitute important export markets and trade competitors for the participating countries. For the regime to prove sustainable, moreover, this must remain the case at least for the foreseeable future.

For most East Asian countries, however, the three industrial regions appear less important as trade competitors than as export markets. In Tables 6.10 and 6.11, the aggregate sum of w_j for the United States, Japan, and the euro area ranges between 43.2 percent (Singapore) and 60.9 percent (China). Measured in terms of our competition indices, however, the corresponding shares fall substantially: the subtotal for the three industrial regions ranges between 35.5 percent (Malaysia) and 50.1 percent (Korea) for v_j^1 and between 38.9 percent (Malaysia) and 50.4 percent (Korea) for v_j^2. The relative share of the three regions also differs substantially across the eight East Asian countries. In Indonesia, for example, the values of v_j^2 for the United States and the euro area are 11.4 and 13.3 percent, respectively. In Korea, however, the corresponding values are 20.9 and 11.5 percent and in the Philippines 20.9 and 10.2 percent. As similar variations exist among other countries, any single set of the weights of the dollar, the yen, and the euro would likely leave at least some countries unsatisfied. Should each country be allowed to choose its own weights, however, there would remain some volatility in the relative value of their currencies, which may also become a source of contention.

More importantly, our computation suggests that for many East Asian countries, Japan is neither the dominant trading partner nor the most important competitor even within the Asian region. As we saw previously, in most countries the share of Japan measured by our composite competition indices, v_j^1 and v_j^2, remained stagnant or fell slightly between 1990 and 2000,[26] whereas those of the ASEAN countries and, in particular, China, have risen sharply. In Tables 6.10 and 6.11, China's values of v_j^1 and v_j^2 are already roughly comparable to those of Japan in Indonesia, Korea, Malaysia, Singapore, and Taiwan. To the extent that the recent trend is more likely to be reinforced than reversed in the near future, the region's policy-makers are likely to find it odd to adopt a collective exchange rate regime that officially elevates only the yen to a special status among the Asian currencies.

For Japan, too, China is an increasingly important trading partner-cum-competitor. In Tables 6.10 and 6.11, we observe that China's v_j^1 and v_j^2 in Japan are roughly as large as those of the euro area and close to the combined shares of Korea and Taiwan. Although the Asian CBP does not require an explicit policy commitment on the part of the Japanese monetary authorities, the adoption of this arrangement by other countries would effectively deny Japan the possibility of adjusting its bilateral trade balance through nominal exchange rate adjustment. In recent years, a number of Japanese policy-makers have openly called on China to revalue the RMB on the grounds that its de facto dollar peg provides Chinese exporters with undue competitiveness vis-à-vis their Japanese counterparts. As the yen has been relatively stable during the past few years against the dollar in nominal terms and hence also against the Chinese RMB, their grievances make little sense unless price-adjusted productivity growth has been substantially faster in China than in Japan. If this is true, however, the CBP implies that Japanese manufacturers progressively lose their price competitiveness to their Chinese rivals unless the yen depreciates against the dollar and the euro continuously and perhaps at a very rapid speed. And that would in turn mean that Japan's monetary policy is dictated to a substantial degree by the need for targeting the yen to the dollar and the euro.

6.4   Intra-industry trade and trade competitiveness

As we noted previously, our trade competition indices reflect closely the state of intra-industry trade between the home country and foreign countries. While our third-market competition indices explicitly recognize the fact that products of two countries compete for customers in other countries as well, these indices are also constructed in a manner analogous to the bilateral competition indices. Although in terms of our indices the East Asian countries are becoming increasingly important competitors to one another, there may be objections to this interpretation. More specifically, although any pair of countries can increase their intra-industry trade and/or exports of similar products to third countries when their industrial structures become genuinely competitive, such trade can expand for other reasons as well. In particular, it is widely recognized that a substantial part of the recent increase in intra-regional trade in East Asia owes itself to the phenomenon known as fragmentation, in which manufacturing firms slice up their production process into distinct stages and locate individual parts in different countries. Fragmentation naturally gives rise to *intra-product* trade – trade in intermediate goods that are used as an input to the next stage of production – and has the effect of expanding trade among countries hosting such production networks.[27] While the presence of intra-product trade does not pose a serious problem to our competition indices as long as intermediate and final goods are classified into independent product categories, the relatively coarse commodity classification of WTD suggests that this is not necessarily the case.[28]

Although it is difficult to quantify rigorously the bias arising from intra-product trade, we should be able to make inferences about its seriousness by calculating our competition indices using trade statistics with different levels of product aggregation and comparing the computed values. As Japan is a major source of foreign direct investment (FDI) in East Asia and engages in substantial intra-product trade with other countries, we take Japan's bilateral trade as an example and conduct this experiment using the Japanese customs data. The Japanese customs data is compiled according to the World Customs Organization's Harmonized System (HS) and permits substantially more detailed product breakdowns than does the WTD. We reestimate Japan's bilateral competition indices w_j^1 and $w_{j'}^2$ j = 1, 2, ..., 23 for 2000,[29] by using data classified according to HS's two-, four-, and six-digit product codes.[30] As the MoF statistics include data for more recent years, we also compute the same indices for 2002, 2003, and 2004[31] and examine whether there has been any noticeable change in Japan's external competitive relationship since 2000.

Tables 6.12 and 6.13 show the results of our computation. By looking at the results for 2000, we find that the estimates obtained with the two- and four-digit data exhibit nonnegligible discrepancies for certain competitor countries. More specifically, the estimates based on the two-digit data are smaller than those based on the four-digit data for Germany and the United States, whereas the converse is the case for China, Malaysia, and Thailand. As the latter countries are major recipients of Japan's manufacturing FDI and likely to engage in substantial production sharing with Japan, our previous concern is perhaps not unfounded. Nevertheless, the estimates based on the four- and six-digit data are not very different from each other. In particular, although using the most detailed six-digit data further increases the estimates for the United States, doing so has little effect on the values for the other countries. It thus seems unlikely that the increasing competition between Japan and the other Asian countries found in Table 6.1 merely reflects an increase in intra-product trade.[32]

In Tables 6.12 and 6.13, we also note that the estimates for greater China have increased sharply during the past few years, whereas those for the United States have fallen by similarly large proportions. Although this partly reflects the rapid growth of the Chinese economy and associated increase in its imports, this does not appear to be the whole story. Between 1999 and 2003, the value of w_j measured with the Japanese customs statistics (not shown in the tables) has risen by 9.3 percent for greater China and has fallen by 7.4 percent for the United States. During the same five-year interval, the values of w_j^1 and w_j^2 for greater China computed with the most disaggregated six-digit HS data have increased by approximately 10.3 percent, whereas the corresponding values for the United States have fallen by 12.7 percent (w_j^1) and 10.5 percent (w_j^2). Although the estimates for 2004 are based on data for the first semester only and thus only indicative, the results in Tables 6.12 and 6.13 suggest that greater China has already replaced the United States as Japan's most important trade competitor, at least as far as bilateral trade is concerned. While we are unsure about what is happening in the other East Asian countries, their trade with

Table 6.12 Trade competition index for Japan (w_j^1)

Competitor (j)	2000			2002			2003			2004		
	HS 2-digit	HS 4-digit	HS 6-digit	HS 2-digit	HS 4-digit	HS 6-digit	HS 2-digit	HS 4-digit	HS 6-digit	HS 2-digit	HS 4-digit	HS 6-digit
Australia	0.4	0.4	0.4	0.3	0.3	0.3	0.3	0.3	0.3	0.3	0.2	0.2
Austria	0.2	0.2	0.1	0.2	0.2	0.1	0.2	0.2	0.1	0.3	0.2	0.1
Belgium (inc. Lux.)	0.6	0.7	0.5	0.5	0.6	0.5	0.7	0.8	0.7	0.6	0.7	0.6
Canada	0.9	0.8	0.7	0.9	0.8	0.7	0.7	0.7	0.6	0.7	0.6	0.5
Greater China	15.5	14.5	14.8	21.9	18.6	19.6	25.5	21.7	23.6	27.9	24.2	26.7
France	1.6	1.7	1.5	1.8	1.8	1.7	1.7	1.9	1.8	1.7	1.9	1.7
Germany	6.1	6.5	5.9	6.3	7.0	6.0	6.9	7.7	6.3	6.8	7.5	6.2
Indonesia	1.9	1.4	1.2	2.0	1.4	1.1	2.0	1.4	1.1	2.0	1.5	1.1
Ireland	0.8	0.6	0.5	0.7	0.4	0.4	0.9	0.4	0.5	0.7	0.3	0.4
Italy	1.3	1.2	1.1	1.3	1.3	1.1	1.3	1.3	1.1	1.4	1.4	1.1
Korea	8.3	8.2	8.1	8.1	9.7	10.3	8.5	10.3	10.6	9.3	11.0	11.0
Malaysia	5.4	3.8	3.8	4.6	3.7	3.9	4.3	3.5	3.5	4.1	3.7	3.4
Mexico	0.7	0.6	0.6	0.7	0.7	0.7	0.6	0.6	0.7	0.5	0.5	0.6
Netherlands	0.9	0.9	0.8	0.8	0.9	0.7	0.7	0.9	0.6	0.6	0.7	0.5
Philippines	3.4	3.2	3.4	3.8	3.5	3.6	3.6	3.4	3.4	3.5	3.4	3.2
Singapore	3.4	3.6	4.1	2.9	2.9	3.0	2.7	2.9	3.1	2.5	2.7	2.9
Spain	0.4	0.4	0.4	0.3	0.3	0.3	0.3	0.3	0.3	0.5	0.5	0.4
Sweden	1.0	0.6	0.5	0.8	0.7	0.4	0.6	0.6	0.4	0.6	0.5	0.4
Switzerland	0.6	0.5	0.4	0.5	0.5	0.3	0.5	0.5	0.3	0.5	0.5	0.4
Taiwan	9.0	8.6	8.7	8.3	8.6	8.7	7.8	8.5	8.6	7.7	8.3	8.5
Thailand	4.1	3.1	3.1	4.5	3.7	3.6	4.6	4.0	3.9	4.8	4.1	4.2
United Kingdom	2.9	3.3	2.9	2.4	2.9	2.8	2.5	3.0	3.0	2.3	3.0	2.9
United States	30.7	35.2	36.4	26.3	29.5	30.0	23.0	25.1	25.6	20.9	22.6	23.1

Notes: Values for 2000 are the average for 1999–2001. Values for 2004 are based on data for the first six months only.
Source: Author's calculation based on customs statistics compiled by Japanese Ministry of Finance.

Table 6.13 Trade competition index for Japan (w_j^2)

Competitor (j)	2000 HS 2-digit	2000 HS 4-digit	2000 HS 6-digit	2002 HS 2-digit	2002 HS 4-digit	2002 HS 6-digit	2003 HS 2-digit	2003 HS 4-digit	2003 HS 6-digit	2004 HS 2-digit	2004 HS 4-digit	2004 HS 6-digit
Australia	0.9	0.7	0.6	0.8	0.5	0.5	0.8	0.5	0.5	0.6	0.4	0.4
Austria	0.3	0.2	0.1	0.3	0.2	0.2	0.3	0.2	0.1	0.3	0.2	0.2
Belgium (inc. Lux.)	0.9	0.8	0.6	0.9	0.8	0.6	1.0	0.9	0.7	1.0	0.9	0.7
Canada	1.3	1.1	0.9	1.2	1.1	0.9	1.1	1.0	0.8	1.0	0.8	0.7
Greater China	15.8	15.1	15.6	21.4	19.7	20.5	24.9	23.2	24.3	26.3	25.1	26.4
France	1.9	1.8	1.6	2.0	2.0	1.7	1.9	2.0	1.8	1.9	2.0	1.7
Germany	5.8	6.1	5.9	5.5	6.0	5.7	5.7	6.3	5.9	5.8	6.4	6.0
Indonesia	1.9	1.5	1.4	2.0	1.6	1.3	2.0	1.6	1.3	2.0	1.7	1.4
Ireland	0.8	0.6	0.6	0.8	0.5	0.5	0.9	0.5	0.5	0.7	0.5	0.5
Italy	1.4	1.4	1.2	1.4	1.4	1.2	1.5	1.4	1.2	1.6	1.5	1.3
Korea	7.7	7.9	7.8	8.0	8.8	9.0	8.5	9.3	9.5	9.3	10.2	10.4
Malaysia	4.0	3.6	3.5	3.5	3.3	3.2	3.2	3.0	3.0	3.1	2.9	3.0
Mexico	0.9	0.7	0.6	0.9	0.7	0.7	0.7	0.7	0.7	0.7	0.7	0.6
Netherlands	1.5	1.3	1.1	1.4	1.2	1.0	1.4	1.2	1.0	1.2	1.0	0.8
Philippines	2.8	2.8	2.9	2.9	3.0	3.1	2.7	2.8	2.9	2.6	2.6	2.7
Singapore	3.7	3.7	3.9	3.0	3.0	3.0	2.8	2.8	2.8	2.8	2.8	2.7
Spain	0.5	0.5	0.4	0.5	0.4	0.3	0.5	0.5	0.4	0.7	0.6	0.4
Sweden	0.8	0.6	0.5	0.6	0.6	0.4	0.6	0.5	0.4	0.5	0.5	0.4
Switzerland	0.7	0.6	0.5	0.6	0.5	0.4	0.6	0.5	0.4	0.7	0.5	0.4
Taiwan	8.3	8.1	8.2	7.7	7.7	7.9	7.6	7.7	7.8	7.9	7.8	8.0
Thailand	3.7	3.3	3.1	4.1	3.8	3.6	4.3	4.0	3.9	4.5	4.2	4.0
United Kingdom	3.3	3.5	3.3	2.9	3.2	3.0	2.9	3.2	3.1	2.8	3.2	3.0
United States	31.3	34.1	35.8	27.7	30.0	31.3	24.1	25.9	27.1	22.0	23.5	24.6

Notes and Source: See Table 6.12.

China has also increased sharply during the past few years (IMF 2004). To the extent that this is the case, it seems likely that the share of greater China measured by our competition indices is rising in these countries as well.[33]

Will China continue to increase its importance as a competitor for Japan and other East Asian countries? While we should be cautious about extrapolating the past trend into the future, it is insightful to look at how the past changes in the *value* of intra-industry trade among the East Asian countries have been accompanied by its *product coverage*. For this purpose, we used the Japanese customs data for 1988–2003 and counted for each year: (1) the number of product categories for which Japan had strictly positive exports to each competitor country; (2) the number of products for which Japan had strictly positive imports from each country; and (3) the number of goods for which there were two-way (i.e. intra-industry) trade between Japan and each country. The results are compiled in Table 6.14.[34]

In the top panel of Table 6.14, we observe that the product coverage of Japan's exports to individual competitor countries has been stable during the past 15 years, except for a few countries (e.g. Australia and Switzerland) for which the coverage has fallen by fairly substantial proportions. This implies that the product coverage of Japan's intra-industry trade with each trading partner cannot increase much unless the latter expands the range of products it sells to Japan. In the middle panel of Table 6.14, we find that this has been the case for most East Asian countries, although the proportionate increase between 1988 and 2003 was particularly large in the ASEAN countries and China. In the bottom panel, we also observe that the number of goods for which Japan had intra-industry trade with these countries have risen significantly, although the pace of increase seems to have slowed in recent years. On the other hand, the number of goods for which Japan has two-way trade with the United States and the EU countries has marginally decreased during the past 15 years. We also note that the substantial increase in the product coverage of Japan's intra-industry trade with the other Asian countries is not concentrated in specific industries for which international production sharing is pervasive (e.g. electronics) but has also occurred in other industries.

As Japan's intra-industry trade with China (and greater China) already covers roughly the same number of products as does its trade with the United States and the EU, the product coverage of the former is unlikely to continue to increase rapidly in the future.[35] This does not necessarily mean, however, that the *value* of the intra-industry trade between Japan and China will also stop increasing soon. Existing studies report that there is often a considerable time lag between the time a country starts to export a certain product to another country and the time when the former achieves a substantial market share in the latter (Bernard et al. 2004). To the extent that this is the case, the value of intra-industry trade between Japan and China may continue to increase at a faster pace than their aggregate trade for at least some years to come.

Table 6.14 Number of goods in Japan's bilateral manufacturing trade

Partner country/region	1988	1991	1994	1997	2000	2003	Change between:			Change (%) between:		
							1988–97	1994–2003	1988–2003	1988–97	1994–2003	1988–2003
Exports from Japan												
Australia	1,762	1,696	1,649	1,581	1,501	1,459	−181	−190	−303	−10.3	−11.5	−17.2
Canada	1,486	1,445	1,337	1,300	1,300	1,283	−186	−54	−203	−12.5	−4.0	−13.7
Indonesia	1,628	1,756	1,698	1,788	1,707	1,709	160	11	81	9.8	0.6	5.0
Korea	2,094	2,169	2,135	2,105	2,104	2,103	11	−32	9	0.5	−1.5	0.4
Malaysia	1,656	1,787	1,808	1,794	1,710	1,694	138	−114	38	8.3	−6.3	2.3
Mexico	1,110	1,203	1,143	1,087	1,114	1,041	−23	−102	−69	−2.1	−8.9	−6.2
Philippines	1,656	1,652	1,703	1,760	1,727	1,695	104	−8	39	6.3	−0.5	2.4
Singapore	1,952	2,000	1,970	1,917	1,844	1,795	−35	−175	−157	−1.8	−8.9	−8.0
Switzerland	1,250	1,259	1,137	1,095	1,094	1,038	−155	−99	−212	−12.4	−8.7	−17.0
Taiwan	2,153	2,148	2,131	2,086	2,082	2,065	−67	−66	−88	−3.1	−3.1	−4.1
Thailand	1,830	1,937	1,917	1,919	1,873	1,874	89	−43	44	4.9	−2.2	2.4
United States	2,078	2,044	2,041	2,012	2,002	2,014	−66	−27	−64	−3.2	−1.3	−3.1
EU	2,026	2,032	1,960	1,972	1,980	1,975	−54	15	−51	−2.7	0.8	−2.5
Euro area	1,957	1,959	1,897	1,898	1,918	1,912	−59	15	−45	−3.0	0.8	−2.3
Greater China	2,147	2,162	2,188	2,172	2,160	2,179	25	−9	32	1.2	−0.4	1.5
China	1,838	1,908	2,018	2,055	2,047	2,084	217	66	246	11.8	3.3	13.4
Hong Kong	2,016	2,040	2,045	2,027	2,011	2,000	11	−45	−16	0.5	−2.2	−0.8
Imports of Japan												
Australia	811	860	948	1,043	991	989	232	41	178	28.6	4.3	21.9
Canada	950	1,053	1,047	1,205	1,185	1,172	255	125	222	26.8	11.9	23.4
Indonesia	421	612	777	984	1,073	1,069	563	292	648	133.7	37.6	153.9
Korea	1,598	1,575	1,679	1,721	1,803	1,825	123	146	227	7.7	8.7	14.2
Malaysia	453	726	847	1,008	1,020	1,018	555	171	565	122.5	20.2	124.7
Mexico	342	423	451	592	651	669	250	218	327	73.1	48.3	95.6
Philippines	371	507	640	855	895	911	484	271	540	130.5	42.3	145.6
Singapore	822	963	1,018	1,056	1,016	1,011	234	−7	189	28.5	−0.7	23.0
Switzerland	1,305	1,302	1,267	1,309	1,257	1,269	4	2	−36	0.3	0.2	−2.8

(Continued)

Table 6.14 (Continued)

Partner country/region	1988	1991	1994	1997	2000	2003	Change between: 1988–97	Change between: 1994–2003	Change between: 1988–2003	Change (%) between: 1988–97	Change (%) between: 1994–2003	Change (%) between: 1988–2003
Taiwan	1,593	1,577	1,645	1,686	1,657	1,648	93	3	55	5.8	0.2	3.5
Thailand	647	889	1,034	1,173	1,235	1,302	526	268	655	81.3	25.9	101.2
United States	2,161	2,193	2,184	2,166	2,151	2,108	5	−76	−53	0.2	−3.5	−2.5
EU	2,234	2,245	2,228	2,208	2,210	2,210	−26	−18	−24	−1.2	−0.8	−1.1
Euro area	2,176	2,206	2,180	2,163	2,178	2,169	−13	−11	−7	−0.6	−0.5	−0.3
Greater China	1,469	1,548	1,740	1,882	1,933	2,005	413	265	536	28.1	15.2	36.5
China	1,230	1,389	1,670	1,840	1,918	1,993	610	323	763	49.6	19.3	62.0
Hong Kong	993	1,024	1,017	1,107	998	962	114	−55	−31	11.5	−5.4	−3.1
Intra-industry trade												
Australia	686	735	752	852	787	783	166	31	97	24.2	4.1	14.1
Canada	739	812	750	862	859	859	123	109	120	16.6	14.5	16.2
Indonesia	283	457	594	827	868	862	544	268	579	192.2	45.1	204.6
Korea	1,480	1,515	1,590	1,647	1,721	1,742	167	152	262	11.3	9.6	17.7
Malaysia	382	639	752	912	888	905	530	153	523	138.7	20.3	136.9
Mexico	201	297	305	381	455	457	180	152	256	89.6	49.8	127.4
Philippines	259	375	505	731	775	783	472	278	524	182.2	55.0	202.3
Singapore	783	924	953	1,010	961	947	227	−6	164	29.0	−0.6	20.9
Switzerland	913	918	842	839	830	807	−74	−35	−106	−8.1	−4.2	−11.6
Taiwan	1,526	1,512	1,571	1,610	1,588	1,573	84	2	47	5.5	0.1	3.1
Thailand	515	774	892	1,066	1,100	1,147	551	255	632	107.0	28.6	122.7
United States	1,948	1,945	1,931	1,928	1,902	1,904	−20	−27	−44	−1.0	−1.4	−2.3
EU	1,957	1,964	1,891	1,909	1,917	1,926	−48	35	−31	−2.5	1.9	−1.6
Euro area	1,861	1,884	1,816	1,826	1,851	1,843	−35	27	−18	−1.9	1.5	−1.0
Greater China	1,380	1,472	1,659	1,811	1,848	1,929	431	270	549	31.2	16.3	39.8
China	958	1,169	1,487	1,684	1,742	1,852	726	365	894	75.8	24.5	93.3
Hong Kong	957	985	979	1,070	978	933	113	−46	−24	11.8	−4.7	−2.5

Note: Numbers of goods are counted for 5-digit codes of SITC Rev. 3.
Source: See Table 6.12.

6.5 Application to effective exchange rates

While our trade competition indicators are of interest in their own right, they can also be used as an input to the construction of other indices that are more directly relevant to issues surrounding exchange rate policy. As an example of such applications, this section uses our competition indices to compute several real effective exchange rate (REER) indices for the East Asian currencies and examines the relationship between nominal exchange rate and external competitiveness.

In general, the REER of the currency of the home country i, defined as a geometric average of its bilateral real exchange rates against those of countries $j = 1, 2, \dots$, can be written as follows:

$$S_t \equiv \prod_j S_{j,t}^{\varpi_{j,t}} \tag{6.15}$$

where

$$S_{j,t} \equiv \frac{E_{j,t} P_{j,t}}{P_{i,t}} \tag{6.16}$$

and

$$\sum_j \varpi_{j,t} = 1 \tag{6.17}$$

In the above, $P_{i,t}$ denotes the price level of country i at time t; $E_{j,t}$ is the nominal exchange rate defined as the price of one unit of foreign country j in terms of the home currency. $\varpi_{j,t}$ represents the weight assigned to the bilateral real exchange rate $S_{j,t}$.

The general REER index in Equation (6.15) allows for a number of choices concerning the price index $P_{j,t}$ and the way in which the currency weight $\varpi_{j,t}$ is calculated. Although their choice should in principle be guided by the type of model one has in mind, it is also constrained by data availability.[36] Here we define the REER specifically as a measure of the price competitiveness of the domestic manufacturing sector vis-à-vis those of foreign countries. While unit labor costs in the manufacturing sector are often the preferred price index for this purpose, reliable data on labor costs is unavailable for most developing countries. We thus use the producer prices index (PPI) for the manufacturing sector as our primary price index and also consider the case of using the more broad-based GDP deflator.[37]

The first choice concerning the construction of the currency weights $\varpi_{j,t}$, $j = 1, 2, \dots$ is whether to fix these values or let them adjust over time to some measure of economic fundamentals. Although fixed weights are convenient, the rapid change in the Asian countries' external competitive relationship observed in the previous sections suggests that time-varying weights are more appropriate. When using time-varying weights, however, we need to modify slightly the canonical REER index in Equation (6.15). To see why, take the ratio of S_t and S_{t-1} in Equation (6.15) and write the result as

$$S_t/S_{t-1} = \prod_j (S_{j,t} / S_{j,t-1})^{\varpi_{j,t}} \times \prod_j S_{j,t-1}^{\Delta\varpi_{j,t}} \tag{6.18}$$

As one can see, even if the bilateral real exchange rates $S_{1,t}$, $S_{2,t}$, ... all remain constant, S_t can fluctuate as long as the values of $\varpi_{1,t}$, $\varpi_{2,t}$, ... change over time. To avoid this problem, we set the value of S_0 arbitrarily and define S_1, S_2, ... recursively as

$$S_t / S_{t-1} = \prod_j (S_{j,t} / S_{j,t-1})^{\varpi_{j,t}} \tag{6.19}$$

If we let s_t and $s_{j,t}$ denote the natural logarithms of S_t and $S_{j,t}$, the preceding equation reduces itself to the familiar expression for the period-to-period proportionate change in the REER

$$\Delta s_t = \sum_j \varpi_{j,t} \Delta s_{j,t} \tag{6.20}$$

where Δ indicates the first difference.

The remaining task is to decide how to set the values of $\varpi_{1,t}$, $\varpi_{2,t}$, ... in each period. In standard REER series provided by national and international agencies, the most common method is to use the shares of country j in the home country's aggregate trade, that is, to use w_j in Equation (6.1). Nevertheless, when the computed REER is meant to represent the home country's external manufacturing competitiveness, this weighting method is not particularly appealing for the reasons discussed in Section 6.2. The indicators of trade competition developed in the preceding sections, w_j^1, w_j^2, z_j^1, z_j^2, v_j^1, and v_j^2, provide reasonable alternatives to this standard method. In what follows, we take w_j^2 and v_j^2 as examples and compare the time-series behavior of the REERs computed using these indices and the corresponding series based on w_j.[38]

As our competition indices treat China and Hong Kong as a single economic area, we only compute the REERs for the currencies of the other eight East Asian countries. We would like to use the computed REERs not only to assess the effect of the choice of currency weights on their time-series behavior but also more generally to examine how the external competitiveness of these eight countries has evolved during the 1990s. Although we would ideally like to examine their behavior on a monthly or quarterly basis, China's PPI became available at such high frequencies only in late 1996. Therefore, we first examine annual REER series of the eight Asian currencies for a relatively long period of 1989–2001, and later present a few quarterly series of the Japanese yen for more recent years as an example of higher-frequency indices.[39]

Figures 6.1 and 6.2 show the annual REER series of the eight East Asian currencies computed with the manufacturing PPI and the GDP deflator. In general, the three series based on w_j, w_j^2, and v_j^2 track one another fairly

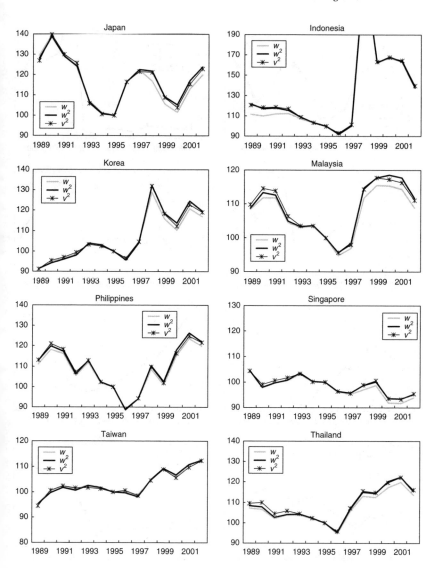

Figure 6.1 Real effective exchange rates of East Asian currencies (based on manufacturing PPI, 1995 = 100)

Note: An upward movement indicates a depreciation of the home currency

Source: Author's calculation based on statistics from IMF, Statistics Canada World Trade Database, CEIC and Bank of Japan

closely, suggesting that the choice of the currency weighting scheme has a relatively minor effect on the computed REERs at least for the currencies and the period considered here. For the years before the Asian crisis, the slight discrepancies among the three series largely reflected the fact that our indices tended

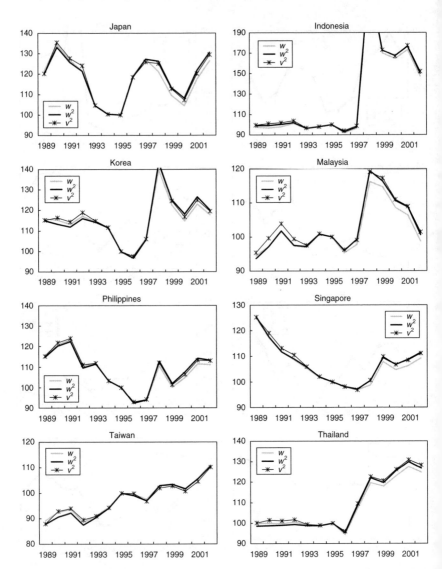

Figure 6.2 Real effective exchange rates of East Asian currencies (based on GDP deflator, 1995 = 100)
Note and Source: See Figure 6.1

to attach a smaller weight to Japan and a larger weight to greater China relative to their gross trade shares. For years after the crisis, the discrepancies among the three series primarily reflect the difference in the weight of Indonesia between our indices and the aggregate trade share.

Although numerous studies have been conducted on the role of exchange rates in the Asian crisis, a number of issues still remain contentious. One issue concerns whether or not the crisis can be regarded as an adjustment toward the long-run equilibrium exchange rate, that is, whether the Thai baht and the other crisis-affected currencies had been sufficiently overvalued in the preceding years as to necessitate the subsequent collapse. As numerous authors point out, many East Asian currencies were effectively pegged to the US dollar between the mid-1990s and the onset of the crisis, during which the nominal US dollar value of the yen fell by some 35 percent.[40] Since most crisis-affected countries also went into a serious export slump in the middle of 1995, some authors claim that the crisis was an inevitable consequence of their loss of competitiveness induced by the divergent movements of the yen and their currencies (Ogawa and Ito 2002).

While a thorough discussion of the foregoing issue is beyond the scope of this chapter, Figures 6.1 and 6.2 suggest that the link between nominal exchange rates and the East Asian countries' export competitiveness is not as straightforward as is often presumed. In terms of the PPI-based REER (our preferred measure of external competitiveness), the four countries that were most severely affected by the crisis – Indonesia, Korea, Malaysia, and Thailand – do appear to have experienced loss of competitiveness before 1997. In Figure 6.1, however, we observe that this process had begun well before 1995 when the yen started to depreciate progressively. Moreover, although the yen had strengthened vis-à-vis the dollar earlier in the 1990s (with the cumulative nominal appreciation of some 50 percent), its effect on the effective value of the other Asian countries is barely perceptible in Figure 6.1. This is due partly to the fact that the trend inflation rates of many East Asian countries had been substantially higher than that of Japan, and partly to the fact that China's PPI started falling in 1994 after surging sharply in the previous year.[41] Furthermore, although the loss of competitiveness measured in our REERs did accelerate in 1996 in most crisis countries, the size of the appreciation looks a little smaller in the series based on our competition indices than in those featuring the aggregate trade shares, apparently reflecting a smaller weight of the yen in the former series.[42]

Another issue that is debated widely is the role of exchange rates in the recovery of the regional economies following the crisis. In particular, despite the collapse of their currencies during the second half of 1997, exports of the crisis countries remained weak in the ensuing months and entered into a clear expansion phase only in mid-1999. According to some observers, this long lag between the nominal depreciation and the export recovery reflects the failure of the former to restore the external competitiveness of the crisis countries (McKinnon 2001; Duttagupta and Spilimbergo 2004). The suggested reasons for its failure include: the yen continued to weaken against the dollar until mid-1998; the nominal depreciation put upward pressures on the export prices of the crisis countries by raising the cost of imported production materials; the collapse of the currencies of the crisis countries prompted other East Asian countries into aggressive cost reductions and offset part of their competitiveness gain.[43,44]

As far as we can see in Figure 6.1, however, the competitiveness gain of the crisis countries during 1997–98 seems to have been substantial and has certainly been more than sufficient to offset any loss incurred during the preceding years. Moreover, the timing of export recovery was largely uniform not only among the crisis countries but also in other countries, suggesting that competitiveness per se had little bearing on their export performance in this period. Interestingly, Figure 6.1 suggests that trade competitiveness measured by our REERs improved in 1997–99 not only in the crisis countries but also in countries like Singapore and Taiwan. This is largely because their currencies also depreciated vis-à-vis the dollar and other industrial-country currencies, albeit by comparatively small proportions. In contrast, Japan seems to have borne a substantial competitiveness loss during this period, notwithstanding the continuation of the yen's depreciation vis-à-vis the dollar.

We next show quarterly REER series for the Japanese yen. In Figure 6.3, we plot our REER index computed using the manufacturing PPI and v^2 as the currency weight,[45] and compare its behavior with two standard REER indices compiled by the IMF and the Bank of Japan (BoJ). The IMF series is computed by weighting the yen's bilaterally real exchange rates with ten industrial-country countries (20 until the introduction of the euro), where the weight of each currency is calculated according to the formula in Equation (6.4);[46] the BoJ series is computed with respect to the currencies of Japan's 15 largest export-market countries, whose weights are computed in terms of the size of imports from Japan. The IMF series employs as the price index the manufacturing unit labor cost (ULC), whereas the BoJ series are based on either the PPI or the wholesale price index (WPI) for export and domestically sold products.

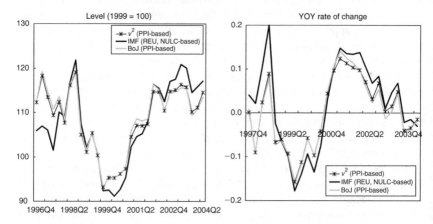

Figure 6.3 Real effective exchange rates of the Japanese yen (quarterly series)
Notes and sources: See Figure 6.1

In Figure 6.3, we find that our REER index and the BoJ index generally remain very close to each other, whereas the IMF index at times deviates substantially from these two series. The discrepancies between the IMF and the other indices are due mainly to the fact the former does not take account of the yen's movement with respect to the other East Asian countries.[47] In particular, although the IMF index indicates a substantial yen depreciation during 1997–98 reflecting the currency's continued fall against the dollar and other industrial-country currencies, its effect is largely offset in the other two indices by the effect of the Asian currency crisis. Similarly, although the yen's effective value fell by close to 30 percent between mid-2000 and early 2002 in terms of the IMF index, its depreciation measured by the other two indices was more limited. This discrepancy reflects the fact that the currencies of some East Asian countries that constitute Japan's important trade competitors, such as Korea and Taiwan, depreciated substantially vis-à-vis the dollar during this period. As is discussed in Chapter 4 of this volume, evidence suggests that many East Asian currencies have become more flexible vis-à-vis the dollar after the crisis and tend to slide in times of weak export performance. To the extent that this is the case, it is more important today to monitor the yen's movement vis-à-vis the other East Asian currencies to accurately measure how nominal exchange rate movements affect Japan's overall external competitiveness.

In Figure 6.3, the time-series profile of our REER index is largely indistinguishable from that of the BoJ index, reflecting the fact that the two series in principle use the same price index and are computed against similar sets of currencies. For most of the period shown in Figure 6.3, the weight assigned to each foreign currency is not very different between the two indices, except for the US dollar.[48] As the two REER indices employ conceptually very different weighting methods, however, there is no reason for this to remain the case in the future. As we saw in the previous sections, the relative importance of the United States and the East Asian countries as Japan's trade competitors appears to be changing more rapidly than what one would surmise from gross trade shares. Although the relative weight of the US dollar and the Chinese RMB is not very important for the yen's effective value as long as the latter remains pegged to the former, this may not necessarily be the case in the future. It thus seems worthwhile to investigate further how alternative combinations of the price index and the currency weighting method influence the behavior of the external values of the yen and other currencies.

6.6   Conclusion

Both the standard OCA theory and its recent extensions suggest that currency union has a better chance of proving successful when member countries engage in extensive intra-industry trade. This chapter developed a series of indices for international trade competition and applied these indices to a set of East Asian countries to examine the state of their external competition and its implication for their exchange rate policy. As trade is just one of many channels through which national economies interact with one another, and as exchange rates influence these channels in myriads of ways, it is not desirable to discuss exchange rate policy solely in terms of its effect on trade. In practice, however, concerns about trade competitiveness figure prominently in discussions about currency regime, as is the case in, for example, recent disputes about China's exchange rate policy.

According to our competition indices, the industrial structure of the East Asian countries has become markedly more competitive during the past decade. During the 1990s, the share of intra-regional trade has increased in some but not all East Asian countries, due in part to the relative stagnation of the Japanese economy. During the same period, however, the collective share of the East Asian countries, measured in terms of our composite competition indices, has risen in almost all countries. In contrast, the United States and Europe are less important as trade competitors than as export markets, a tendency that seems to have strengthened in recent years. While our estimates may be biased somewhat by growing production sharing and intra-product trade, there seems to be little doubt that East Asian manufacturers increasingly find their main competitors in other regional economies.

It is not clear, however, what this implies for the region's monetary arrangement in the future. It is conceivable that the growing sense of export rivalry motivates the region's policy-makers to seek a common exchange rate policy to lock in the relative value of their currencies. It seems equally possible, however, that rising trade flows and perceived competitive pressure within the region makes the policy-makers wary of forswearing adjusting their external balance through natural and/or forced changes in nominal exchange rates. Moreover, although numerous authors recommend the CBP as an alternative to the status quo, this regime implies an awkward policy asymmetry between Japan and the other Asian countries and would not be incentive-compatible for the participating countries unless they perceive Japan to be an exceptionally important trade partner-cum-competitor. In many East Asian countries, however, China figures increasingly prominently both as a market for their products and as a competitor in their and other countries. Even for Japan, greater China now rivals the United States as its export market and competitor, with their relative importance apparently changing rapidly in favor of the former. It seems likely, therefore, that the attention of the region's monetary authorities will increasingly gravitate toward the Chinese RMB, not the Japanese yen.

The penultimate section examined the evolution of the overall competitiveness of the East Asian countries during the 1990s by computing a series of REER indices that embed our competition indices. While the REER is widely used as a measure of external competitiveness, this interpretation is valid only when an appropriate choice is made about the underlying price index and the weight attached to each bilateral exchange rate. Although the choice of the price index is discussed extensively in the literature, there exists less research concerning the optimal currency weight. Whereas the behavior of our REER indices appeared fairly insensitive to changes in the currency weights, this may not be the case for other currencies and/or periods. Moreover, although we computed our REER indices using only aggregate price indices, it would be interesting to use more disaggregated industry price data so as to better exploit detailed product information incorporated in our competition indices.

Notes

1 The author would like to thank Mr Satoru Okuda of Institute of Developing Economies, Japan External Trade Organization (IDE-JETRO), for sharing some of the data used in this chapter.

2 In this chapter, "East Asia" refers to ten East and Southeast Asian countries of China, Hong Kong, Indonesia, Japan, Korea, Malaysia, the Philippines, Singapore, Taiwan, and Thailand. Our use of this term merely follows the convention of the literature and should not be construed as suggesting that these countries constitute an economically meaningful entity.

3 See Chapter 4 of this volume for a sample of recent proposals for regional exchange rate management in East Asia.

4 "Goods produced in foreign countries j" include goods produced by a subsidiary in country j of a firm headquartered in the home country. The following discussion of trade competition is based on the domestic rather than national concept of countries.

5 The International Monetary Fund (IMF) computes nominal and real exchange rate indices for a set of industrial-country currencies using this weighting method. The US Federal Reserve Board (FRB) uses a simplified version of this scheme to compute the effective value of the US dollar.

6 Although we can easily devise a multiproduct version of Equation (6.4), actual computation requires detailed data on sectoral output and consumption that is not available in many countries.

7 To be more precise, adjustment is conducted region by region, not between individual importer and export countries. See Bordé (1999) for details.

8 See, for example, van Marrewijk (2002: Chapter 10).

9 Although there are similar concerns about Singapore's trade, we conduct no arbitrary adjustment to its statistics assuming that the problems arising from entrepôt trade are less acute for Singapore than for Hong Kong. However, as Singapore does not report its trade with Indonesia, the WTD statistics on Singapore–Indonesia trade are likely to contain large margins of errors. See Ng and Yeats (2003) for other difficulties concerning the East Asian countries' trade statistics.

10 We treat Luxembourg as part of Belgium as WTD does not provide separate data for these two countries.

11 To remove distortions due to short-run factors, we computed these values in terms of the arithmetic averages for 1989–91 and 1999–2001.

12 Although the values in each column sum to 1 in our original definition, we multiply these values by 100 so that each number can be read as a percentage share among the 23 countries.

13 Deviations of z_j^1 and z_j^2 from w_j tend to be particularly salient when competitor j is a relatively large economy such as the United States and Japan. This is not

surprising since these countries provide a large market for their trade partners but do not necessarily compete with the latter in third countries.

14   When, however, there is a large (manufacturing) trade imbalance between the home country and country j, the values of w_j^1 and w_j^2 occasionally exhibit a non-negligible gap. In some countries this is the case when country j is Japan or the United States.

15   In Indonesia, the values of w_j^1 and w_j^2 for the United States have risen marginally between 1990 and 2000. Their low values in 1990 were due partly to disproportionately large shares of greater China. The latter in turn reflected substantial two-way trade in textiles and related products between Indonesia and China, of which a large part seems to have been mediated by Hong Kong.

16   This seems to reflect the fact that the United States' major export markets, such as Canada and Mexico, are not important markets for the exporters of the Asian countries.

17   The relatively modest shares of the Asian countries measured in terms of z_j^1 and z_j^2 reflect the large shares assumed by the European countries.

18   We note, however, that this is not a problem unique to our indices. The index in Equation (6.4), for example, shares the same difficulty.

19   To see why, suppose that the home country engages in intra-industry trade in good k with countries $j = 1$ and 2 where the following inequalities hold: $X_1^i(k) > X_1^i(k)$ and $X_i^2(k) < X_2^i(k)$. If we treat these countries as independent competitors, the contribution of trade in k to the numerator in Equation (6.6) is $X_1^i(k)$ for country 1 and $X_i^2(k)$ for country 2. If, on the other hand, we treat these countries as a single economic area, the contribution of the above trade to the numerator of w_j^1 will clearly be larger than $X_1^i(k) + X_i^2(k)$. If, on the other hand, we compute z_j^1 for this composite competitor, its value tends to fall short of the sum of the values calculated independently for the two countries, because $\min[X_i^1(k), X_2^1(k)]$ and $\min[X_i^2(k), X_1^2(k)]$, $k = 1, 2, \ldots$ no longer appear in the numerator of Equation (6.10).

20   As in Tables 6.1–6.9, all values are the arithmetic average of the estimates for 1999, 2000, and 2001.

21   Although Japan's trade dependency ratio (the sum of imports and exports divided by GDP) is very low, evidence suggests that its exchange rate policy has been influenced heavily by concerns about external competitiveness (Cargill et al. 1997).

22   There are observers who question the merits of an Asian monetary union even as a long-term project; see Eichengreen (2003) and Chapter 4 of this volume.

23   See, for example, Ogawa and Ito (2002). There is, however, considerable doubt about this view, as discussed extensively in Chapter 4 of this volume.

24   Another assumption implicit in the CBP proposal is that Japan's economy is not sufficiently open to justify a fixed exchange rate regime. Although CBP implies an awkward asymmetry in terms of monetary policy autonomy between Japan and the other Asian countries, most proponents of the scheme regard this to be an intermediate step toward a full Asian monetary union, in which Japan will also participate (Kawai and Takagi 2000; Ogawa and Ito 2002).

25   Most East Asian countries have been relatively free from monetization of fiscal deficits, although the Philippines might be a marginal exception in this respect. The inflation rate of some countries (e.g. Singapore) has in fact been lower than the average of industrial countries during the past few decades.

26   Although this is partly because of Japan's economic stagnation and slow import growth in the 1990s, it is hard to believe that this trend will be reversed completely in the future.

27 See Ng and Yeats (2001) for evidence on fragmentation and intra-product trade in East Asia.

28 As noted previously, this chapter adopts the domestic rather than national concept of countries. There is thus no conceptual inconsistency in, for example, taking intra-industry trade between Japan and China as evidence of their competition even when China's export goods are produced by a Chinese subsidiary of a Japanese multinational corporation. If, however, this subsidiary utilizes intermediate goods imported from Japan, and particularly if both the intermediate and final goods are classified into the same product category, this intra-firm trade will become a source of concern.

29 Again these values are computed in terms of the average for 1999, 2000, and 2001. We note that the results presented in this section are not directly comparable with those in Table 6.1 since WTD's export data is primarily based on importer statistics. Import data in the Japanese statistics also deviates from WTD since the former include transport and insurance costs.

30 In the current version of HS, the number of product categories for manufacturing goods are approximately 70 (2-digit), 1000 (4-digit) and 4400 (6-digit).

31 The result for 2004 is for the first six months only.

32 As the level of WTD's product aggregation falls somewhere between those of the HS's 2- and 4-digit codes, however, there remains a possibility that the results of the previous section entailed some bias.

33 In Tables 6.12 and 6.13, the estimates for the other East Asian countries have been relatively stable during the past few years. However, the fact that exports to China have also risen sharply in such countries as Korea and Taiwan suggests that Japanese exporters are now in more intense competition with their Korean and Taiwanese rivals in China. It thus seems likely that the values of z_j^1 and z_j^2 are also increasing for these countries.

34 As the HS's coding system underwent major revisions in 1996 and 2000, we cannot accurately assess the time-series evolution of these numbers in terms of the original HS codes. We thus computed all numbers using data recompiled into the 5-digit SITC rev. 3 code, in which the maximum number of manufacturing goods is approximately 2400.

35 Given China's disproportionately large population and geographical proximity to Japan, however, the product coverage of Japan's intra-industry trade with China might ultimately settle at a level beyond the current coverage for its trade with the United States and Europe.

36 See, for example, Hinkle and Montiel (1999). In the existing literature, the method for determining the currency weight receives less attention than the choice of the price index. A relatively small number of studies that focus on the former include Ellis (2001) and Ha and Fan (2003).

37 Although the export price index is another possibility, export prices are not exogenous to exchange rates, particularly in countries whose exports are invoiced in foreign currencies. For countries for which a suitable manufacturing PPI is unavailable, we used the wholesale price index (WPI) for domestic and export goods.

38 Although we also computed the REERs based on w_j^1 and v_j^1, the dynamic behavior of these series was very similar to those based on w_j^2 and v_j^2.

39 In Equation (6.20), the rate of change in the home currency's REER is defined as a weighted average of the corresponding rates of change in the home currency's bilateral real exchange rates with the currencies of $j = 1, 2, ...$ When the home

currency is, for example, the Japanese yen, the latter include the real exchange rate between the yen and the (notional) currency of greater China. The rate of change in the latter was approximated by taking a weighted average of the rates of change in the yen/Chinese RMB real exchange rate and the yen/Hong Kong dollar real exchange rate, where the weights were computed by the shares of China and Hong Kong in their aggregate US dollar GDP. China had maintained a dual exchange rate system until 1993 and switched to the current system at the beginning of 1994. For the period prior to 1994, the rate of change in the RMB exchange rate was approximated by averaging those based on the official and market exchange rates with the weights of 0.2 and 0.8; see Fernald et al. (1999).

40 The Korean won depreciated against the dollar by about 18 percent during the same period.

41 There is, however, evidence that China's PPI was behaving very differently from its export prices during this period (Kumakura 2005).

42 By comparing Figures 6.1 and 6.2, we find that the PPI and GDP deflator REERs were trending differently in some countries. Although the cumulative inflation of the PPI was larger than that of the GDP deflator in all Asian countries (reflecting faster productivity growth in the manufacturing sector than in other industries), the discrepancy between the two differs substantially across the countries. Among the four crisis countries, the gap between the PPI and the GDP-deflator inflation rates was relatively small in Indonesia, Malaysia, and Thailand, as reflected in the near stability of their currencies' GDP-deflator REERs and the progressive appreciation of their PPI REERs. This observation suggests that these countries would have found it difficult to concurrently achieve the *internal* and *external* competitiveness of their tradable sector whatever policy had been taken about their nominal exchange rates. See Athukorala and Rajapatirana (2003) for the internal exchange rates of the Asian currencies during the lead-up to the crisis.

43 The Singapore government launched sweeping cost-cutting measures in 1998 to restore the country's international competitiveness (Jin 2000).

44 Other authors stress supply-side factors, such as exporters' temporary credit constraints (Boorman et al. 2000).

45 As we have the values of v_j^2 only up to 2001, those for 2002 onward were extrapolated by fitting a quadratic time trend model on the series for 1985–2001.

46 These weights are, however, computed using data for 1989–91 and fixed over time.

47 Turner and Golub (1997) extend the IMF's ULC-based REERs by including 23 developing-country currencies.

48 In 2000, the weight of the US dollar in the BoJ index was 32.3 percent, whereas its weight in our REER index was only 23.6 percent.

References

Allen, C., M. Gasiorek, and M. A. M. Smith, 1998, "The Competition Effects of the Single Market in Europe," *Economic Policy*, 13: 440–86.

Armington, P., 1969, "A Theory of Demand for Products Distinguished by Place of Production," *IMF Staff Papers*, 16: 159–78.

Athukorala, P. C. and S. Rajapatirana, 2003, "Capital Inflows and the Real Exchange Rate: a Comparative Study of Asia and Latin America," *World Economy*, 26: 613–37.

Baldwin, R., 1989, "On the Growth Effects of 1992," *Economic Policy*, 1: 247–81.

Bernard, A. B., J. B. Jensen, and P. K. Schott, 2004, "Forecasting the Timing of Market Entry by Low-wage Countries," Tuck School of Business Working Paper, Dartmouth College.

Boorman, J., T. Lane, M. Schulze-Ghattas, A. Buliř, A. R. Gosh, J. Hamann, A. Mourmouras, and S. Phillips, 2000, "Managing Financial Crises: the Experience in East Asia," IMF Working Paper WP/00/107.

Bordé, F., 1999, "A Database for Analysis of International Markets." A companion article for Statistics Canada, World Trade Analyzer.

Cargill, T. F., M. M. Hutchison, and T. Ito., 1997, *The Political Economy of Japanese Monetary Policy*, Cambridge, Mass.: MIT Press.

Duttagupta, R. and A. Spilimbergo, 2004, "What Happened to Asian Exports during the Crisis?" *IMF Staff Papers*, 51: 72–95.

Eichengreen, B., 2003, "What to do with the Chiang Mai Initiative," *Asian Economic Papers*, 2: 1–52.

Ellis, L., 2001, "Measuring the Real Exchange Rate: Pitfalls and Practicalities," Research Discussion Paper 2001–04, Economic Research Department, Reserve Bank of Australia.

Feenstra, R. C., W. Hai, W. T. Woo, and S. Yao, 1999, "Discrepancies in International Data: an Application to China–Hong Kong Entrepot Trade," *American Economic Review Papers and Proceedings*, 89(2): 338–43.

Fernald, J., H. Edison, and P. Loungani, 1999, "Was China the First Domino? Assessing Links between China and the Rest of the World," *Journal of International Money & Finance*, 18(4): 515–35.

Frankel, J. and A. Rose, 1998, "The Endogeneity of the Optimum Currency Criteria," *Economic Journal*, 108: 1009–25.

Ha, J. and K. Fan, 2003, "Alternative Measures of the Real Effective Exchange Rate," *Hong Kong Monetary Authority Quarterly Bulletin*, March.

Hinkle, L. E. and P. J. Montiel, 1999, *Exchange Rate Misalignment: Concepts and Measurement for Developing Countries*, New York: World Bank and Oxford University Press.

International Monetary Fund, 2004, "China's Growth and Integration into the World Economy: Prospects and Challenges," IMF Occasional Paper No. 232.

Jin, N. K., 2000, "Coping with the Asian Financial Crisis: the Singapore Experience," Visiting Researchers Series No. 8 (2000), Institute of Southeast Asian Studies.

Kawai, M. and S. Takagi, 2000, "Proposed Strategy for a Regional Exchange Rate Arrangement in Post-crisis East Asia," World Bank Policy Research Working Paper No. 2503.

Kumakura, M., 2005, "Trade, Exchange Rates, and Macroeconomic Dynamics in East Asia: Why the Electronics Cycle Matters," IDE Discussion Paper No. 34, Institute of Developing Economies, Japan External Trade Organization (IDE-JETRO).

McKinnon, R., 2001, "After the Crisis, the East Asian Dollar Standard Resurrected," in J. Stiglitz and Y. Y. Shahid (eds), *Rethinking the East Asian Miracle*, New York: Oxford University Press, pp. 197–246.

Ng, F. and A. Yeats, 2001, "Production Sharing in Asia: Who does What for Whom, and Why," World Bank Policy Research Working Paper No. 2197.

Ng, F. and A. Yeats, 2003, "Major Trade Trends in East Asia," World Bank Policy Research Working Paper No. 3084.

Ogawa, E. and T. Ito, 2002, "On the Desirability of a Regional Basket Currency Arrangement," *Journal of the Japanese and International Economies*, 16: 317–34.

Spilimbergo, A. and A. Vamvakidis, 2000, "Real Effective Exchange Rate and the Constant Elasticity of Substitution Assumption," IMF Working Paper WP/00/128.

Turner, A. G. and S. S. Golub, 1997, "Toward a System of Multilateral Unit-labor Cost-based Competitiveness Indicators for Advanced, Developing and Transition Countries," IMF Working Paper WP/97/151.

van Marrewijk, C., 2002, *International Trade and the World Economy*, Oxford: Oxford University Press.

7
Effects of Exchange Rate Revaluation under Price Controls and Endogenous Quality Adjustment

Kaku Furuya

7.1 Introduction

When a country under a fixed exchange rate system – whether *de jure* or de facto – exhibits large and persistent current account surpluses, it is often pressed to revaluate the exchange rate (i.e. let the home currency appreciate against foreign currencies). Well-known examples are West Germany in the 1960s (which ended up revising the dollar–Deutschemark rate in 1961 and 1969) and Japan in the early 1970s (which acquiesced in the Smithsonian Agreement to revise the dollar–yen rate in 1971). More recently, China has been under intense pressure from its major trading partners to revaluate the renminbi.

While the popular discourse on international relations tends to focus on the nominal exchange rate (hereafter denoted by E), it is the real exchange rate (defined as EP^*/P, where P^* and P are the foreign and domestic CPI) that ultimately matters to resource allocations including the current account balance. It is thus important to examine how a nominal revaluation (a reduction of E) will affect the real exchange rate (EP^*/P), holding the foreign CPI (P^*) constant.

The standard theory offers two different predictions regarding the relationship between the nominal and real exchange rates, depending on the flexibility of prices. When there is downward rigidity in goods prices, the domestic CPI (P) after a nominal revaluation will not fall as much as the value of foreign currency (E), causing a real appreciation of the home currency (a fall in EP^*/P); this provides an implicit basis for Keynesian analysis (e.g. one using the Mundell–Fleming model). In contrast, when goods prices are completely flexible, a nominal revaluation (a fall in E) will cause an equiproportionate fall in the domestic CPI (P), leaving the real exchange rate (EP^*/P) unchanged; this is a representation of monetary neutrality in the international context, often dubbed the purchasing power parity (PPP). In any case, the standard theory predicts that the nominal exchange rate will have a weakly positive effect on the real rate ($d(EP^*/P)/dE \geqslant 0$).

This chapter argues that, contrary to the commonly held views, the nominal and real exchange rates can move in opposite directions ($d(EP^*/P)/dE < 0$) if there exist government-imposed price controls. More specifically, the chapter considers a small open economy with tradable and nontradable sectors, where the tradable price P_T is determined by the nominal exchange rate E and the international price $P_T{}^*$, while the nontradable price P_N is capped by a ceiling $\bar{P}_N$ (i.e. $P_N \leqslant \bar{P}_N$). The quality of the tradable good is assumed to be constant, while the quality of the nontradable good (hereafter measured by z) is assumed to be adjustable, enabling the nontradable sector to eliminate excess demand even when the price ceiling happens to be binding ($P_N = \bar{P}_N$).[1] The domestic CPI (P) will depend not only on the goods prices (P_T, P_N) but also on the quality of the nontradable good (z).[2] Suppose now that the economy is initially in a distorted equilibrium with a binding price ceiling and a suboptimal good quality in the nontradable sector. Then it can be shown that a *nominal revaluation* (a *fall* in E) will lead to a *real depreciation* (an *increase* in EP^*/P), causing the quality-adjusted CPI (P) to fall more than the nominal exchange rate (E).

The above result, which might seem a little odd at the first sight, is actually quite intuitive. In the initial equilibrium, the binding price ceiling in the nontradable sector is depressing the relative price (P_N/P_T), forcing the quality level (z) to be suboptimal. The revaluation and the subsequent fall in the tradable price (P_T) will mitigate the initial distortion, enabling the nontradable producers to raise the quality of their products in return for the higher relative price. Thus, the revaluation reduces the quality-adjusted CPI not only by causing a lower tradable price (lower P_T) but also by inducing quality improvement (higher z); the existence of the latter effect causes the fall in P to outweigh the fall in E in magnitude, thereby causing the real exchange rate (EP^*/P) to depreciate.

The result of this chapter teaches us a lesson that the effect of exchange rate policy on the real economy can be influenced by institutional factors in a nontrivial way: those who simplistically believe that nominal revaluations should reduce current account surpluses could end up deceiving themselves if the economy is distorted by a price ceiling in the first place. This lesson seems particularly relevant to developing countries (including economies in transition), where the incidence of government control over prices is reportedly high (Mishkin 2000).[3]

The remainder of the chapter is organized as follows: the next section (Section 7.2) presents a simple closed-economy model to illustrate how a price ceiling interacts with quality of the good. This is to set the stage for a more complex, open economy analysis. Section 7.3 develops a two-sector model of a small open economy under a fixed exchange rate system. Using the model, the general equilibrium with a binding price ceiling is characterized and the effect of a nominal revaluation on the real exchange rate is analyzed. Section 7.4 briefly discusses policy implications of the model, focusing on the possible revaluation of the Chinese renminbi. Section 7.5 concludes the chapter.

7.2 Price ceiling and quality adjustment – an illustration

This section incorporates a price ceiling into the endogenous quality model by Rosen (1974) to illustrate the interaction between price and quality. The economy consists of large numbers of identical households and firms. (For simplicity, the population sizes of the households and the firms are both assumed to be one.) The households are endowed with a numéraire good with constant quality (hereafter called M good), which – in the hands of the firms – can be turned into another kind of consumption good with variable quality (hereafter called C good).

The representative household's preferences are defined over the amount of C good consumed (c), its quality (z), and the amount of M good (m). Assume (without loss of generality) that the representative household has the following Gorman utility:

$$U = u(c, z) + m \qquad (7.1)$$

where u is a strictly concave function of c and z. Maximizing the utility function (7.1) subject to the budget constraint

$$pc + m = \overline{M} \qquad (7.2)$$

(where p is the price of C good and $\overline{M}$ is the amount of M good endowed), we get the following first-order condition:

$$\frac{\partial}{\partial c} u(c^o, z) = p \qquad (7.3)$$

Equation (7.3) in the above gives the demand for C good as a function of the price (p) and quality (z):

$$c^o = c^o(p, z) \qquad (7.4)$$

Substituting Equations (7.2) and (7.4) back into (7.1) yields the indirect utility function:

$$V = u[c^o(p, z), z] + \overline{M} - pc^o(p, z) \qquad (7.5)$$

Following Rosen (1974), the goods markets are assumed to be perfectly competitive. The representative firm producing C good of quality z has a CRS (constant returns to scale) technology, where the marginal cost τ is strictly convex in z:

$$\tau = \tau(z) \qquad \tau'(z) > 0 \qquad \tau''(z) > 0 \qquad (7.6)$$

Equation (7.6) means that as the firm raises the quality of its product, the marginal cost will increase. The profits of the representative firm can thus be written as

$$\pi = pQ - \tau(z)Q \qquad (7.7)$$

where Q is the amount of C good (of quality z) produced. Maximizing (7.7) with respect to Q leads to the following supply function of C good:[4]

$$p = \tau(z) \tag{7.8}$$

When the quality level z is exogenous and invariant, the demand equation (7.4) and the supply equation (7.8) can determine the equilibrium price p^0 that clears all the markets. When z is variable, however, there will be numerous combinations of (p, z) that equilibrate the goods markets. In order to determine the quality level endogenously, we need another boundary condition which guarantees that no entity can improve his or her position by accepting a different pair of (p, z). Such a boundary condition can generally be written as

$$\left.\frac{\partial p}{\partial z}\right|_{dV=0} = \left.\frac{\partial p}{\partial z}\right|_{d\pi=0} \tag{7.9}$$

which can be rewritten here (by using the indirect utility function (7.5) and profit function (7.7)) as

$$\frac{u_z(p, z)}{c^o(p, z)} = \tau'(z) \tag{7.10}$$

where u_z is the partial derivative of u with respect to z. The LHS of Equation (7.10) indicates how much price increase households will be willing to bear in return for a marginal improvement in quality, while the RHS of (7.10) indicates how much it will cost for the firms to marginally improve product quality. If the LHS (u_z/c^o) exceeds the RHS ($\tau'(z)$), then the firms can make positive profits (while leaving the households as well-off as before) by marginally improving quality at the cost of $\tau'(z)$ and raising the price by u_z/c^o. However, the positive profits will induce increases in production and excess supply of C good. These in turn will cause decreases in p and increases in z (to eliminate excess supply) until the equality in Equation (7.10) is restored. A similar arbitrage argument can be made for the opposite case (LHS < RHS). Thus one can verify that the equilibrium is achieved only when Equations (7.4),(7.8), and (7.10) are satisfied simultaneously.

Let us now introduce into the model a government-imposed ceiling on the price of C good. The economy will be described by the following system:

(Demand equation) $\dfrac{\partial}{\partial c} u(c^o, z) = p$ $\hspace{2cm}$ (7.3)

(Supply equation) $p = \tau(z)$ $\hspace{3.5cm}$ (7.8)

(Boundary condition) $\dfrac{u_z(c^o, z)}{c^o} = \tau'(z)$ $\hspace{2cm}$ (7.10)

(Price ceiling) $p \le \bar{p}$ $\hspace{3.8cm}$ (7.11)

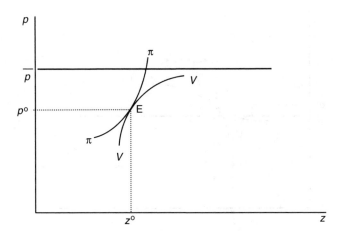

Figure 7.1 Equilibrium when price ceiling is not binding

When Equation (7.11) is not binding ($p < \bar{p}$), three equations (7.3), (7.8), and (7.10) will determine the equilibrium values of c^o, p, and z. In contrast, when (7.11) is binding ($p = \bar{p}$), the boundary condition (7.10) cannot be satisfied. The quality will be constrained to a suboptimal level $\underline{z}$ such that $\pi(\underline{z}) = \bar{p}$, raising the LHS of Equation (7.10) (due to higher marginal utility with respect to z and lower c) and lowering the RHS of Equation (7.10).[5]

The effect of the price ceiling [Equation (7.11) in the above] can be best understood in graphs. Figure 7.1 depicts the equilibrium in the (z, p) space when the price ceiling is not binding ($p < \bar{p}$). The steeper curve labeled $\pi\pi$ is an iso-profit curve consistent with the supply equation (7.8). The region above this curve (characterized by higher prices and lower quality) corresponds to positive profits. The flatter curve VV is an indifference curve derived from the indirect utility function (7.5). The region below this curve (characterized by lower prices and higher quality) corresponds to higher utility levels. The equilibrium levels of z and p [(z^o, p^o) in the figure] are indicated by point E, where the iso-profit curve $\pi\pi$ and the indifference curve VV are tangential to each other. This result comes from the boundary condition (7.10), which requires that the households' marginal valuation of quality is equal to the marginal cost of quality improvement. The horizontal line indicates the price ceiling. Since it is not binding, the equilibrium price (p^o) lies below the statutory maximum ($\bar{p}$).

Figure 7.2 describes the case when the price ceiling is binding ($p = \bar{p}$). The equilibrium is given by point $\underline{E}$ in the figure, where the horizontal price ceiling line and the iso-profit curve $\pi\pi$ intersect. The quality level is given by $\underline{z}$ in the figure. Notice that point $\underline{E}$ lies to the southwest of point E, which represents the unconstrained optimum. Thus, the indifference curve going through point $\underline{E}$ (labeled $\underline{V}\,\underline{V}$) lies above the one going through point E (labeled VV), meaning that the households will be worse off than at the unconstrained optimum.

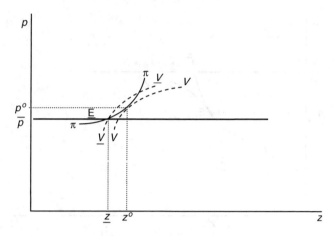

Figure 7.2 Equilibrium when the price ceiling is binding

7.3 The model

Let us now extend the closed-economy model in the previous section to a small open economy with a fixed exchange rate. Production of goods now takes place in two sectors, tradable and nontradable. The quality of the tradable good is fixed, while that of the nontradable good (measured by z) is adjustable. The tradable price P_T is determined by the nominal exchange rate E and the international price P_T^*, where the complete pass-through guarantees the following equation to always hold:

$$P_T = EP_T^*$$ (7.12)

The nontradable price P_N is subject to a price ceiling

$$P_N \leq \bar{P}_N$$ (7.13)

where $\bar{P}_N$ is exogenously set by the government.

7.3.1 Households

The utility function of the representative household is assumed to have the following weakly separable form:

$$U = U\left[u\left(c, \frac{m}{P}\right), l\right]$$ (7.14)

where c is the composite consumption index, (m/P) is the real money balances, l is the amount of labor supplied, and u is the subutility function homogeneous of degree one in terms of the two arguments. Assume (without loss of generality) that Equation (7.14) has the following simple form:

$$U = U\left[u\left(c, \frac{m}{P}\right), l\right] = \frac{1}{(1-k)^{1-k}k^k} c^{1-k} \left(\frac{m}{P}\right)^k - l^\phi \tag{7.15}$$

The composite consumption index c depends on tradable consumption c_T, nontradable consumption c_N and nontradable quality z and is homogeneous of degree one in terms of c_T and c_N. Assuming (again without loss of generality) a CES preference structure

$$c = \Omega\left(c_T, c_N, z\right) = [(c_T^{(\theta-1)/\theta} + (z^{1/(1-\theta)}c_N)^{(\theta-1)/\theta}]^{\theta/(\theta-1)} \qquad (\theta > 0) \tag{7.16}$$

we can obtain the corresponding CPI

$$P = \varphi(P_T, P_N, z) = [P_T^{1-\theta} + z^{-1}P_N^{1-\theta}]^{1/(1-\theta)} \tag{7.17}$$

Notice that the above CPI depends negatively on the nontradable quality level z.

In addition to labor, households own an amount $\overline{K}$ of physical capital (all of which is supplied inelastically) and an amount $\overline{M}$ of money stock (the supply of which is controlled by the government so that it will be consistent with the nominal exchange rate E).[6] The budget constraint of the representative household can thus be written as

$$P_T c_T + P_N c_N + m = Wl + R\overline{K} + \overline{M}(\equiv Z) \tag{7.18}$$

where W and R are (nominal) wage and rental, respectively.

Maximizing the utility function (defined by Equations (7.15)–(7.17)) subject to the budget constraint (7.18) yields the following relations:

$$\text{(Tradable demand)} \quad c_T = \left(\frac{P_T}{P}\right)^{-\theta} (1-k)\left(\frac{Z}{P}\right) \tag{7.19}$$

$$\text{(Nontradable demand)} \quad c_N = \left(\frac{P_N}{P}\right)^{-\theta} \frac{(1-k)}{z}\left(\frac{Z}{P}\right) \tag{7.20}$$

$$\text{(Money demand)} \quad m = kZ \tag{7.21}$$

$$\text{(Labor supply)} \quad l = \left(\frac{1}{\phi}\right)^{1/(\phi-1)} \left(\frac{W}{P}\right)^{1/(\phi-1)} \tag{7.22}$$

where Z is the nominal value of total endowment given by Equation (7.18). Using Equations (7.19)–(7.22) in the above, the indirect utility function of the representative household can be written as

$$V = \frac{1}{1-k} \frac{Wl + R\overline{K}}{P} - l^\phi \tag{7.23}$$

where l is optimally chosen according to Equation (7.22).

7.3.2   Firms

The production side of the economy has fairly standard features; perfect competition and CRS technology are assumed for all the sectors. Without loss of generality, we assume the following production functions for the tradable and nontradable sectors:

$$Q_T = F(L_T, K) = \frac{1}{(1-\alpha)^{1-\alpha}\alpha^\alpha} L_T^{1-\alpha} K^\alpha \tag{7.24}$$

$$Q_N = G(L_N, z) = \frac{1}{\tau(z)} L_N \tag{7.25}$$

where Q_i and L_i (i = T, N) are the levels of output and employment in sector i. Profits of the representative firm in each sector are thus given by

$$\pi_T = P_T Q_T - W L_T - R K \tag{7.26}$$

$$\pi_N = P_N Q_N - W L_N \tag{7.27}$$

Maximizing the profit functions (7.26)–(7.27) subject to (7.24)–(7.25) will yield the following supply equations:

$$P_T = W^{1-\alpha} R^\alpha \tag{7.28}$$

$$P_N = \tau(z) W \tag{7.29}$$

7.3.3   General equilibrium

Market clearing of consumption goods, labor, and capital requires that

$$c_T = Q_T \tag{7.30}$$

$$c_N = Q_N \tag{7.31}$$

$$L_T + L_N = l \tag{7.32}$$

$$W = P_T \frac{\partial}{\partial L_T} F(L_T, \overline{K}) \tag{7.33}$$

$$R = P_T \frac{\partial}{\partial K} F(L_T, \overline{K}) \tag{7.34}$$

Furthermore, the endogenous determination of quality requires the boundary condition

$$\left. \frac{\partial P_N}{\partial z} \right|_{dV=0} = \left. \frac{\partial P_N}{\partial z} \right|_{d\pi_N=0} \tag{7.35}$$

Finally, the fixed exchange rate requires that the money supply should be set such that

$$\overline{M} = \frac{k}{1-k}\left[Q_T + \left(\frac{P_N}{P_T}\right)Q_N\right]P_T * E \qquad (7.36)$$

The above conditions (7.30)–(7.36), together with the auxiliary equations (7.12), (7.17)–(7.25), (7.28)–(7.29), and the price-ceiling constraint (7.13) constitute an equations system which determines the general equilibrium of this economy.

By introducing normalized variables such as $p \equiv (P_N/P_T)$, $\bar{p} \equiv (\overline{P}_N/P_T)$, $q \equiv (P/P_T)$, and $\omega \equiv (W/R)$, the above system can be further simplified as follows:

(Relative demand)
$$\frac{\overline{K}}{\alpha}\frac{1}{\omega}\left\{\omega^\alpha \frac{p^{-\theta}\tau(z)}{z} + (1-\alpha)\right\}$$
$$= \left(\frac{1}{\phi}\right)^{1/(\phi-1)}\left[\frac{\omega^\alpha}{(1+z^{-1}p^{1-\theta})^{1/(1-\theta)}}\right]^{1/(\phi-1)} \qquad (7.37)$$

(Relative supply) $p = \tau(z)\omega^\alpha$ \qquad (7.38)

(Boundary condition) $\left.\dfrac{\partial p}{\partial z}\right|_{dV=0} = \left.\dfrac{\partial p}{\partial z}\right|_{d\pi_N=0}$ \qquad (7.39)

$$V = \frac{1}{1-k}\frac{\omega^\alpha l + \omega^{\alpha-1}\overline{K}}{q} - l^\phi \qquad (7.40)$$

$$l = \left(\frac{1}{\phi}\right)^{1/(\phi-1)}\left[\frac{\omega^\alpha}{(1+z^{-1}p^{1-\theta})^{1/(1-\theta)}}\right]^{1/(\phi-1)} \qquad (7.41)$$

$$q = (1+z^{-1}p^{1-\theta})^{1/(1-\theta)} \qquad (7.42)$$

(Price ceiling) $p \le \bar{p}$ \qquad (7.43)

It should be noted that the normalized system (7.37)–(7.43) in the above closely resembles the closed-economy system (7.3), (7.8), (7.10), (7.11) in Section 7.2. As before, the system yields two types of equilibria, depending on whether or not the price ceiling (7.43) is binding. Once we eliminate ω from the system (i.e. solving ω for p, z, and $\overline{K}$ in (7.37) and substituting it into (7.38) and (7.40)), graphical analysis given in Figures 7.1 and 7.2 can be used to determine the equilibrium levels of p and z, in exactly the same way as in Section 7.2.

7.3.4   Effects of revaluation on relative price and real exchange rate

We are now ready to analyze the effects of a revaluation (a reduction of E). First, let us take a brief look at what will happen to the equilibrium levels of relative price p ($=P_N/P_T$) and quality z.

Figures 7.3 and 7.4 depict the effects of a revaluation with and without the initial distortion. Figure 7.3 corresponds to the case in which the price ceiling is not binding in the initial equilibrium, while Figure 7.4 corresponds to the

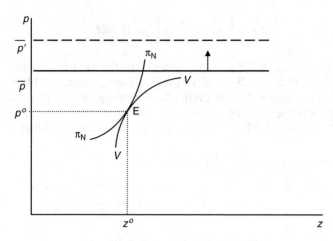

Figure 7.3   Effects of revaluation when the price ceiling is initially not binding

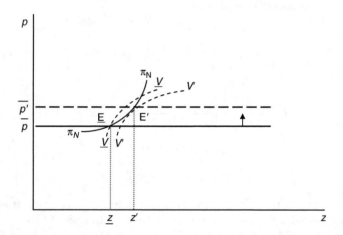

Figure 7.4   Effects of revaluation when the price ceiling is initially binding

case in which the price ceiling is initially binding. In both cases, the revaluation will shift up the solid horizontal line representing the price ceiling ($p = \bar{p} \equiv (\bar{P}_N/P_T)$). This is because a decrease in E and the resulting fall in the tradable price $P_T(=EP_T^*)$ will raise the relative value of ceiling $\bar{P}_N$.

The effects on the equilibrium levels of p and z can be easily seen from Figures 7.3 and 7.4. When the price ceiling is not binding in the first place (as in Figure 7.3), the revaluation and the resulting increase in $\bar{p}$ will have no effect on the equilibrium levels of p and z; the equilibrium will remain at point E. In contrast, when the price ceiling is binding in the initial equilibrium (as in Figure 7.4), a revaluation and the resulting increase in $\bar{p}$ will cause the equilibrium point to slide along the iso-profit curve $\pi_N \pi_N$. The equilibrium levels of p and z will increase accordingly.

Let us now turn to the effect of a revaluation on the real exchange rate. Noting that the domestic and foreign CPIs can be decomposed as

$$P = P_T \, q \tag{7.44}$$

$$P^* = P_T^* q^* \tag{7.45}$$

we can rewrite the real exchange rate as

$$\frac{EP^*}{P} = \frac{EP_T^* q^*}{P_T q} = \frac{q^*}{q} \tag{7.46}$$

where q, the ratio of the CPI and the tradable price, is given as a function of p and z as in Equation (7.42) in the above. Since q^* is exogenous, our task boils down to determining how q will change in response to a fall in the nominal exchange rate E.

Again, the relationship between E and q depends crucially on the initial state. When the price ceiling is not binding in the initial equilibrium (as in Figure 7.3), a decrease in E and the resulting increase in $\bar{p}$ will have no effect on p or z. Hence, q (which is the function of p and z) will also be unaffected. Recalling Equation (7.46) in the above, we can see that the real exchange rate (EP^*/P) will stay at the same level; the only effect the revaluation causes is equiproportionate falls in P_T and P_N.

When the price ceiling is binding in the initial equilibrium (as in Figure 7.4), the effect of a revaluation on the real exchange rate is harder to determine, since the increases in p and z will have conflicting effects on q (see Equation (7.42)). One can verify, however, that a sufficiently small decrease in E will reduce q, causing the real exchange rate to depreciate:

Proposition 1: *If the economy is initially in a distorted equilibrium where the price ceiling is binding, then a revaluation of the nominal exchange rate will lead to a depreciation of the real exchange rate.*

Proof: See Appendix 7A.

The intuition behind the above proposition can be described as follows: when the price ceiling is initially binding, a revaluation will reduce the distortion in the relative price, enhancing both consumptive and productive efficiency, and making the households better off than before. At the margin, this improvement of welfare has to be materialized by a fall in the CPI beyond what would be predicted by the purchasing power parity. Thus, a decrease in P will be greater in magnitude than that in P_T, which implies that $q = P/P_T$ must be falling.

7.3.5 Effect of revaluation on current account

The analysis so far has revealed that a nominal exchange rate revaluation (in an economy under a binding price ceiling) could cause a decrease in the quality-adjusted CPI and a depreciation of the real exchange rate. A question which naturally follows is what this result implies for the current account balance. In order to address this question, we will need to extend the preceding static model to a dynamic one. Here we will consider the simplest two-period model, keeping as much as possible the structure of the original static model.

Let J denote the representative household's lifetime utility

$$J = u\left(c_0, \frac{m_0}{P_0}\right) + \beta u\left(c_1, \frac{m_1}{P_1}\right) \tag{7.47}$$

where $\beta \in (0,1)$ represents the discount factor and the period utility function u_t ($t = 0,1$) has a CRRA form with an elasticity of intertemporal substitution $\sigma\ (>0)$

$$u\left(c_t, \frac{m_t}{P_t}\right) = \frac{1}{1-(1/\sigma)}\left[\frac{c_t^{1-k}\left(m_t/P_t\right)^k}{(1-k)^{1-k}k^k}\right]^{1-(1/\sigma)} \tag{7.48}$$

The households inelastically supply an amount l of labor in both periods 0 and 1. The budget constraints are given by

$$\begin{aligned} P_0c_0 + P_{T0}b + m_0 &= Z_0 \\ P_1c_1 + m_1 &= P_{T1}b(1+r) + Z_1 \\ Z_t &\equiv W_t l_t + R_t \overline{K}_t + \overline{M}_t \quad (t = 0,1) \end{aligned} \tag{7.49}$$

where b is the amount of consumption bonds (measured in units of tradable goods) purchased by the households, and r is the world interest rate in terms of tradable goods. All other notations and assumptions are the same as before.

The optimal consumption path $\{c_t\}$ ($t = 0,1$) can be obtained by maximizing the lifetime utility (7.47)–(7.48) subject to the budget constraints (7.49). To derive the first-order condition, let us define an auxiliary variable x_t as

$$x_t = c_t + \frac{m_t}{P_t} \tag{7.50}$$

Then the budget constraints (7.49) can be rewritten as

$$\begin{aligned} P_0x_0 + P_{T0}b &= Z_0 \\ P_1x_1 &= P_{T1}b(1+r) + Z_1 \end{aligned} \tag{7.51}$$

which can be further simplified as

$$x_0 + \frac{1}{1+r_C}x_1 = \frac{Z_0}{P_0} + \frac{1}{1+r_C}\frac{Z_1}{P_1} \tag{7.52}$$

where r_C is the consumption-based real interest rate defined as[7]

$$\begin{aligned} 1 + r_C &= (1+r)\frac{q_0}{q_1} \\ q_t &\equiv P_t/P_{Tt} \end{aligned} \tag{7.53}$$

Recalling from (7.48) that c_t and (m_t/P_t) can be expressed in x_t as

$$c_t = (1 - k)x_t$$
$$m_t/P_t = kx_t \tag{7.54}$$

we can also rewrite the lifetime utility as

$$J = u_0 + \beta u_1$$
$$u_t = \frac{x_t^{1-(1/\sigma)}}{1 - (1/\sigma)} \quad (t = 0, 1) \tag{7.55}$$

The households' task thus boils down to maximizing (7.55) subject to (7.52)–(7.53), which yields the following Euler equation in terms of x_t:

$$x_1 = \beta^\sigma (1 + r_C)^\sigma x_0 \tag{7.56}$$

Recalling (7.54) and the CES preference structure

$$c_{Tt} = \left(\frac{P_{Tt}}{P_t}\right)^{-\theta} c_t \tag{7.57}$$

the Euler equation (7.56) can be rewritten as

$$c_{T1} = \beta^\sigma (1 + r)^\sigma \left(\frac{q_0}{q_1}\right)^{\sigma - \theta} c_{T0} \tag{7.58}$$

Since the markets for nontradable goods and real money balances will have to clear in each period, the budget constraint (7.52) in equilibrium can be simplified as

$$c_{T0} + \frac{1}{1+r} c_{T1} = Q_{T0} + \frac{1}{1+r} Q_{T1} \tag{7.59}$$

where Q_{Tt} is the amount of domestically produced tradable good in each period. Substituting the Euler equation (7.58) into the simplified budget constraint (7.59) yields the optimal consumption levels

$$c_{T0} = \gamma \left(Q_{T0} + \frac{1}{1+r} Q_{T1}\right)$$
$$c_{T1} = (1 - \gamma)(1 + r)\left(Q_{T0} + \frac{1}{1+r} Q_{T1}\right) \tag{7.60}$$

where γ is the marginal propensity to consume (MPC) given by

$$\gamma = \frac{1}{1 + \beta^\sigma (1+r)^{\sigma-1} \left(q_0/q_1\right)^{\sigma-\theta}} \tag{7.61}$$

Equation (7.61) above indicates an important link between q_0 (the tradable-based CPI in period 0) and γ (MPC). Holding q_1 constant, a fall in q_0 – and hence a depreciation of the real exchange rate e_0 ($\equiv q_0^*/q_0$) – will have two conflicting effects on the MPC: on the one hand, it will reduce the consumption-based real interest rate r_C [$\equiv (1 + r)(q_0/q_1) - 1$] and boost current consumption c_{T0} relative to future consumption c_{T1}; on the other hand, it will make tradable goods more expensive (relative to nontradable goods), causing the households to switch their spending from tradable to nontradable goods. The net effect depends on the magnitude of these two effects and is generally indeterminate. However, if the elasticity of intratemporal substitution is greater than that of intertemporal substitution ($\theta > \sigma$), then the second effect (intratemporal substitution) will win out over the first effect (intertemporal substitution), and a lower q_0 will be associated with a lower γ (and hence a decrease in current tradable consumption c_{T0}).

In equilibrium, the current account (measured in terms of tradable goods) is given by the difference between production and consumption in the tradable sector:

$$b = Q_{T0} - c_{T0} = (1 - \gamma) Q_{T0} - \gamma \frac{Q_{T1}}{1+r} \qquad (7.62)$$

where Equation (7.60) is used to obtain the last expression. Equation (7.62) in the above can be used to assess the current account effect of a nominal revaluation.

Starting from an initial equilibrium path where the price ceiling is binding only in period 0 (and not in period 1), suppose that a revaluation of the home currency gives rise to a real depreciation (i.e. a fall in the tradable-based, quality-adjusted CPI, q_0). Then, by Equation (7.61), this real depreciation (with a sufficiently high θ such that $\theta > \sigma$) will lead to a decrease in the MPC ($\gamma\downarrow$), which will in turn lead to an increase in the current account ($b\uparrow$ in Equation (7.62)) for *given levels of* Q_{T0} *and* Q_{T1}. It must be noted immediately that both Q_{T0} and Q_{T1} are endogenous variables whose changes could weaken (or even overturn) the positive effect of the nominal revaluation on the current account. In particular, the change in the relative price (P_{N0}/P_{T0}) induced by the revaluation could cause relocation of labor from the tradable to nontradable sector, lowering the period 0 tradable output Q_{T0} and giving rise to a downward pressure on the current account. (See Equation (7.62).) However, as long as the labor share in the tradable sector [$(1 - \alpha)$ in production function (7.24)] is sufficiently small, the fall in tradable output will be limited in magnitude and the current account will increase due to the decrease in the MPC.

To sum up, a nominal exchange rate revaluation (under a binding price ceiling and quality adjustment in the nontradable sector) is likely to increase the current account when (1) the elasticity of intratemporal substitution is greater than that of intertemporal substitution ($\theta > \sigma$) and (2) the labor share ($1 - \alpha$) in the tradable sector is sufficiently low.

7.4 Discussion

The model developed above has a straightforward implication for the much-debated revaluation of the Chinese yuan renminbi.[8] Those who vociferously demand the revaluation – especially the lobby of manufacturers displaced by Chinese imports – seem to have a presumption that it will cause a real appreciation of the yuan, reducing the Chinese current account surplus. However, if China happens to be in a distorted equilibrium (with depressed prices and suboptimal quality in the nontradable sector), then the revaluation of the yuan could set off a fall in the quality-adjusted CPI and a depreciation of the real exchange rate (a decrease in $q \equiv P/P_T$ in the above model). This real depreciation could cause Chinese households to increase savings, which (with other things being equal) will place an upward pressure on the Chinese current account surplus, contrary to the intention of the pro-revaluation lobby.

The model has another interesting implication that lifting the binding price ceiling (while keeping the exchange rate unchanged) will have the same effect on the real exchange rate as the revaluation. Even when E and P_T are held constant, an increase in $\bar{P}_N$ (or complete removal of the price ceiling) will cause an increase in $\bar{p}(\equiv \bar{P}_N/P_T)$ in the model; thus the graphical analysis in Section 7.3.4 will remain valid; the equilibrium levels of p and z will both increase, reducing the tradable-based CPI q ($\equiv P/P_T$) and depreciating the real exchange rage EP^*/P.[9] To sum up, even a minor revaluation could lead to a substantial real depreciation (and possibly an upward pressure on the current account surplus) if it is accompanied by deregulation. This may be highly relevant to present China, where the government is apparently very reluctant to depart from the status quo but is fairly aggressive in implementing regulatory reforms (OECD 2002).

7.5 Concluding remarks

In popular discourse, it is often presumed that a revaluation of a currency under the fixed exchange rate system will cause (if anything) a real appreciation. This chapter shows that such a presumption will be incorrect if the initial equilibrium is distorted by a price ceiling in the nontradable sector, which drives down the quality of the nontradable good to a suboptimal level. The revaluation and the resulting fall in the price of the tradable good will mitigate the distortions in the relative prices, enabling the nontradable good producers to adjust the quality level upward. This quality improvement will lower the quality-adjusted CPI more than what would be implied by the purchasing power parity, causing the real exchange rate to depreciate. Put differently, the presence of price controls may cause the nominal and real exchange rate to move in opposite directions. Applying this finding to contemporary China, we can see that the revaluation of the renminbi may not lead to a real appreciation but to a real depreciation. In this case, those who lobby for the renminbi revaluation in expectation of a real appreciation and reduction in the current account surplus may end up with an outcome totally opposite to their goal.

Appendix 7A   Proof of Proposition 1

When the price ceiling is binding and the nontradable quality is at a suboptimal level, it must be true that

$$\left.\frac{\partial p}{\partial z}\right|_{dV \sim 0} > \left.\frac{\partial p}{\partial z}\right|_{d\pi_N = 0} \tag{7A.1}$$

In Figure 7.4 in Section 7.3.4, the above condition (7A.1) can be described as the slope of the indifference curve $\underline{V}\,\underline{V}$ at point $\underline{E}$ being steeper than that of the iso-profit curve $\pi_N \pi_N$.

A revaluation (a decrease in E) will raise the price ceiling and cause (z, p) to rise along the iso-profit curve $\pi_N \pi_N$. Let dy denote a vector of the resulting change in z and p

$$dy = \left(dz, \left.\frac{dp}{dz}\right|_{d\pi_N = 0} dz\right) \tag{7A.2}$$

and ∇V denote the gradient of the indirect utility V. (See Figure 7A.1.) Then, (7A.1) implies that

$$\nabla V \cdot dy > \nabla V \cdot dx = 0 \tag{7A.3}$$

where dx is a vector tangential to the indifference curve $\underline{V}\,\underline{V}$.

Recall from Equation (7.40) that indirect utility V depends on the tradable-based CPI $q\ (\equiv P/P_T)$, wage rental ratio ω, and labor supply l. Since the household takes factor prices (hence ω) as given and the labor supply l is chosen optimally (given ω and q), the first-order effect of the revaluation on indirect utility V will take place through a change in q. Therefore,

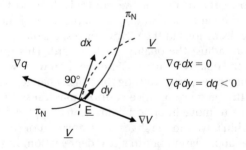

Figure 7A.1   Diagrammatic Proof of Proposition 1

$$\nabla V = V_q \cdot \nabla q \tag{7A.4}$$

where V_q (<0) is the partial derivative of V with respect to q (a negative scalar) and ∇q is the gradient vector of q.

Combining (7A.3) and (7A.4) yields

$$dq = \nabla q \cdot dy = V_q^{-1} \cdot \nabla V \cdot dy < 0$$
$$\because V_q^{-1} < 0 \qquad \nabla V \cdot dy > 0 \tag{7A.5}$$

which indicates that a revaluation will cause q to fall. Since the real exchange rate is expressed as

$$\frac{EP^*}{P} = \frac{EP_T^* q^*}{P_T q} = \frac{q^*}{q} \tag{7A.6}$$

(where q^* is held constant), the decrease in q will lead to a real depreciation.

Notes

1 Examples of such quality adjustment under a price ceiling are low amenity in rent-controlled housing, chronic congestion in public transportation, long waiting time at hospitals, and unreliable supplies of public utilities.

2 It should be noted that, *ceteris paribus*, a quality improvement (an increase in z) will lead to a fall in the quality-adjusted CPI (a decrease in P). This can be easily understood if one recalls an often mentioned upward bias on the measured CPI at the times of rapid innovations in personal computers.

3 Devereux and Connolly (1993) make a similar point and go further to analyze the effect of a relaxation in price control on the real exchange rate. However, their model does not allow quality adjustment, yielding an ambiguous prediction.

4 Since the technology is linear in labor, this condition also means that price equals the average cost. Equation (7.8) can be thus interpreted as the zero profit condition.

5 One way to motivate the price ceiling as in (7.11) is to assume that some households (with strong political power) gain no utility from quality improvement above $\underline{z}$ and oppose an increase in p above $\bar{p}$ (or any form of price discrimination).

6 Both labor and physical capital are assumed to be immobile across countries, although this assumption can be relaxed without altering the results of the chapter qualitatively. One should also note that the money here is assumed to be an inconvertible, fiat money which is not demanded abroad (i.e. does not serve as international reserves). This (combined with immobility of factors across countries) implies that domestic tradable consumption c_T cannot exceed domestic production Q_T (i.e. the home currency cannot be "traded" for foreign tradable goods). This assumption essentially eliminates the difference between small and large open economies, making the results of this section equally applicable to a large open economy. When we allow monetary transactions across countries (especially the possibility of financing trade deficits by money balances), the equivalence breaks down: the perfect path-through in small open economies will not generally hold in large economies – for example, a 10 percent revaluation of the home currency (a fall in E) will not lead to equiproportionate fall in the tradable price P_T. This is because the revaluation will cause a shift in the money stock from

home to abroad, raising the foreign tradable price P_T^* and partially offsetting the fall in E. (Recall from Equation (7.12) that $P_T = E P_T^*$.)

7   The notations of the interest rates follow Obstfeld and Rogoff (1996).

8   The assumption of a small open economy made in the model may seem problematic for China, given its increasing presence in the world market. As discussed in note 6, however, the results of the model will remain valid for large open economies as long as a nominal revaluation causes leads to *some* (not necessarily an equiproportionate) decrease in the domestic tradable price.

9   Since the nominal exchange rate E is assumed to be kept unchanged, the fall in the domestic CPI will stem solely from the quality improvement.

References

Devereux, John, and Michael Connolly, 1993, "Public Sector Pricing and Real Exchange Rate," *Economica*, 60(3): 295–309.

Mishkin, Frederic, 2000, "Inflation Targeting in Emerging Market Countries," *American Economic Review*, 90(2): 105–9.

Obstfeld, Maurice, and Kenneth Rogoff, 1996, *Foundations of International Macroeconomics*, Boston: MIT Press.

OECD, 2002, *China in the World Economy: the Domestic Policy Challenges*, Paris: OECD.

Rosen, Sherwin, 1974, "Hedonic Prices and Implicit Market: Product Differentiation in Perfect Competition," *Journal of Political Economy*, 82(1): 34–55.

Index